Deconstructing Dads

Deconstructing Dads

Changing Images of Fathers in Popular Culture

Edited by
Laura Tropp and Janice Kelly

LEXINGTON BOOKS
Lanham • Boulder • New York • London

Published by Lexington Books
An imprint of The Rowman & Littlefield Publishing Group, Inc.
4501 Forbes Boulevard, Suite 200, Lanham, Maryland 20706
www.rowman.com

Unit A, Whitacre Mews, 26-34 Stannary Street, London SE11 4AB

British Library Cataloguing in Publication Information Available

Library of Congress Cataloging-in-Publication Data

Names: Tropp, Laura, editor.
Title: Deconstructing dads : changing images of fathers in popular culture / edited by
    Laura Tropp and Janice Kelly.
Description: Lanham : Lexington Books, 2015. | Includes bibliographical references
    and index.
Identifiers: LCCN 2015039111| ISBN 9781498516037 (cloth : alk. paper) |
    ISBN 9781498516044 (electronic)
Subjects: LCSH: Families in mass media. | Fathers. | Fatherhood. | Families. |
    Popular culture.
Classification: LCC P94.5.F34 D43 2015 | DDC 306.874/2—dc23 LC record available at
    http://lccn.loc.gov/2015039111

∞™ The paper used in this publication meets the minimum requirements of American
National Standard for Information Sciences—Permanence of Paper for Printed Library
Materials, ANSI/NISO Z39.48-1992.

Printed in the United States of America

To My Husband, Michael, who knows as well as
I the meaning of the phrase "The Second Shift"

—LT

In loving memory of Edward Lee Herring
To My Pop: Charles D. Storer
To my loving Husband and son Michael Herring
& Michael E. Herring Jr.

—JK

Contents

Acknowledgments

We would like to thank Lindsey Porambo, our editor, for her commitment to this collection and guidance through the process. We would also like to thank our contributors for their diverse and thought-provoking work. Finally, we would like to thank Arevik Torosian who has been indispensable in her assistance with the formatting of this manuscript.

Janice would like to acknowledge her deep gratitude to her coeditor and friend, Dr. Laura Tropp, without whom my work on *Deconstructing Dads*, would not have been possible. Throughout the writing of this book, Laura's support and encouragement helped move this project from a concept to a reality. Thank you for your time, wisdom and direction, my dear friend. I want to thank my mentor, Kenneth Braswell, President of Fathers Incorporated for his generosity and inviting me to serve as a board member where I gained further insight into the fatherhood movement.

My family has always been the driving force behind my work. My mother, June Kelly-Storer, my grandmother, Katherine Kirby (a mighty force) and my sister Jamie Grujic and niece Jennifer Leonard have supported my intellectual pursuits. Drs. Nireata Seals, Lisa Newland, Pat Mason, Felicia Moore-Mensha, Lisa Johnston, M.D., Zandra Alexander, and Janet Douglas-Pryce hold a special place in my heart, and I thank them for their encouragement along with my colleagues at Molloy College. I am thankful for the fathers that resemble wonderful role models for me to observe: Derek Johnston, Vincent Grujic, Clarence Haynes, and Rick Freeman. Lastly, to my loving son, Michael Edward Herring Jr., you are blessed to have such a strong and loving role model like your dad. To my husband, Michael Herring, who supports, loves and encourages me, you are my foundation and inspiration.

Laura would like to thank her coeditor Janice for her commitment to this manuscript and her constant optimism and enthusiasm, which was contagious.

I would also like to thank my colleagues at Marymount Manhattan College for their support and insights during the writing of this collection. A special thanks goes to my children, Ethan, Maya, and Gillian for playing on their own while mommy worked on this book. I am also grateful to my mother for watching the children when they wouldn't play on their own. My father, Charles Tropp, deserves special acknowledgment for spending a significant portion of his "retirement" formatting and indexing this book. Finally, thank-you to my husband Michael, my always-faithful editor and co-parent.

Introduction

Changing Conceptions of the Good Dad in Popular Culture

Janice Kelly and Laura Tropp

The film *Mr. Mom* premiered in 1983. It starred Michael Keaton as a husband and father who lost his job and was forced to become a stay-at-home dad while his wife returned to work. The film began by showing his lack of competence in everything from dropping his kids off at school to buying groceries at the store. He had to deal with the sexual advances of predatory moms and battle a vacuum cleaner, all while attempting to maintain his masculinity. By the end of the film, he had learned to confidently care for his children and household. The movie both mocked and reinforced the stereotypes of the bumbling dad while it simultaneously reinforced the framework that fatherhood could only be understood in relation to mothers. In 2014, Lake Superior State University listed "Mister Mom" on its list of top words to banish.[1] These days, media stories, television shows, and advertising all wrestle with contradictions and ideologies concerning what should be the roles and expectations of fathers in the twenty-first century.

Father involvement now begins even before the baby is born. A 2015 viral video shows a man informing a woman she is pregnant. Suspecting she might be pregnant, he waited until she went to the bathroom without flushing, and he used a pregnancy test to surprise her.[2] The public was shocked with this turning of tables of a man being able to inform a woman that she was pregnant. This video, though, illustrates a desire on the part of the man to be included in the fatherhood process much earlier than ever before. The explosion of ultrasound equipment during pregnancy has fathers touting pictures of their fetuses and anticipating fatherhood, when pregnancy previously was the primary domain of the mother's body and imagination.[3] At the birth, fathers are no longer waiting outside the birthing room as they used to, nor sitting behind video cameras. They are a part of the birth process, cutting the cord, live-tweeting updates, and welcoming their babies into the world. After birth, fathers reaffirm their private moments with public postings on blogs, Facebook, Instagram, Twitter, and other social media.

Popular media, which help to both shape and reflect reality, are depicting fathers as having an increased presence in the lives of their children. Television, films, blogs, and other media within popular culture showcase the father in all his roles. *Modern Dads, blackish, Raising Hope, Up All Night, Guys with Kids, See Dad Run,* and *Baby Daddy* all have fathers who are the main presence in the house during the day. Stay-at-home dads have been the stars of their own show, like in A&E's *Modern Dads.* The bumbling fatherhood image, once a staple of many programs, including *Home Improvement, The Simpsons, Married With Children,* and *Everybody Loves Raymond,* is now more complicated with characters like Phil in *Modern Family,* where the audience is a part of the joke in mocking Phil's ineptitude.

For more than a decade, men's social and political organizations such as Promise Keepers, Focus on the Family, and the Million Man March events, as well as pro-masculine grassroots organizations protested that network television and popular culture in general portray American fathers in a negative and limited way.[4] Failing to recognize the contribution that fathers make in the household is said to have created a media bias where mothers are the powerful parent and fathers are the oppressed. However, today society no longer accepts without question the incompetent father figure.

More recently, media campaigns have been forced to respond to negative portrayals of fathers. When a new Huggies campaign featured dads alone with their babies and unable to handle diaper changing, parents created a petition to protest this negative and unrealistic portrayal of fathers. Huggies responded by modifying their campaign to show more positive representation.[5] When Ragu started a twitter campaign with moms talking about the limits of dads in the kitchen, offering Ragu as an answer to this problem, dads protested the representation, offering how they are frequently the dominant cook in the kitchen these days.[6]

Terms such as Baby Mama and Baby Daddy, which did not exist decades ago, are now used by people and within popular culture to express relationships with children that move beyond a commitment between a man and a woman. Will Farrell can walk onto the 2013 Emmy Awards with his children making a joke about not being able to locate a babysitter, and the audience laughs. Fathers who were once thought of as babysitting when they cared for their own children now share the burden of childcare.

There are different reasons for the shift in the representation of fathers. Cultural shifts in expectations of fatherly involvement have gained momentum as the woman's movement encouraged more women to become employed. In difficult economic times, some families have had little choice but to send women into the workforce because, in some cases, they have an easier time obtaining jobs than men.[7] Scholarly work discussing working women and the challenge of balancing family and career is so pervasive, it has now reached public debate. When Anne Marie Slaughter wrote "Why Women Can't Have it All" for *The Atlantic*,[8] 75,000 Facebook users shared it.[9] After Sheryl Sandberg, the chief operating officer of Facebook, published *Lean In*, she sparked a dialogue among people about women in the workforce. Less discussed, though, is the other side of the women and workforce equation. As more women enter traditionally "male spheres," more men are required to share the burden of childcare and join what are traditionally defined as "women spheres." The Pew Research Center says that the number of stay-at-home dads has almost doubled to 2 million since 1989.[10]

Aside from these economic changes, society has changed how it thinks about notions of masculinity and femininity. Books like *Do Fathers Matter? What Science is Telling Us About the Parent We've Overlooked* explore the biological side of fatherhood, using scientific studies to examine how fathers influence children.[11] Studies have appeared that demonstrate men may have biological changes in levels of estrogen and testosterone when they become fathers.[12] What used to be traditionally defined as masculine and feminine domains are now becoming blurred. New moments that defy gender expectations show fathers and daughters polishing each other's toenails or fathers playing with dolls, as seen in the *Huffington Post* piece "Real Men Play with Barbies." Notions of gender and sexuality have also been changing. Gay men who are fathers are represented more in shows like *The New Normal* and *Modern Family,* and gay dads are appearing more frequently in ads, including the brands JC Penney and Coca Cola.

We also live in a new media age when social media and the Internet are providing new places for fathers to engage in conversations with others about their parenting. Countless blogs, including *DadStreet, Dada Rocks, Dad or Alive, DIY Father, Hanging with Dad* and others are devoted to exploring personal narratives of fatherhood and offer advice, product suggestions, or even just an ear to listen to other fathers. Apps now solve every kind of potential dad problem, including the "Baby-Cry Translator" or the "Forget Me Not Kid Alarm."

Marketers have realized the power of this new consumer group and have begun to direct marketing campaigns to fathers. A specific type of branding has emerged around millennial dads described as "influencing parenthood. These enthusiastic parents are spending more time with their kids, doing a larger portion of the household shopping and spending lots of money."[13] The toy manufacturer Mattel, for example, has introduced a new line of Barbie dolls that encourage fathers to play with their daughters. Last year, a "Fatherhood Expo" in Columbus, Ohio brought together companies, organizations, and dads to discuss the topic of fatherhood. The Dove-campaign realized the

power of "dad marketing" by using pictures of "real dad moments" with contributors sharing photos of what they believe fatherhood looks like.[14]

As opportunities for fathers to engage with their children become more visible, contradictions appear within society over the expectations of dads and
views of masculinity, gender, laws, and policies regarding men and fatherhood. An example of this can be found in baseball: since Major League Baseball is a male-dominated field, some may consider it encouraging when the
organization decided in 2011 to create a more family-friendly policy regarding players taking leaves. Fathers in the MLB now had a 72-hour paternal
leave policy. However, when Daniel Murphy of the New York Mets decided
to miss the first two games of the season to be with his wife and newborn son,
the talk radio circuit criticized his lack of commitment to his team and fans.
Murphy actually is one of the lucky ones because his high pay status allows
him to take off this time. Most fathers work in companies that do not offer
paternal leave and must simply take unpaid family leave when they have a
newborn, if they even feel comfortable doing that. In fact, recognizing the
importance of parental leave for both parents, Netflix announced a flexible
policy that included both fathers and mothers for up to a year of leave time.[15]

In other ways, our laws also lag behind our expectations of fathers.
Increased use of sperm donation raises new social questions of what makes
a father and becomes the premise of programs such as MTV's *Generation
Cryo* and films like *Delivery Man*. Jason Patric appeared on media to argue
for his paternal rights and question a California law that allowed his former
girlfriend to declare him as only the sperm donor of his son, with no other
parental rights. A *New York Times* op-ed piece titled "A Man's Right to
Choose" raised questions about what rights a man should have to be a potential father if a woman does not want to have a baby.[16] The question of father's
rights is one being raised in a variety of fronts over custody battles, the right
to choose not to be a father, and the custodial rights arising from sperm and
egg donation.

The Families and Work Institute's National Study of the Changing Workforce reported that nationwide, "Men now experience more work-family
conflict than women." In the article "The New Male Mystique," the authors
explore underlying reasons, including the fact that men and women have
more egalitarian roles, but men still feel pressure to conform to traditional
patriarchal notions of the role of breadwinner.[17] The Boston College Center
for Work and Family indicates that men who choose to be stay-at-home parents continue to face a social stigma.[18] Al Watts, president of the National At-
Home Dad Network, decided to combat this stigma by creating "man cards"
fathers can hand out. They read, "As an actively involved dad, you are the
manliest of men."[19] Earlier images of the bumbling dad, who, compared to
moms, could not do anything right, still exist in part with characters like Hal

in *The Middle* or Dre in *blackish*, but the new emasculated dad, a man who seems too feminine when engaged in traditional "womanly" activities, also has emerged. The opening of the A & E reality show, *Modern Dads*, contrasts images of macho men with their current role of fathers, implying that caretaking is, in some ways, emasculating. Popular culture is struggling with new questions arising from the intersection of caretaking and masculinity.

Despite the pervasive images of fatherhood, scholars are examining what society means by "good" fathers. Stony Brook University has just started a new graduate program on Men and Masculinities, led by the scholar Michael Kimmel, well known for his work exploring fatherhood.[20] Shifting notions of fatherhood necessitate debate and conflict over the meaning and consequences of these changes. Researchers have attempted to develop a construct of positive fatherhood, alternatively calling it "good fathering." Several synonyms have been forwarded in the literature, including "involved fathering," "developmental fathering," "generative fathering," and "responsible fathering."[21] Scholars have explored the different dimensions of good fathering, paternal engagement, accessibility, and responsibility.[22] Yet, more traditional research has explored questions of accessibility and expectations about the authoritarian nature of fatherhood. and masculinity.[23]

While scholars continue to debate representations of "good" fathering, advocacy organizations are trying to instill notions of strong fathering among men. President Obama started a national campaign for Responsible Fatherhood. This organization encourages fathers to sign a "fatherhood pledge," promising to be active in the lives of their children. Other organizations, such as the National Fatherhood Initiative, also advocate for fathers to become involved. While the root of these efforts is the desire to help fathers from different social economic backgrounds, there is still a question over how effective these efforts are in helping low-income fathers, incarcerated fathers, or fathers who lack access to their children for a variety of reasons. Additional groups with religious affiliations, such as the Promise Keepers, also promote strong fatherhood but see it as aligned within traditional patriarchal structures. Notions of race, class, ethnicity, and access differ among fathers but have yet to be represented adequately in popular culture.

Emerging debates about mothers and motherhood are now leading to larger societal discussions about work-life balance and how to better support mothers. The researchers of motherhood studies have spent decades trying to make the lives of mothers more visible, since so much of that work flies under the radar. Words now exist to describe the challenges and experiences of motherhood: terms such as The Second Shift, the Maternal Wall, the Feminine Mystique, and Having-It-All serve to help women identify the varying conflicts in their lives and the way society presents expectations for motherhood. The field of fatherhood studies has yet to coin corresponding terms for fathers, and these challenges are not as widely publicized within popular culture. Moreover, still ignored in much of this debate are the social and familial expectations that place great emphasis on the financial and provider role of fathers. This book explores both how popular culture represents "new" fatherhood while reinforcing dominant ideologies of masculinity and traditional notions family structures.

The following chapters explore how different types of programs confront the questions of what makes a good father, how fatherhood is framed in relation to feminism and gender expectations, and what contradictions appear in popular media's representations of fatherhood. This book is divided into three sections: the first section examines the evolution of the father figure within popular culture. Ralph LaRossa, a seminal writer in fatherhood studies, explores changing definitions within the culture of fatherhood during social change. LaRossa questions the current media proclamation of a "new fatherhood" by revisiting the second wave fatherhood movement and its celebration of men and expectations of paternal responsibilities during this period. He concludes that the cultural expectations of fatherhood contrast with the everyday practices of fathers. Laura Tropp examines television and film programs to explore how fatherhood, responsibility, and participation are framed surrounding the issue of sperm donation. She concludes that media representations of sperm donors both reinforce traditional understandings of fatherhood and show how new reproductive technologies can threaten existing family structures. In chapter 3, Laura C. Prividera and John W. Howard study expectations of fatherhood and masculinity when considering media coverage of military dads. They examine the challenges of being a good soldier while also living up to notions of a good dad. They conclude that news media ultimately creates a gap in reflecting the challenges and reality of life as a military dad by showcasing idealized moments of connection and inspiration within their stories. Previous historical studies reveal that the nature of change in fatherhood has never been and may never be as revolutionary as media hype implies. In chapter 4, Janice Kelly traces representations of the sitcom dad. Her study finds that young viewers are not passive receivers of TV images or messages, but instead are critical of media portrayals of TV fathers and the ideology it propagates.

In the second section of the book, contributors explore fatherhood in different media genres. In chapter 5, Peter Schaefer examines advertising to study the leisure gap in workload expectations of mothers versus fathers. He argues that television ads create a "privilege of play" that both favor recreational activities with children as the way to be a good dad while simultaneously leaving women to shoulder more household work. Sarah Kornfield outlines the portrayal of masculinity and fatherhood in crime dramas such as *Bones* (Fox), *Fringe* (Fox), *The Mentalist* (CBS), and *Castle* (ABC) that feature male detectives who have been celebrated in popular media for their nurturing nature. Ultimately, her examination of these programs finds the introduction of paternal figures who engage in little caregiving and feature traditionally strong masculine components, affirming traditional gender roles. In chapter 7, Justin Hendricks, Heidi Steinour, William Marsiglio, and Deepika Kulkarni search magazines for depictions of fatherly involvement in the health of their children. They discover that fathers are shown more often as entertainers of their children rather than having active roles in the administrative functions of parenting, particularly related to health. While public health discourse often highlights the father's role as a protector of their children's health, popular magazines mostly fail to demonstrate that representation. In chapter 8, Fernando Gabriel Pagnoni Berns and Canela Ailen Rodriguez Fontao investigate the portrayal of fatherhood in horror films to demonstrate the reconfiguration of paternity in a post-9/11 society. They show how the economic crisis and the fear of unemployment threaten the father figure. The contributors find a challenge in representation that reflects these external societal fears, where fathers are expected to function as nurturers but have not yet been given the necessary skillset to do so and must engage in these new acts of fathering within societies that remain quite traditional.

The third section of this collection discusses representation of race, gender, and identity within constructed notions of fatherhood. In chapter 9, Shirley Hill and Janice Kelly explore the evolution of African-American fatherhood and the problematic portrayals of fathers as irresponsible and unattached to their children. They demonstrate that the influence of social class are diversifying portrayals of African American families and fathers in particular. Lynda Goldstein chronicles the history of gay dads on network television and uses the shows *Modern Family* and *The New Normal* to argue that queer dads complicate social expectations of masculine and feminine narratives when they enter domestic spaces. These shows destabilize representations from earlier decades, foregrounding the new possibilities of fatherhood. Finally, in chapter 11, Leandra Hernandez explores Mexican American fathers in popular films to understand how media represents the Latino father. She studies the image of the father in the films *Mi Familia, A Better Life, Quinceañera,* and *La Mission.* Hernandez argues that, though the films reflect nurturing and caring fathers, they often conform to pre-existing media stereotypes.

For most in the United States, popular culture continues to remain the primary space to find representations of fatherhood in our society. There is no question that fathers are becoming involved in the lives of their children in more and different ways than in the past. This book, however, questions the idea that a "new" fatherhood has emerged and explores contradictions in media representations that seem to challenge dominant notions of masculinity and fatherhood while simultaneously maintaining these very ideologies. This collection questions what it means to be a father in modern media today, and how that meaning is conveyed to viewers.

NOTES

1. "Lake Superior Banished Word List: 2014." Lake Superior State University, http://www.lssu.edu/banished/current.php.

2. "Husband Shocks Wife with Pregnancy Announcement," You Tube Video, 7:55, posted by Sam and Nia, August 5, 2015, https://www.youtube.com/watch?v= GODw8TuinNQ.

3. Laura Tropp, *A Womb with a View*, (Westport, CT: Praeger Publishers, 2013).

4. William Marsiglio, Paul Amato, Randal D. Day and Michael E. Lamb, "Scholarship on fatherhood in the 1990s and beyond," *Journal of Marriage & Family, 62* no. 4 (2000): 1173–1192.

5. Josh Levs, "No More Dumb Old Dad: Changing the Bumbling Father Stereotype." *CNN*. 15, June 2, 2012, Retrieved from www.cnn.com/2012/06/12/living/dumb-dad-stereotype/.

6. C. C. Chapman, Blog Post, Retrieved on July 30, 2014 from http://www.cc-chapman.com/2011/ragu-hates-dads/.

7. Hannah Rosin, "Who Wears the Pants in This Economy: When Jobs Go Away, Husbands and Wives Make a New Deal," *The New York Times Magazine*, September, 2 (2012): 22–38.

8. Anne Marie Slaughter, "Why Women Can't Have It All," *The Atlantic*, July 13, 2012, http://www.theatlantic.com/magazine/archive/2012/07/why-women-still-cant-have-it-all/309020/.

9. Beth J. Harpaz, "Record Hits on Mag's 'Can't Have It All' Story," *AP: The Big Story*. June 22, 2012, http://bigstory.ap.org/article/record-hits-mags-cant-have-it-all-story-0.

10. Gretchen Livingston, "Growing Number of Dads Home with the Kids," Pew Research Center Social & Demographic Trends, 2014, http://www.pewsocialtrends.org/2014/06/05/growing-number-of-dads-home-with-the-kids/.

11. Paul Raeburn, "Do Fathers Matter? What Science is Telling Us About the Parent We've Overlooked," New York: *Scientific American*, 2014.

12. Sandra J. Berg and Katherine E. Wynne-Edwards, "Changes in Testosterone, Cortisol, and Estradiol Levels in Men Becoming Fathers," *Mayo Clinic Proceedings* 76, no. 6 (2001): 582–592.

13. Kasi Bruno,"Millennial Dads are Real, and So Is Their Spending Power: Three Trends Among Millennial Dads Markets Should Watch," Ad Age, http://adage.com/article/digitalnext/millennial-dads-real-spending-power/297782/. Retrieved March 27, 2015.

14. Julia Ingersoll, "Dove Men + Care Shares Real Dad Moments," posted June 11, 2014 www.allegorystudios.com.

15. Emily Steel, "Netflix Offers Expanded Maternity and Paternity Leave," *New York Times*, August 4, 2015, Web. Retrieved August 6, 2015.

16. Dalton Conley, "A Man's Right to Choose," *New York Times*, Od-Ed. December 1, 2005.

17. Ellen Galinsky, Kerstin Aumann, and Kenneth Matos, *The New Male Mystique*, (New York: Families and Work Institute, 2011). Retrieved from http://familiesandwork.org/downloads/NewMaleMystique.pdf : 1.

18. Brad Harrington, Fred Van Deusen, and Beth Humberd, "The New Dad: Caring, Committed and Conflicted," *The Boston College Center for Work & Family*, (2011), Retrieved from http://www.bc.edu/content/dam/files/centers/cwf/pdf/FH-Study-Web-2.pdf: 6.

19. Brigid Schulte, "Don't Call Them Mr. Mom: More Dads at Home With Kids Because They Want to be," *Washington Post*, June 5, 2014, Retrieved at http://www.washingtonpost.com/news/parenting/wp/2014/06/05/dads-who-stay-home-because-they-want-to-has-increased-four-fold/.

20. Jessica Bennett, "A Master's Degree in . . . Masculinity?," *New York Times*, August 8, 2015, http://www.nytimes.com/2015/08/09/fashion/masculinities-studies-stonybrook-michael-kimmel.html?_r=0.

21. William J. Doherty, Edward F. Kouneski, and Martha Farrell Erickson," Responsible Fathering: An Overview and Conceptual Framework, *Journal of Marriage & Family, 60*, no. 2 (1998): 277–292.; DOI: 10.2307/353848.

22. Rob Palkovitz, "Involved Fathering and Child Development: Advancing Our Understanding of Good Fathering," in Natasha J. Cabrera and Catherine S. Tamis-LeMonda, eds., *Handbook of Father Involvement: Multidisciplinary Perspectives* (Mahwah, NJ: Lawrence Erlbaum Associates 2002), 119–140.

23. Ibid., 119–140.

BIBLIOGRAPHY

Bennett, Jessica. "A Master's Degree in . . . Masculinity?" *New York Times*, August 8, 2015. http://www.nytimes.com/2015/08/09/fashion/masculinities-studies-stony-brook-michael-kimmel.html?_r=0.

Berg, Sandra J., and Katherine E. Wynne-Edwards. "Changes in Testosterone, Cortisol, and Estradiol Levels in Men Becoming Fathers." *Mayo Clinic Proceedings* 76 (2001): 582–592.

Bruno, Kasi. "Millennial Dads are Real, and So Is Their Spending Power: Three Trends Among Millennial Dads Markets Should Watch." *Ad Age*. Accessed March 27, 2015. http://adage.com/article/digitalnext/millennial-dads-real-spending-power/297782/.

Chapman, C. C. Blog Post. Accessed July 30, 2014. http://www.cc-chapman.com/2011/ragu-hates-dads/.

Conley, Dalton Conley. "A Man's Right to Choose." *New York Times*, December 1, 2005. Op-Ed.

Doherty, William J., Edward F. Kouneski, and Martha Farrell Erickson. "Responsible Fathering: An Overview and Conceptual Framework." *Journal of Marriage & Family 60*, no. 2 (1998): 277–292. doi:10.2307/353848.

Galinsky, Ellen, Kerstin Aumann, and Kenneth Matos. "The New Male Mystique."*Families and Work Institute*, 2011. Accessed February 12, 2015 http://familiesandwork.org/downloads/NewMaleMystique.pdf.

Harpaz, Beth J. "Record Hits on Mag's 'Can't Have It All' Story." *AP: The Big Story*. Accessed June 22, 2012. http://bigstory.ap.org/article/record-hits-mags-cant-have-it-all-story-0.

Harrington, Brad, Fred Van Deusen, and Beth Humberd. "The New Dad: Caring, Committed and Conflicted." *The Boston College Center for Work & Family*, (2011), Accessed September 9, 2016. http://www.bc.edu/content/dam/files/centers/cwf/pdf/FH-Study-Web-2.pdf: 6.

"Husband Shocks Wife with Pregnancy Announcement." You Tube Video, 7:55, posted by Sam and Nia, August 5, 2015, https://www.youtube.com/watch?v= GODw8TuinNQ.

Ingersoll, Julia. "Dove Men + Care Shares Real Dad Moments." Posted June 11, 2014 www.allegorystudios.com.

"Lake Superior Banished Words List: 2014. "Lake Superior State University. http://www.lssu.edu/banished/current.php.

Levs, Josh. "No More Dumb Old Dad: Changing the Bumbling Father Stereotype." *CNN*. 15, Jun 2, 2012, Retrieved from www.cnn.com/2012/06/12/living/dumb-dad-stereotype/.

Livingston, Gretchen. "Growing Number of Dads Home with the Kids." Pew Research Center Social & Demographic Trends, 2014. http://www.pewsocial-trends.org/2014/06/05/growing-number-of-dads-home-with-the-kids/.

Marsiglio, William, Paul Amato, Randal D. Day, and Michael E. Lamb. "Scholarship on fatherhood in the 1990s and beyond." *Journal of Marriage & Family 62* no. 4 (2000): 1173–1192.

Palkovitz, Rob. "Involved Fathering and Child Development: Advancing Our Understanding of Good Fathering." In Natasha J. Cabrera and Catherine S. Tamis-LeMonda, eds., *Handbook of Father Involvement: Multidisciplinary Perspectives*. Mahwah, NJ: Lawrence Erlbaum Associates 2002: 119–140.

Raeburn, Paul. "Do Fathers Matter? What Science is Telling Us About the Parent We've Overlooked." New York: *Scientific American*, 2014.

Rosin, Hannah. "Who Wears the Pants in This Economy: When Jobs Go Away, Husbands and Wives Make a New Deal." *New York Times Magazine*, September 2 (2012): 22–38.

Schulte, Brigid. "Don't Call Them Mr. Mom: More Dads at Home With Kids Because They Want to be." *Washington Post*, June 5, 2014. Accessed September 12, 2015. http://www.washingtonpost.com/news/parenting/wp/2014/06/05/dads-who-stay-home-because-they-want-to-has-increased-four-fold/.

Slaughter, Anne Marie. "Why Women Can't Have It All." *Atlantic*, July 13, 2012. Accessed April 14, 2015. http://www.theatlantic.com/magazine/archive/2012/07/why-women-still-cant-have-it-all/309020/.

Steel, Emily. "Netflix Offers Expanded Maternity and Paternity Leave." *New York Times*, August 4, 2015. Accessed August 6, 2015. http://www.nytimes.com/2015/08/05/business/netflix-offers-expanded-maternity-and-paternity-leave.html?_r=.

Tropp, Laura. *A Womb with a View*. Westport, CT: Praeger Publishers, 2013.

Section I

THE EVOLVING DAD IN POPULAR CULTURE

Chapter 1

The Culture of Fatherhood and the Late-Twentieth-Century New Fatherhood Movement

An Interpretive Perspective

Ralph LaRossa

Throughout the media are journalistic pieces spreading the message that being a father today is so much different than it ever was before. As the author of a 2008 *Parents Magazine* article put it, twenty-first century fathers—by which he meant men who had recently transitioned to parenthood—wear "spit-up" on their shoulders as a "battle scar" rather than an "embarrassing stain." These guys, unlike their predecessors, are not "satisfied with a supporting role in [their] children's lives," but make a point of "attending childbirth classes, memorizing the pediatrician's number, . . . helping pick out baby gear, . . . staying home when a child is sick, doing the daycare drop-off, and enrolling in programs like 'Time for Dads' [a parental support group]."[1]

Some of what is reported in these pieces is true. Research does suggest that the *culture of fatherhood* (the norms, values, beliefs, and expressive symbols pertaining to fatherhood) and the *conduct of fatherhood* (what fathers actually do when they try to act "fatherly") have changed in recent years.[2] Culture-wise, more fathers are being asked, and in some cases being pressured, to be hands-on caregivers; and increasing numbers of men see their parental role as more important than their breadwinning role, rather than the other way around. Conduct wise, time-diary studies have revealed an increase in father-involvement as of late (with the rising percentage of stay-at-home dads being a notable trend), while other studies have showcased men who, though they may not reside with their kids and be an everyday presence in their lives, are doing their best to connect or reconnect with daughters and sons.[3]

Often missing in the journalistic pieces, however, is a deep appreciation for the history of fatherhood and a basic knowledge of how fatherhood as a social institution has fluctuated over the years.[4] Particularly puzzling is the selective inattention—some might say mnemonic decapitation—of what went on in America's families just a generation ago.[5] Today's tyro fathers—most of whom were born and raised in the 1960s, 1970s, or 1980s—are not simply characterized as nurturing dads but are said to be light years ahead of their fathers (as well as their grandfathers and great grandfathers). If the pundits are to be believed, yesterday's dads were not expected to do much childcare at all. Scanning the pieces, we could easily conclude that it is only in recent years that *anyone* has thought to write about fathers and that the very idea of a man enrolling in a childbirth class or staying home from work to care for a youngster with the flu is totally unprecedented.

The truth of the matter is the popular press has been proclaiming the arrival of the so-called "new father" for well over hundred years, and has repeatedly applauded each generation of fathers for being a "vast improvement" over generations before. It is curious how much print (and now online) journalists have embraced this story, so much so that they tell it over and over again. In their doing so, they make the mistake of failing to establish a phenomenon before explaining it.[6]

Not everyone is disposed to commit this error. Researchers generally recognize the importance of historical context. Most know that, without that context, what initially might be thought of as "progress" could be found, after careful analysis, to be "more of the same"; or an "advancement" could prove to be a subtle variation on a decades-old pattern. Probing the past also provides leads on how to investigate the present, and helps us to identify when an emerging phenomenon, even with its historical links, deserves to be categorized as "novel."

Based on the premise that a firm understanding of fatherhood today requires a deep appreciation for what fatherhood was like before, this chapter aims to shed light on the social realities of fatherhood in a prior time. For reasons that will soon be clear, my temporal focus is on the 1960s, 1970s, and 1980s, while my analytical focus is primarily on the culture of fatherhood, secondarily on the conduct of fatherhood, and tertiarily on the culture-conduct connection (or lack thereof).

In the main, two questions guided this project: What kinds of parental expectations were directed to fathers in the 1960s, 1970s, and 1980s? What can we learn from a close analysis of these expectations?

AN INTERPRETIVE PERSPECTIVE ON THE SOCIAL REALITIES OF FATHERHOOD

Scholars have devoted a fair amount of attention to the historical study of fatherhood in the 1960s, 1970s, and 1980s, not because they necessarily wanted to know what families were like when twenty-first-century fathers were born and raised (an important question, to be sure) but because they were interested in charting the effects of the social and political upheavals that characterized the times. The 1960s, 1970s, and 1980s saw earnest efforts to expand the rights of women and racial and sexual minorities, and were a witness as well to a veritable "youth quake," as baby boomers challenged traditional views on these and other issues and stood in defiance of the US government and its involvement in the Vietnam War.[7] Economic and technological changes, along with philosophical and aesthetic shifts, furthermore prompted—or at the very least fueled—a rejection of "modern" ways of thinking and led to what some have called the "postmodern" age.[8]

As a by-product of these events and transformations, the 1960s, 1970s, and 1980s ushered in a *new fatherhood movement*, which was analogous (but not identical) to an earlier movement that dated back to the 1910s, 1920s, and 1930s.[9] The aim of these movements was to communicate to men that although economic providing was central to being a good father, being a reliable wage earner, by itself, was not sufficient. A good father, it was said, also had to regularly spend time with his kids and nurture them. How kid-time should be measured and what qualified as nurturance were not given, but shifted in people's minds from one decade to the next.

In the early-twentieth-century new fatherhood movement, emphasis was given to the idea that, along with being a breadwinner, a father should be a male role model and companion or playmate to his children. Personally caring for youngsters was included in the combination; but, more often than not, it was assumed that, when a father did in fact get involved, he would serve as a "helper" or "stand-in" for the mother.[10] In the late-twentieth-century new fatherhood movement, being a breadwinner, male role model, and companion/playmate continued to be valued components, but the care aspects of fatherhood received heightened attention, too. Now, a good father was expected, on top of his other duties, to minister to his children on a routine basis and see himself not so much as an assistant to, but as a co-tasker with, the mother.[11]

What might have been prescribed for fathers in the 1960s, 1970s, and 1980s was not always practiced; that is, there was a disjunction between culture and conduct. Whereas the culture of fatherhood exhibited a progressive slope from the 1960s to the 1970s and 1980s, men's contribution to childcare generally showed little or no change; and, throughout the era, the care level of fathers remained substantially below the care level of mothers.[12]

Explanations for the disparity often have pointed to women's greater physical attachment to infants during pregnancy and breastfeeding, and to sexist patterns of socialization (e.g., the message that "girls should play with dolls, and boys should play with trucks"). These explanations, we recognize now, are not sufficient. As research on fatherhood and motherhood began to build, other factors—more structural in nature—were discovered to be in play. One outgrowth of this research is that scholars have increasingly employed an *interpretive perspective* to make sense of the division of childcare in the home.

An interpretive perspective is a theoretical approach that underscores the value of closely examining discourse or language, and the role of "accounts" or "rationalizations" (as ideologies) in the social movement and resistance process. Central to the perspective is the observation that men frequently have been granted a license to excuse and justify levels of paternal involvement that fail to coincide with certain norms and values.[13] An interpretive perspective also acknowledges the fragmentary nature of culture and leaves room for the fact that different, even contradictory, views can appear in a single text and be selectively appropriated by social actors to achieve desired ends. Because it sees advantage in focusing on the symbolism in words and on the power and politics that pervade the deployment of ideas, an interpretive perspective stresses the necessity of linking micro- and macro-phenomena. Thus, whereas excuses and justifications are delivered on an interpersonal plane, it is their availability in the larger supermarket of ideas that makes their strategic utilization possible. "Men are not skilled at taking care of babies" is an account/rationalization that is readily available for appropriation, whereas "Men should avoid changing diapers because Jupiter is not aligned with Mars" is not likely to be a script on the shelves. Needless to say, the fact men have the power to stock the cultural supermarket with an assemblage of accounts/rationalizations that suit their interests cannot be discounted. Indeed, it is instrumental to the process.[14]

An interpretive perspective was a major part of this project from its inception. Relying on the perspective, I scrutinized elements of the culture of fatherhood in the late twentieth century when the second wave of the new fatherhood movement was in full swing, by analyzing popular magazine and newspaper articles (and, in some instances, commercial-oriented journal articles) that were written on the subject of fatherhood and listed in the *Reader's Guide to Periodical Literature* from 1960 to 1989 (N = 161). My analysis of the articles was qualitative in scope, and entailed the application and development of concepts, dimensions, and hypotheses.[15]

A full-scale interpretive study of the culture of fatherhood and the late-twentieth-century new fatherhood movement would draw on a wide range of cultural objects to plot continuities and changes (i.e., not just popular periodicals, but also child-rearing manuals, storybooks, advertisements, posters, comic strips, greeting cards, films, plays, radio and television shows, interviews with fathers and mothers, etc.).[16] A full-scale interpretive study also would explore a wide range of views on fatherhood—both good and bad—in order to best capture the multifaceted world of fatherhood. My focus is tapered, in that I am mainly interested in popular periodical articles published during a thirty-year period—articles which, in connection with the late-twentieth-century new fatherhood movement, tended to highlight the positive aspects of fatherhood. A full-scale interpretive study of the culture of fatherhood, in addition, would examine racial, ethnic, sexual, and class variations. The articles I looked at, however, for the most part did not explore these variations.[17] The articles also tended to ignore the upheavals of the 1960s, 1970s, and 1980s. (Popular periodical articles on fatherhood historically have been insular.)[18]

Although the materials for the current project are restricted to one set of cultural objects and although my emphasis is on a particular social movement at a particular time, the materials and emphasis have the potential to yield valuable information, as prior studies have demonstrated that popular periodical articles, if carefully analyzed, can serve as a barometer of trends, and that even within a single and ostensibly monochromatic collection of texts, a range of important messages can be discerned and dissected.[19]

MEN AND INFANT CARE

Longitudinal studies of popular periodical articles on fatherhood published in the latter part of the twentieth century have highlighted the upward shift in the ratio of articles that referenced nurturing versus economic providing, and documented the increase in the percentage of articles that cited the self-fulfilling versus the fun aspects of fathering. What is noteworthy about the patterns reported in the first study was the dramatic rise in the ratio of articles that referenced men nurturing their children. In the 1950s and 1960s, the ratios were 1.4 and 1.3, respectively, whereas in the 1970s and 1980s, the ratios were 3.3 and 2.8.[20] In the second study, the percentage of articles from the 1920s to the 1960s that cited the self-fulfilling aspect of fathering was consistently low (never reaching more than 14 percent), but then intensified in the 1970s and 1980s (first coming close to 20 percent and then moving up to around 30 percent).[21]

In my analysis of popular periodical articles on fatherhood from the 1960s, 1970s, and 1980s, I saw change, too, but what stood out was the percentage of articles that talked about men's role in infant care. In the 1960s, the percentage of articles that focused on infant care (if not in the entire article then at least in part of it) was slight (around 9 percent among the items in my sample), whereas in the 1970s and 1980s the percentage was much higher (around 48 percent).[22]

Besides the change in the focus of the articles, what stood out also was the shifting tone of the infant care narratives. In the 1960s, the tendency was to characterize any infant care that a dad might provide as a poor substitute for what a mom could do. In the 1970s and 1980s, however, the articles leaned more toward communicating that infant care was a task that a good father should not only willingly undertake but also strongly believe he could do as well as anyone else. I say "leaned toward" to describe a shift that was perceptible but not a reversal from the attitudes that had existed before.

A 1960 article talked about father-present "natural" childbirth (which would become increasingly common in 1960s, 1970s, and 1980s) and offered as a reflection, "When a wife decides on natural childbirth, a husband must be prepared for anything—from breathing exercises to doll diapering."[23] Illustrations for the article depicted several fathers wearing smocks (atop their suits and ties) and looking befuddled as they tried to change a diaper on a small doll. (The nurse standing nearby had a facial expression that further buttressed the message that men were clueless caregivers.) Said the author about the prenatal class he was taking: "Aproned and shaking, I practiced changing diapers the right way (stick the pins into the diaper not the baby), washing the baby (with soap and water) and, of course, the art of burping (don't get in the way). As I wrestled a shirt onto the rubber baby a nurse cheerfully informed me that it would be easier with my own baby since his arms would bend easier (and break easier, too, I thought)."[24]

In a second article, published in 1966, a father said that, with his first child, he "was spared any [immediate] role in the feeding schedule" because his wife had chosen to breastfeed," but that when his son graduated from breast to bottle, "the workload became too heavy for [him] to ignore and [he] took over bottle preparation."

> Fumbling around like a sorcerer's apprentice, I sterilized, measured and capped, in great clouds of steam. I folded diapers on demand, too. But somehow I managed to avoid directly ministering to the baby. [In time, however] I got in the habit of letting my wife sleep through two or three mornings a week. It wasn't long before I was serving some daytime bottles, spoonfeeding every now and then, and changing a diaper occasionally. . . . When . . . our second child arrived, . . . I did my part, although it was mostly keeping our older boy from feeling neglected.[25]

A 1968 article initially said, "When a young father regularly takes a hand in caring for the baby it gives him a chance to get acquainted with the new family member," suggesting an endorsement of the axiom that men should be involved in infant care from the start. But then the article offered, as a qualification: "Of course, no father can or should be expected to give as many bottles or change as many diapers as mother does, but more and more fathers are taking over some of the baby's physical care. They find it not only comfortable, but possible, to be helpful fathers and real men at the same time." In addition, the article rationalized: "Some men feel awkward and shy about doing anything for a tiny newborn, and there's no point making an issue out of it. For these men fatherhood takes a little growing into. Even if dad does not take on any of the baby's physical care, he performs one important function as a new father when he gives his wife needed moral support."[26]

In the 1970s, the fatherhood discourse in the articles changed and evidenced, on the whole, a broad-mindedness not generally seen in the articles published in the 1960s. (This is not entirely surprising. Some may think of the 1960s as a "decade of liberation," but, in matters of gender, the decade was a fairly traditional time.)[27] References to men's contribution to infant care as subsidiary or ancillary (i.e., not equal to women's contribution) could still be found in the 1970s, but these were partially offset by articles that spoke about the value of co-tasking infant care, and about men who became "house-persons" in order to care for their babies.

A 1970 article, which offered a case study of a husband and wife in the throes of their transition to parenthood, maintained, "A happy offshoot of women's 'lib' is the increasing demand on the part of new fathers to take on their fair share in active parenting." The article went on to say: "[T]he old definitions of mothering and fathering have broken down. The idea that the mother is soft, flexible, and forgiving, the father strong, authoritative and firm; the mother always at home and the father at work—these distinctions are no longer clear. By their own choice, the parenting roles assumed by many couples today change and overlap."[28] Along with the text was a series of photos of a father skillfully bathing a baby and changing a diaper.

Another article, published in 1976, noted the observations of a grandmother and how impressed she was by her son's fathering skills and commitments.

Jenny is my granddaughter, and I had come to visit and help right after the birth. But to my surprise and deep pleasure, Jenny's Dad, Michael, who is my son, had graciously declined my offer to look after the baby. He was happy to have me take over the running of the house while my daughter-in-law, Lee, rested, but when it came to the baby-care tasks, Michael was eager to take over. And so he did, using several days of his vacation in order to share with Lee the responsibility and joy of looking after their newborn infant. . . . [And later in the article] At home, Lee nursed the baby, and Michael took on the job of changing Jenny's diapers, bathing her (a thing most men are afraid to do), and sharing with Lee the satisfaction of comforting their baby when she cried. After Michael went back to work, he still spent time with Jenny every evening. Usually they had a quiet playtime together while Lee prepared dinner. Sometimes, when Jenny was in a fretful mood, Michael would rock her until she fell asleep.[29]

The grandmother did say also, "Naturally, a father's relationship to his child will be different from that of a mother's," but the gist of her remarks was that fathers should "take an active hand in parenting during the first months of their children's lives."[30]

A 1984 article stressed as well the importance of fathers, and told the story of a couple whose flexible jobs offered an opportunity to engage in tag-team parenting.

> Gary Johnson and his wife, Becky, knew when their son, Jake, was born last year that *each* wanted as much involvement as possible with his upbringing. So Gary, a graduate student at the University of Pittsburgh and Becky, a teacher at the Western Pennsylvania School for the Deaf, scheduled their working hours so that they could share Jake's care. Becky teaches every weekday morning, so Gary stays home. He studies, part of the time, and does laundry, washes dishes, makes beds, cooks—and feeds, changes, bathes, hugs, and plays with Jake. Becky takes over in the afternoons and evenings while Gary goes to the university.[31]

And in a 1987 article, an author talked about how great a father he was and how fatherhood was all the rage; but he said also that he was angry that those around him seemed not to notice the terrific job he was doing. What he appeared to suggest was that, by not acknowledging the effort men were making, people were standing in the way of meaningful social change. The father, for example, thought that a baby nurse, who helped him and his wife navigate through the first few weeks of the transition to parenthood, had failed to fully appreciate his dedication to being involved with his son.

> I'd stand there by the table as she showed us how to change [baby Benjamin]. Serious I was, intent on learning. But it was clear that she thought the whole thing was just a lark to me, and that any minute I'd go into the next room and watch a football game. She'd say, "Oh, the baby likes his daddy. Would Daddy like to hold the baby?" And I'd hold him for two seconds and then, just as he and I were getting comfortable, she'd whisk him away, saying, "He loves his daddy." And then she'd Twinkle at me [by which he meant she would give him the "that look" that says, "Ooh, aren't new daddies *cute*"]. Don't get me wrong. I rather like being cute. . . . What makes me crazy is that on the outside people take you very seriously, but underneath they sort of regard this daddy-involved-with-baby business like they did the Hula-Hoop; fun for now, but in a couple of months it will be gathering dust in the garage. . . . In the meantime, I continue to do my fair share with Benjamin, and I love it."[32]

Several articles in the 1970s and 1980s told stories of stay-at-home dads. These articles tended to center on men caring for preschool children, and they often spoke of an epiphany the men felt they had experienced from having to care for a baby on a prolonged basis. Infant care, they had discovered, took a lot of effort.[33] "Without seeming to be 'work,' parenting was actually a physically demanding and mentally consuming job," said one father in a 1975 article.

> When and where does a homebound parent get tired? How, by the end of the day, had I earned the dull stiffness in my legs, the kink in my back? Was it the result of my 14th trip upstairs? Perhaps it was the 23rd trip that did it. . . . There is a mental side too. . . . The parent is always on the job. Even when the parent is asleep a state of being 'on call' exists. The sound of coughing, steps in the hall, doors closing—any and every sound must be heard and evaluated before it can be dismissed. The mind is prevented from getting so involved in some one thing that it shuts out the surroundings.[34]

Another dad in a 1977 article reported:

> In no time at all, I became an irritable mother. I had been led to believe that babies just ate, slept and messed diapers their first month. Perrie [his daughter] ate and messed but she never learned to sleep. . . . [F]or all the good times I enjoyed as a surrogate mother, there were as many depressing days. Perrie's crankiest moments coincided with the cold and windy days left in the season. I'd no sooner sit down to read when Perrie would break into a long whining session.[35]

And yet another dad in a 1980 article talked about what he called his "adventures in full-time fatherhood":

> I had much to learn about babies—more than I wanted to know. They wake up early, no matter what time they've gone to bed. They have the habit of spilling things on their clothes—especially those you just washed. . . . Since I have truly become a parent, I have learned how demanding and self-less a task it is, especially in those unseen and unheralded moments where many mothers have spent much of their time and energy.[36]

Finally, there was the "full-timer" who had concluded: "It's hard work. Anyone who belittles a woman for staying home with the kids is off his rocker."[37]

ENGAGEMENT, ACCESSIBILITY, AND RESPONSIBILITY: TRADITIONAL AND FEMINIST MESSAGES

Although the articles offered a glimpse of the culture of fatherhood in the 1960s, 1970s, and 1980s and about how it was changing, they were fairly restricted in their attention and perhaps more revealing (as cultural objects) for what they failed to say than for what they did say. Granted, infant care is one of the most challenging aspects of parenthood and the tasks associated with it exemplify how nurturing children can sometimes be, literally, "dirty work." Still, if we are to talk about infant care in its totality, we must include, at a minimum, three dimensions: engagement, accessibility, and responsibility.[38]

Engagement is direct contact with a child and includes, among other things, the tasks of feeding, cleaning, clothing, carrying, and comforting. *Accessibility* denotes being ready and able to provide direct care; that is, being ready to be engaged. Staying close by when a baby is asleep so we can hear it when it cries is an example of accessibility. *Responsibility* means being "in charge" of a child's care. Keeping track of when immunizations are needed, deciding when it is time to move to the next-size diaper, scoping out the qualifications of a baby sitter, visiting and evaluating possible day care settings, and worrying about and feeling ultimately answerable for a child's growth and development (i.e., feeling that the buck stops with *you*) all are subsumable under responsibility. It is responsibility that was largely shouldered by women in the 1960s, 1970s, and 1980s, even in cases where women were co-economic providers, and it is responsibility that continues to be largely shouldered by women today.[39] For these and other reasons, responsibility for children is a dimension that cannot and should not be ignored.

Consider, however, the articles thus far discussed. Virtually all of them concentrated on parental engagement, with hardly any mention of parental responsibility and only slight reference to parental accessibility (e.g., "Even when the parent is asleep a state of being 'on call' exists"). When I saw this, I decided to look at the entire set of articles again, with an eye toward identifying the articles that did address responsibility. To allow a finer analysis and to plot incremental continuities and changes, I also divided the sample into half-decade sectors (i.e., 1960 to 1964, 1965 to 1969, 1970 to 1974, etc.).

What I found was that none of the articles from the 1960s made the case that responsibility should be examined alongside engagement and accessibility, while some of the articles from the 1970s and 1980s did. One of the articles from the late 1970s quickly caught my attention. It offered a feminist critique of "liberated husbands" and commented on how seemingly caring dads frequently were only semi-involved. Discussing research that recently had reported on "men [who] were assuming more household responsibilities," the article rejoined:

> The most interesting change discussed [in the study] was the increased amount of time these fathers felt they were spending with their children, *while still leaving the primary responsibility for parenting to their wives.* . . . [Then, after

referring to a father in the study who talked about men as "babysitters"] The word "babysitting" is used repeatedly by these men. They see themselves as babysitters, their children see them as babysitters, and perhaps even their wives see them as babysitters . . . These fathers are not consciously denying parenthood, but, by using the term "babysitter," the effect is virtually the same. The issue is not whether these men love and care about children, but, rather, their view that *they do not hold ultimate responsibility for the child's welfare.*[40]

A telling aspect of the article is that it was published not in *Parents Magazine* or *McCalls* or *Ladies Home Journal* or in any number of other magazines that parents might pick up from the newsstand, but in *Intellect*, a journal that was sponsored by the Society for the Advancement of Education. In the June issue of the journal in which the article appeared, there also were essays on terrorism, urban life in Sweden, water conservation, and Gertrude Stein. *Intellect* may have been targeted to a larger public, but it was not the kind of periodical that parents generally turned to for childcare advice.

What about the periodicals that parents were likely to buy and have in their home? Did any of them bring up the question of parental responsibility? Again, some did. But with the exception of an article published in *Psychology Today* in 1977 and another article published in the *Ladies Home Journal* in 1979, feminist critiques of the division of infant care generally were not offered until the 1980s (and, in particular, not until the late 1980s).

The *Ladies Home Journal* article, the more mass-market oriented of the two, centered on dads who were single parents. The *Psychology Today* article, written by two psychologists, discussed fatherhood research that had been conducted in the 1970s and the gender differences in styles of parenting that were observed.[41] The author of the *Ladies Home Journal* article said that men who were the sole caregivers acquired an understanding of childcare that other fathers often did not have. In making her point, the author drew on the work of a researcher who had recently completed a study of men who by themselves were raising children.

What, in essence, are these mean learning? They are learning to acquire what Boston psychologist Harry Keshet calls "parental consciousness." Keshet points out that most men, even ones who do a lot of diaper changing, function as mother's helpers. They rarely assume executive responsibility that requires total awareness of a child's physical and emotional needs. Acquiring "parental consciousness," explains Keshet, . . . means learning to remember to make a doctor's appointment for a child, calling the babysitter, buying diapers—in short, taking responsibility for the thousands of practical tasks associated with child-rearing. It means learning to tune in to what a child needs on an emotional level, even when he or she can't explain what's wrong.[42]

By my count, nine of the articles in the late 1980s' subsample offered feminist (or somewhat-feminist) critiques of the division of infant care, and many, like the 1979 *Ladies Home Journal* article, drew on social and behavioral science research. What was happening is that, first in the 1970s but especially in the 1980s, scholars began to investigate the new fatherhood movement and were finding that men's involvement typically was restricted to engagement and accessibility, with responsibility for the most part ignored.[43] Interestingly, two of the articles—both published in 1987, one in *Parents Magazine* and the other in *McCalls*—were individually authored by Michael Lamb and James Levine, two members of the research team that had first proposed that we differentiate engagement, accessibility, and responsibility.[44] Said Lamb: "When it comes to overall responsibility and planning for children's needs, . . . many studies show that fathers are essentially uninvolved in the day-to-day concerns as: Does my child need new clothes? Is a dental checkup due? How will she get to ballet or Little League today? Who will babysit on Saturday night?" Echoed Levine: "It's one thing for Dad to change a diaper. But who does the thinking about the diaper supply? Put succinctly, it's not just who carries the baby in the backpack that counts, but who carries the baby in heart and mind."[45]

The attention given to engagement and/or accessibility and/or responsibility was not consistent. Some articles, though critical, failed to talk much about who had responsibility for infants. For example, a 1985 article commented:

> [M]any news dads [are] taking advantage of the fact that fatherhood is "in" these days. Men whose wives recently delivered their first babies are not just writing books, they're appearing on the covers of magazines, giving speeches and going on TV talk shows to tell us how unexpectedly pleased they are to be parents. . . . These nouveau daddies can spoon baby food, change diapers and sing lullabies with the best of them. They call home five times a night when they've left the baby with a sitter. They hate to go to work in the morning for fear of missing some milestone in their children's lives. Well, guys, enough already. I'm tired of hearing about it. . . . Why are we heaping them with so much praise? Everywhere we look somebody is writing or talking about these paragons, from the ones who actually stay at home to the more common variety who just do something more than put their feet up when they come home at night. We are constantly telling them what a swell bunch of guys they are.[46]

Note the fact that the critique focused not on parental responsibility but on the idea that men were being praised for doing what women had been doing for years. "[H]ow often," the author asked, "did we read articles praising women for holding down two full-time jobs?"[47]

In a 1989 article, published as a part of a series, "Can This Marriage Be Saved?," a mother voiced her frustration that her husband would not "do his part," when it came to caring for their daughter Kate who was almost a year old. The mother thought the father should be willing to take the child to the doctor and "remember" to "put diapers on the [shopping] list if he notices that [they] were out." Still, her attention was mostly directed to her partner's lack of parental engagement and accessibility, as opposed to his level of responsibility. "I do 99 percent of the child care and housework," exclaimed the mother. And later: "Even when he's home, he's not there. Last week, it was his turn to watch the baby while I took a nap. As soon as my head hit the pillow, I heard Kate crying. When I raced into the living room, Steve was lying on the sofa reading the paper while Katie screamed." Given a chance to reply, the husband offered as an excuse: "I try to *help* out. I try to pick up Katie when she's crying, but she keeps craning her neck to see where [her mother] is. She doesn't want me, she wants her mommy. So what am I supposed to do?" And as a justification: "How about a little credit for the things I do? . . . I spend a lot of time in the grocery store, making sure to buy everything on *her* list."[48]

An article published in 1985 in *Ms. Magazine* addressed the "cult of fatherhood," but, despite the magazine being feminist oriented as a matter of policy, the article talked more about engagement and accessibility than about responsibility. The author (a father who was married to an obstetrics resident working "100 hours a week") complimented himself for the level of infant care he provided: "I'm not a househusband; I take Nick to day care five days a week. But I come as close to house-husbandry as I care to. I am what you might call a nontraditional father." He also maintained that he had "go[ne] beyond the cult of fatherhood." What he primarily discussed, however, was the litany of infant care activities in which he was engaged. He did use the word "responsibility" or "responsibilities" in the piece (as in "[M]y career [as a writer] has taken off just as my responsibilities as a father have hit their peak"), but it is not clear whether he was speaking about responsibility in contrast to engagement and accessibility, or whether he was equating responsibility with engagement.[49]

Interesting, too, was an episode described in the article where the father did address responsibility, as researchers have defined the term. But when he did so, he seemed to convey that, in his mind, responsibility was more his wife's domain. The couple's son had cut his forehead on a metal toy while in the home of a babysitter and was rushed to the emergency room. Both parents felt terrible that they were away and could not drive the child to the hospital. However, the father rationalized that his guilt over not being with his son during the crisis was less than the mother's guilt. "This is one of the differences I have discovered between mothers and fathers," he remarked. "Deep inside [my wife's] psyche lies a powerful message that she belongs at home, that if she is not with her child, she is terribly irresponsible. I feel guilty only occasionally. Deep within my psyche . . . the most powerful message is that I belong at work, that if I am not making my mark on the world I am worth nothing."[50]

THE MULTIPLE MESSAGES IN THE CULTURE
OF FATHERHOOD AND THE COMPLEXITIES
OF CONTINUITY AND CHANGE

Looking back at the new fatherhood movement of the 1960s, 1970s, and 1980s, we may wonder how revolutionary it was. Was it all that different from the new fatherhood movement of the 1910s, 1920s, and 1930s? Had the second wave, compared to the first, in fact, "challenged men to share equally the nurture and daily care of their offspring"?[51] If we examine certain writings or certain segments of some writings in the late twentieth century, the answer to these questions would seem to be a *yes*. However, if we scrutinize the range of opinions not just across different sets of cultural objects but also within a single set of cultural objects (e.g., among the articles reviewed here), the answer would have to be (optimistically) a *qualified yes* or (skeptically) a *qualified no*.[52]

This is not to imply that the culture of fatherhood was impervious to change over the course of the twentieth century or that it failed to budge from one decade to the next in the latter part of the twentieth century. In both instances, shifts were clearly evident. But the nature of change was more contradictory than consistent, and the texture of change was more serrated than smooth.[53]

Parallels can be found in the conduct of fatherhood. Careful examinations of conduct over time show less of a difference between "then" and "now," as we learn that fathers in the past were more involved in childcare than has been generally acknowledged, and that fathers in the present are not as involved as they may appear to be at first glance. Historical studies of the conduct of fatherhood also show more variation in the behavior of yesterday's dads than the stereotypes imply.[54]

Likewise, changes in the culture of fatherhood may not be as dramatic as they would appear to be initially. The culture of fatherhood in prior times was more progressive than many imagine, while the culture of fatherhood in later times is more traditional than some of us would wish. I am not discounting the fluctuating pattern in the culture of fatherhood that historical research has uncovered. I am speaking, for the moment, about a "best-fitting" gradient for a specific point in time.[55]

The combination of traditional and feminist messages in the culture of fatherhood in the 1960s, 1970s, and 1980s may help us sort out why changes in the conduct of fatherhood were so minimal. With the culture of fatherhood being a mélange of ideas, parents have the opportunity to pick and choose from an array of accounts/rationalizations in the supermarket of ideas to suit their strategic purposes.[56] Even more so than I have been able to show here, focusing as I have on popular periodicals alone, a comprehensive examination of a host of cultural objects from the 1960s, 1970s, and 1980s likely would reveal a variety of concepts associated with the culture of fatherhood, with some strongly feminist, some strongly traditional, and some falling in between.

For the fathers and mothers who read and digested feminist-oriented cultural objects (especially, feminist-oriented scholarship-based articles), the rules for being a "good father" might include not only being engaged and accessible but also being responsible (if not completely at least to an important degree). The failure of a father to live up to this standard would put him in the position of having to account for his less than stellar performance. If the excuses and justifications offered to his partner provided a license for a father to renege on his commitments, his level of parental involvement likely would remain lower than his partner (and perhaps he) would define as ideal. Negotiations along these lines would help to explain the unequal division of infant care that was found in the homes of progressive middle-class couples in the 1960s, 1970s, and 1980s.[57]

What about the fathers and mothers who held strongly traditional ideas on the division of childcare and who were hardly exposed, if at all, to the enlightened notions on fatherhood and motherhood that were being circulated in the 1960s, 1970s, and 1980s? Among these individuals we are likely to find men whose participation in childcare was fairly low. The pattern of father involvement in this group, upon being added to the aggregate, would have the effect of dampening the overall level of father involvement.

There is another group (in truth, there are many groups), one that in the 1960s, 1970s, and 1980s was probably larger than the first and maybe also larger than the second. This group would be made up of the fathers and mothers who read and digested the kinds of traditional *and* feminist messages that many of the popular magazine articles on fatherhood seemed to convey. This group, however, might be inclined to appropriate the messages that were more traditional, disregarding or downplaying the feminist messages also available in the texts, because they preferred to believe *from the outset* that a traditional (or somewhat traditional) division of childcare served their interests. The scenario here is that in the supermarket of ideas, there is something for everyone and each of us can readily find some precept to excuse and/or justify an already-chosen path of action.

The content of the cultural objects tells a story, too. Populating a number of the articles, especially in the 1970s and 1980s, were men who were feeding, cleaning, clothing, carrying, and comforting infants. Seeing this, we might surmise that the amount of childcare that men did in the 1970s and 1980s had to be dramatically higher than it was in the 1960s. Yet studies indicate it was not.[58] Why?

Apart from the fact that culture and conduct are not the same and that culture is variegated enough to support virtually any behavior, the answer may come down to how we measure *care*. If we tabulate the number of soiled diapers a father changes compared to the number of soiled diapers a mother changes (and some parents do keep track of this to determine if things are "fair") the division of childcare can appear to be "balanced."[59] If, however, we tabulate the number of minutes and hours that a father and mother actually devote to childcare *and* also include in the tabulation instances of engagement, accessibility, and responsibility (where responsibility would be assessed in terms how much time is devoted to thinking about the children and anticipating their needs), the division of childcare is likely to be one sided, with mothers shouldering most of the work. Responsibility for infants was generally left out of the culture of fatherhood as it was represented in popular periodical articles in the 1960s and 1970s, and given only scattered attention in the 1980s. Responsibility for infants generally was not a central component of the conduct of fatherhood either.

Another possible reason that the conduct of fatherhood was not significantly different in the 1970s and 1980s than in the 1960s may be related to the emphasis that was given to men's infant care activities. This would seem to be counterintuitive, in that infant care is often considered a dependable sign of just how involved men actually are. Would men's contribution in this regard not show how serious fathers were about being involved? Perhaps. Or perhaps not.

Consider, first, how much the fathers in the articles bragged about their infant feeding, cleaning, clothing, carrying, and comforting. The men appeared to wear these activities as badges of honor. In the same way that fathers in the 1970s and 1980s publicly displayed their infants (e.g., proudly pushing them in a stroller) and received social approval in the process— exhibiting what may be called *baby parading*—so also those who broadcast their infant care activities may be seeking commendation. (Parading thus can be accomplished via self-report as well as performance.)[60]

Notable, too, is how much diaper changing, compared to overall comforting, was dwelled upon. Diapering no doubt was a large part of what fathers did for infants in the 1960s, 1970s, and 1980s (and before). But how much time does it take to change a diaper as opposed to comfort an infant (even with the acknowledgment that two may occur simultaneously)? Comforting is a process that can require considerable effort and energy, not to mention know-how. Diapering, in comparison, though it can be a challenge to a neophyte, typically takes but a few minutes.

That said, diapering could have *symbolic* value to fathers. If engaging in diapering is amplified in a father's mind, while other baby-care chores are diminished, we can picture a father who does relatively little but credits himself for doing a lot. Consider the case, recounted in a 1972 article, of a father and mother who left the maternity ward with their baby and, upon arriving home, *together* changed a diaper. Though the couple had worked jointly, it was concluded in the article, "From that moment on, Dad was a full-fledged baby tender."[61] What is curious about this statement is that it suggests that diapering, by itself, equated to "full-fledged" tendering, *but only for the father.* (Presumably, the mother would have had to do more to earn the accolade.) A message that readers might have gleaned: change a diaper, expect a lot of points, if you are a guy.

Central to the symbolism that diapering might have had, and a crucial element as to why other paternal activities, besides diapering, might have been magnified as well, was the fictive narrative that prior to the 1960s, 1970s, and 1980s, fathers did hardly any childcare at all. This had the effect of making whatever fathers did in the way of infant care, even it were negligible, seem enormous. Thus, a 1973 article began: "What kind of man makes a good father? Until recently, such a question was not even raised?"[62] Began another in 1986: "Barely a generation ago, a father was supposed to be a good provider, a stern disciplinarian ('Just wait till your father gets home') and a kind of overgrown playmate. . . . None of these roles, however, involved him in the day-to-day reality of rearing children."[63] Said a third in 1989: "It's official—fathers are no longer the invisible parent."[64]

Claiming to be "the first" generation of men to care for infants not only was self-aggrandizing but also lowered the bar for fathers, allowing them to provide less infant care than mothers provided, and less infant care than they might have chosen to provide (or been pushed to provide) if they were held to a higher standard.[65]

LOOKING BACK, LOOKING FORWARD

The new fatherhood movement continued into the 1990s. Illustrative of its momentum was the 1993 *Time Magazine* story, "Bringing Up Father," and the accompanying cover photo of a father holding his young daughter in his arms and looking thoughtfully into her eyes. The child returns the gaze and is shown smiling and lightly touching her dad's cheeks. Superimposed on the portrait was the caption, "Fatherhood: The guilt, the joy, the fear, the fun that come with a changing role."[66] Other articles in the 1990s reiterated this theme, with titles such as "The New Father" (1991), "Dad: New and Improved" (1991), "How Fathers Feel" (1993), "Remaking Fatherhood"

(1994), "The New Family Man" (1995), "World's Greatest Dads" (1995), "Building a Better Dad" (1996), "Make Room for Daddy" (1996), "Becoming a Dad" (1997), and "The Good Father" (1999).[67]

The new fatherhood movement continued also into the twenty-first century. In Winter 2012/2013, two fathers of infant sons launched *Kindling Quarterly*, a magazine with the expressed aim of "present[ing] a thoughtful dialogue about fatherhood that is missing from our cultural landscape." Said the editor: "We offer no dramatic manifestos or grand theories about what it means to be a father, just simple explorations of creative individuals whose role as a parent—whether stay at home, working full time, or everywhere in between—is intrinsic to their life, and often their career."[68]

Kindling Quarterly is not the first periodical to be addressed to fathers, and it probably will not be the last. Before its arrival, there was *Dad*, *Modern Dad*, and *Dads*, to name just a few.[69] Sharing cultural space with *Kindling Quarterly* is the academic journal *Fathering*, which began publication in 2003, and a variety of websites devoted to "all things paternal." One of the sites, *Fatherly*, is pitched as "a parenting resource for men who understand that embracing what they've become doesn't mean giving up who they are."[70]

Articles from the 1960s, 1970s, and 1980s help to place today's articles in context. It is clear that there is precedence for current discussions about "new-and-improved" fatherhood. It is clear, too, that at least some twenty-first-century fathers grew up in homes where their own fathers were expected to attend childbirth classes, pick out baby gear, take a child to the doctor, ferry youngsters back and forth to school (as well as after-school programs), and, in some instances, join informal groups that discussed what it meant to be a dad. As for how much hands-on care fathers actually provided, and how much responsibility they had for kid-related activities, investigations into the conduct of fatherhood indicate that corners were cut.[71]

Researchers have analyzed popular periodical articles on fatherhood today and found many of the same patterns that historians have discovered in their examination of articles from the past. Some studies reveal broad changes in the culture of fatherhood (e.g., more intensity nowadays in the "messages about fathers participating in and even enjoying the routine care of children"). Other studies show that fathers continue to be perceived as "mother's helpers" and often are not expected to have equivalent responsibility for childcare. In short, there is evidence of both change and resistance to change—much as there was before.[72]

And so it goes. As the future unfolds and as the reproduction of culture continues, we may be surprised at the direction that fatherhood takes. Then again, we may not.

ACKNOWLEDGMENT

I appreciate the research assistance provided by Christina E. Barmon and Bobby Jo Otto, and the constructive feedback from Maureen Mulligan LaRossa and Margaret K. Nelson.

NOTES

1. Doug Most, "The New Face of Fatherhood," *Parents Magazine*, June 2008.

2. The culture of fatherhood and conduct of fatherhood are terms first employed in Ralph LaRossa, "Fatherhood and Social Change," Family Relations 37 (October 1988): 451–457. See also Ralph LaRossa, *The Modernization of Fatherhood: A Social and Political History* (Chicago: University of Chicago Press, 1997); Ralph LaRossa, *Of War and Men: World War II in the Lives of Fathers and Their Families* (Chicago: University of Chicago Press, 2011).

3. For evidence of the changing culture of fatherhood in recent times, see Suzanne M. Bianchi, John P. Robinson, and Melissa Milkie, *Changing Rhythms of American Family Life* (New York: Russell Sage Foundation, 2006), 128; Ralph LaRossa, Charles Jaret, Malati Gadgil, and G. Robert Wynn, "The Changing Culture of Fatherhood in Comic Strip Families: A Six-Decade Analysis," *Journal of Marriage and Family* 62 (May 2000): 375–387; Melissa A. Milkie and Kathleen E. Denny, "Changes in the Cultural Model of Father Involvement: Descriptions of Benefits to Fathers, Children, and Mothers in Parents' Magazine, 1926–2006," *Journal of Family Issues* 35 (January 2014): 223–253. On fathers who see their parental role as more important than their breadwinning role, see Gayle Kaufman, *Superdads: How Fathers Balance Work and Family in the 21st Century* (New York: New York University Press, 2013). For evidence on the changing conduct of fatherhood in recent times, see Bianchi et al., *Changing Rhythms of American Family Life*, 63, 160. The rise in father (and mother) involvement reported in this volume continued into the twenty-first century (Suzanne Bianchi, personal communication, September 21, 2010). On the increase in the percentage of stay-at-home dads, see Gretchen Livingston, "Growing Number of Dads Home with the Kids: Biggest Increase Among Those Caring for Family," *Pew Research Center*, June 5, 2014, http://www.pewsocialtrends.org/2014/06/05/growing-number-of-dads-home-with-the-kids/. For stories of nonresident fathers and their involvement with their children, see Kathryn Edin and Timothy J. Nelson, *Doing the Best I Can: Fatherhood in the Inner City* (Berkeley, CA: University of California Press, 2013); William Marsiglio and Kevin Roy, *Nurturing Dads: Social Initiatives for Contemporary Fatherhood* (New York: Russell Sage Foundation, 2012).

4. On the fluctuations in the history of fatherhood, see LaRossa, *The Modernization of Fatherhood*; LaRossa, *Of War and Men*. On fluctuating images of fatherhood, in particular, see Ralph LaRossa, Betty Anne Gordon, Ronald Jay Wilson, Annette Bairan, and Charles Jaret, "The Fluctuating Image of the 20th Century American Father," *Journal of Marriage and the Family* 53 (November 1991): 987–997; LaRossa et al., "The Changing Culture of Fatherhood in Comic Strip Families."

5. On mnemonic decapitation in historical narratives, see Eviatar Zerubavel, *Time Maps: Collective Memory and the Social Shape of the Past* (Chicago: University of Chicago Press, 2003).

6. On stories of fatherhood repeatedly told, see Ralph LaRossa, "The Historical Study of Fatherhood: Theoretical and Methodological Considerations," in *Fatherhood in Late Modernity: Cultural Images, Social Practices, Structural Frames*, ed. Mechtild Oechsle, Ursula Müller, and Sabine Hess (Germany: Barbara Budrich Publishers, 2012), 37–58. See also LaRossa, *The Modernization of Fatherhood*; LaRossa, *Of War and Men*. On the importance of establishing a phenomenon before explaining it, see Robert K. Merton, "Three Fragments from a Sociologist's Notebooks: Establishing the Phenomenon, Specified Ignorance, and Strategic Research Materials," *Annual Review of Sociology*, 13 (1987):1–28.

7. Steven Mintz, *Huck's Raft: A History of American Childhood* (Cambridge, MA: Harvard University Press, 2004); Arlene Skolnick, *Embattled Paradise: The American Family in an Age of Uncertainty* (New York: Basic Books, 1991).

8. Steven Best and Douglas Kellner, *Postmodern Theory: Critical Interrogations* (New York: Guilford, 1991); Jefferson Cowie, *Stayin' Alive: The 1970s and the Last Days of the Working Class* (New York: New Press, 2010); Judith Stacey, *In the Name of the Family: Rethinking Family Values in the Postmodern Age* (Boston: Beacon Press, 1996).

9. Research on the history of fatherhood in the 1960s, 1970s, and 1980s includes: Maxine A. Atkinson and Stephen P. Blackwelder, "Fathering in the 20th Century," *Journal of Marriage and the Family* 55 (November 1993): 975–986. Randal D. Day and Wade C. Mackey, "The Role Image of the American Father: An Examination of a Media Myth," *Journal of Comparative Family Studies* 17 (Autumn 1986): 371–388; Robert L. Griswold, *Fatherhood in America: A History* (New York: Basic Books, 1993); LaRossa et al., "The Changing Culture of Fatherhood in Comic Strip Families"; Milkie and Denny, "Changes in the Cultural Model of Father Involvement." The late-twentieth-century fatherhood movement was part of general men's movement that, to some scholars, was one of the most important cultural transformations in U.S. history. See Philip Jenkins, *Decade of Nightmares: The End of the Sixties and the Making of Eighties America* (New York: Oxford University Press, 2006); Bruce J. Schulman, *The Seventies: The Great Shift in American Culture, Society, and Politics* (New York: Da Capo Press, 2001).

10. On the early-twentieth-century new fatherhood movement, see Griswold, *Fatherhood in America*; LaRossa, *The Modernization of Fatherhood*.

11. Ibid; LaRossa, "Fatherhood and Social Change"; Ralph LaRossa and Maureen Mulligan LaRossa, *Transition to Parenthood: How Infants Change Families* (Beverly Hills, CA: Sage, 1981).

12. LaRossa, "Fatherhood and Social Change"; Bianchi et al., *Changing Rhythms of American Family Life*. Joseph Pleck did find evidence of certifiable, though not very large, increases in men's involvement in childcare, but he also acknowledged that "fathers remain[ed] a long way from parity with mothers." Joseph H. Pleck, "Paternal Involvement: Levels, Sources, and Consequences," *The Role of the Father in Child Development*, ed. Michael E. Lamb (New York: John Wiley), 66–103.

13. An *account* is "a linguistic device employed whenever an action is subjected to valuative inquiry" and as "a statement made by a social actor to explain unanticipated or untoward behavior." In common parlance, an account is equivalent to a *rationalization*. One type of an account is an excuse; another type is a justification. In an *excuse*, "one admits that the act in question is bad, wrong, or inappropriate but denies full responsibility." In a *justification*, "one accepts responsibility for the act in question, but denies the pejorative quality associated with it." Marvin B. Scott and Stanford M. Lyman, "Accounts," *American Sociological Review* 33 (February1968): 46–62.

14. For an example of an interpretive perspective being applied to understanding the division of childcare during the late twentieth century and demonstrating how accounts/rationalizations figure into a "traditionalization" process during the transition to parenthood, see LaRossa and LaRossa, *Transition to Parenthood*. Other examples of an interpretive perspective being employed in the study of fatherhood and motherhood include Kathryn C. Backett, *Mothers and Fathers* (New York: St. Martin's Press, 1982); Anna Dienhart, "Make Room for Daddy: The Pragmatic Potentials of a Tag-Team Structure for Sharing Parenting," *Journal of Family Issues* 22 (November 2001): 973–999; Andrea Doucet, *Do Men Mother? Fathering, Care, and Domestic Responsibility* (Toronto: University of Toronto Press, 2006); LaRossa, *The Modernization of Fatherhood*; Ralph LaRossa and Cynthia B. Sinha, "Constructing the Transition to Parenthood," *Sociological Inquiry* 76 (November 2006): 433–457; Martha McMahon, *Engendering Motherhood: Identity and Self-Transformation in Women's Lives* (New York: Guildford, 1995); Deborah Lupton and Lesley Barclay, *Constructing Fatherhood: Discourses and Experiences* (London: Sage, 1997); Jane Sunderland, "Baby Entertainer, Bumbling Assistant, and Line Manager: Discourses of Fatherhood in Parentcraft Texts," *Discourse and Society* 11 (April 2000): 249–274; Susan Walzer, *Thinking about the Baby: Gender and Transitions to Parenthood* (Philadelphia: Temple University Press, 1998). Critical to the argument presented here is the idea that "chunks of culture" are deployed for strategic purposes. A theoretical basis for the argument can be found in Ann Swidler, "Culture in Action: Symbols and Strategies," *American Sociological Review* 51 (April 1986): 273–286.

15. On the application and development of concepts, dimensions, and hypotheses in qualitative research, see Ralph LaRossa, "Writing and Reviewing Manuscripts in the Multidimensional World of Qualitative Research," *Journal of Marriage and Family* (August 2012): 643–659; also Ralph LaRossa, "Thinking About the Nature and Scope of Qualitative Research," *Journal of Marriage and Family* (August 2012): 678–687.

16. A *cultural object* "is a socially meaningful expression that is audible, or visible, or tangible, or can be articulated." Wendy Griswold, *Cultures and Societies in a Changing World* (Thousand Oaks, CA: Pine Forge Press, 1994), 11.

17. In terms of class, the new fatherhood movement was, for the most part, a middle-class movement, and magazine articles on parenthood often presumed middle-class privilege. LaRossa, *The Modernization of Fatherhood*; LaRossa, "Fatherhood and Social Change."

18. For example, articles on fatherhood published during the Great Depression generally did not mention the economic crisis; and those published during the 1950s

generally did not mention the postwar civil rights movement. LaRossa, *The Modernization of Fatherhood*; LaRossa, *Of War and Men*.

19. LaRossa, "The Historical Study of Fatherhood."

20. Atkinson and Blackwelder, "Fathering in the 20th Century."

21. Milkie and Denny, "Changes in the Cultural Model of Father Involvement."

22. The fact that a sizable percentage of articles in the 1970s and 1980s attended to infant care is striking, given that a recent study of a year's worth of articles (from September 1999 to June 2000) in a Canadian newspaper found "a lack of emphasis on the importance of fathers' connection to, and time spent with, infants and young children." Glenda Wall and Stephanie Arnold, "How Involved is Involved Fathering?: An Exploration of the Contemporary Culture of Fatherhood," *Gender and Society* 21 (August 2007): 508–527.

23. On the history of the "natural" or "prepared" childbirth movement, see Judith Walzer Leavitt, *Make Room for Daddy: The Journey from Waiting Room to Birthing Room* (Chapel Hill, NC: University of North Carolina Press, 2009). The rise in the number of fathers present in delivery rooms probably explains in part why popular magazines increased the amount of attention they gave to men and infant care in the 1970s and 1980s.

24. Hal Higdon, "Dad Had It!" *Parents Magazine*, June 1960.

25. Patrick Parish, "The Day I Really Became a Father," *Parents Magazine*, February 1966.

26. "Father's Day with Baby," *Parents Magazine*, June 1968. Interesting here is that some of the wording in the article is very similar to what could be found in the 1968 edition of Benjamin Spock's manual *Baby and Child Care* (New York: Hawthorne Books, 1968). Said Spock: "Some fathers have been brought up to think that the care of babies and children is the mother's job entirely. But a man can be a warm father and a real man at the same time. . . . Of course, I don't mean that the father has to give just as many bottles or change just as many diapers as the mother. But it's fine for him to do these things occasionally" (pp. 30–31). The wording in the manual was not new to the 1968 edition but was a carryover from the 1946 (first) edition and 1957 (second) edition (which was a slightly-altered version of the original text). Benjamin Spock, *The Common Sense Book of Baby and Child Care* (New York: Duell, Sloan, and Pearce, 1946); Benjamin Spock, *The Common Sense Book of Baby and Child Care* (New York: Duell, Sloan, and Pearce, 1957). On comparisons between the first and second edition of *Baby and Child Care*, see LaRossa, *Of War and Men*.

27. Stephanie Coontz, *A Strange Stirring: The Feminine Mystique and American Women at the Dawn of the 1960s* (New York: Basic Books, 2011).

28. Veryl Rosenbaum, "Fair Play for Fathers," *Parents Magazine*, December 1970.

29. K. Davis, "The Power of Positive Fathering," *Parents Magazine*, April 1976.

30. Ibid.

31. Janice Gibson, "Fathers are Important, Too," *Parents Magazine*, October 1984. On social patterns of tag-team parenting, see Anna Dienhart, "Make Room for Daddy."

32. Richard Greene, "I'm a New Father Who Takes His Role Seriously," *Glamour*, June 1987.

33. On the social logic of epiphanies and the semiotic structure of awakening stories, see Thomas DeGloma, *Seeing the Light: The Social Logic of Personal Discovery* (Chicago: University of Chicago Press, 2014).

34. Reese Sarda, "Reflections of a Father Who Became a Mother," *Redbook*, November 1975.

35. Edward Susman, "I Was a Mother for Six Months," *Good Housekeeping*, July 1977.

36. Wayne Grice, "Fathers Mother Too!" *Essence*, June 1980.

37. Robert B. McCall, "Fulltime Father: Staying Home with Baby," *Parents Magazine*, February 1984.

38. Michael E. Lamb, Joseph H. Pleck, Eric. L. Charnov, and James A. Levine, "Paternal Behavior in Humans," *American Zoologist* 25 (3, 1985): 883–894. The authors use the term "availability" rather than "accessibility," but in a subsequent publication, Lamb refers to "accessibility." Michael E. Lamb, "Introduction: The Emergent American Father," in *The Father's Role: Cross-Cultural Perspectives*, ed. Michael E. Lamb (Hillsdale, NJ: Lawrence Erlbaum, 1987, 3–25). My preference is to conceptualize the dimension as "accessibility," because then the dimension can be linked to patterns of temporal accessibility, which are pivotal to the workings of continuous coverage social systems. See Eviatar Zerubavel, *Patterns of Time in Hospital Life* (University of Chicago Press, 1979). For an example of how continuous coverage social systems can become operative in certain family situations, see LaRossa and LaRossa, *Transition to Parenthood*.

39. Bianchi et al., *Changing Rhythms of American Family Life*, 170, 178; Doucet, *Do Men Mother?*

40. Lola Hillman, Miriam Raskin, and Karen Orloff-Kaplan, "The Liberated Husband: Father or Babysitter?" *Intellect*, June 1978, my italics.

41. Geraldine Carro, "When He Keeps the Kids," *Ladies Home Journal*, April 1979; Ross Parke and Douglas B. Sawin, "Fathering: It's a Major Role," *Psychology Today*, November 1977.

42. Carro, "When He Keeps the Kids."

43. LaRossa, "Fatherhood and Social Change."

44. Lamb et al., "Paternal Behavior in Humans."

45. Michael Lamb, "Will the Real 'New Father' Please Stand Up?" *Parents Magazine*, June 1987; James A. Levine, "The New Fatherhood," *McCalls*, June 1987.

46. Robert Crittenden, "Two Cheers for the 'New Fathers,'" *McCalls*, August 1985.

47. Ibid.

48. Margery D. Rosen, "I'm Still Doing Everything," *Ladies Home Journal*, November 1989, my italics.

49. David Osborne, "Beyond the Cult of Fatherhood," *Ms.*, September 1985.

50. Ibid.

51. Griswold, *Fatherhood in America*, 245.

52. Looking, in particular, at feminist writings, especially those outside of popular periodicals, we can see a direct challenge to men. For example, in the 1970s, Jessie Bernard critiqued the division of childcare and pointed out that men may care for a

baby, but rarely have overall responsibility for a baby. "A considerable number of fathers are willing to help their wives. They will give an infant a bottle; they will even change a diaper. They will carry the baby in its shoulder pack. They will babysit several evenings a week. But these contributions—not to be undervalued as helping wives to bear their load—are not the same as role sharing, not the same as sharing responsibility, and it is responsibilities of the mother role that make integrating it with the worker role so difficult. Just helping, which does not relieve the mother of any of her responsibilities, is therefore not enough." Jessie Bernard, *The Future of Motherhood* (New York: Dial Press, 1974), 175. Not everyone who contributed to the culture of parenthood was as firm in challenging men.

53. Contradictions and serrations in the culture of fatherhood have been observed in other historical periods as well. LaRossa, *The Modernization of Fatherhood*; LaRossa, *Of War and Men*.

54. Ibid

55. Ibid; LaRossa et al., "The Fluctuating Image of the 20th Century American Father."

56. Cf., Swidler, "Culture in Action."

57. LaRossa and LaRossa, *Transition to Parenthood*.

58. LaRossa, "Fatherhood and Social Change"; Bianchi et al., *Changing Rhythms of American Family Life*.

59. On the mental calculations that parents may do to believe that their workload is "fair" or "equitable," see LaRossa and LaRossa, *Transition to Parenthood*.

60. LaRossa, "Fatherhood and Social Change"; David F. Lancy, "Baby-Parading: Childcare or Showing Off?" *Psychology Today*, https://www.psychologytoday.com/blog/benign-neglect/201207/baby-parading-childcare-or-showing. Post originally published in *Benign Neglect: An Anthropologist Looks at Contemporary Parenting* (July 2012).

61. "Father Takes a Turn at Baby Care," *Parents Magazine*, April 1972.

62. Ruth Winter, "Psychologists Sound Off on What Makes a Good Father," *Science Digest*, June 1973.

63. Sondra Forsyth Enos, "A New Kind of Father," *Ladies Home Journal*, June 1986.

64. Roger M. Barkin, "The Changing Role of Fathers," *USA Today*, July 1989 (not the newspaper but the magazine that is published monthly by the Society for the Advancement of Education).

65. LaRossa, *The Modernization of Fatherhood*; LaRossa, *Of War and Men*.

66. Nancy R. Gibbs, "Bringing Up Father," *Time Magazine*, June 28, 1993.

67. Erik Larson, "The New Father," *Parents Magazine*, June 1991 ("Today's dads are more involved than ever before"); Lisa Schroepfer, "Dad: New and Improved," *American Health*, June 1991; Richard Louv, "How Fathers Feel," *Parents Magazine*, December 1993; Richard Louv, "Remaking Fatherhood," *Parents Magazine*, December 1994; Catherine Cartwright, "The New Family Man," *Working Mother*, June 1995; "World's Greatest Dads," *Ebony*, June 1995; J. Adler, "Building a Better Dad," *Newsweek*, June 17, 1996; "Make Room for Daddy," *Redbook*, June 1996 ("It used to be tough just to get a guy to change a diaper"); Nancy Seid and Annis Golden,

"Becoming a Dad," *Parents Magazine*, February 1997; David Shribman, "The Good Father," Life, June 1999 ("The new models are different").

68. *Kindling Quarterly* (Winter 2012/2013), inside front cover, 12.

69. *Dad* initiated publication in February/March 1990. *Modern Dad* began in Summer 1995. *Dads* premiered in June/July 2000. None of these magazines is still in operation.

70. *Fatherly*, https://www.fatherly.com/sp/about-us.html

71. LaRossa and LaRossa, *Transition to Parenthood.*

72. Milkie and Denny, "Changes in the Cultural Model of Father Involvement"; Sunderland, "Baby Entertainer, Bumbling Assistant, and Line Manager"; Wall and Arnold, "How Involved is Involved Fathering?"

BIBLIOGRAPHY

Adler, Jerry. "Building a Better Dad." *Newsweek*, June 17, 1996.

Atkinson, Maxine P. and Stephen P. Blackwelder. "Fathering in the 20th Century." *Journal of Marriage and the Family* 55 (November 1993): 975–986.

Backett, Kathryn C. *Mothers and Fathers.* New York: St. Martin's Press, 1982.

Barkin, Roger M. "The Changing Role of Fathers." *USA Today*, July 1989

Bernard, Jessie. *The Future of Motherhood.* New York: Dial Press, 1974.

Best, Steven and Douglas Kellner. *Postmodern Theory: Critical Interrogations.* New York: Guilford, 1991.

Bianchi, Suzanne M., John P. Robinson, and Melissa Milkie. *Changing Rhythms of American Family Life.* New York: Russell Sage Foundation, 2006.

Carro, Geraldine. "When He Keeps the Kids." *Ladies Home Journal*, April 1979.

Cartwright, Catherine. "The New Family Man." *Working Mother*, June 1995.

Coontz, Stephanie. *A Strange Stirring: The Feminine Mystique and American Women at the Dawn of the 1960s.* New York: Basic Books, 2011.

Cowie, Jefferson. *Stayin' Alive: The 1970s and the Last Days of the Working Class.* New York: New Press, 2010.

Crittenden, Robert. "Two Cheers for the 'New Fathers.'" *McCalls*, August 1985.

Davis, K. "The Power of Positive Fathering." *Parents Magazine,* April 1, 1976.

Day, Randal D. and Wade C. Mackey. "The Role Image of the American Father: An Examination of a Media Myth." *Journal of Comparative Family Studies* 17 (Autumn 1986): 371–388.

DeGloma, Thomas. *Seeing the Light: The Social Logic of Personal Discovery.* Chicago: University of Chicago Press, 2014.

Dienhart, Anna. "Make Room for Daddy: The Pragmatic Potentials of a Tag-Team Structure for Sharing Parenting." *Journal of Family Issues* 22 (November 2001): 973–999.

Doucet, Andrea. *Do Men Mother? Fathering, Care, and Domestic Responsibility.* Toronto: University of Toronto Press, 2006.

Edin, Kathryn and Timothy J. Nelson. *Doing the Best I Can: Fatherhood in the Inner City.* Berkeley, CA: University of California Press, 2013.

Enos, Sondra Forsyth. "A New Kind of Father." *Ladies Home Journal*, June 1986.

"Father Takes a Turn at Baby Care," *Parents Magazine*, April 1972.

Fatherly, https://www.fatherly.com/sp/about-us.html.

"Father's Day with Baby," *Parents Magazine*, June 1968.

Gibbs, Nancy R. "Bringing Up Father." *Time Magazine*, June 28, 1993.

Gibson, Janice. "Fathers are Important, Too." *Parents Magazine*, October 1984.

Greene, Richard. "I'm a New Father Who Takes His Role Seriously." *Glamour*, June 1987.

Grice, Wayne. "Fathers Mother Too!" *Essence*, June 1980.

Griswold, Robert L. *Fatherhood in America: A History*. New York: Basic Books, 1993.

Griswold, Wendy. *Cultures and Societies in a Changing World*. Thousand Oaks, CA: Pine Forge Press, 1994.

Higdon, Hal. "Dad Had It!" *Parents Magazine*, June 1960.

Hillman, Lola, Miriam Raskin and Karen Orloff-Kaplan. "The Liberated Husband: Father or Babysitter?" *Intellect*, June 1978.

Jenkins, Philip. *Decade of Nightmares: The End of the Sixties and the Making of Eighties America*. New York: Oxford University Press, 2006.

Kaufman, Gayle. *Superdads: How Fathers Balance Work and Family in the 21st Century*. New York: New York University Press, 2013.

Kindling Quarterly (Winter 2012/2013). Inside front cover, 12.

Lamb, Michael. "Will the Real 'New Father' Please Stand Up?" *Parents Magazine*, June 1987.

Lamb, Michael E., Joseph H. Pleck, Eric. L. Charnov and James A. Levine. "Paternal Behavior in Humans." *American Zoologist* 25 (3, 1985): 883–894.

Lamb, Michael E. "Introduction: The Emergent American Father. In *The Father's Role: Cross-Cultural Perspectives*, ed. Michael E. Lamb. Hillsdale, NJ: Lawrence Erlbaum, (1987): 3–25.

Lancy, David F. "Baby-Parading: Childcare or Showing Off?" *Psychology Today*, https://www.psychologytoday.com/blog/benign-neglect/201207/baby-parading-childcare-or-showing. Post originally published in *Benign Neglect: An Anthropologist Looks at Contemporary Parenting* (July 2012).

LaRossa, Ralph. "Fatherhood and Social Change." *Family Relations* 37 (October 1988): 451–457.

LaRossa, Ralph. *Of War and Men: World War II in the Lives of Fathers and Their Families*. Chicago: University of Chicago Press, 2011.

LaRossa, Ralph. *The Modernization of Fatherhood: A Social and Political History*. Chicago: University of Chicago Press, 1997.

LaRossa, Ralph. "Thinking About the Nature and Scope of Qualitative Research." *Journal of Marriage and Family* (August 2012): 678–687.

LaRossa, Ralph. "Writing and Reviewing Manuscripts in the Multidimensional World of Qualitative Research." *Journal of Marriage and Family* (August 2012): 643–659.

LaRossa, Ralph. "The Historical Study of Fatherhood: Theoretical and Methodological Considerations," in *Fatherhood in Late Modernity: Cultural Images, Social*

Practices, Structural Frames, ed. Mechtild Oechsle, Ursula Müller, and Sabine Hess. Germany: Barbara Budrich Publishers, (2012): 37–58.

LaRossa, Ralph and Maureen Mulligan LaRossa. *Transition to Parenthood: How Infants Change Families*. Beverly Hills, CA: Sage, 1981.

LaRossa, Ralph, Betty Anne Gordon, Ronald Jay Wilson, Annette Bairan and Charles Jaret. "The Fluctuating Image of the 20th Century American Father." *Journal of Marriage and the Family* 53 (November 1991): 987–997.

LaRossa, Ralph, Charles Jaret, Malati Gadgil, and G. Robert Wynn. "The Changing Culture of Fatherhood in Comic Strip Families: A Six-Decade Analysis." *Journal of Marriage and Family* 62 (May 2000): 375–387.

LaRossa, Ralph and Cynthia B. Sinha. "Constructing the Transition to Parenthood." *Sociological Inquiry* 76 (November 2006): 433–457.

Larson, Erik. "The New Father," *Parents Magazine*, June 1991.

Leavitt, Judith Walzer. *Make Room for Daddy: The Journey from Waiting Room to Birthing Room*. Chapel Hill, NC: University of North Carolina Press, 2009.

Levine, James A. "The New Fatherhood." *McCalls*, June 1987.

Livingston, Gretchen. "Growing Number of Dads Home with the Kids: Biggest Increase Among Those Caring for Family." *Pew Research Center*, June 5, 2014. http://www.pewsocialtrends.org/2014/06/05/growing-number-of-dads-home-with-the-kids/.

Louv, Richard. "How Fathers Feel." *Parents Magazine*, December 1993.

Louv, Richard. "Remaking Fatherhood." *Parents Magazine*, December 1994.

Lupton, Deborah and Lesley Barclay. *Constructing Fatherhood: Discourses and Experiences*. London: Sage, 1997.

"Make Room for Daddy." *Redbook*, June 1996.

Marsiglio, William and Kevin Roy. *Nurturing Dads: Social Initiatives for Contemporary Fatherhood*. New York: Russell Sage Foundation, 2012.

McCall, Robert B. "Fulltime Father: Staying Home with Baby." *Parents Magazine*, February 1984.

McMahon, Martha. *Engendering Motherhood: Identity and Self-Transformation in Women's Lives*. New York: Guildford, 1995.

Merton, Robert K. "Three Fragments from a Sociologist's Notebooks: Establishing the Phenomenon, Specified Ignorance, and Strategic Research Materials." *Annual Review of Sociology*, 13 (1987): 1–28.

Milkie, Melissa A. and Kathleen E. Denny. "Changes in the Cultural Model of Father Involvement: Descriptions of Benefits to Fathers, Children and Mothers in Parents' Magazine, 1926–2006." *Journal of Family Issues 35* (January 2014): 223–253.

Mintz, Steven. *Huck's Raft: A History of American Childhood*. Cambridge, MA: Harvard University Press, 2004.

Most, Doug. "The New Face of Fatherhood." *Parents Magazine*, (June 2008).

Osborne, David. "Beyond the Cult of Fatherhood." *Ms.*, September 1985.

Parish, Patrick. "The Day I Really Became a Father." *Parents Magazine*, February 1966.

Parke, Ross and Douglas B. Sawin. "Fathering: It's a Major Role." *Psychology Today*, November 1977.

Pleck, Joseph H. "Paternal Involvement: Levels, Sources, and Consequences." *The Role of the Father in Child Development*, ed. Michael E. Lamb. New York: John Wiley, 66–103.

Rosen, Margery D. "'I'm Still Doing Everything.'" *Ladies Home Journal*, November 1989.

Rosenbaum, Veryl. "Fair Play for Fathers." *Parents Magazine*, December 1970.

Sarda, Reese. "Reflections of a Father Who Became a Mother." *Redbook*, November 1975.

Schroepfer, Lisa. "Dad: New and Improved." *American Health*, June 1991.

Schulman, Bruce J. *The Seventies: The Great Shift in American Culture, Society, and Politics*. New York: Free Press, 2001.

Scott, Marvin B. and Stanford M. Lyman. "Accounts." *American Sociological Review* 33 (February 1968): 46–62.

Seid, Nancy and Annis Golden. "Becoming a Dad." *Parents Magazine*, February 1997.

Shribman, David. "The Good Father." *Life,* June 1999.

Skolnick, Arlene. *Embattled Paradise: The American Family in an Age of Uncertainty*. New York: Basic Books, 1991.

Spock, Benjamin. *The Common Sense Book of Baby and Child Care*. New York: Duell, Sloan, and Pearce, 1946.

Spock, Benjamin. *The Common Sense Book of Baby and Child Care*. New York: Duell, Sloan, and Pearce, 1957.

Spock, Benjamin. *Baby and Child Care*. New York: Hawthorne Books Inc., 1968.

Stacey, Judith. *In the Name of the Family: Rethinking Family Values in the Postmodern Age*. Boston: Beacon Press, 1996.

Sunderland, Jane. "Baby Entertainer, Bumbling Assistant, and Line Manager: Discourses of Fatherhood in Parentcraft Texts." *Discourse and Society* 11 (April 2000): 249–274.

Susman, Edward. "I Was a Mother for Six Months." *Good Housekeeping*, July 1977.

Swidler, Ann. "Culture in Action: Symbols and Strategies." *American Sociological Review* 51 (April 1986): 273–286.

Wall, Glenda and Stephanie Arnold. "How Involved is Involved Fathering?: An Exploration of the Contemporary Culture of Fatherhood." *Gender and Society* 21, no. 4 (August 2007): 508–527.

Walzer, Susan. *Thinking about the Baby: Gender and Transitions to Parenthood*. Philadelphia: Temple University Press, 1998.

Winter, Ruth. "Psychologists Sound Off on What Makes a Good Father." *Science Digest*, June 1973.

"World's Greatest Dads," *Ebony* 50, (Issue 8, June 1995).

Zerubavel, Eviatar. *Time Maps: Collective Memory and the Social Shape of the Past*. Chicago: University of Chicago Press, 2003.

Zerubavel, Eviatar. *Patterns of Time in Hospital Life*. Chicago: University of Chicago Press, 1979.

Chapter 2

Who's Your Daddy

Sperm Donation and the Cultural Construction of Fatherhood

Laura Tropp

Thirty years ago, the word "sperm" was generally a term one only heard at a medical office. These days, sperm has become a regular part of popular vernacular. One can buy t-shirts with pictures of sperm with the phrase "my boys can swim." Sperm donation, once confined to married couples who had difficulty conceiving, is now also used by non-heteronormative couples and single women who want to become moms. News media cover cases when the law wrestles with the new culture of sperm donation. The actor Jason Patric founded the organization Stand Up for Gus after his former girlfriend challenged his parental rights in court and labeled him as simply a sperm donor.[1] Other issues involving sperm donation include whether sperm banks should be required to limit the number of times a sperm donor is permitted to donate.[2] In another case, the state of Kansas has sued a man for child support after he donated sperm to a lesbian couple and the child later needed state-supported services.[3] While these are some more newsworthy cases, more families are grappling with questions about sperm donation, such as when, or even whether, to inform their children, and what role the sperm donor will play in their child's life, if any. This chapter explores how popular culture represents the phenomenon of the sperm donor, and how it works through constructions of fatherhood, paternity, genetics, masculinity, and how sperm donation both reinforces and changes our notion of parenting.

SPERM DONATION, FATHERHOOD, AND A CHANGING CULTURE

Sperm donation has been a more common subject in popular media for a variety of reasons. While sperm donation has been in use for some time,

31

more advances with different types of fertility assistance have resulted in increased opportunities to use donated sperm, including *in vitro* fertilization and surrogacy. In addition, an expanded range of family structures beyond the traditional heterosexual couple has expanded the market for sperm donation. Single Mothers by Choice is an organization dedicated to serving women who decide to have babies on their own, sometimes through adoption but often through sperm donation. Jennifer Egan reports in an article about sperm donation that, "The California Cryobank, the largest sperm bank in the country, owed a third of its business to single women in 2005, shipping them 9,600 vials of sperm, each good for one insemination."[4] In addition, lesbian couples use sperm donors to start families, and even gay men participate in the process of *in vitro* fertilization, contributing their sperm to combine with donated eggs.

While additional opportunities and use of sperm donation have appeared, the growth of the Internet and social media has created a society in which secrets are difficult to keep. In the past, an offspring's sperm donor may have been kept secret for their entire life. Now people often use resources available through the Internet and social media to seek out their donor. Professor Joanna Grossman argues, "Even if the adults involved in donor conception continue to prefer anonymous donations, technology may simply make permanent secrecy impossible."[5] The Donor Sibling Registry was created to help siblings who share sperm donors to find each other. Established in 2000, the organization reasoned that, though the sperm donor himself may have elected to remain anonymous, siblings are not constrained by the same limitation. Though they are not comfortable in referring to their donors as "fathers," children of sperm donation have less trouble with using the term "sibling" to describe other children created from the same sperm donor.[6] This may not be as surprising as it seems, as traditional families often have more than one sibling, but the idea of a second father often raises questions of definition and relations.

The profile of the typical sperm donor is also changing. Newer studies are questioning the assumption that sperm donors simply do it only for the cash with no thought as to the consequences. In contrast, in some cases sperm donors are longing to find out more about the children they have fathered.[7] However, scholar Rene Almeling, who studies comparative perspectives of sperm and egg donors, has found that expectations of these different types of donors conform to traditional gender expectations. While egg donors are expected to possess altruism as the main motive for their donation, in contrast, the managers of sperm banks did not require that sperm donors exhibit any other motivation other than the desire for financial compensation.[8] She writes, "The danger is in accepting these sentiments at face value, especially in sites like commercial fertility agencies, in which the very product for sale is made possible by sexual differences between males and females, making the conflation of sexual and gender difference more likely."[9] The difference in expectations of women who donate eggs versus men who donate sperm also reinforce the gendered roles we have assigned mothers and fathers. If egg donors are expected to demonstrate a profound commitment to motherhood, as Almeling argues, sperm donors have been treated as an afterthought or as a secondary parent, which conforms to the history of how society has viewed fatherhood.

Sperm donation itself raises questions about who is what we have labeled "the father" of the children produced. A long history of scholarship has explored fatherhood as a social construction, as expectations and definitions of fathers have changed over time. Fatherhood scholars like Ralph LaRossa have examined the difference between the culture of fatherhood and the conduct of fatherhood, indicating that our cultural expectations of fathers often change faster than actual practices.[10] Other scholars focused on media representation have mapped the tropes of fatherhood, which include the pervasive perception of fathers as bumbling or part-time parents.[11] Some have explored the way society genders expectations of parenthood, including the "flexibility stigma" that fathers experience when reducing their employment to focus on their families.[12] Recent research assesses how sperm donation may raise new challenges for legal definitions of fatherhood.[13] Much as in the legal sphere, popular media has not yet caught up to changes in definitions and participants of fatherhood.

Fiction media forms also have represented sperm donation with increasing frequency. Feature films are sometimes ripped from the headlines to explore phenomena like 150 children fathered from the same donor or the complications that ensue when a child searches for their sperm donor.[14] Within these depictions, however, films and television programs also explore what fatherhood means when genetics are divorced from the social obligations of fathers. This study examines films and television programs in which sperm donation is the central premise. The programs include four films: *Delivery Man, The Switch, Made in America*, and *The Kids Are All Right*, one reality television program, MTV's *Generation Cryo*, and one fiction television series, *Seed*, produced and viewed in Canada.[15] The content of these programs often depict how the construct of fatherhood adapts outside of a heteronormative family structure.

QUEST FOR YOUR SPERM DONOR

A key theme that runs through all of these narratives is the need to find one's sperm donor in order to fill in a missing piece of oneself. This journey becomes the premise of the reality program *Generation Cryo*, where Breanna (Bree) looks for her half-siblings in an effort to enlist their help in finding their sperm donor. This quest is also the theme of *Made in America* where Zora, a young woman of color, searches to identify her sperm donor and is surprised to find he is Caucasian. A similar journey is the subject of *The Kids Are All Right* in which the son, Laser, convinces his sister Joni to search for their birth father. The film comedy *Delivery Man* creates dueling quests: a sperm donor's children look for him while he simultaneously searches for them. *The Switch* provides a variation of the familiar quest. In the film, Kassie's friend Wally struggles to find a way to reveal to her that he is the father of her child after he had accidently spilled the sperm donor's sample when he was drunk and secretly replaced it with his own. In *Seed,* Harry's two children find him in the first episode; by the third episode, another woman using his donated sperm is pregnant with his child, and she accidentally stumbles upon him prior to confirming the pregnancy.

Although the plots of these stories vary, each program illustrates the need of a child to know the identity of their sperm donor. Many of these characters express a sense of missing a piece of themselves that only the discovery of their sperm donor will fulfill. In some cases, children are presented as lacking father figures, which starts them on their search. In *Seed*, Harry is found by two of his donor children: Billy, the child of two lesbian moms, and Anastasia, the daughter of a heterosexual couple in which her father was infertile. Throughout the series, Harry provides advice from a male perspective for Billy. The program implies Billy needs this guidance because two women are raising him. One episode shows Harry trying to change Billy's favorite hobby of scrapbooking; in another, Harry tries to help Billy be more cool in school.

The child in *The Switch*, Sebastian, collects picture frames with the stock photos still inside, which he pretends are his family members. The father figure he desires has translated to a desperate grasping for any depiction of a family. Sebastian's missing father is contrasted with the origin story Kassie recites. She tells him, "Mommy didn't have a husband but wanted you so very much that she couldn't wait another day." The film contrasts the mother's obtaining the sperm as a simple business transaction with the child yearning for a more emotional connection with his biological father. This becomes the impetus for Kassie to begin a relationship with the man whom she believes to be the sperm donor, though the audience is aware that Wally is the true sperm donor. In *Delivery Man*, one child describes his desire to find a father as, "I want to have a part of myself." In *Made in America*, Zora rushes off to find her father after a blood test conducted as a science experiment in school reveals that her deceased father could not have been her biological father. Her mother tries to downplay the role of the sperm donor, but Zora immediately imagines him as a potential parent: "But Mom, I could have a father." The desire to fulfill a missing part of one's identity with a father figure appears often in *Generation Cryo*, where for 17-year-old Bree this quest becomes an important moment in her transition to adulthood.

Common in the construction of these programs is that idea that, though the children often have had strong parental role models and a happy childhood, they still feel a need to find their biological selves, which in these cases is represented as knowing the identity of their sperm donors. The quest in each film helps to connect social lives with the biological self. Kassie's perceived sperm donor in *The Switch* is unable to connect with Sebastion, while the child's relationship with his true sperm donor seems much more effortless. In a similar fashion, the instant connection in *Seed* between Harry and Billy, who are regularly shown hanging out together after their first meeting, represents the "natural" way that the sperm donor can connect with a child.

Perhaps because it was produced as an independent film, *The Kids Are All Right* questions the "natural" connection between sperm donor and child more than the other stories examined here. Laser had spurred the search for his and his sister's sperm donor, but he does not discover an instant connection to Paul. Laser's sister Joni, who had expressed less interest in meeting the donor, however, is drawn in by his "coolness." By the end of the film, both children have bonded with him in different ways but are also disillusioned by him. Joni tells Paul, "I wish you were better."

The legal obligations of the sperm donor are explored in *Delivery Man*, as children petition to unseal papers to reveal the identity of their sperm donor. The film depicts moments when one of his children wants more from him than he feels he can give. The conflict reflects an American culture where the identity of a sperm donor is oftentimes still guarded in secrecy, unlike other countries that have updated their regulations to entitle a future child to have the right to know his or her sperm donor.[16]

Though ideological norms assert that to be a good father a man must play an active role in the nurturing of their child, the central quest in these narratives argues the opposite. These sperm donor plots imply that there often exists an instant connection between a child and sperm donor and a role waiting to be fulfilled because of the genetic connection that they share.

FATHERLY THREAT

As children in these stories search for their donors in order to feel more fully knowledgeable about themselves or to fill in a missing piece in their lives, the search itself is portrayed as disrupting and threatening the internal family structure. Diane Ehrensaft coined the term "birth other" as a term "for the outside person who offers gametes or uterus so that someone else can procreate. . . ."[17] This phrase reflects the confusion that the sperm donor poses for family structure. Though most of the programs continually reassert the love present within the family that is raising or has raised the child, they ultimately raise questions about who should be considered to be the "true" father by representing the sperm donor as a significant threat.

Indekeu et al. describe the challenges of families and sperm dona-tion: "Living in a socio-cultural context that highly values genetics made it challenging to negate the genetic origin of the child—being partly the sperm donor, while the system of donor anonymity—separating donor and recipient—hindered the existence of the donor."[18] These narratives reflect the challenge of finding a place for the sperm donor within an already con-structed family by portraying the search for the donor as having a component of secrecy. This is apparent in *Made in America*, where Zora sneaks off to the sperm bank to look for her sperm donor and then has to break the news to her mother that he seems to be a terrible man. As the oldest of the stories studied here, Zora does not have access to a digital search and must physically hide in the sperm bank to try to sneak access to the information, all the while trying to hide the search from her mother, whom she knows would not approve.

Though the search for the sperm donor is physically easier in *Generation Cryo* because it can involve computer databases and Internet searches, the threat to the family is no less present. In fact, many of the siblings acknowl-edge the threat outright. One sibling, Molly, says, "It's so much better when the dads say it's okay," acknowledging the ambivalent feelings that come up when searching for a donor that does not want to be found.[19] Even though some of the families are not troubled by a child's search for their donor, the program spends a significant amount of time on the conflict between donor sibling Jonah and his father, who is threatened by the Jonah's and Bree's search for their donor. While the reality program may be using this conflict for dramatic purposes, the result of this emphasis is the constant reminder of the possibility that the revelation of the sperm donor may threaten the stasis of the family.

Even for non-heteronormative families that have no father to be threat-ened, children still worry about offending their parents. Bree, the daughter of a lesbian couple, worries that Sherry, her nonbiological mom, will be more threatened by the donor than her mom who has a biological connection. In a fictional depiction of a family with two lesbian moms, Laser asks his sister Joni to help him find their sperm donor in *The Kids Are All Right* because she is of legal age and is permitted to initiate the search. She agrees to help only if he promises to keep it quiet, because "That could really hurt moms' feelings." The children in *Seed* have kept their search for their sperm donor a secret from their parents, but in each case, once Harry is found, the nonbiological parental figure acts more vulnerable by the emergence of the sperm donor.

Anastasia's father cautions Harry to "stay away from my family,"[20] offers to pay him off to stay out of their lives,[21] and becomes upset when he finds out his daughter revealed to other kids at her school that she is the product of a sperm donation.[22]

Children in these narratives often suggest medical or biological reasons for their search, hoping that this rational concern will not be perceived as much of a threat to their current father figure. Jonah, who is not that interested in finding his sperm donor but helps his half-sister with the search, says that he is most interested in finding out more information about possible hereditary traits, such as addiction. In *Made in America*, Zora tells her mother that she could have a father out there, expressing dissatisfaction with the lack of a father figure in her life.

The films and television programs also portray the sperm donor as a sexual threat to the family. Most of the male donors depicted in these programs are emphasized as having a strong sexual appetite. They are seen as womanizers (Harry in *The Seed*, Hal in *Made in America*, and Paul in *The Kids Are All Right*) or as simply having a strong virility, such as the delighted shock in *Generation Cryo* when the children find their donor had written that he "likes sex" on an information form. Despite the fact that, in all of these donor situations, no sex ever was involved during the donation process, the mother of Paige and Molly describes feeling strange "that she had another man's sperm inside me." She admits to feeling like she had cheated on her husband in some way by accepting the donation.[23] In *Made in America*, Hal exploits the fact that Sarah used his donation to conceive as a reason to consummate their relationship. He tells her, "My sperm has been in your body."

Scholars studying sperm donation notice a pattern in the way male figures in heterosexual couples feel threatened: "Even though men are more likely to define themselves by their work, their competence as a family provider is also a measure of their 'manhood.' As a result, not being able to provide the essence of life that defines their manhood and their wives' womanhood is demoralizing and self-effacing to men."[24] This emotion is reflected in *Generation Cryo,* where Jonah's father explains his trepidation with his children meeting the sperm donor: "Am I secure enough in who I am to say we had to use donor sperm? I couldn't do it. The one manly thing that every man is expected to do." The son asks his father whether raising the kids is the manly thing, and father counters by saying "from a human evolution perspective, those that couldn't produce died out. So that was the single most manly thing that took place."[25] Of all those featured in the program, this father is the most threatened by the sperm donor, despite what seems to be a healthy and close relationship with his children.

Ironically, the most outright sexual threat appears in the film *The Kids Are All Right* when Paul engages in a sexual affair with one of the lesbian moms, Jules. This moment nearly destroys the internal structure of the family. Toward the end of the film, the other mom, Nic, confronts Paul: "This is not your family. This is my family. . . . You don't know and you know . . . because you're a f****** interloper. If you want a family so much, you go out and make your own."

Though each of the stories represents the sperm donor as some type of threat, by the end of each one, a more traditional notion of family has reasserted itself. Jennifer Maher writes, ". . . Hollywood romantic comedies of the (wonders) of reproductive technology paradoxically function, as does much contemporary discourse, to reinstate the 'natural' romance of the patriarchal family."[26] In these sperm donor representations, popular media either reinforce the patriarchal family as indicated by Maher, or in some cases, when that is not possible, finds an alternative way to reassure audiences that despite the presence of a sperm donor, a nuclear family will remain intact.

David announces in a pivotal speech in *Delivery Man*, "It's not anyone but me who can decide if I am a father or not." He implies that in some way he will watch over all of the children for whom he donated sperm. The film ends with him celebrating his new family made up of his girlfriend and newborn baby, and many of his children admiring the baby through the window in the newborn nursery. In *The Switch*, Kassie has broken up with Roland, the originally intended sperm donor, and the film ends with a scene that establishes the new family of Kassie, Wally, and Sebastion, complete with a picture frame holding a photograph of his family as part of his collection. Sara, Hal, and Zora publicly acknowledge their new family at Zora's graduation in *Made in America*, despite the fact that they find out that Hal is not her true sperm donor. In *Seed*, the lesbian parents of Billy and the heterosexual parent of Anastasia remain their primary caretakers, with Harry providing support in the form of advice and outings. Harry even reassures Anastasia's father, Jonathan: "You make the sacrifices. You're her real father. Everyone knows that."[27] Harry, though, is now playing the father/husband role in the life of Rose, and it is clear that a love interest is brewing that will be explored more in Season Two. *The Kids Are All Right* is the only representation that does not have a father figure presented at the conclusion, but it does offer the reassurance that the original family structure will remain intact. While the ending is more ambiguous in *Generation Cryo*, a happy ending is implied in that the siblings had found their donor, who is willing to communicate with them, and he no longer seems as threatening to their existing caregivers. Bree's mother, Sherry, tells her that this guy "is part of her soul."[28] The mother says she would love to meet and thank him. While these media representations ultimately reassure audiences that the sperm donor will not destroy the family structure, the threat itself remains a central plotline for many of these films.

INSTANT FATHERHOOD AND THE
SELF-ACTUALIZATION OF MEN

Another theme appearing throughout much of the representation of sperm donation in popular media is that once a man meets the children of his donor sperm, he shifts from an irresponsible or self-absorbed person to become a more responsible, caretaker figure. This theme situates fatherhood as an essential life stage for men to pass through in order to become a self-actualized adult.

The opening scenes of all these films portray the sperm donors as childlike, with unrealized potential, or living a life that is too self-indulgent. In the opening scene of *The Switch*, a mentally ill homeless man calls Wally a "beedy-eyed little man boy." During conversations with Kassie, he appears neurotic and self-absorbed. His irresponsible nature is evident when he becomes jealous that Kassie is passing him over as her sperm donor, becomes drunk, and accidently spills her sperm sample and replaces it with his own. The childish man theme is also the premise of *Delivery Man*, where David is represented as not acting as a real adult. He works for his dad, and his parents and siblings bemoan his lack of responsibility. He owes a large debt which puts his life at risk, and he cannot hold down a stable relationship, though his girlfriend has announced she is pregnant by him.

The irresponsible father is also on display in *Seed*. The woman Harry is with in the opening scene tells him to "grow up" while he plays video games. In *Made in America*, the audience is introduced to Hal as the ultimate irresponsible man, with junk food, alcohol and cigarettes as well as his overly extended id and sexual interest. Finally, in *The Kids Are All Right*, Paul is shown at the beginning of the film as living the life of a bachelor. He flirts with women and showcases his sexuality and virility. The fear of commitment and accompanying self-absorption seems to be a key component of the sperm donor; they are all depicted without a family, are not successful often within relationships or even desiring a commitment. Hal describes two failed marriages and a hedonistic lifestyle: "I live to enjoy myself." Even in *Generation Cryo*, when the half-siblings locate their donor, they find him to be a single man who never had married.

At the beginning of each narrative, most of the sperm donors seem to resist the father role in some way. In *Seed*, Harry tries to avoid a connection with the kids: "The kids are in my head and I don't like it, but I will not let that get in the way of my hooking up with emotionally needy women."[29] Yet, in each episode, he ends up more involved and vested in the lives of his children, even visiting their schools and participating in their extracurricular activities. Wally resists getting to know Kassie's son, but he's depicted as unable to avoid interaction once he's forced in situations together with him. He gives Sebastian advice and, in a pivotal moment in the film, he has no choice but to care for Sebastian overnight and deal with his case of lice. The scene presents a voiceover of Kassie giving Wally step-by-step instructions on how to handle the lice. In filling this fatherly role, Wally bonds with Sebastian and grows a bit. In *Delivery Man*, David at first denies that he has fathered 533 children through his sperm donation and files a lawsuit to avoid being identified. By the end of the film, however, he feels compelled to find his children and vows to "be their guardian angel." He helps one fight drug addiction, provides care to a disabled child, and proudly visits and applauds the children who are performers or actors.

It is this involvement with the children that allows the men to grow and, in some cases, prepare to become responsible fathers. At the beginning of *Delivery Man*, David's girlfriend, after announcing she is pregnant, rejects him as a possible father figure because of his irresponsible nature. Observing him as he takes on responsibilities for his donor children, she says at the end of the film, "I'm going to declare you the father on probation." By the end of *Seed*'s first season, Harry's friend tells him, much to his shock, that he's become a "responsible adult" because of his commitment to preparing for the birth of his child and supporting Rose, the mother of his child. *Made in America* implies that Hal will settle down with Sarah, Zora's mother. Even in *The Kids Are All Right*, which as an independent film is less likely to follow dominant ideological norms, the film shows Paul longing for domesticity as he looks through the window at the family he could have had.

Fatherhood, which brings along the culmination of adulthood, is depicted in these stories as achievable only through a full transformation from a boyish, self-absorbed man-child to a new man who is selfless, more likely to commit to a relationship, and most importantly, able to appreciate the art of sacrifice, which these stories set up as an attribute required for parenting. The transformation of fatherhood is not a new subject for media. Films such as *Knocked Up* (2007), *The Back-Up Plan* (2010), and *What to Expect when You're Expecting* (2012) all showcase a man learning how to become a father. Sperm donor films take the same transformation but shift the parameters. The birth itself no longer separates the man-child from the transformed father; children of various ages showing up in a donor's life become the new point of demarcation. However, men still must pass through stages where they learn to embrace monogamy (not always with the mother of the child) and temper their sexuality. They must learn to be less self-absorbed and begin to sacrifice for their children. This new stage of fatherhood is not reached through a pregnancy journey but an inner process triggered by the knowledge and acceptance of a child in one's life. Sperm donor films depict instant fatherhood as a first step toward true fatherhood and adulthood through an inner transformation conforming to idealized assumptions about the self-sacrificing, caring father figure.

FATHERLY ROLES AND FUNCTIONS

Sperm donation itself raises questions about who should be designated the father. Many children already have a father who has raised them, but their sperm donor is another person who shares their genetic code. Other families have no formal father figure. Most of these sperm donor narratives fall into dominant ideological assumptions about the roles of the father. These fall into three categories: to provide a strong protector role, particularly with female children, to teach sons to protect and defend their masculinity and engage in masculine activities, and to bring a level of coolness and fun to the child's life.

The protector role is evident within *Made in America*, *Delivery Man*, and *Seed*. Scenes in each of these films show a sperm donor protecting his daughter against a sexual interest that he perceives as a threat to her girlhood. In *Made in America*, Hal threatens the teen about to take Zora out on a date, and is proven right when the teen makes sexual advances despite Zora asking him to stop. David is bothered by men ogling his daughter in *Delivery Man*, and Harry in *Seed* rushes to save Anastasia from a sexually charged party. The sperm donor in each of these stories provides masculine protection for his daughter as an expression of fatherhood.

In contrast to their female offspring, sperm donors teach their male children the skills necessary to be able to defend themselves in the world. The first two episodes of *Seed* show Harry teaching his son how to avoid being bullied. In *The Switch*, Sebastian reaches out to Wally because he is being bullied and wants his guidance on how to stop it. Though each of these boys have loving and involved parents, because they do not have a father figure, these stories present the missing masculine role as hampering the boys from being equipped with necessary defense skills. The masculine role model also is reinforced in *The Kids Are All Right*, in which Laser hangs out with Clay, a friend who is a bad influence on him. Though his mothers have tried to warn Laser about Clay, it is only when Paul criticizes the friend that Laser listens. Paul advises Laser not to hang out with Clay because he doesn't like how Clay talks down to him. In these cases, the depictions show how the sperm donor can connect to the children in ways that their families have been unsuccessful. In some cases the stories imply that a man is needed to fulfill the functions of a male father figure in order to successfully raise children.

While these stories imply that father figures are necessary for the full socialization of the child, sperm donors are often represented as making poor choices or providing bad advice. In *The Switch*, Wally tells Sebastian to act crazy to the bully because, "No one messes with the crazy guy." David tells one of his sons in *Delivery Man* to go for an audition while he stands in for him at his job, but he works so poorly that he almost gets his son fired. In

Seed, Harry forces Billy to give up scrapbooking, a hobby that he deems too feminine.[30]

The sperm donors in these texts also provide fun, risk, and excitement into children's lives. Paul takes his daughter for a motorcycle ride in *The Kids Are All Right*, much to the shock of her mother. In a similar scene, Harry wants to take both his children out on a motorcycle despite the protests of the children's parents.[31] Anastasia's mother complains that Harry is turning her father into "the lame dad."[32] In another scene, Anastasia is in trouble at school and has them call Harry, hoping to pretend he is her father.[33] In both *Seed* and *The Kids Are All Right*, the sperm donor's coolness is contrasted with rigid rules the parents have established. The standard trope of the bumbling father who is not as effective as mothers in their parental duties is absorbed the sperm donor, who may fulfill some fatherly functions but cannot be as self-less as the parents who raised the children from birth. The donors may bring risk and excitement to the life of the children, but the parents' safety concerns ultimately prove the stronger force.

These stories contend with the notions of masculinity and fatherhood. In her study, Maher describes romantic comedies featuring the use of reproductive technology as preserving the role of masculinity in some way:

> Without abandoning it entirely, then, masculinity must be somehow rehabilitated in order to not appear obsolete in this new (post-feminist) world order of sperm for sale. As such, the male character in these films must be seen as retreating from traditional masculinity even as they embody it through their roles as white biological fathers and romantic partners.[34]

With men not needed for their role as sexual mate, Maher argues that media are representing men as filling more than the roles traditionally assigned to them. In *The Kids Are All Right*, the filmmakers wrestle with notions of masculinity with the character of Paul because his activities evoke more hospitable pursuits, such as his involvement in the restaurant business and tending to his own organic garden. In addition, during a conversation with his donor son, he boldly declares his lack of interest in team sports. David's inability to function as a provider in *Delivery Man* is compared with his girlfriend, who appears in the traditionally masculine role of police officer. Wally, who does not seem to be overly masculine, is contrasted with the extreme masculinity of the intended sperm donor.

However, these media representations also showcase scenes of the sperm donors exhibiting traditional masculine identities. David is excited to see that one of his donor children plays professional sports, and he tries to teach another son how to play basketball. In *Seed*, Harry's sexual desires often prevent him from exercising a commitment to his children, such as when he brings a date to Rose's ultrasound or makes Billy sign up for rhythmic gymnastics so he can hit on the teacher.[35] Though these depictions shift the meaning of masculinity and its place within fatherhood, the roles and functions of traditional fatherhood are reinforced while introducing a new character who can pick and choose from these roles to both endanger and invigorate the family unit.

FATHERHOOD AS A CONSUMER TRANSACTION

Sperm donation complicates the nature of fatherhood in part because components of the process are commoditized. Jennifer Egan has interviewed women who have used sperm donors. She writes:

> Despite the obvious parallels between shopping for sperm and dating online, there is finally no comparing them—a sperm donor is providing *half the DNA for your child,* and whether or not you choose to think about it, he'll be there forever in the child's tastes and choices and personality. No one wants a decision like that to feel arbitrary.[36]

The search for a sperm donor is not constrained by the same choices that may go into one's requirements for a spouse. The women or couples selecting a donor may focus solely on the product (the child) that they want and choose the type of sperm that can help them achieve their desired goal. These media depictions imagine how the decision to select a particular donor is made, whether the commoditized process of donor selection can be trusted, and what happens when the expectations for the sperm donor are not met.

The media depictions all explore what motivates men who donate their sperm. Conforming to Almeling's finding that society assumes sperm donors are motivated by financial compensation, these stories describe the reasons why men donated sperm. In *The Kids Are All Right*, Laser, who first is suspicious of Paul, asks him why he donated. "I loved the idea of helping people," Paul replies. "People who were in need who wanted to have a kid and couldn't." Laser looks disbelieving and asks Paul how much he got paid. "I got paid $60 bucks a pop, and that was a lot of money to me." Paul adds, "I'm glad I did it." As the half-siblings search for their donor in *Generation Cryo*, they compare the different applications he had completed to discover a more complete picture of him. His motivations were money, and he had written, "I like sex." When asked why he is donating, Roland, the intended sperm donor in *The Switch*, says he is doing it for the money, although he is married and claims to be in love with his wife, whom he describes as his "soul mate." In fact, the only donor not shown as financially motivated seems to be Wally, in *The Switch*, who substitutes his sample when he accidently spills the one Roland contributed. *Delivery Man* states at its beginning that Hal received $24,254 for all his sperm donations.

The financial motivation of the sperm donor is contrasted with the expectation of those seeking the sperm. They want not just a child, but also one that fits a particular genetic profile. These media depictions represent the selection process as all about choosing paternity, as opposed to fatherhood. In choosing a particular sperm sample, women imagine the influence of the DNA contained within. All recognize its importance, and some are more specific than others. In *Made in America,* the main character Sarah (played by Whoopi Goldberg) tells her daughter that she went to the sperm bank and asked them for "the best that they have." Kassie in *The Switch* expresses a strong desire for a specific type of sperm donor; she rejects her best friend Wally because she thinks he is too neurotic. Instead, she seeks someone who is tall and has a sense of humor. Her choice is a blond man who works as an assistant professor. At this stage in the process, the worth of the donor is in his DNA.

All the media depictions show this process as a simple transaction. Ehrensaft describes strategies couples use to interact with donors, including to "reduce the donor to a vial of sperm or an egg in a dish or shrink the surrogate to a disembodied uterus" to both eliminate any sexual threat and placate fears of an interloper that can demand parental rights.[37] *Generation Cryo*'s opening title sequence matter-of-factly states the transaction: "Two moms, neither of them had a penis. Plan B. One day some mystery guy did his thing in a cup, tall, athletic, and intelligent." Likewise, the title of the television series *Seed* evokes what is collected from a donor in order to grow a family. Harry reassures his daughter of his pride in fatherhood by telling her that, "Best thing I've ever done involved five minutes into a Styrofoam cup in a sperm bank."[38] Hal reduces his paternity to "conception in a plastic cup." *Delivery Man* refers to both Hal's occupation and the idea of sperm donation as a transactional process.

Once the sperm donor is found in these media representations, he transforms from a paternity figure to having the expectations of a father, complicating the original transaction. In fact, these stories connect the inherited genetic similarities between father and child to the push toward fatherhood. For example, Wally and Sebastian in *The Switch* seem to share characteristics that may be either hereditary or socially constructed. Wally explains how, as a hypochondriac, he is always worrying about having a disease. Sebastian says, "Oh, my God. I have that." They both hum as they eat. Even after Wally tells a stranger on a bus that they are not related, she says to him, "He's a little you." In *Seed*, Harry and Billy look alike. Jules tells Paul in *The Kids Are All*

Right, "I keep seeing my kids' expressions in your face," and she later sleeps with him. These stories suggest that genetics create an unavoidable draw between donor and child.

Once the sperm donor is discovered, the stories shift to the way the donor transitions from sperm provider to fatherhood and plays with the ambiguities between inherited and socially constructed traits. The media representations also wrestle with the disappointment parents sometimes face when confronted with a sperm donor who does not live up to their expectations. At dinner together in *The Kids Are All Right*, Paul does not match the image the moms imagined from what was written on donor forms. When Nic questions Paul about his International Studies major, he admits to her that he did not finish college, and he confesses that he is not in a committed relationship. Though Nic never vocalizes her fears then, she expresses disappointment that Paul does not match her expectations and may have provided them with a "defective" product. Likewise, Anastasia's parents in *Seed* question whether Harry lied to them on his application because he does not seem to possess all the qualities he listed. They blame their daughter's academic troubles on him and make Harry take an IQ test to prove his claims of intelligence.[39] In *Made in America*, Sara is clearly upset that she had been given sperm from a white instead of black donor and calls the sperm bank to complain about their process. Wally spends much of *The Switch* worried about how he can tell Kassie he is the real donor, imagining her disappointment at the information. In *Generation Cryo*, the possibility of knowing her father frightens Paige because she used to use her image of him to attribute any of her traits, good or bad.[40] Having expressed little interest in learning about his donor, in the fifth episode Jess refuses to admit how they look alike, but by the next one he begins to acknowledge that they share physical traits.

In all these media representations, the sperm donor shifts from the commoditized role of providing a product of bodily fluid to fulfilling some role of fatherhood. Though some of the stories make clear that the sperm donor will not take the place of the primary family unit, they also assert a genetic connection between the members that moves beyond the control of either participant. In *Delivery Man*, David insults one of his donor children by referring to his "real" family, prompting the child to protest that David does not see him as real. The genetic storyline reveals this sense of familial obligation on the part of the sperm donor, with only *Delivery Man* using the lawsuit to outright question a donor's legal obligation. Though the law finds in David's favor to remain anonymous, in the end he reveals himself to the children after all. These storylines assert an inevitable pull toward the quest for finding one's genetic origin.

CONCLUSION

Sperm donation disrupts the notion of the natural, normative family structure. Writing on fertility and reproduction issues, Bridget Taylor argues:

> The major change that NRTs [new reproductive technologies] have brought about is that kinship can no longer be viewed as purely biological and marital relatedness. The means of achieving relatedness is no longer solely dependent on biology, for NRTs contain the possibility of rendering biological or blood ties immaterial.[41]

While the initial process of sperm donation sets up the role of sperm donor as functioning in a simple commoditized transaction, after the sperm donor and children are reunited, the sperm donor shifts from a paternal to potential father figure. However, the meanings of paternity and fatherhood are ambiguous in these representations, particularly concerning what should be the expectations of their role and how their genetic contribution may influence the child. This ambiguity is best expressed in *Generation Cryo*, when one of Bree's half-siblings Paige says about the donor, "He's a parent but he's never filled that parent role."[42] While the sperm donor originally is represented as a menace to the family, all the media representations examined here eventually contain the threat by either bringing the sperm donor into the family, confining him to outsider status, or having him function as a secondary father figure. Sperm donation has the potential to reimagine the family structure, yet most of these media representations continue to be bound by traditional notions of fatherhood.

NOTES

1. Standupforgus.org. retrieved July 27, 2015.
2. Jacqueline Mroz, "One Sperm Donor, 150 Offspring," *New York Times*, September 5, 2011. www.nytimes.com.
3. Associated Press, "Kansas: Sperm Donor is Ordered to Pay Support," *New York Times*. January 2, 2013. www.nytimes.com.
4. Jennifer Egan, "Looking for Mr. Good Sperm," New York Times Magazine, March 19, 2006, 46.
5. Joanna L. Grossman, "Sperm Donors on the Large and Small Screen," *Verdict: Legal Analysis and Commentary from Justia*, November 27, 2013.
6. Amy Harmon, "Hello, I'm Your Sister. Our Father is Donor 150," *New York Times*, November 20, 2005. http://www.nytimes.com/2005/11/20/us/hello-im-your-sister-our-father-is-donor-150.html?_r=0.
7. Stephanie Fairyington, "Today's Sperm Donor isn't a Broke 20-Something." *Daily Beast*, September 20, 2014, http://www.thedailybeast.com/articles/2014/09/20/today-s-sperm-donor-isn-t-a-broke-20-something.html.

8. Rene Almeling, "'Why do you want to be a donor?': gender and the production of altruism in egg and sperm donation," *New Genetics and Society* 25, no. 2 (2006) 150.

9. Ibid., 155.

10. Ralph LaRossa. "Fatherhood and Social Change," In *Men's Lives*. Ed. Michael S. Kimmel and Michael A. Messner. (Needham Heights, Massachusetts: Pearson, 1995): 448.

11. Jane Sunderland, "Baby Entertainer. Bumbling Assistant and Line Manager: Discourses of Fatherhood in Parentcraft Texts," *Discourse Society*, 11, no. 2 (2000): 249–274; Jessamyn Neuhaus. "Dad Test: Gender, Race, and "Funny Fathers" in Disposable Diaper Advertising from the 1970s to 2012," *Advertising & Society Review* 14, no. 2 (2013).

12. Scott Coltrane, Elizabeth C. Miller, Tracy DeHaa, and Lauren Stewart, "Fathers and the Flexibility Stigma," *Journal of Social Issues* 69, no. 2 (2013): 279–302.

13. Nancy E. Dowd "Multiple Parents/Multiple Fathers" *J.L. & Family Studies 231* 9 (2007).

14. Jacqueline Mroz, "From One Sperm Donor, 150 Children," *New York Times*, September 6, 2011, D1.

15. *The Switch*, Blu Ray, directed by Josh Gordon and Will Speck (2011; USA: Lionsgate Films, 2011); *Made in America*, DVD, directed by Richard Benjamin (1993; USA; Warner Home Video, 2004) *The Kids Are All Right*, DVD, directed by Lisa Cholodenko (2010; USA: Universal Studios Home Entertainment, 2010), *Delivery Man*, DVD, directed by Ken Scott (2013; USA: Walt Disney Studios, 2014); Though most of the programming was focused within the United States, an exception was made for the Canadian program Seed, which is a sitcom dealing with a man whose children from sperm donation seek to find him.

16. Sheila Pike and Allan Pacey, "Sperm Donation: Coping with Change," *Human Fertility* 8, no. 3 (2005): 173–174.

17. Diane Ehrensaft, "When Baby Makes Three or Four or More: Attachment, Individuation, and Identity in Assisted-Conception Families," *Psychoanalytic Study of the Child* 63 (2009): 3–23.

18. Astrid Indekeu, Thomas D'Hooghe, Ken R. Daniels, Kris Dierickx & Peter Rober. "When 'sperm' becomes 'donor': Transitions in parents' views of the sperm donor" *Human Fertility* 17, no. 4 (2014): 274. DOI: 10.3109/14647273.2014. 910872.

19. *Generation Cryo*, "One Last Trip," no. 6, Season 1, first broadcast December 23, 2013, by MTV.

20. Seed, "Ill Conceived," no. 1, Season 1, directed by James Genn and written by Joseph Raso (Port Washington, NY: Entertainment One Film USA, 2013), DVD.

21. *Seed*, "The Rhythmic Gymnastic Method," no. 3, Season 1, directed by James Dunnison and written by Joseph Raso. Port Washington, NY: Entertainment One Film USA, 2013).

22. *Seed*, "The Ultra Sound and the Fury," no. 4, Season 1, directed by James Dunnison and written by Joseph Raso (Port Washington, NY: Entertainment One Film USA, 2013).

23. *Generation Cryo*, "Where's Your Family," no. 3, Season 1, first broadcast December 9, 2013, by MTV.

24. Patricia Mahlstedt, Kathleen LaBounty, and William Thomas Kennedy, "The View of Adult Offspring of Sperm Donation: Essential Feedback for the Development of Ethical Guidelines within the Practice of Assisted Reproductive Technology in the United States," *Fertility and Sterility* 93, no. 7 (2010): 2236–2246.

25. Generation Cryo, "Who's Your Daddy," no. 1, Season 1, first broadcast November 19, 2013, by MTV.

26. Jennifer Maher, "Something Else Besides a Father: Reproductive Technology in Recent Hollywood Film," *Feminist Media Studies* 14, no. 5 (2014): 855. http://dx.doi.org/10.1080/14680777.2013.831369http://dx.doi.org/10.1080/14680777.2013.831369.

27. *Seed*, no. 4, Season 1.

28. *Generation Cryo*, no. 6, Season 1.

29. *Seed*, no. 1, Season 1.

30. *Seed*, no. 3, Season 1.

31. Ibid.

32. Ibid.

33. *Seed*, no. 4, Season 1.

34. Maher, "Something Else Besides a Father,": 858.

35. *Seed*, nos. 3 and 4, Season 1.

36. Egan, "Looking for Mr. Good Sperm," 50.

37. Ehrensaft, "When Baby Makes Three or Four."

38. Seed, no. 1, Season 1.

39. Seed, no. 2, Season 1.

40. *Generation Cryo*, no. 6, Season 1.

41. Bridget Taylor, "Whose Baby is it? The Impact of Reproductive Technologies on Kinship" *Human Fertility* 8 (September 2005): 194.

42. *Generation Cryo*, no. 6, Season 1.

BIBLIOGRAPHY

Almeling, Rene. "'Why do you want to be a donor?': Gender and the production of altruism in egg and sperm donation." *New Genetics and Society* 25, no. 2 (2006): 143–157. doi:10.1080/14636770600855184.

Associated Press. "Kansas: Sperm Donor is Ordered to Pay Support." *New York Times*. January 2, 2013. www.nytimes.com.

Coltrane, Scott, Elizabeth C. Miller, Tracy DeHaa, and Lauren Stewart. "Fathers and the Flexibility Stigma." *Journal of Social Issues* 69, no. 2 (2013): 279–302. doi:10.1111/josi.12015

Delivery Man. Directed by Ken Scott. Written by Ken Scott and Martin Petit. Produced by Touchstone Pictures, DreamWorks Pictures and Reliance Entertainment. Original release 2013. USA: Walt Disney Studios Motion Pictures 2014. DVD.

Dowd, Nancy E. "Multiple Parents/Multiple Fathers." *J.L. & Family Studies* 231 (2007): 231–263. http://scholarship.law.ufl.edu/facultypub/459.

Ehrensaft, Diane. "When Baby Makes Three or Four or More: Attachment, Individuation, and Identity in Assisted-Conception Families." *Psychoanalytic Study of the Child* 63 (2009): 3–23.

Egan, Jennifer. "Looking for Mr. Good Sperm." *New York Times Magazine*. March 19, 2006: 46.

Fairyington, Stephanie. "Today's Sperm Donor isn't a Broke 20-Something." *Daily Beast*. September 20, 2014. http://www.thedailybeast.com/articles/2014/09/20/today-s-sperm-donor-isn-t-a-broke-20-something.html.

Generation Cryo. Episodes 1-6, Season 1. MTV. Original broadcast November 2013.

Grossman, Joanna L. "Sperm Donors on the Large and Small Screen." *Verdict: Legal Analysis and Commentary from Justia*. (2013). https://verdict.justia.com/2013/11/27/sperm-donors-large-small-screen.

Harmon, Amy. "Hello, I'm Your Sister. Our Father is Donor 150." *New York Times*. November 20, 2005. http://www.nytimes.com/2005/11/20/us/hello-im-your-sister-our-father-is-donor-150.html?_r=0.

Indeku, Astrid, Thomas D'Hooghe, Ken R. Daniels, Kris Dierickx, and Peter Rober. "When 'sperm' becomes 'donor': Transitions in parents' views of the sperm donor." *Human Fertility* 17, no. 4 (2014): 269–277. doi:10.3109/14647273.2014.910872.

The Kids Are All Right. Directed by Lisa Cholodenko. Written by Lisa Cholodenko and Stuart Blumberg. Original release 2010. USA: Universal Studios Home Entertainment, 2010. DVD.

LaRossa, Ralph. "Fatherhood and Social Change." In *Men's Lives*, ed. Michael S. Kimmel and Michael A. Messner, 448-460. Needham Heights, Massachusetts: Pearson, 1995.

Made in America. Directed by Richard Benjamin. Written by Marcia Brandwynne, Nadine Schiff and Holly Goldberg Sloan. Original release 1993. USA: Warner Home Video. 2004. DVD.

Maher, Jennifer. "Something Else Besides a Father: Reproductive technology in recent Hollywood film." *Feminist Media Studies* 14, no. 5 (2014): 853–867. doi:10.1080/14680777.2013.831369

Mahlstedt, Patricia, Kathleen LaBounty, and William Thomas Kennedy. "The View of Adult Offspring of Sperm Donation: Essential Feedback for the Development of Ethical Guidelines within the Practice of Assisted Reproductive Technology in the United States." *Fertility and Sterility* 93, no. 7 (2010): 2236–2246. doi: http://dx.doi.org/10.1016/j.fertnstert.2008.12.119

Mroz, Jacqueline. "One Sperm Donor, 150 Offspring." *New York Times*, September 5, 2011. D1.

Neuhaus, Jessamyn. "Dad Test: Gender, Race, and 'Funny Fathers' in Disposable Diaper Advertising from the 1970s to 2012." *Advertising & Society* Review 14, no. 2 (2013). doi:10.1353/asr.2013.0014

Pike, Sheila and Allan Pacey. "Sperm Donation: Coping with Change." *Human Fertility* 8, no. 3 (2005): 173–174. doi:10.1080/14647270500200067.

Seed. Episodes 1–13, Season 1. Directed by James Genn. Written by Joseph Raso and Mark Farrell. CW Network and City. Original broadcast February 2013. Port Washington, NY: Entertainment One Film USA, 2013. DVD.

Stand Up For Gus. www.standupforgus.org. Website. Accessed July 27, 2015.
Sunderland, Jane. "Baby Entertainer, Bumbling Assistant and Line Manager: Discourses of Fatherhood in Parentcraft Texts." *Discourse Society* 11, no. 2 (2000): 249–274. doi:10.1177/0957926500011002006.
The Switch. Directed by Josh Gordon and Will Speck. Written by Allan Loeb. Produced by Mandate Pictures and Echo Films. Original release 2010. USA: Lionsgate Films, 2011. DVD.
Taylor, Bridget. "Whose Baby is it? The Impact of Reproductive Technologies on Kinship." *Human Fertility* 8 (September 2005): 189-195. doi:10.1080/14647270 500277693.

Chapter 3

Soldiers and Fathers

Archetypal Media Representations of Service, Family, and Parenting

Laura C. Prividera and John W. Howard

Contemporary society is seeing a trend toward increased involvement of fathers in family life. The traditional model of the breadwinner spending the day away from family and spending the evening engaged in a break from work while occasionally playing with the children is disappearing as the social norm. Father involvement increasingly takes the form of participating in children's lives as mentor, disciplinarian, coach, and a domestic partner sharing household duties. Today, fathers are multidimensional. They are stay-at-home dads, active participants as breathing coaches to their pregnant partners, participants in paternity leave, and individuals who navigate work-family and work-life balance issues.

The challenges with balancing parenting and one's occupational obligations are well documented. Yet, the trend toward greater involvement is not so easily executed for all fathers. Fathers in military service are met with significant challenges to being present as a partner and parent. Consequently, father-soldiers are a unique population for how they parent during pregnancy and child-rearing. Few professions simultaneously situate the father away from home for extended periods and also entail high risks of injury or death. Their sacrifices are uniquely played out as they may be away from home for extended periods yet still are "dads" even as their ability to serve in that capacity may be diminished or a least altered by their absence. This places father-soldiers in a distinct double-bind whereby their duty to country is placed at odds with duty to family. However, as important as the military dads' experiences are, it is the portrayal of those experiences in the mass media that informs soldiers and civilians alike how to father and soldier simultaneously.

Using media stories of father-soldiers, our chapter contributes to the young dialogue about fatherhood and military service though the following inquiries: First, what are the mediated expectations of the male soldiering parent? Second, how are the inherent contradictions of being a good soldier and good father resolved in media coverage? Our analysis reveals how the contradictions are navigated, as archetypal models of "soldier" and "father" are used in tandem to frame media coverage of father-soldiers during and following the conflicts in Iraq and Afghanistan.[1] We conclude with a critique of the challenges that result from these constructions and recommendations for recasting soldiering fathers as media icons and social members.

THE PREVALENCE OF MILITARY FATHERS

According to the U.S. Department of Defense, men comprise 85.1% of the active duty military force in the United States.[2] In 2013, 42.7 % of active duty personnel were reported to have children—a number that has risen over the last decade.[3] The largest percentages of military children are between birth and 5 years, which is a critical time in child (and parent) development. During this same time frame, the Department of Defense report on "The Impacts of Deployed Members of the Armed Forces on Their Dependent Children," noted that not since Vietnam have so many families been impacted by military conflicts.[4] The report goes on to state that "family separation due to deployment is a major life event, which could cause a great deal of stress for military children."[5] Indeed, since the start of the "war on terror," the lives of military children have changed dramatically with their parents experiencing increased and multiple deployments, greater use of Reserve and Guard members, increases in physical and mental combat injuries, and even death. It is clear why with ongoing military conflicts in the Middle East, there is significant concern regarding the impact on military children.[6]

Even more challenging are the complex and diverse effects of combat duty. As revealed in the 2008 RAND study by Terri Tanielian and Lisa Jaycox, approximately 14% of soldiers returning from Iraq and Afghanistan experience PTSD or depression and about 19% experience a traumatic brain injury (TBI).[7] According to the Department of Veteran Affairs, approximately 1.4 million service people have left active duty service and about half of these individuals have sought medical services for physical and/or mental health issues.[8] Of those seeking services, the most common diagnoses were diseases of the musculoskeletal nervous, endocrine, and digestive systems; mental disorders with posttraumatic stress disorder (PTSD), depressive disorders and neurotic disorders being the most common; and a series of undefined conditions.[9] Expert help is critical in diagnosis yet not all personnel seek help and others may find the accessibility of services limited or inadequate to satisfy their complex needs. In all cases, the consequences of combat service affect fathering and family participation.

MILITARY PARENTING

The consequences of military service (particularly combat deployment) are unique and significant yet military dads and their families are understudied populations. The complexities begin with fathers' absences being characterized and experienced in diverse ways for children and family members. Furthermore, military dads and their families experience periods of adjustment and change in preparing for deployment, during the deployment itself, as well as reintegrating the post-deployment father and family. As Elaine Willerton et al. state in their article "Military Fathers' Perspectives on Involvement," "active-duty personnel are on call 24/7, frequently work long and unpredictable hours, and their service imposes a distinct lifestyle on the whole family given the communal character of the organization and its emphasis on discipline and control."[10] These obligations have unique impacts on attachment and child development outcomes.

The potential effects of this lifestyle are most obvious in young children. Charles Zeanah et al. note that attachment processes between parent and child begin early in life and are critical to a child's growth and development.[11] Active caregiving early on by central caregivers (i.e., parents) is predictive of healthy child development outcomes later in life.

Today's father spends time with his children while sharing an equivalent workload with the mother.[12] Mark Morman and Kory Floyd found in their research that fathers experience a closer, more affectionate, and more satisfying relationship with sons than in previous generations.[13] They further argue that conceptions of fatherhood have evolved from the authoritative and detached father to a more nurturing and involved one. This is echoed in the work of John Duckworth and Patrice Buzzanell who state that "contemporary fathers are expected to nurture, devote daily time and resources to, and to coach their children in activities."[14] Moreover, scholars have found that the style of father's interactions can enhance children's self-esteem.[15] Yet, these benefits are not universally realized as military dads are often physically absent during early childhood development.

In "Online Fathering," Kathleen Schachman discusses how fathers experience and navigate parenting challenges via technology and communication. Schachman argues that while much research is done on the importance of men being present for a child's birth as well as the benefits of them being present, little is known about how military men, many of whom are deployed, experience this critical familial transition. Through her interviews with military dads, she found two main themes: disruption of the protector/ provider role and restoration of the protector/provider role. For the former, men experienced worry about the childbirth process, lost opportunities with family, guilt for being absent, fear of their own death, and concern for family if they died. The men "felt an obligation to protect and to provide for their wives and children, and their absence interfered with their ability to fulfill this role." The second theme revealed how they used communication technologies to restore the protector role, maintain bonding experiences, and relieve some of their fear and anxiety. Communication through e-mail was most common although YouTube, instant messaging, and social networking sites such as Facebook and MySpace were also used.[16]

Ashley Louie and Lisa DeMarni Cromer found in their research on military families that it is important for ongoing attachment processes to prepare children in age appropriate ways for deployment. For example, pictures can be useful for infants or a piece of clothing with their father's scent to promote attachment while dad is not physically present.[17] Such techniques can allow father and child to continue bonding in the face of deployments.

In "Fathering after Military Deployment: Parenting Challenges and Goals of Fathers of Young Children," Tova Walsh et al. found two prominent themes from their interviews with military dads: they were motivated to be good fathers but they also experienced many challenges in returning to their father role. Military dads were receptive to support and assistance in fathering after extended periods away from the familial home due to deployment. The challenges they experienced after returning from deployment(s) included reconnecting with their child, navigating regret about missing parts of their child's development, changing their expectations from a military context to a civilian context and co-parenting after deployment and reunification. Even more challenging was that, many fathers reported having to deal with the effects of trauma from their time in the military as well as transitioning from the extremes of a regimented military life to a more dynamic and fluid civilian life.[18]

Good support systems are needed for military dads. Like Tova Walsh et al., Shawna Lee et al. found that military fathers were highly motivated to be good fathers in spite of demanding work schedules, deployments and frequent moves. They were also receptive to training on parenthood but were unaware of services to assist them. The authors concluded that using mentors would be effective for delivering parenting information and normalizing the frustrations experienced by being a father-soldier. Furthermore, the authors found that delivering information using digital technologies may be useful and practical for military dads.[19]

Although scholarship is revealing more about the experiences and challenges faced by father-soldiers, much more of the social understanding obtained by civilians, policy makers, and soldiers themselves is framed via media stories. Consequently, it is important to examine those framings in the context of such scholarship to gain a more comprehensive understanding of the father-soldier.

FRAMING POPULAR MEDIA

Through story selection and construction, news media effectively tell consumers what to think and what to think about. These constructions are not value-free synopses of events but are value-laden interpretations that frame story content.[20] Maxwell McCombs has described framing as second-level agenda setting, focusing on the characterizations journalists make in their discussions of the topics they have chosen to cover.[21] Erving Goffman observed in his book *Frame Analysis* that individuals actively seek to organize, understand, and interpret information to make sense out of their experiences in the social world. He states that frames allow individuals "to locate, perceive, identify, and label" the vast array of societal information.[22] Such frames are used to construct media stories and are adopted by media consumers. As explained by Robert Entman in his widely cited article on "Framing:" "To frame is to select some aspects of a perceived reality and make them more salient in a communication text, in such a way as to promote a particular problem definition, causal interpretation, moral evaluation and/or treatment recommendation for the item described."[23]

Media producers are faced with constraints of time and space. Consequently, it is typical for news media to deliver content using frames—and even actively seek out a frame to aid in media consumer sensemaking. In fact, Zhongdang Pan and Gerald Kosicki argue that "we may conceive a news media frame as a cognitive device used in information encoding, interpreting, and retrieving; it is communicable. . . ."[24] Moreover they argue that framing can "be studied as a strategy of constructing and processing news discourse."[25] Scholars argue that consistent media frames are (re)produced daily in the news and such repetition influences media consumers' perceptions on specific topics. One of the myriad available framing techniques is the archetype.

ENDURING ARCHETYPES

Archetypal models have significant influences on expectations for social actors. The archetype is a perfect model to which actors may aspire. There is an innumerable list of archetypes available for social actors (e.g., mother, hero, martyr, scapegoat, leader, teacher, soldier).

That human beings understand things in terms of archetype has been widely explored in the work of Carl Jung and Joseph Campbell and a cadre of literary critics and theorists. Jung argues that archetypes are foundational and embedded in the psyche and foundational to social structure via the collective unconscious.[26] Consequently, the archetypal "hero," "warrior," "mother," or "father," experiences differences in articulation and expression across times and cultures. Fundamental to the expression of archetypes are myths (or narratives). Archetypes emerge from narratives and frequently, narratives are constructed around archetypal plots and characters. Jack Lule observes that myths reproduced in journalistic stories tend to support the social order and understanding of things.[27] This notion is supported in the work of Walter Fisher who argues that social activity and understanding occur in narrative form—we are storytelling beings.[28] In short, narratives and archetypes are vehicles for creating understanding and reinscribing ideologies. The two archetypes most relevant to this discussion are the "father" and the "warrior-hero."

In his discussions of archetypes, Jung observes that the father is a familial authority figure. Jung's father has suggestions of negativity as powerful and stern.[29] However, in other expressions the father is a positive authority figure who serves as leader and protector of the family. Though not defined primarily by warmth or nurturing, the father is a caring provider and preserves family well-being. Consequently, today's archetypal father still retains his gendered roots and contrast with "mother" but is also a connected and engaged family member capable of (and expected to) love, protect, and guide the family.

As discussed by John Howard and Laura Prividera, the soldier archetype to emulate is the "warrior-hero."[30] The warrior-hero is physically and mentally strong, sexually and physically potent, and fiercely independent and resilient. "He" is the protector of our nation and secures our freedom and such bravery and selflessness is celebrated through our common rhetoric of "supporting the troops." Furthermore, as noted by Rachel Woodward, the warrior-hero is one of the ideals among ideals.[31] Consequently, it has great significance as a symbol for that which is good, patriotic, and noble. As stated by John Howard and Laura Prividera, in their framing analysis of military personnel, "What constitutes an appropriate archetypal role model or narrative conclusion is presupposed in the ideological values embraced by the narrator and audience."[32] Consequently, the only weakness the warrior-hero can display and remain the warrior-hero is compassion (typically the protection of others unable to protect themselves). In contrast, the father archetype is one of protection, provision, instruction, and compassion itself. It is in the navigation of these archetypal models that the father-soldier may find his own ideologically appropriate archetypal expression.

METHOD

Using the LexisNexis database, we retrieved news transcripts from ABC, CBS, and NBC using keyword searches for "military fathers" and "military dads" from September 2001 to May 2015. Only transcripts that included stories on these subjects were included in our data set.

We selected these sources because they are widely accessible. In most areas throughout the United States, these major news networks can be viewed without cable or satellite programming. Furthermore, these news networks are widely aired in public venues and appear with high frequency throughout the day. A total of 616 pages of data were generated. Specifically, ABC produced 212 pages, CBS produced 195 pages, and NBC produced 209 pages.

Recurrent patterns in news transcripts were used to identify common themes in the data. Consistent with David Altheide's (1996) discussion in his book *Qualitative Media Analysis*, our research was "systematic . . . but not rigid."[33] We examined each news transcript closely with a focus on the language used to describe and characterize military fathers/dads. Altheide goes on to state that "themes are the recurring typical theses" that appear throughout the texts.[34] We developed our themes using the "constant comparative method." Two important aspects of the constant comparative method as described in Thomas Lindlof's book *Qualitative Research Methods* are that "it specifies the means by which theory grounded in the relationships among data emerges through the management of coding (hence, grounded theory), and it shows explicitly how to code and conceptualize as field data keep flowing in."[35] Patterns in language, descriptions, and characterizations of military dads and military families that occurred in at least one-third of the data were used to define common elements. In subsequent coding passes, elements collapsed together and generated the emergence of themes in the data.

MEDIA CONSTRUCTIONS OF MILITARY DADS

As we reviewed our data set, it became clear that media stories were not explicitly defining what it was to be a father-soldier. Although some stories directly inquired about dad's role and the specific challenges of that dad's absence, a much more frequent pattern was to frame the father in relation to family members, the nation, or military service. Consequently, the media construction of father-soldiers is performed largely through the foils of partners and children of father-soldiers and the news personalities that ask the questions of those family members. Four themes emerged in the data: daddy—defined by deployment, absence as service, ensuring attachment and maintaining dad's presence, and hedging hardship. Our analysis reveals the tension created by the competing demands of being a soldier and father and poignantly illustrates the profound effect media texts have in constructing an image of the father-soldier.

DADDY—DEFINED BY DEPLOYMENT

Father-soldiers were most frequently described in the context of their time away from family. Shifts in familial burdens, what dad meant to the family (and what the family meant to dad), and changes to routines and relational dynamics collectively framed what it was to be a military dad. The specifics of what constituted "dad" were largely characterized by the types of events the dad was missing during deployment. Fathers and families expressed how important it was to be present at births, graduations, holidays, and other familial milestones. Furthermore, media personalities themselves drew attention to these missed events with statements like: "So many months apart and milestones missed," which aired on *Good Morning America*.[36] Even missed mundane activities characterized deployments. Andrea Garcia noted her children do not "get their dad to make them pancakes that he used to make them every Sunday, things that normal parents do for their kids."[37] Sgt. Denver Smith said "I'd give anything for just—just the normal things, you know? Just mowing the grass with . . . [his son] . . ."[38] Children themselves shared these feelings. Corey Hill noted, "If I'm having a bad day or something. I'll wish he was there just so I could ask some advice."[39]

In essence, these stories highlight much of what is expected of a father— presence, love, and participation. These in-the-moment experiences and expectations are curtailed during deployments and other extended obligations away from home. Such characterizations do challenge traditional forms of masculinity and more closely embrace participatory fatherhood yet their enactment proves difficult due to the nature of the profession.

Domestic activity is another area in which father-soldiers find it difficult to live up to modern expectations. This is clear in how fathers were defined via the extra work shifted to the mother and family as a function of deployment. Mundane activities like changing diapers, cooking, and caring for the home were cited as tasks deployed fathers could not assist with that then fell upon the partner, children, or other family members. The significance of the burden was reinforced in fathers' talk, as expressed by Sgt. Devon Weaver, "I think my wife is one of the strongest women I've ever had in my presence."[40] Other partners were cited as being "troopers" or doing "the real work" all of which serves as a reminder of what the father-soldier was unable to contribute while away.

Expressions of concern by family members were also vehicles for characterizing the father-soldier. The love and attachment of partners and children to the father was near-universal in the transcripts. In numerous interviews, family members shared that they "were worried" or "scared" or "afraid" for their father's well-being. The depth of stress and attachment were sometimes expressed in vivid detail. *ABC News* reporter, Deborah Roberts, asked a group of children about their concerns and, in particular, if they had nightmares. One boy replied "I dreamed of, like, that my dad driving a tank and someone dropped a bomb on it."[41] His concerns were echoed by innumerable others who feared their father would be hurt or killed. Deborah Roberts concluded "even though they are not on the front lines, children of those in the military are fighting their own battle with fear, loneliness, abandonment, and often, say psychologists, a sense of impending death."[42] Fathers themselves expressed concerns about not returning to their families and how their passing would be a permanent absence for the family.

The traditional conceptualizations of masculinity upon which soldiering is based (e.g., working away from the home, a bifurcation of domestic and public activity, self-reliance, and child-rearing as a feminine activity) are at odds with modern expectations of fathers as sharing the burden of work and domestic life with their partners. Yet, what could be an irreconcilable double-bind whereby father and soldier are placed in opposition was instead reinterpreted through a uniquely militarized lens that allowed for the father-soldier identities to function in tandem. Part of this reinterpretation is illustrated in our second theme regarding how families reconciled the tensions created by fathers' absences.

ABSENCE AS SERVICE

Father-soldiers, by definition, experience time away from family for training, TDYs/TADs, operations at sea, and, of course, deployments, which were most frequently discussed in our data. Although such absences are disrupting and challenging for the family, they are accepted and revered for what they mean. As one military wife noted, "it's bittersweet most of the time as a military spouse, but it's part of the job."[43] When asked about the hardship of her husband being deployed another military wife responded, "Yes, it's very, very difficult, but we understand the situation. It is an honor for us to be serving everybody else in America. So someone in the family has to do it, and we're proud that he's doing it for us."[44] The general characterization was "this is what military families do." The assumption that absence is expected and noble is embedded in a question asked to a soldier's child on

ABC News: If you could tell your dad one thing about how proud you are of him, what would you tell him?"[45] The absences were expressions of a central part of soldier (and military family) identity: service. Service characterized by the sacrifices made by dads and families for the good of the nation.

Father-soldiers navigated the tensions in various ways. Some fathers, for instance, noted their families would "always be on my mind" while deployed. Others noted that they could not think of family because they needed to be completely present to serve. As articulated by Sgt. William Hamrick on *Good Morning America*, "I miss my family. I do. I'd, I'd love to see my daughter and hold her, but, you know, I'm still in Iraq and that's where my head's got to be."[46] A poignant example comes from Hal Sellars' interview on *Good Morning America*. He chose to deploy after much dialogue with his wife even though his son needed heart transplant surgery. In his words:

> It was a difficult decision to make. But at the end of the day I think both my wife and I believe that the place where I could do the most good, where I needed to be was with, was with my unit and the Marines that deployed. Unfortunately, there wasn't a whole lot I could do for, for Dillon. Leaving, obviously, left my family to have to deal with a lot of that. But again, it was, it was a mutual decision and I don't really have any regrets whatsoever. . . .[47]

The stories present father and family as extensions of one another and the military through service. Dan Ahern articulates the connection on *Saturday Today*, "the soldier's only as strong as the strength of its family, we say."[48] Ahern's statement reifies the notion that "military families" are truly unique in their definition. The support the family provides the soldier is that soldier's strength and the protection the father provides the "national family" (nation) is framed as an essential component of the father-soldier.

The father-soldier exists in a space defined by family which both fills the void left by the father's absence and consequently serves with the father. As described by one wife on *Good Morning America*, "Nobody understands what he's going through like I do. And nobody understands what I'm going through like he does. And so that just makes it, I mean, it's just bonded our marriage and our family."[49] In many cases, the stories focused on the parent-child bond in service. In the words of Gene Joiner on *Sunday Morning*, "The kids serve, too, and that's really important that people understand that these kids are struggling at times, but also that these kids are resilient."[50]

The idea that the family is an extension of the father-soldier is particularly salient in how the shifts of family member obligations occurred during deployments. Many stories noted how the children "grow up fast." Frequently, sons were invoked as the "man of the house" in daddy's absence. The increased pressure to grow up was not lost on the fathers as noted by

SSgt. Ernesto Escobar on *Good Morning America*, "after I, I leave he's gonna take over being the man of the house. He's gonna have more responsibilities than he has now." He continued, "It's a lot of, it's a lot of pressure to put, put on an 11-year-old."[51] The reality of it and the desire for it to be truly temporary was expressed well by Josh Lyon, "I guess I had to kind of take that role as the man of the house or whatever, but once my dad comes back, I—it's fine with me. I don't really want to be anymore."[52]

The pressures are real and "you are the man of the house" can have profound manifestations as discovered by Master Sergent Albert Brown and his wife Staff Sergant Octavia Brown who were both deployed and had their son living with his grandmother. During their deployments, 12-year-old Ty called 911 more than 20 times to help his grandmother who was experiencing health complications from diabetes. On a call to his step-father, Ty reassured him of his grandmother's status "Ty said, 'Hey, hey, Dad, she's in good hands. I will let you know if we need you.'" The story showed how even as an adolescent Ty was serving and supporting his deployed parents. Furthermore, the broadcast noted that Ty's family situation wasn't that unusual; according to the Pentagon 67,000 children had both parents in the military.[53]

Even when spouses and children expressed frustrations, the sense of duty and service as a military family rang through. In the words of one son on *ABC News*, "I feel so angry because he, he left the family. I don't, I don't like it when he leaves the family."[54] Even so, he concluded with "but that's his job. He has to protect the world from the terrorists."

Reframing "father" through the lens of soldier allowed for absences to be understood and embraced as part of fatherhood. Furthermore, by shifting the role of "man of the house" to the male child the importance of the father is maintained and traditional notions of masculinity are reinscribed. Rhetorically, the shift allows the father to leave and fulfill soldiering duties and there still be a masculine presence in the home. Yet, as illustrated above, the framing does not provide relief from the real pressures faced by the interim "man of the house" or the military families. The absence is understood—but as further illustrated in our third theme the need for presence endures.

ENSURING ATTACHMENT AND MAINTAINING DAD'S PRESENCE

Although fathers were primarily defined via absence, their characterization was supplemented by how they maintained presence. Families committed a significant amount of effort to keep fathers integrated with their daily lives. The importance of those connections for families is difficult to overstate as shared by one soldier live on *Good Morning America*:

Kim, I just want you to know how much I love you and miss you. I think about you every day. I look forward to every time we talk on the phone. And I look forward to your letters and your care packages and they mean everything to me. I just want you to know how much I love you.[55]

His wife, Kimberly, gave an impassioned monologue about how she missed him and how she wanted to share (via the broadcast) an ultrasound of their unborn child. Other partners echoed the importance of hearing from their soldiers and what it meant to them and their children.

The most discussed strategy for maintaining presence was phone calls (satellite and cell) particularly in being present for family milestones. Many stories were told of conversations with soldiers via satellite phone connections like Dusty Cook who was able to converse with his wife during the birth of their child as told by wife Samantha on *Today,* "My mom held up my phone on speaker for the last hour of labor and Dusty was able to hear our son being born."[56] Satellite phone connections formed the basis of stories about the joys of hearing from dad in the remote spaces of rural Afghanistan or Iraq.

Not all connections were so novel. Many soldiers and their families were able to enjoy more regular and stable conversations from areas with better infrastructures. So common and important was cell service that a not-for-profit organizations like Freedom Calls featured on *Today* provided calling cards to military personnel to help them keep in touch with their loved ones for everything from major life events like births to routine conversations.[57]

Conversely, the frustration and anxiety created by a missed call or dropped connection due to the instability of satellite communication brought home the reality that even with a technological tether dad was still thousands of miles away in a space that was potentially life-threatening. Luke Simerly says of his dad's calls, "It's devastating. It's—you know, because he is making the effort to reach out to you a lot of times. We'll answer the call and the connection won't go through."[58]

Web-based technologies such as Skype[59] and FaceTime[60] were also employed. Sgt. Ken Pompilli shared his story with *Good Morning America* on being by his wife's side for 17 hours while she gave birth to their first child.[61] Technology was employed by nonfamily groups as well. School graduations have, with increasing frequency, been televised or streamed for soldiers overseas.[62] Furthermore, in some cases the fathers themselves were able to be streamed back to the events so the graduate could have dad present for the big day. Social networking sites like Facebook and MySpace were also cited as ways to keep family close. Even YouTube was used to host family videos for sharing.[63]

Mail and e-mail were also heavily used ways to keep in touch. Sgt. Jared Roth noted that he and his family used "A lot of email." He continued "and writing letters and cards so that the mail's always flowing both from them to me and me to them."[64] When asked about receiving mail and packages Sgt. Jared Roth said, "I got so much mail while I was over there, and just getting these kind of things, you know, reminded me that, you know, why I'm over there. I have a great family to come home to and it made the time go by real fast." His spouse, Sgt. Tammy Roth, focused on the value of "snail mail" for soldiers as well "It's the mail. The mail's real important over there."[65]

The idea that tangible artifacts have special meaning carried over into discussions of photos. Many families cited having photos around as ways of keeping close. So important are photos to families that Operation Love Reunited sponsors photo shoots for deploying soldiers and their families. The value of this presence is noted by soldier Denny Rindel on *Saturday Today,* "It's being able to hold a piece of home in your hand and keep it with you and it makes the days go by, helps them go by quicker."[66] Reporter Kristen Dahlgren observes of Rindel's son later in the same broadcast the photos are "a simple gift that for awhile will be a little boy's link to his dad." Photos are of equal value to the family and the father.[67]

Some of the artifacts that maintained presence were very personal. On *ABC News*, one daughter spoke of wearing her dad's clothes "I wear, like, his shirts to bed and his socks to school."[68] A son noted on *ABC News* that his dad "sprayed my sister's little chocolate moose with his cologne. I wish I could smell that" he continued. "She sleeps with it at night."[69] Another family featured on *Good Morning American* put a tracing of their father's hand on the refrigerator so that the children "could experience his trademark high five when they did something good."[70]

Father-soldiers were able to maintain a surprising level of physical presence through items designed specifically for soldiers. Numerous stories focused on the recorded father as a presence in the family's life. "Daddy Dolls" were one such innovation that made headlines. The dolls had recordings of the fathers built in so they could speak to the family in their absence. The dolls are not simply symbolic of dad's presence in the family—they were emotionally connected in many cases. Cassidy Fisher's husband did the recordings of his voice for his 5-year-old son, Shane, "the day that he left. So, it was an emotional time for him anyway, and so, and you can kind of even hear it a little bit in his voice."[71] Many talked about using "Build-a-Bears"[72] in the same fashion. Other stories highlighted campaigns like "United Through Reading"[73] and "Reach out and Read"[74] where the father was recorded into a storybook so the child could be read to by dad while he was deployed. Many of these examples took planning on the part of the dad pre-deployment and planning on the part of the family at home to utilize "daddy" objects.

There were even less technologically advanced ways military fathers were incorporated into the lives of their families. Historically, photos and mementos have served the role of reminding families of their loved ones. However, one group took the idea of photos as presence and expanded upon it—literally. The "Flat Daddy"[75] is a full-sized cardboard backed poster of the soldier. One family told how their Flat Daddy went out to dinner, sat at the table at home, attended church, and participated in many family functions. The family wrote on the back the places Flat Daddy had been, what happened, and even attached e-mails about him. This allowed for dad to be present in the moment and also allowed for dad to have a record of the memories to see and share with the family upon his return.

All of these strategies showcased the importance of presence and maintaining attachment. Yet, by attending to personal(ized) artifacts, photos, and their familial connections, the stories maintain viewer focus upon the "human interest" to the minimization of government and not-for-profit activities that attempt to fill the gap that remains when fathers are deployed. The significance of this is exposed in those stories that specifically address interventions and activities to help cope with a deployed daddy.

HEDGING HARDSHIP

When noted, the challenges experienced by father-soldiers and families nearly always manifest as generalities. Instead, the stories frequently shifted focus to support. In Dan Augustine's words "I think a lot of people disregard how difficult it is for the—for the Guard members to transition back and forth. Military families need some support while they're—while they're gone. Not just the soldier, the military family needs some support."[76] When discussing her husband's deployment and how her family was coping one military wife observed, "I got a crew of women ready to be there for me, tons of family willing to come out, as well. So it's a big support network that we have here in the military."[77] When asked about hardships many families noted that there was a "wives' club" of other military mothers whom they could turn to. Betsy Sellers noted as her son Dillon went through surgery that her family was a support "and so were all the military wives. They really rallied around and offered me any kind of help that I needed."[78]

As the father-soldier derives strength from his family the military family derives strength from the military community. Family is constructed as a web of connections and support whereby those that remain behind help fill the gaps left by those who have deployed. Thus, the framed father-soldier is validated for absence based in service and that absence is less tangible because of the support network he leaves behind. Even so, some stories illustrate how the gaps are not fully filled.

The military itself provides additional support for families and, in particular, children. "Operation Military Kids is a US Army program to help children of deployed parents develop coping skills."[79] "The Department of Defense itself spends billions of dollars per year on support for military families."[80] That there is a need for family support is not lost on the educational institutions that serve military populations. Bill Hefner Elementary school serves Ft. Bragg and actively works with students to cope with deployments; "they are taught how to support and comfort each other."[81] Programs for support, counseling, and intervention were common at the schools near bases. A counselor at Nolan Richardson Middle School in El Paso, Texas created the "worry wall"[82] where students write down (anonymously if they like) their fears and concerns about a parent's deployment.

Many not-for-profit programs supported needs for children of deployed parents such as the summer camps of Operation: Purple, which serve only that population.[83] Dimanique Thomas (an Operation Purple participant) noted "It's just good to talk to someone who can understand."[84] Sponsored by an NHL player, Defending the Blue Line[85] provides hockey training, ice time, equipment, and transportation for players in need who have a parent serving.

A handful of stories highlighted the even more unique experiences of National Guard and Reservist soldiers whose families do not live on base and who also have jobs and financial situations that add even more complexity and risk than active duty soldiers. As noted by Shellen MacDermid, "The support structures that are in place were designed at a time where we didn't have deployments like this."[86] The absence of support from military families was obvious in the struggles of National Guard and Reserve soldiers. For them, the absence of the military family/community is an added challenge when dad is deployed.

The community involvement that fills in the void left by soldiers is probably best summed up in the words of Erin Miller, "it takes a village to send a man to war."[87] As framed, the father-soldier has unique professional commitments but the military family has unique ways of coping with those commitments.

MEDIATING FATHER-SOLDIER STORIES

Media constructed father-soldiers are not simple reifications of the traditional breadwinning dad, nor are they constructed as hypermasculine warriors. Instead, they are soldiers engaged with their families, present at births, providing socioemotional support, sharing the whole of their being, and have community support to make it all work. That media coverage of the most masculine of professions showcases such practices is an encouraging message for those who seek to promote parenting practices that are fluid, equitable, and flexible. Additionally, it is comforting for media consumers to feel that the tensions between fatherhood and military service can be effectively navigated and that families embrace and support that service to the nation. Finally, it is inspiring to see the media caring for the soldiers and families as well via showcased events like televised graduations, on-air reunions, messages from family and troops to one another, and coverage of the holidays when loved ones were apart.

In the end, this rendering showcases real positives, attachments, and practices that show how, even in a challenging environment, a good father role model can exist with innovation, family support, and community support. The father-soldiers showcased in our data truly went to great lengths to participate, and be present with their families in exceptionally challenging conditions. In sum, media constructions of the father-solder tell a satisfying story that fits with audience predispositions and ideological definitions about what is ideal or ought-to-be for soldiers, fathers, and families.

Yet, what makes the story so satisfying is not the reality but the *framing* of soldiering and fathering that implies the two are compatible and harmonious activities. The compatibility is created by ordering the archetypes wherein the warrior-hero supersedes and assimilates the father. This ordering is revealed through the themes as the tensions are either essentialized as part of the father-soldier identity (defined by deployment); are internalized by the family and celebrated as an honorable activity (absence as service); are directly met (by maintaining presence); or are met through community action (in hedging hardship). In this framing the warrior-hero and father archetypes collapse into the "warrior-father" who remains physically and mentally strong, resilient, and self-reliant in deployment yet is able to retain compassion and connection in his presence with the family. Most importantly the warrior-father is successful in both domains because he serves the family *by* serving the nation. Moreover, the family itself celebrates this commitment and supports the nation and soldier.

Unfortunately, this inspiring media narrative is eloquently tidy to a fault. The coverage implies that connection is more the norm than disconnection, fear and concern are vanquished by phone calls and homecomings, and father and soldier expectations are congruent rather than discordant. Thus, in practice, media coverage does little to create a real understanding of the long-term and significant consequences of soldiering commitments and fathers' absences (particularly in combat zones) and overstates the level of support received by those fathers and their families while simultaneously understating its need. A handful of stories noted serious consequences for soldiers and their families including the increased rates of divorce, abuse, aggression in children of deployed parents, permanent disability, mental illness, and substance abuse, that are the realities for many soldiers and their families. Furthermore, the framing places unreasonable expectations on father-soldiers and their families by making the ideal seem easily obtainable.

This divide between the image and the reality has material consequences for father-soldiers and their families. The support is simply inadequate for the volume of fathers and families that need it. Yet, the narrative fuels political, organizational, and social misconceptions, which leaves potential program donors, supporters, and policy makers with the distinct sense that the military father and family are indeed having their needs met. Consequently, the narrative implies that changes in support programs, veteran's benefits, and health care are unnecessary. Furthermore, the real fathers and families that struggle post-deployment fall outside the narrative making them easy to label as failing or flawed because they did not fit the archetypal narrative.

To address this, media stories need to problematize the experiences of the father-soldier and military family. Stories need to feature the joy and challenges of coming home. Return from a combat zone means a return to safety and a realization of the dream of having daddy home but it also entails a reintegration with family and civilian society. It means coping with unhealthy experiences, mental and physical wear and tear (and disability), changed family members and dynamics, and (for many) a lifetime of care and dedication to maintain familial health. The stories need to feature how families truly succeed in such challenging environments by benefiting from social and governmental support. Stories also need to illustrate the real consequences for the families and soldiers who lack such support.

So often media stories portray the successes and nobility of military life to the end of honoring soldiers and their families. An archetypal warrior-father is what is featured. Yet, accurate and complete reporting of the challenges and hard work, and dispelling the illusion that soldier-fathers and their families are innately able to manage these tensions as de facto practice is the only way to truly honor their service and sacrifice in the long run.

NOTES

1. Operation Iraqi Freedom is the term used to describe the beginning of the war in Iraq in 2003. Operation Enduring Freedom is used to refer to the global war on terrorism. Operation New Dawn is used to refer to the period of time in Iraq after 2010.

2. U.S. Department of Defense, 2013 Demographics: Profile of the military community. Retrieved from http://download.militaryonesource.mil/12038/MOS/Reports/2013-Demographics-Report.pdf 2003: v.

3. U.S. Department of Defense, 2013 vi.

4. U.S. Department of Defense (October, 2010). Report on the Impact of Deployment of Members of the Armed Forces on Their Dependent Children. [Report to the Senate and House Committees on Armed Services]. Retrieved from http://download.militaryonesource.mil/12038/MOS/Reports/Report_to_Congress_on_Impact_of_Deployment_on_Military_Children.pdf 1.

5. U.S. Department of Defense (October, 2010) 3.

6. U.S. Department of Defense (October, 2010) 1.

7. Terri Tanielianm and Lisa Jaycox, "Invisible Wounds of War: Psychological and Cognitive Injuries, their Consequences, and Services to Assist Recovery," *RAND, Center for Military Health Policy Research* (2008) Retrieved from http://www.rand.org/pubs/monographs/MG720.html xxi.

8. Department of Veterans Affairs (2012). Analysis of VA Health Care Utilization Among Operation Enduring Freedom, Operation Iraqi Freedom, and Operation New Dawn Veterans. Retrieved from http://www.publichealth.va.gov/docs/epidemiology/healthcar e-utilization-report-fy2012-qtr1.pdf 5.

9. Department of Veterans Affairs (2012). 9.

10. Elaine Willerton et al., "Military Father' Perspectives on Involvement," *Journal of Family Psychology* 25, no 4 (2011): 521. doi: 10.1037/a0024511.

11. Charles H. Zeanah et al., "Practitioner Review: Clinical Applications of Attachment Theory and Research for Infants and Young Children," *Journal of Child Psychology* 52 (2011): 819. doi: 10.1111/j.1469–7610.2011.02399.x.

12. Suzanne M. Bianchi, John P. Robinson, and Melissa Milkie, *Changing Rhythms of American Family Life* (New York: Russell Sage Foundation, 2006), 1.

13. Mark T. Morman and Kory Floyd, "A 'Changing Culture of Fatherhood': Effects on Affectionate Communication, Closeness, and Satisfaction in Men's Relationships with their Fathers and their Sons," *Western Journal of Communication* 66, no 4 (2002): 405.

14. John D. Duckworth and Patrice M. Buzzanell, "Constructing Work-Life Balance and Fatherhood: Men's Framing of the Meanings of Both Work and Family," *Communication Studies*, 60, no 5 (2009): 560.

15. Lynn Webb et al., "Perceived Parental Communication, Gender and Young Adults Self-Estemm: Male, Female and Universal Path Models," In Philip Backlund and Mary Rose Williams (Eds.), *Readings in Gender Communication* (pp. 197–224). Belmont, CA: Wadsworth, 2004, 214.

16. Katheleen A. Schachman, "Online Fathering: The Experience of First-Time Fatherhood in Combat-Deployed Troops," *Nursing Research*, 59, no 1 (2010): 13, 16.

17. Ashley Louie and Lisa DeMarni Cromer, "Parent-Child Attachment During the Deployment Cycle: Impact on Reintegration Parent Stress," *Professional Psychology: Research and Practice* 45, no 6 (2014): 500–501. doi.org.jproxy.lib.ecu.edu/10.1037/a0036603.

18. Tova B. Walsh et al., "Fathering after Military Deployment: Parenting Challenges and Goals of Fathers of Young Children," *Health and Social Work* 39, no 1 (2014): 36,39,40. doi: 10.1093/hsw/hlu005.

19. Shawna Lee et al., "Sources of Parenting Support in Early Fatherhood: Perspectives of United States Air Force Members," *Children and Youth Services Review* 35, (2013): 913. doi.org.jproxy.lib.ecu.edu/10.1016/j.childyouth.2013.02.012.

20. See Douglas Kellner, "The Media and the Crisis of Democracy in the Age of Bush-2," *Communication and Critical/Cultural Studies,* 1 (2004); Deepa Kumar. "Media, War, and Propaganda: Strategies of Information Management During the 2003 Iraq War," *Communication and Critical/Cultural Studies* 3 no 1, (2006). doi: 10.1080/14791420500505650; and Jim A. Kuypers, Framing Analysis. In Jim

A. Kuypers (Ed.), *The Art of Rhetorical Criticism* (pp. 186–211). Boston: Allyn & Bacon, 2005.

21. Maxwell McCombs, "New frontiers in agenda setting: Agendas of attributes and frames," *Mass communication review* 24, no. 1/2 (1997): 32–52.

22. Erving Goffman, *Frame Analysis: An Essay on the Organizational of Experience* (New York: Harper Row, 1974), 21.

23. Robert Entman, "Framing: Toward Clarification of a Fractured Paradigm," *Journal of Communication* 45, no. 4 (1993): 53.

24. Zhongdang Pan and Gerald Kosicki, "Framing Analysis: An Approach to News Discourse," *Political Communication* 10, no 1 (1993): 57.

25. Ibid.

26. Carl G. Jung, *The Archetypes and the Collective Unconscious (Collected works of C.G. Jung vol. 9 part 1)* (G. Adler & R. F. C. Hull, Trans.) (Princeton, NJ: Bollingen, 1981, Original works published 1934–1954).

27. Jack Lule, *Daily News, Eternal Stories: The Mythological Role of Journalism* (New York: Guilford Press, 2001), 15.

28. Walter Fisher, *Human Communication as Narration: Toward a Philosophy of Reason, Value, and Action* (Columbia: University of South Carolina Press, 1987).

29. Jung, *The Archetypes and the Collective.*

30. John Howard and Laura Prividera, "Rescuing Patriarchy or Saving 'Jessica Lynch:' The Rhetorical Construction of the American Woman Soldier," *Women & Language,* 27, no 2 (2004): 90.

31. Rachel Woodward, "Warrior Heroes and Little Green Men: Soldiers, Military Training, and the Construction of Rural Masculinities," *Rural Sociology* 65 (2000): 644.

32. John Howard and Laura Prividera, "The Fallen Woman Archetype: Media Representations of Lynndie England, Gender and the (Ab)uses of U.S. female soldiers." *Women's Studies in Communication* 31 (2008): 292–293. doi:10.1080/074 91409.2008.10162544.

33. David L. Altheide, *Qualitative Media Analysis* (Thousand Oaks, CA: Sage, 1996), 16, 31.

34. Ibid., 31.

35. Thomas Lindlof, *Qualitative Communication Research Methods* (Thousand Oaks, CA: Sage, 2005), 222–223.

36. "Operation Christmas: Down Home Holiday Cheer," *Good Morning America,* ABC (December 7, 2006).

37. "GMA Homecoming Live!; Military Family's Christmas Miracle," *Good Morning America*, ABC (December 12, 2012).

38. "Wives and Children Think of Their Soldier Dads."

39. "In Depth; Stresses Faced by Military Families," *NBC Nightly News,* NBC (January 12, 2008).

40. "Today's Call to Action; Sergeant Devon Weaver and wife Amanda Show the Difficulties of One Parent Serving in Iraq," *Today*, NBC (June 4, 2009).

41. "Special Report: War With Iraq Introduction," *ABC News Special Report*, ABC (March 24 2003).

42. "A Mother's Joy; The Child of the Fallen," *Nightline,* ABC (February 19, 2007).

43. "Getting to the Heart of Christmas; Surprises for Expectant Military Mothers," *Today*, NBC (December 23, 2010).

44. "Travis Peterson and His Wife and Daughters Discuss His Surprise Homecoming from Afghanistan at His Daughter's School," *The Saturday Early Show*, CBS (April 5, 2008).

45. "Special Report: War with Iraq Introduction."

46. "Gift of Life Soldier Views Birth Via Web Cam," *Good Morning America,* ABC (August 12, 2005).

47. "Dillon Sellers, "Update on Child Heart Transplant Patient," *Good Morning America, ABC* (March 22, 2004).

48. "The Families of Service Members in Afghanistan Being Taken Care of at Fort Bragg," *Saturday Today*, NBC (September 18, 2010).

49. "Message From Home; On the Front Line With Our Troops," *Good Morning America,* ABC (December 6, 2010).

50. "Operation Purple's Summer Camp for Children of Soldiers Deployed Overseas," *Sunday Morning,* CBS (July 1, 2007).

51. "Brink of War Family Where Both Parents are in the Military," *Good Morning America*, ABC (March 19, 2003).

52. "In Depth; Stresses Faced by Military Families," *NBC Nightly News*, NBC (January 12, 2008).

53. "Twelve-year-old Boy Forced to Grow up Quickly to Take Care of His Family While Parents are Deployed in Iraq," *NBC Nightly News*, NBC (October 15, 2004).

54. "Special Report: War with Iraq Introduction."

55. "Operation Christmas; GMA."

56. "Everyone Has a Story; Samantha Cook and Her Husband Dusty Discuss their Son Chance Being Born While Dusty was Deployed in Afghanistan," *Today*, NBC (June 3, 2010).

57. "Freedom Calls Allows Military Families to Keep in Touch," *Sunday Today,* NBC (August 23, 2009).

58. "For November 10, 2013," *CBS Evening News Sunday Edition*, CBS (November 10, 2013).

59. "Dillon Sellers, "Update on Child Heart Transplant."

60. "For November 10, 2013."

61. "A Father's Wish; Soldier Sees Baby's Birth," *Good Morning America*, ABC (December 24, 2010).

62. "Soldiers from Ft. Hood Now Serving in Iraq get to See Their Sons and Daughters Graduate Via the Internet," *CBS Evening News,* CBS (May 31, 2004).

63. "Hero's Homecoming; Emotional Reunion," *Nightline*, ABC (December 23, 2009).

64. "The Roth Family and Elmo Discuss Remembering Military Families Who Have Loved Ones Deployed," *Today,* NBC (December 25, 2006).

65. "The Roth Family."

66. "Operation Love Reunited Has Professional Photographers Take Free Pictures for Military Families, *Saturday Today*, NBC (November 26, 2011).

67. "Operation Love Reunited."
68. "Special Report: War with Iraq Introduction."
69. "Special Report: War with Iraq Introduction."
70. "Daddy Dolls; Eases Kids' Separation Pain," *Good Morning America*, ABC (June 5, 2008).
71. "Daddy Dolls."
72. "Operation Christmas; GMA."
73. "Readings From the Front; United Through Reading," *World News Saturday,* ABC (December 11, 2010).
74. "Reach Out and Read Program Keeps Military Families Connected," *Saturday Today,* NBC (October 15, 2011).
75. "Bailey Family Carries Life-Size Cutout of Husband and Father Craig, Who's Serving in Kuwait, to Various Events," *The Early Show*, CBS (September 21, 2006).
76. "Making a Difference; Augustine and Sons Farm Helping Employee Who Serves in National Guard," *NBC Nightly News,* NBC (September 1, 2010).
77. "Getting to the Heart of Christmas; Surprises for Expectant Military Mothers," *Today*, NBC (December 23, 2010).
78. "Dillon Sellers, "Update on Child Heart Transplant."
79. "For November 9, 2011," *The Early Show*, CBS (November 9, 2011).
80. "For November 10, 2013."
81. "Children at Bill Hefner Elementary Near Fort Bragg, North Carolina, Show Stress as Their Parents Go Off to War," *Today,* NBC (March 28, 2003).
82. "Children at a School Near Fort Bliss Army Base in El Paso, Texas, Find a Way to Cope With Their Worries About Loved Ones in Iraq," *Today: The Battle For Baghdad*, NBC (April 4, 2003).
83. "Summer Camps for Children of Those Deployed in Iraq and Afghanistan," *Today*, NBC (June 21, 2007).
84. "Making a Difference; Operation Purple Provides Camp For Children of Deployed Soldiers," *NBC Nightly News*, NBC (July 27, 2009).
85. For November 10, 2013."
86. "National Guard Families Lack Support Structure of a Base to Deal With Long Deployments," *NBC Nightly News*, NBC (June 5, 2007).
87. "War With Iraq the Struggles of US Military Families," *Good Morning America*, ABC (April 6, 2003).

BIBLIOGRAPHY

ABC News Special Report. "Special Report: War With Iraq Introduction." ABC. March 24 2003.
Altheide, David L. *Qualitative Media Analysis.* Thousand Oaks, CA: Sage, 1996.
Bianchi, Suzanne M., John P. Robinson, and Melissa Milkie. *Changing Rhythms of American Family Life.* New York: Russell Sage Foundation, 2006.
Campbell, Joseph. *The Hero with a Thousand Faces.* Princeton, NJ: Princeton University Press, 1949.

CBS Evening News. "Soldiers from Ft. Hood Now Serving in Iraq get to See Their Sons and Daughters Graduate Via the Internet." CBS. May 31, 2004.

CBS Evening News Sunday Edition. "For November 10, 2013." CBS. November 10, 2013.

Department of Veterans Affairs (2012). Analysis of VA Health Care Utilization Among Operation Enduring Freedom, Operation Iraqi Freedom, and Operation New Dawn Veterans. Retrieved from http://www.publichealth.va.gov/docs/epide-miology/healthcar e-utilization-report-fy2012-qtr1.pdf.

Duckworth, John D., and Patrice M. Buzzanell. "Constructing Work-Life Balance and Fatherhood: Men's Framing of the Meanings of Both Work and Family." *Communication Studies*, 60. no 5. (2009): 558–573.

The Early Show. "Bailey Family Carries Life-Size Cutout of Husband and Father Craig, Who's Serving in Kuwait, to Various Events." CBS. September 21, 2006.

The Early Show. "For November 9, 2011." CBS. November 9, 2011.

Entman, Robert. Framing: Toward clarification of a fractured paradigm. *Journal of Communication* 43, no 4 (1993): 51–58.

Fisher, Walter. *Human Communication as Narration: Toward a Philosophy of Reason, Value, and Action.* Columbia: University of South Carolina Press, 1987.

Goffman, Erving. *Frame Analysis: An Essay on the Organizational of Experience.* New York: Harper Row, 1974.

Good Morning America. "Gift of Life Soldier Views Birth Via Web Cam." ABC. August 12, 2005.

Good Morning America. GMA Homecoming Live!; Military Family's Christmas Miracle." ABC. December 12, 2012.

Good Morning America. "A Father's Wish; Soldier Sees Baby's Birth." ABC. December 24, 2010.

Good Morning America. "Brink of War Family Where Both Parents are in the Military." ABC. March 19, 2003.

Good Morning America. "Daddy Dolls; Eases Kids' Separation Pain." ABC. June 5, 2008.

Good Morning America. "Dillon Sellers, "Update on Child Heart Transplant Patient." ABC. March 22, 2004.

Good Morning America. "Message From Home; On the Front Line With Our Troops." ABC. December 6, 2010.

Good Morning America. "Operation Christmas: Down Home Holiday Cheer." ABC. December 7, 2006.

Howard, John and Laura Prividera. "The Fallen Woman Archetype: Media Representations of Lynndie England, Gender and the (Ab)uses of U.S. Female Soldiers." *Women's Studies in Communication* 31, (2008): 287–311. doi:10.1080/07491409. 2008.10162544.

Howard, John and Laura Prividera. "Rescuing Patriarchy or Saving 'Jessica Lynch:' The Rhetorical Construction of the American Woman Soldier." *Women & Language* 27, no. 2 (2004): 89–97.

Jung, Carl G. *The Archetypes and the Collective Unconscious (Collected works of C.G. Jung vol. 9 part 1).* G. Adler & R. F. C. Hull, Trans. Princeton, NJ: Bollingen, 1981. Original works published 1934-1954.

Kellner, Douglas. "The Media and the Crisis of Democracy in the Age of Bush-2." *Communication and Critical/Cultural Studies* 1, no 1 (2004): 29–58.

Kumar, Deepa. "Media, War, and Propaganda: Strategies of Information Management During the 2003 Iraq War." *Communication and Critical/Cultural Studies* 3, no 1 (2006): 48–69. doi: 10.1080/14791420500505650.

Kuypers, Jim A. Framing Analysis. In Jim A. Kuypers (Ed.), *The Art of Rhetorical Criticism* (pp. 186–211). Boston: Allyn & Bacon, 2005.

Lee, Shawna J., Tova B. Neugut, Katherine L. Rosenblum, Richard M. Tolman, Wendy J. Travis, Margaret H. Walker. "Sources of Parenting Support in Early Fatherhood: Perspectives of United States Air Force Members." *Children and Youth Services Review* 35, (2013): 908–915. doi.org.jproxy.lib.ecu.edu/10.1016/j.childyouth.2013.02.012.

Lindlof, Thomas. *Qualitative Communication Research Methods.* Thousand Oaks, CA: Sage, 2005.

Louie, Ashley and Lisa DeMarni Cromer, "Parent-Child Attachment During the Deployment Cycle: Impact on Reintegration Parent Stress." *Professional Psychology: Research and Practice* 45, no 6 (2014): 500–501. doi.org.jproxy.lib.ecu.edu/10.1037/a0036603.

Lule, Jack. *Daily News, Eternal Stories: The Mythological Role of Journalism.* New York: Guilford Press, 2001.

McCombs, Maxwell. "New frontiers in agenda setting: Agendas of attributes and frames." *Mass communication review* 24, no. 1/2 (1997): 32–52.

Morman, Mark T., and Kory Floyd, "A 'Changing Culture of Fatherhood': Effects on Affectionate Communication, Closeness, and Satisfaction in Men's Relationships with their Fathers and their Sons." *Western Journal of Communication* 66, no 4 (2002): 395–411.

NBC Nightly News. "In Depth; Stresses Faced by Military Families." NBC Universal. January 12, 2008.

NBC Nightly News. "Making a Difference; Augustine and Sons Farm Helping Employee Who Serves in National Guard." NBC Universal. September 1, 2010.

NBC Nightly News. "Making a Difference; Operation Purple Provides Camp For Children of Deployed Soldiers." NBC Universal. July 27, 2009.

NBC Nightly News. "National Guard Families Lack Support Structure of a Base to Deal With Long Deployments." NBC Universal. June 5, 2007.

NBC Nightly News. "Twelve-year-old Boy Forced to Grow up Quickly to Take Care of His Family While Parents are Deployed in Iraq." NBC Universal. October 15, 2004.

Nightline. "Hero's Homecoming; Emotional Reunion." ABC. December 23, 2009.

Nightline. "A Mother's Joy; The Child of the Fallen." ABC. February 19, 2007.

Pan, Zhongdang and Gerald Kosicki. "Framing Analysis: An Approach to News Discourse." *Political Communication* 10, no 1 (1993): 55–75.

The Saturday Early Show. "Travis Peterson and His Wife and Daughters Discuss His Surprise Homecoming from Afghanistan at His Daughter's School." CBS. April 5, 2008.

Schachman, Kathleen. "Online Fathering: The Experience of First-Time Fatherhood in Combat-Deployed Troops." *Nursing Research*, 59, no 1 (2010): 11–17.

Sunday Morning. "Operation Purple's Summer Camp for Children of Soldiers Deployed Overseas." CBS. July 1, 2007.

Tanielianm, Terri and Jaycox, Lisa. "Invisible Wounds of War: Psychological and Cognitive Injuries, their Consequences, and Services to Assist Recovery." *RAND, Center for Military Health Policy Research* (2008). Retrieved from http://www.rand.org/pubs/monographs/MG720.html.

Today. "The Battle For Baghdad: Children at a School Near Fort Bliss Army Base in El Paso, Texas, Find a Way to Cope With Their Worries About Loved Ones in Iraq." NBC Universal. April 4, 2003.

Today. "Children at Bill Hefner Elementary Near Fort Bragg, North Carolina, Show Stress as Their Parents Go Off to War." NBC Universal. March 28, 2003.

Today. "Everyone Has a Story; Samantha Cook and Her Husband Dusty Discuss their Son Chance Being Born While Dusty was Deployed in Afghanistan." NBC Universal. June 3, 2010.

Today. "Getting to the Heart of Christmas; Surprises for Expectant Military Mothers." NBC Universal. December 23, 2010.

Today. "The Roth Family and Elmo Discuss Remembering Military Families Who Have Loved Ones Deployed." NBC Universal. December 25, 2006.

Today. "Summer Camps for Children of Those Deployed in Iraq and Afghanistan. NBC Universal. June 21, 2007.

Today. "Today's Call to Action; Sergeant Devon Weaver and wife Amanda Show the Difficulties of One Parent Serving in Iraq." NBC Universal. June 4, 2009.

Today Saturday. "The Families of Service Members in Afghanistan Being Taken Care of at Fort Bragg." NBC Universal. September 18, 2010.

Today Saturday. "Operation Love Reunited Has Professional Photographers Take Free Pictures for Military Families." NBC Universal. November 26, 2011.

Today Saturday. "Reach Out and Read Program Keeps Military Families Connected." NBC Universal. October 15, 2011.

Today Sunday. "Freedom Calls Allows Military Families to Keep in Touch." NBC Universal. August 23, 2009.

U.S. Department of Defense. (October, 2010). Report on the Impact of Deployment of Members of the Armed Forces on Their Dependent Children. [Report to the Senate and House Committees on Armed Services]. Retrieved from http://download.militaryonesource.mil/12038/MOS/Reports/Report_to_Congress_on_Impact_of_Deployment_on_Military_Children.pdf

U.S. Department of Defense, 2013 Demographics: Profile of the military community. Retrieved from http://download.militaryonesource.mil/12038/MOS/Reports/2013-Demographics-Report.pdf 2003: v.

Walsh, Tova B., Carolyn J. Dayton, Michael S. Erwin, Maria Muzik, Alexandra Busuito and Katherine L. Rosenblum. "Fathering after Military Deployment: Parenting Challenges and Goals of Fathers of Young Children," *Health and Social Work* 39, no 1 (2014): 35-44. doi: 10.1093/hsw/hlu005.

"War With Iraq the Struggles of US Military Families." *Good Morning America.* ABC. April 6, 2003.

Webb, Lynn et al., "Perceived Parental Communication, Gender and Young Adults Self-Estemm: Male, Female and Universal Path Models," In Philip Backlund and Mary Rose Williams (Eds.), *Readings in Gender Communication* (pp.197–224). Belmont, CA: Wadsworth, 2004, 214.

Willerton, Elaine, Rona Schwarz, Shelley Wadsworth and Mary Oglesby, "Military Fathers' Perspectives on Involvement." *Journal of Family Psychology* 25, no 4 (2011): 521-530. doi: 101037/a0024511

"Wives and Children Think of Their Soldier Dads as Father's Day Approaches." *Today,* NBC, (June 18, 2004)Woodward, Rachel. "Warrior Heroes and Little Green Men: Soldiers, Military Training, and the Construction of Rural Masculinities." *Rural Sociology* 65, 2000: 640-657.

World News Saturday. "Readings From the Front; United Through Reading." ABC. December 11, 2010.

Zeanah, Charles, H., Lisa Berlin, and Neil Boris. "Practitioner Review: Clinical Applications of Attachment Theory and Research for Infants and Young Children." *Journal of Child Psychology* 52, (2011): 819-833. doi: 10.1111/j.1469-7610.2011.02399.x.

Chapter 4

Decoding Comedic Dads

*Examining How Media and Real Fathers
Measure up with Young Viewers*

Janice Kelly

A sentiment exists that fathers are devalued in the media, and the media appear to be in conflict with the portrayals of real fathers. Fathers today are more involved in childcare, household chores, carpooling, P.T.A. meetings, school activities and the emotional development of their children than their fathers were, according to the National Fatherhood Initiative Study.[1] However, failing to recognize the contribution fathers make in the household is said to have created a media bias where the mothers are the powerful ones and the fathers are the oppressed. Some communication scholars have claimed that the primary role men play on these domestic shows is as a one-dimensional character whose primary role is that of financial provider not an emotional supporter.[2] This is a contrast to the golden age of television when fathers were authoritarian and problem-solvers. In fact, TV fathers like Jim Anderson from *"Father Knows Best"* were described as the "good father."[3] The promulgation of the "good father" image broadcast throughout mass media may contain a middle-class bias that presupposes fathers have sufficient time to devote to the domestic sphere. Fathers with marginal incomes may have to work two or three jobs to make ends meet, precluding them from achieving the ideal lifestyle.[4] However, cultural media critic, Mark Crispin Miller stated, "in the 1970s television father's authority became passe."[5]

One popular theory to explain the rise of the bumbling dad portrayal on television directly relates to the shift in the American economy during the 1970s. Men's wages declined or remained the same at a time when an increasing number of women entered the workforce. Women's income increased 10 percent (relative to men) in both manual and nonmanual jobs in industry between 1970 and 1976, with the greater part of that increase taking place toward the end of this period.[6]

Family composition changed from the sole breadwinners to a dual-income household. As a result, fathers had to share in domestic responsibilities and some of their social status was diminished. Watching TV fathers burn the evening dinner or ruining the laundry became the focal point of the jokes. Focusing on domestic chores allowed more and more TV fathers from all socioeconomic brackets to become the center of the laugher implying man's domain is the world of work and not the domestic sphere.[7] And this television scripted formula continues as the newest situation comedy on TBS-TV, *The Jim Gaffigan Show* portrays himself as the doofus dad.[8] Petroski and Edley state, "the media will create a fatherly role that is not accurate just to get some laugh."[9]

Yet, others like Coontz, who wrote the popular book: *The Way We Never Were: American Families and the Nostalgia Trap,* argue that the media continues to support a paternalistic ideology where the men are still in a powerful position despite their funny antics.[10] For example, during an episode of *Everybody Loves Raymond*, Ray Barone told his wife that he was the breadwinner and the sole provider of the house and that he therefore determines the family vacation destination.[11] Similarly, on one episode on *Mike and Molly*, Molly decided to quit her job as a teacher to become a writer, and her husband, Mike commented that he was the breadwinner and made the final decision regarding resource allocation.[12] Coontz would claim these attitudes are not solely reflective of economic resources but describes power structures in the family as well.[13]

Perceptions of paternal roles in the media do not only affect individuals whose personal experience is in a family where there is a father in residence, but those without. Media images have a pronounced impact on the 24 million children in this country who do not live with their fathers. With no paternal role model at home, these children gather impressions of fatherhood from media fathers.[14] As a result, some children without fathers may believe these are accurate portrayals because they don't have a father or male role model in their life to compare them to.

Television has the power to shape our attitudes, beliefs, and perceptions.[15] Psychologist, Albert Bandura, claims children seek out role models to emulate.[16] Yet children in general are exposed to conflicting images of fatherhood. Christopher Brown, President of the National Fatherhood Initiative explores how media primes the public to interpret fatherhood in negative and positive ways.[17]

Although the discussions about the portrayal of fathers are contained in academic and political arenas (primarily with regard to social policy), a better way to assess how real fathers have changed is to ask their children. They have a fundamental understanding of their relationship, or lack thereof, with their fathers. Therefore, they should be good reporters about the nature of the relationship. Understanding father-child dyads through the lens of their children's eyes can help communication educators better develop practical family scripts useful in parenting programs that particularly target young fathers, as well as lessons on how to deconstruct unrealistic images of what fathers ought to or should be. This exploratory study raises questions such as, what is the relationship between media images of fathers and the perception of fathers as experienced by their children? In addition, it explores socio-emotional support (guidance, communication and affection), such as to what is the relationship between media images of fathers and the perception of fathers as experienced by their children? How does the media portray TV fathers? The study gives a partial answer to the question of to what extent does the construction of fatherhood in family situation comedies relate to the experienced-based perceptions of fatherhood in actual families?

FATHER INVOLVEMENT—ITS DEFINITION IS BASED ON WHOM YOU ASK?

Researchers have attempted to develop a construct of positive fatherhood, alternately calling it "good fathering." The development of this construct is prima facie evidence of serious issues surrounding fatherhood. If sociologists identify responsible fathering, the concept must have boundaries outside of which exist irresponsible fathering, which constitutes a social problem.[18]

Good fatherhood has three major dimensions: paternal engagement, accessibility and responsibility.[19] Yet, other research suggests two major dimensions: functionality and authoritativeness. First, to what extent is the relationship functional to the positive development of the child? Functionality covers the issue of paternal engagement and accessibility. The second concept focuses on paternal responsibility. Authoritarian, punitive, negative parenting tend to result in children who have trouble with social relations and who are aggressive. Involved fathers who practice "authoritative parenting" have more contact, provide more caregiving, play with the children more, establish limits, provide more emotional support, take more responsibility and greater opportunity for positive growth. Involvement is described as a parent actively involved in the daily activities of their child's life. However, some social scientists are debating the definition of involvement when it relates to fathers since it is narrowly defined to mean economic resources.

Coley and Morris analyzed predictors of father involvement with their children in a sample of 228 urban, low-income, predominately minority couples with at least one preschool child.[20] They reported a high rate of consensus between father-mother pairs on the rate and nature of fathers' involvement; however, mothers rated father's involvement consistently lower than the fathers' self-ratings. Factors that influenced the magnitude of discrepancy between fathers' and mothers' ratings were greater discrepancies for older fathers as compared to younger fathers. The higher the mothers' education was, the greater the discrepancy. Discrepancies were higher among employed mothers compared to unemployed mothers. The greater the conflict between the couple, the higher the discrepancy score. Although mothers' perceptions and fathers' perceptions of fathers' involvement behaviors are strongly correlated, mothers consistently rate the level of fathers' involvement lower than do fathers. This illustrates the bias in the reporting by mothers as they describe the role fathers play with their children.

FATHER'S ROLES AND RESPONSIBILITIES IN FAMILIES

Hofferth using data gathered from several large-scale national studies reported that when asked about responsibilities for caregiving, fathers reported that they had much more responsibility than what the mothers perceived of these fathers.[21] For example, regarding discipline, 19% of fathers indicated that it was primarily their responsibility, while only 6% of the mothers agreed. 77% of the fathers said that it was a shared responsibility compared to 59% of the mother; 4% of the fathers said that it was the mother's responsibility primarily compared to 35% of the mothers.[22] This pattern held true for basic caregiving, playing with children, emotional support, and monitoring children as well.

Researchers have recently explored how fathers respond to their parenting role. For example, Paisley, Futris, and Skinner examined the relationships between commitment and psychological centrality on fathering behaviors by surveying a sample of 186 upper-middle class, predominately white fathers with children under the age of 18.[23] Data indicated that in general fathers believed that their wives viewed them positively as parents, and they viewed themselves competent as parents. They were highly satisfied with parenting as a role. They reported having an extensive social support network for their roles as fathers. Additionally, most fathers viewed their role as a parent as central to their identity. Affective communication explained 28% of the variance in psychological centrality and the two variables together explained 38% of the variance in role performance as a father. Thus, among fathers, the greater the commitment to the family and perceptions of a centralized role in their children's lives, the more positive was the role performance.[24]

Fathers living with their children change on the basis of their social involvement from informal social relationships to greater participation in community organizations. No differences were found among those living with their children and those who were not in terms of life satisfaction and physical health.

THE CONCEPT OF FAMILY TIME

Daly noted that "family time" is an ideological construct shaped by Western ideas of family togetherness, positive engagement, and child centeredness.[25] It is a construct that is difficult to be realized in today's world in which adult members' time is taken up with occupational obligations. The contradiction between the ideological construct and actually lived family time leads parents to believe that things would get better if they had more time. However, they felt that spending adequate and quality family time was just beyond their grasp because of outside activities like work. Both men and women experience similar levels of guilt. Therefore, family time is problematized as something in which there is always a scarcity.

Family time is a subject in which there is a great deal of tension, negotiation, and guilt. As American families have increasingly become smaller and extended family relationships more tenuous, greater normative expectations devolve on mothers and fathers for child-rearing. In societies where quite literally children are raised by the village through the efforts of extended and fictive kin, such pressures are less prevalent.

The research suggests that the cultural level of social expectations on father's role performance is increasing while simultaneously at the material level of social reproduction, incomes have stagnated or declined creating demand for longer work weeks to shore up the family's financial situation, along with a divorce rate hovering around 50% for the last 25 years.[26] The analysis of the study will yield useful and relevant information on the ideological construction of fatherhood that is communicated through the television medium.

METHODOLOGY

This study asked students from all ethnic, racial, urban and suburban environments and socioeconomic groups who lived with their fathers continuously between the ages of 15 and 18. Students who lived away from their fathers for more than four years were ineligible to participate in the study in order to enhance the validity of the findings. Long separation from their fathers might influence participations' perceptions, possibly leading to idealization or vilification of their fathers. Participants were divided into two groups and asked to watch domestic situation comedy shows found on syndicated cable such as *The Simpsons, Family Guy, George Lopez Show, My Wife and Kids, Fresh Prince of Bel-Air, Full House, Bernie Mac, Family Matter, Everyone Loves Raymond and the Cosby Show.* From this list, three episodes from each situation comedy were randomly selected. The fifteen episodes were considered a random sampling of mediated images of fathers as portrayed in situation comedies. Thus, participants watched a total of 69 minutes of television shows, without intervening commercials. Viewings were approximately five minutes apart. This gave students time to take notes if they so desired. The viewing of the video sequences was conducted in a large classroom.

They were asked four questions:

1. In what ways is the media father like your own father?
2. In what ways is the media father different from your own father?
3. Include your own comments comparing your fathers and those presented on sitcoms.
4. How do you define support?

The majority of participants were white n = 12 and African American n = 8. The other participants were Hispanic n = 4 and Asian n = 2.

Response to Open-Ended Question

1. In what ways is the media father like your own father?
    Participant —"My dad loves to tell stories and give me advice. He's involved in me and knows my friends and my daily activities. He sends me cards and tells me he loves me."
    Participant —"My dad is a great father, family-oriented like Cliff Huxtable. I love his interaction with his children; his support and dedication to his family."
    Participant —"I know he's not the best role model, but my father is like Homer Simpson cause he puts his family first when he needs to gets involved with his children's activities to an extent, and in times of need, is always there." Homer doesn't understand Lisa but he tries to."
    Participant —"The fathers I know don't read to their children, don't help them with their homework, don't get too involved in their lives and they are too busy working two jobs and putting food on the table."
    Participant—"As an American Born Chinese, I wished my dad was more like TV fathers. TV dads listen to their children talk about their day. I have a linear relationship with my dad. My parents don't listen to me."

The second most frequently mentioned commonality was that both media fathers and actual fathers provided moral regulation. Under this category

Table 4.1 Frequencies and Distributions of Responses on Similarities between Actual and Media Fathers (*n* = 26)

Similar Father Behaviors	n	%
Emotional Presence		
Support	8	12.3
Humor	6	9.2
Caring/Love	5	7.7
Aloof	3	4.6
Causes Guilt	3	4.6
Verbally abusive	2	3.1
Absent	1	1.5
Rude	1	1.5
Blames others	1	1.5
Moral Regulation		
Guidance	8	12.3
Moral enforcement	5	7.7
Strict	3	4.6
Participation		
Involved	7	10.8
Household Chores	1	1.5
Attend Meetings	1	1.5
Achievement Pressure	1	1.5
Concern/Responsibility		
Family oriented	4	6.2
Work oriented	2	3.1
Weak	2	3.1
Practical	1	1.5
Responsible	1	1.5
Total	**65**	**100.0**

were providing guidance (23%), moral reinforcement (7.7%) and being strict (4.6%).

Participant—"My father is most like Carl Winslow of *Family Matters,* and Michael Kyle. My father is hard working just like Carl and he tries to instill good values in his kids. He likes to joke around with us but he is more concerned with you."

Participant—"He compared his father to Phil on *Fresh Prince of Bel-Air* stating 'He's trying hard for his kids to achieve their full potential. He knows when to be strict and when to be funny.'"

Participant—"My father is sort of like Phil he wants to set you on the right path and gives me advice on what not to do in the future. He's quiet but if he sees you going the wrong way or doing something wrong he has lots to say."

Participant—"My parents are just like those on TV where my dad tries to be the bad cop and has to discipline us and my mom is the good cop."

In general, the comments about the commonalities between media fathers and actual fathers were overwhelmingly positive, with the possible exception of emotional support. Participants favorably compared their fathers with media fathers. They appreciated their support, and humor, caring, family involvement, concern for others, provision of guidance and behavioral boundaries. A plurality of study participants used the comparison of media and actual fathers negatively. The major complaints against fathers were their physical and emotional absence and verbal abusiveness. One participant compared her father to George Lopez: "Lopez reminds me of my father because he's so silly with his children and he blames his rude behavior on his mother and not having a father and trying to figure out how to be a good father on trial and error which is an excuse."

DIFFERENCES BETWEEN MEDIA AND ACTUAL FATHERS

When the participants were asked to compare their real fathers with media fathers, media fathers earned some merit for their portrayal. The media fathers had more positive attributes than actual fathers. The data are presented in Table 4.2.

Four (10.5%) comments related to socioeconomic status. All agreed that, in general, media fathers were more highly educated, had better jobs, and earned more money than their own fathers. Half of the comments related to role performance. Participants commented in several veins. First, participants commented about the unfavorable depiction of media fathers. Three examples were:

Homer Simpson doesn't provide a stable environment. Doesn't seem supportive.

Table 4.2 Frequencies and Distributions of Responses on Similarities of Actual and Media Fathers by Category and Valence (*n* = 26)

Parental Realm	N	%
Emotional Presence	29	44.6
Moral Regulation	16	24.6
Participation	10	15.4
Concern/Responsibility	10	15.4
Behavioral Valence		
Positive	52	80.0
Negative	13	20.0
Total	**65**	**100.0**

The father from *Family Guy* is the most disturbing father I have ever seen. He doesn't show support for his kids, his language sense is awful and he isn't a good role model.

Peter Griffen, *Family Guy*: This media father is a poor excuse of a parent. He shows absolutely no responsibility within the family and shows his poor judgment calls.

Second, participants shared some of the negative comparisons of their actual fathers with media fathers:

They are more talkative than my father. They are always in their kids business and doing silly things. TV fathers are more like friends to their children than parents. My dad doesn't want to be my friend and he says that a lot, he's my father.

TV fathers allow their children to make mistakes. My dad wants me to avoid them.

[Media fathers] seem like they have a lot more time at home than real fathers. [They] want to know what's going day to day, not [just] when things happen, like my dad.

Third, some of the participants had positive comments about their fathers which made comparisons that included gender roles and behaviors connected to culture:

[My father is] not silly or inept at home. Can cook and take care of the kids. He lets you talk about everything and anything. He helps my mom all the time. Why is this laughable?

[My father] treats me different than my brothers and on TV fathers treat their children equally. Muslim fathers don't open up and talk about their past; that's an American thing.[Muslim] fathers are strong, admired and wise.

A second category of comparison was how positively participants compared their fathers to media fathers. There were only two participants who viewed their fathers more positively than the media fathers. For example, one participant implied that his family would disown the father if he behaved this way. He stated, "My father could not be anything like [the Family Guy] if he wanted to continue to hold the title of father."

Some of the participants complained that media fathers were unrealistic or that making comparisons between their father and the media fathers were unfair:

TV fathers are unrealistic. The majority of real fathers I know work hard and struggle to have time to spend with their kids. Bernie Mac and [George] Lopez spend too much time with their children and more with their sons.

Too perfect! Real fathers do not pamper their sons like Cosby or Bernie Mac. TV fathers relate to their family in a more superficial way meaning that TV fathers do not have to go through all the changes and attitudes of an actual growing adolescent.

The third category of comparisons was emotional support, accounting for 39.5% of the comments. In this particular area, media fathers were viewed far more supportive than actual fathers. Below were two comments:

Children can express their feelings, which doesn't happen in my family. They use humor a lot too; not my father. He's serious all the time.

[Media fathers are] patient with their children but my dad tries to be with us but having six brothers and sisters he doesn't have it. He doesn't bark orders but when he calls you, you better go to him.

In summary, the participants viewed media fathers as having higher social status, being more adept in performing the role of the father, and manifesting more emotional support. Of the 21 statements about media fathers, 16 indicated that media fathers were economically better off than actual fathers. Of the 17 statements about actual fathers, 10 compared them negatively to media fathers' time with their children. However, certain media fathers, especially those in cartoons, such as Homer Simpson and the Family Guy, were criticized for their ineptitude, egoism, and lack of judgment. Several participants commented on the artificiality of the situations of media fathers, noting that they did not have to deal with real-world problems or that they inhabited the role of father too perfectly.

Table 4.3   Comments on Media and Actual Fathers

Comments	n	%
Unrealistic	9	24.3
Good father	6	16.2
Unfair	6	16.2
Reflect Social Norms	3	8.1
Racial Imbalance	3	8.1
Different than Actual Fathers	3	8.1
Negative Image of Fathers	3	8.1
Accurate	2	5.4
Narrow Depiction of Fathers	2	5.4
Total	37	100.0

General Comments

Participants were invited to include their own comments comparing their fathers to those presented in situation comedies. Their responses are enumerated in Table 4.4. The most common comment (24.3%) was that the portrayal of fathers in the media was unrealistic.

Similarly, comments from some of the participants revealed their views of media fathers: For example one participant stated, "I think that television fathers are more of a fantasy of how people expect fathers these days to behave (those positive fathers)." Similarly, another wrote: "I believe some media give fathers too much credit. They make them look too good, when in life their not as good. It's sort of life a fairy tale."

The second largest category was tied between those who seemed to think that the media portrayed father's ideals and those that thought the portrayal of fathers was unfair (16.2%). An example of the former was: "Parents in real life are different than TV portrayed parents. Parenthood is almost like a perfect family, which is impossible in real life."

Several participants thought that portrayals of fathers in the media were unfair. Typical comments were:

The media is unfair to real fathers because it paints what and how fathers should be.

Media is unfair to real fathers. Fathers struggle with their jobs to make a living; many of them don't spend as much time with their families. In the Hispanic community this is what fathers do. My dad and I hang out on the weekends and that works for me.

Media is unfair; it's Candyland because it's different from reality.

Some participants, such as the first commenter in the list above, suggested that the media images of fathers are attempts to socialize the larger population by presenting ideals or holding up exaggerated negative examples for ridicule.

TV provides rules and models of what is normal. Some of them are not ethically and morally doing the right thing by our norms. Too many conflicting messages of what is a good father.

Of all the comments by the participants, the above statement was the most analytical and sociological. The comment suggests that the media present contradictory images about what constitutes appropriate fatherly behavior.

Numerous commentators reported that media images were unfair to actual fathers, primarily because media fathers have the luxury of unlimited time to interact with their families. This is regardless of whether they are role ideals like Heathcliff Huxtable or buffoons, such as Homer Simpson or the Family Guy, as suggested in previous comments.

Three (8.1%) participants commented on the racial/ethnic imbalance in family situation comedies, even though several situation comedies were ostensibly about African American or Hispanic families. As one participant stated, "[The media present a] narrow view of fathers and it's based on the White fathers' values [with] no other cultural perspectives. These shows don't represent my family experience."

Although three (8.1%) participants mentioned that media fathers were different than actual fathers, many of those comments were enumerated above in terms of reflecting ego ideals and represented by fathers who seemed not to be limited by extensive working hours. Three participants (8.1%) also mentioned that television media presented negative images of fathers in contradiction to those who thought that media fathers were "too good." In addition, two (5.4%) participants indicated that the media portrayed fathers fairly accurately. As one participant said, "Fathers are 85% accurately portrayed."

It is apparent that participants selected different media fathers to comment upon. In some cases, such as Homer Simpson, some participants viewed him as a positive father image because he always put his family first, perhaps reluctantly, given his self-indulgence. He always demonstrated his love for his wife and children, even though at times he has been shown strangling his son, Bart. Even though sorely tempted, he always did the right thing in the end. However, other viewers may focus on his buffoonery, gross ineptitude, and selfishness. So is Homer Simpson an ego ideal or a negative stereotype? The answer apparently lies in the eye of the beholder.

In contradiction to the participant who stated that the media presented too many conflicting images of fatherhood, two (5.4%) comments were that the depiction of fathers was too narrow. In addition to the participant who claimed that the norm was white fathers even when the characters were ostensibly black, one participant commented that the media image of the father was: "A narrow perspective-Dads are silly and distant from their children— no cultural perspective. All of them are the same."

In summary, the comments from the participants on media fathers were contradictory. Many thought they were unrealistic while others thought they were accurate. Many thought that the image of the media fathers was overly positive while others thought that the images were too negative. Some thought that the spectrum of fathers was too broad and contradictory while others thought that they were too narrow. The consensus was that TV fathers were more privileged than their own in that they had more time to spend with their family, and they seemed to have more psychological resources to deal positively with other family members.

Table 4.4   Definitions of Support

Support	N	%
Emotional/caring/loving	16	37.2
Financial/Material	14	32.6
Behavioral	9	20.9
Instructional	4	9.3
Total	43	100.0

The final question was divided into four subquestions in which the participants were asked to define: (a) support, (b) guidance, (c) acceptance, and (d) opposition. When asked about the definitions of support, nearly 7 out of 10 (69.8%) mentioned either emotional (37.2%) or material support (32.6%). Another 20.9% mention behavioral support which was defined as participation and interaction with their children, and 9.3% mentioned help with school or academics. The data are presented in Table 4.4.

Of prime importance in the definition was emotional support, which was also defined as caring, showing love, and being available when needed. Some typical comments were:

When [at] times [they] come home from work just [to] talk with their kids . . . and if they need help he's home for you.

No matter how bad you do on something they should always keep telling you to try. Help your self-esteem.

I believe that a father should always be there for his family's time(s) of need. Even adolescents look to their fathers on certain life decisions.

Similarly, some typical comments or examples of material support included: "financial support-food, clothing and rent," or "buys my affection with items," or "financial support, however little else." These last two comments reflected a certain amount of cynicism in relation to material support. The second participant seems to suggest that her father bribes her; the third participant indicates that his father provides only financial support. However, a fourth participant had a softer view of her father, by stating that her real father: "Supports the family financially. Mom doesn't work. He works two jobs."

Behavioral support was primarily defined as "being there." For example, three statements were shared from participants:

Always being there; being at basketball games.

There for their sons when he is really needed like street trouble.

Attends every school event that his kid participates in.

Educational support was always mentioned with other kinds of support. For example, one participant mentioned that "Education is important-won't talk about personal stuff, just job and money issues," and another expressed that "financial and religious support" were given by his Muslim father.

CONCLUSION

Network television's portrayal of the American father matters to young viewers. Television content influences viewers' expectations of family life and family relations. They can establish an ideological notion of what fathers ought to or should be. For example, the father is a common target for conflict in family situation comedies given the current cultural paradigm of male ineptitude in the management of intimate and interpersonal relationships.[27]

When asked to compare and contrast their own fathers with media fathers, only two participants support the thesis that the media portray fathers in a positive light and they identified as first generational Americans. Many participants complain that the portrayal of media fathers is unfair to actual fathers, who did not have the luxury of time to spend with their families. Some characterize family situation comedies as mere fantasy. In family situation comedies, the father almost always has an occupation; however, the work never seems to interfere with family time. They are rarely seen at work, even though in real life work occupies a minimum of one-quarter of one's waking hours.[28] Perhaps another ideological function of family situation comedies is to underplay the deleterious effects of long work hours on the family.

Fathers are expected to be more involved in their families than they were in previous generations. They are expected to be attentive to the emotional lives of their children as well as providers of material support and moral guidance.[29] Authority in the new age family is supposed to be democratic and involve consultation and negotiation. This is most clearly exemplified in the comments of first-generation immigrant participants whose fathers behave in a traditional role in which social distance between fathers and children are very high, where fathers are authorities in all realms of family living, and children are expected to revere them.

IMPLICATIONS OF THE STUDY

By and large, television and other media significantly influence the lives of the American public and impact perceptions of individuals and families alike. The implications resulting from this study, although it's a small sample size, provide a framework and context for using fathers as presented by the media as case studies for teaching courses on television fathers and effective family functioning. Further, these television depictions determine the ideological function of the media with its portrayals of family life. Implications that are derived from this study are presented in two sections: (1) media literacy/ family-life education, and (2) directions for further research.

MEDIA LITERACY AND FAMILY LIFE EDUCATION

The study reveals that the media portrays both positive and negative images of television fathers. These portrayals were a touchstone, causing participants to open up and talk about how they compared their real fathers with TV fathers in terms of communication, involvement, and affection. Studies that focus on media viewing will benefit by providing participants with the tools to deconstruct these images along with their understanding of patriarchal notions of family life. Thus, media literacy involves a critical and careful attention to what messages and images are communicated and how these messages and images become socializing means for youth and young adults. Opportunities for dialogue about images and messages can provide a forum to discuss the complex view of family life. These dialogs can embrace cultural, racial and ethnic differences and provide an alternative to the middle-class white stereotype of family life.

FURTHER RESEARCH

Additional research is needed to focus on young children. A specific empha-sis should be applied to children between the ages 2 and 12 who spend hours in front of a television and other media exposure and are greatly influenced by its content. It will be interesting to learn about their relationships with their fathers in comparison to the media portrayals. Further research should conduct a comparative study between those living with their fathers and those without fathers who watch family situation comedies. Their perceptions of family life and fathers in general would be highly informative. This will be particularly interesting in determining how youngsters use or model their parenting skills after television fathers because of the absence of fathers from their lives.

The use of commercial television in courses on fatherhood should be explored for its utility as accessible case studies within the classroom. This form of media evaluation may be employed as an aid in teaching parenting programs targeted to young fathers. Again, television media is a powerful tool for learning, and other forms of television programming such as the family drama series, which are watched by many young viewers and young adults, may provide yet another rich source of the impact of images of family life and fathers. Thus, this study provides informative data that could lead to additional studies about the extent of the impact of media, especially television media, on images of fatherhood and family.

NOTES

1. "National Fatherhood Initiative Study," 2008. http://www.fatherhood.org retrieved August 12, 2015.

2. Kimberly R. Walsh, Elfriede Fursich, and Bonnie Jefferson, "Beauty and the Patriarchial Beast: Gender Role Portrayal in Sitcoms Featuring Mismatch Couples," *Journal of Popular Film and Television*, 36 (2008): 123–132; William Douglas and Beth Olson, "Beyond Family Structure: The Family in Domestic Comedy," *Journal of Broadcasting and Electronic Media*, 39 (1995): 236–262.

3. June M. Frazer and Timothy C. Frazer, "Father Knows Best and The Cosby Show, Nostalgia and the Sitcom Tradition," *Journal of Popular Culture*, 27 (2004): 163–172.

4. John Honeycutt, Lynn B. Wellman, and Mary S. Larsen, "Beneath Family Role Portrayals: An Additional Measure of Communication Influence Using Time Series Analyses of Turn at Talk on a Popular Television Program," *Journal of Broadcasting & Electronic Media,* 41 no. 1 (1997): 40–57.

5. Mark Crispin Miller, "Dads Through the Decades: Thirty Years of TV Fathers," Center for Media Literacy, 48, 1986. http://www.medialit.org/reading.../ dads-through-decades-thirty-years-tv-father.com.

6. Aileen McColgan, *Just Wages for Women* (Oxford: Clarendon Press, 1997), p. 91.

7. Erica Scharrer, "From Wise to Foolish, The Portrayal of the Sitcom Father: 1950s-1990s," *Journal of Broadcasting and Electronic Media,* 45 (2001): 25–40.

8. *The Jim Gaffigan Show,* "Super Great Daddy Day," directed by Todd Biermann and written by Jim Gaffigan and Jeannie Gaffigan, TBS-TV, August 12, 2015.

9. David J. Petroski and Paige P. Edley, "Stay-at-Home Fathers: Masculinity, Family, Work, and Gender Stereotypes." *The Electronic Journal of Communication*, 16 (2006). http://www.cios.org/EJCPUBLIC/016/3/01634.HTML.

10. Stephanie Coontz. *The Way We Never Were: American Families and the Nostalgia Trap,* (New York, NY. BasicBooks 1992).

11. *Everybody Loves Raymond*, "The Checkbook," directed by John Fortenberry and written by Philip Rosenthal and Tom Caltabiano, TBS-TV, February 2, 1998.

12. *Mike and Molly*, "Molly Unleashed," directed by Phil Lewis and written by Mark Roberts, CBS-TV, November 4, 2013.

13. Coontz. *The Way We Never Were.*

14. "National Fatherhood Initiative Statistic Report," National Fatherhood Initiative, http://www.fatherhood.org, accessed August 12, 2015.

15. Richard J. Harris, *A Cognitive Psychology of Mass Communication* (Mahwah, NJ: Lawrence Erlbaum Associates, Publishers, 1999), p. 107.

16. Harris, *A Cognitive Psychology*, p. 20.

17. Ryan Sanders, "How Mass Media Portray Dads and What You Can Do About It," National Fatherhood Initiative, July 2, 2015. http://www.fatherhood.org.

18. William Marsiglio, Paul Amato, Randal Day, and Michael Lamb, "Scholarship on Fatherhood in the 1990s and Beyond," *Journal of Marriage and Family*, 64 (2000): 1173–1191; Ronald Palkovitz, "Involved Fathering and Child Development: Understanding," in *Handbook of Father Involvement: Multidisciplinary Perspectives*, eds., Catherine S. Tamis-LeMonda and Natasha Cabera (Mahwah NJ: Lawrence Erlbaum Associates, 2000), pp. 119–131.

19. Palkovitz, "Involved Fathering," pp. 119–131.

20. Rebekah Levine Coley and Jodi E. Morris, "Comparing Father and Mother Reports of Father Involvement Among Low-Income Minority Families," *Journal of Marriage and Family* 64 (2002): 1741–3737.

21. Sandra L.Hofferth, "Race, Ethnic Differences in Father Involvement in Two-Parent Families Culture, Context, or Economy?," *Journal of Family Issues*, 24 (2003): 185–216.

22. Coley and Morris, "Comparing Father and Mother Reports of Father Involvement Among Low-Income Minority Families," 1741–3737.

23. Kay Pasley, Ted G. Futris and Martie L. Skinner. "Effect of Commitment and Psychological Centrality on Fathering," *Journal of Marriage and Family*, 64 (2002): 130–138.

24. Ibid.

25. Kerry L. Daly, "Deconstructing Family Time: From Ideology to Experience," *Journal of Marriage and Family*, 62 (2001): 283–295.

26. Rose M. Kreider and Tavia Simmons, *Marital Status, 2000,* (Washington: United States Census Bureau, 2003).

27. Nancy Signorelli, N., & Michael Morgan. "Television in the Family: The Cultivation Perspective." In *Television and the American Family,* edited by Jennings Bryant & J. A. Bryant, 333–351. Mahwah, NJ: Lawrence Erlbaum, 1990.

28. Kerry L. Daly, "Deconstructing Family Time: From Ideology to Experience," *Journal of Marriage and Family*, 62 (2001): 283–295.

29. David J. Eggebeen & Chris Knoester. "Does Fatherhood Matter for Men?" *Journal of Marriage & Family,* 63 (2001): 381–394.

BIBLIOGRAPHY

Coley, Rebekah Levine and Jodi E. Morris. "Comparing Father and Mother Reports of Father Involvement Among Low-Income Minority Families." *Journal of Marriage and Family,* 64 (2002): 1741–3737.

Coontz, Stephanie. *The Way We Never Were: American Families and the Nostalgia Trap,* New York, NY: BasicBooks, 1992.

Daly, Kerry L. "Deconstructing Family Time: From Ideology to Experience." *Journal of Marriage and Family,* 62 (2001): 283–295.

Douglas, William and Beth Olson. "Beyond Family Structure: The Family in Domestic Comedy." *Journal of Broadcasting and Electronic Media,* 39 (1995): 236–262.

Eggebeen, David J. and Chris Knoester. "Does Fatherhood Matter for Men?" *Journal of Marriage & Family*, 63 (2001): 381–394.

Everybody Loves Raymond. "The Checkbook." directed by John Fortenberry and written by Philip Rosenthal and Tom Caltabiano, TBS-TV, February 2, 1998.

Frazer, June M. and Timothy C. Frazer. "Father Knows Best and The Cosby Show, Nostalgia and the Sitcom Tradition." *Journal of Popular Culture*, 27 (2004): 163–172.

Harris, Richard J. *A Cognitive Psychology of Mass Communication*. Mahwah, NJ: Lawrence Erlbaum Associates Publishers, 1999.

Hofferth, Sandra L."Race, Ethnic Differences in Father Involvement in Two-Parent Families Culture, Context, or Economy?" *Journal of Family Issues* 24 (2003): 185–216.

Honeycutt, John, Lynn B. Wellman, and Mary S. Larsen. "Beneath Family Role Portrayals: An Additional Measure of Communication Influence Using Time Series Analyses of Turn at Talk on a Popular Television Program," *Journal of Broadcasting & Electronic Media* 41 no. 1 (1997): 40–57.

Mike and Molly. "Molly Unleashed." directed by Phil Lewis and written by Mark Roberts, CBS-TV, November 4, 2013.

"National Fatherhood Initiative Study." 2008. http://www.fatherhood.org retrieved August 12, 2015.

The Jim Gaffigan Show. "Super Great Daddy Day." directed by Todd Biermann and written by Jim Gaffigan and Jeannie Gaffigan, TBS-TV, August 12, 2015.

Kreider, Rose M. and Tavia Simmons. *Marital Status, 2000*. Washington: United States Census Bureau, 2003.

Marsiglio, William, Paul Amato, Randal Day, and Michael Lamb. "Scholarship on Fatherhood in the 1990s and Beyond." *Journal of Marriage and Family* 64 (2000): 1173–1191

McColgan, Aileen. *Just Wages for Women*. Oxford: Clarendon Press, 1997.

"National Fatherhood Initiative Statistic Report," National Fatherhood Initiative, http://www.fatherhood.org, accessed August 12, 2015.

Pasley, Kay, Ted G. Futris and Martie L. Skinner. "Effect of Commitment and Psychological Centrality on Fathering." *Journal of Marriage and Family* 64 (2002): 130–138.

Palkovitz, Ronald. "Involved Fathering and Child Development: Understanding," in *Handbook of Father Involvement: Multidisciplinary Perspectives*, eds., Catherine S. Tamis-LeMonda and Natasha Cabera. Mahwah NJ: Lawrence Erlbaum Associates, 2000. 119–131.

Petroski, David J. and Paige P. Edley. "Stay-at-Home Fathers: Masculinity, Family, Work, and Gender Stereotypes." *The Electronic Journal of Communication*, 16 (2006). http://www.cios.org/EJCPUBLIC/016/3/01634.HTML

Sanders, Ryan. "How Mass Media Portray Dads and What You Can Do About It." National Fatherhood Initiative, July 2, 2015. http://www.fatherhood.org.

Scharrer, Erica. "From Wise to Foolish, The Portrayal of the Sitcom Father: 1950s–1990s." *Journal of Broadcasting and Electronic Media*, 45 (2001): 25–40.

Signorelli, Nancy N., & Michael Morgan. "Television in the Family: The Cultivation Perspective." In *Television and the American Family,* edited by Jennings Bryant & J. A. Bryant, 333–351. Mahwah, NJ: Lawrence Erlbaum, 1990.

Walsh, Kimberly R., Elfriede Fursich, and Bonnie Jefferson. "Beauty and the Patriarchial Beast: Gender Role Portrayal in Sitcoms Featuring Mismatch Couples." *Journal of Popular Film and Television* 36 (2008): 123–132

Section II

DADS ACROSS POPULAR
CULTURE GENRES

Chapter 5

Watching the Leisure Gap

Advertising Fatherhood with the Privilege of Play

Peter Schaefer

A recent study by the Pew Research Center reveals that fathers tend to have three more hours per week of leisure time than mothers, and the study found that dads spend the bulk of this excess leisure time watching television.[1] The persistence of the leisure gap attests to the undue burden placed on mothers and what Arlie Hochschild refers to as the "stalled revolution" of feminism.[2] Women have entered the workforce only to remain primarily responsible for domestic labor in two-career families. Taking the Pew study and its connections between the leisure gap and television watching as a starting point, this essay looks to contemporary advertising's use of the theme of dads at play to explore gender inequality in heteronormative parenting practices in the United States. An analysis of commercials broadcast on television in 2014 and the first half of 2015 shows that representations of fatherhood help legitimate the leisure gap by emphasizing play as a primary parenting task. The phrase "privilege of play" works in two ways. First, ads tend to privilege recreational activities with kids as the way to be a good dad. Second, men have the privilege to identify parenting with play because women remain inordinately responsible for household work. Furthermore, there is a sophisticated and wide-ranging set of emotions mobilized during depictions of play-based activities between dads and kids. These affective clusters work to build brand associations and to enlist fathers as content creators for promotional purposes. This corporate appropriation of paternal carework undermines the possibility that changes in representations of fatherhood could be enough to close the leisure gap.

Representations of fatherhood in advertising are on the rise. In more and more commercials, dads are shown as hands-on caretakers who build emotional relationships with their kids.[3] During the 2014 and 2015 Super Bowls, for example, multiple ads featured fathers in caretaking roles, a marked change from the mostly absent or hands-off paternal role models of years prior.[4] The increased quantity of representation for active paternal caretakers offers a way of understanding shifting attitudes in the United States where more dads identify as emotionally responsible for the well-being of their children.[5] However, it's not enough to focus on the quantity of these representations, for dads tend to be shown more as the fun-loving parent who plays with kids more so than the parent who does the household chores. Contemporary television advertising depict fatherhood as a world that is emotionally rich and full of play, but these largely idealized representations neglect the physical labor needed to maintain a household.

Gender-based wage inequality remains a significant social problem as does the inequality in parental leisure time. For decades, women have been taking on more of a role in bringing income to two-parent families, and numerous studies demonstrate the fact that the division of labor in the home has not changed as fast as the demographics of labor outside the home.[6] *The Second Shift* by Arlie Hochschild, published in 1989, offered the first systematic look at the lag between private and public labor practices. Hochschild writes, "Just as there is a wage gap between men and women in the workplace, there is a 'leisure gap' between them at home. Most women work one shift at the office or factory and a 'second shift' between them at home."[7] Unfortunately, since the book's publication in 1989, this leisure gap remains such that women bear the brunt of this second shift when "58 percent of women say the division of labor in modern families is not fair to them, while 11 percent of men make a similar claim."[8] Clearly there is still progress that needs to be made so that men and women equally share domestic labor.

The past several decades have seen dramatic changes in the composition of American families. The traditional family consisting of a mother, a father, and 2.5 kids is less the norm than ever, despite the fact that parental representations in advertising still strongly favor this traditional model. In regard to employment practices, marriages are much more fluid, and even two-income households rely less and less on two careers.[9] Instead, parents of both genders are more likely to have a series of short-term employment. The unpredictable employment patterns for young parents means that equality in the second shift is more important than ever since clearly communicated and delineated divisions of domestic labor will alleviate anxieties that come from changes in work outside the home since "gender flexibility provides an indispensable way for a rising number of families to prepare for and adapt to twenty-first-century uncertainties."[10] Contemporary advertising presents a biased depiction of domestic labor for parents that hampers progressive notions of gender flexibility for work inside the home.

This study refers to the parental caretaking for children as "carework," a term borrowed from Zimmerman, Litt, and Bose who define it as "the multifaceted labor that produces the daily living conditions that make basic human health and well-being possible."[11] These authors identify particular tasks that comprise the bulk of this vital labor. "Carework includes home management, housekeeping, and related domestic tasks such as laundry, clothing repair, and meal preparation. It also includes the care of others—that is, nursing the sick, looking after and nurturing children, and assisting the disabled and elderly."[12] This study focuses on an integral element of carework: the nurturing of children. Carework is both physical labor and emotional labor, and the caring of children involves engaging with them as feeling creatures in need of a range of stimulating activities, one aspect of which is play. In other words, playing with children and engaging in other leisure-based activities are included under the umbrella of carework as well as household chores.[13] While there are historical and cultural dimensions to carework that link these practices to women and femininity, carework is "neither 'natural' for women to do nor 'essential' to their being."[14] And while contemporary advertising is showing more men caring for children, only play-based paternal carework tends to be shown.

Before proceeding to the analysis, a few words need to be said about how contemporary advertising relates to the persistent leisure gap and representations of paternal carework. Modern media such as television serve as the bridge between the consumers and producers of goods by creating the mythological world of advertising that represents products as ways to fulfill the emotional needs of consumers.[15] The relationship between consumer and product has deepened in emotional resonance with the rise of what Banet-Weiser calls "brand culture" that she defines as the way contemporary marketing, products, and consumers form relationships that "have increasingly become cultural contexts for everyday living, individual identity, and affective relationships."[16] Recently father-child relationships have been deployed as marketing tools as a means to garner market share for the adult male demographic by depicting these relationships as emotionally complex. "Brand cultures facilitate 'relationships' between consumers and branders and encourage an affective connection based on authenticity and sincerity."[17] Dads and their kids are depicted as having sincere and authentic relationships, and these depictions bolster brand identity but do nothing to redress gender-based labor inequalities in the home.

METHOD

This study used the following research questions to explore advertising representations in relation to gender inequality in domestic work.

1. How is fatherhood represented in contemporary advertising?
2. What are the types of paternal carework represented?
3. What are the functions of paternal carework representations from a branding perspective?

This study uses a purposive sample of fatherhood representations, looking to advertisements broadcast on television from January 2014 to July 2015. The ads are examined via a textual analysis that takes these promotional tools as cultural constructions that reflect and sustain ideological notions of what it means to be a father in contemporary culture. In addition, the essay reviews discourse through which these ads circulate to make a stronger connection between the texts themselves and shared beliefs about the concept of fatherhood. Advertisements were identified for analysis using iSpot.tv, a television commercial tracking website that catalogs ads shown on the top 110 U.S. cable networks. Analysis was done on the ads returned via the following search terms: "dad," "daddy," "father," and "fatherhood." For an advertisement to be included in the sample it had to show a man doing carework to at least one child (estimated to be eighteen years and younger). In the case of having both English and Spanish language versions of an ad, only one of the versions was included in the analysis. Ads are categorized based on the type of carework performed and which family member performs the carework. The type of carework is divided into leisure-based and non-leisure based. Following Zimmerman, Litt, and Bose non-leisure-based carework includes tasks such as cleaning, laundry, and meal preparation. Leisure-based carework includes activities such as playing with toys, playing sports, and other relaxation activities.[18]

FINDINGS

Using the sample criteria listed above, this study examines sixty ads that show men performing carework with one or more children ages eighteen years or younger. Table 5.1 details the product being advertised, the name of the advertisement, and whether the father or mother is represented doing leisure-based carework. The ads promote a broad range of products from multiple sectors of the economy such as the automotive, entertainment, food, pharmaceutical, retail, banking, and defense industries. Out of these ads, thirty-three (55 percent) show fathers doing carework that is exclusively leisure based; twenty (33 percent) show fathers doing a mix of leisure-based and non-leisure-based carework; and seven (12 percent) show fathers doing only non-leisure-based carework.

Table 5.1

Product	Ad Name	Father Leisure-Based Carework?	Mother Leisure-Based Carework?
Allegra	Dad	Yes	N/A
Amica Auto Insurance	Toy Plane	Yes	N/A
Bass Pro Shops	Gifts for Dad	Yes	N/A
Cabela's	Dad!	Yes	N/A
Cabela's	Father & Son Archery	Yes	N/A
Cascade Platinum	Non-Stick	No	No
Cheetos	Tan Lines	Yes	Yes
Chili's	Table 9	Yes	N/A
CiCi's Pizza Buffet	Daughter Pays	Yes	N/A
Citi Thank You Preferred Card	Everybody Wins	Yes	N/A
Clorox	Dads	Yes	N/A
Dove Men + Care	Makes a Man Stronger	Yes	N/A
Dove Men + Care	Real Strength	Mixed	N/A
Dove Men + Care Bodywash	Stronger Skin	Yes	N/A
Dove Men + Care Clean Comfort Antiperspirant	Superman	Yes	N/A
Extra Spearmint	Oragami	Mixed	No
Fisher Price's Little People City Skyway	Boy's Drive with Dad	Yes	N/A
Frosted Flakes	Catch with Dad	Yes	N/A
Frosted Flakes	T-I-G-E-R	Yes	N/A
Gerber Pudding Grabbers	Who's Your Daddy?	No	N/A
GoGurt	Dad's Way	No	N/A
GoGurt	Sticky Notes	No	N/A
Grand Canyon University	Working Dad	Yes	N/A
Frigidaire Gallery	Saving Innovations	No	No
Home Depot	Superhero Dad	Mixed	Mixed
Honda Generators	My Dad	Mixed	Mixed
Honest Company, The	Honestly Transparent	No	No
Honey Maid	Time	Mixed	Mixed
Hotwire	Mexico	Yes	N/A
Huggies Little Movers	Daddy Daycare	Yes	N/A
Hunt's Manwich	Dads and Sons	No	N/A
Hyundai Genesis	Dad's Sixth Sense	Mixed	N/A
JCPenny	Love Dad Sale	Yes	N/A
KFC Original Recipe Boneless Chicken	Dad Ate the Bone	Yes	N/A
Kohl's	Summer Fun for Dad	Yes	N/A
Liberty University	My Dad	Yes	No
Lowe's	Celebrate Dad	Mixed	N/A
Nintendo Mario Kart 8	Dad vs. Kids	Yes	N/A
Mass Mutual	Dad	Mixed	N/A
McDonald's	Like Father, Like Son	Yes	N/A
Metamucil	Orange Blob	Yes	N/A
NBATickets.com	Sold Out Tickets	Yes	N/A
Nikon D3300	Capture the Moment	Mixed	N/A
Old Spice	Dad Song	Mixed	Mixed

(Continued)

Table 5.1   (Continued)

Product	Ad Name	Father Leisure-Based Carework?	Mother Leisure-Based Carework?
Olympic Elite	Interruptions	Yes	Yes
Realtree	Thanks Dad!	Yes	N/A
Ritz Bitz Crackers	Life's Rich: Karate	Yes	N/A
Safelite Auto Glass	Dance Recital	Mixed	N/A
Snuggle Fresh Spring Flowers	Family Snuggle	Mixed	Mixed
Subaru Legacy	Can You Fix It?	Yes	N/A
State Farm	Never	Mixed	Mixed
Swiffer WetJet	Big Jerry	Mixed	N/A
Toyota Camry	My Bold Dad	Mixed	N/A
Travelers Auto Insurance	Growing Up	Mixed	N/A
TriCalm	Dad and Summer Itches	Yes	N/A
US Army	Moment of Independence: Baseball Game	Yes	N/A
US Army	Moment of Independence: Water Slide	Yes	N/A
Wells Fargo	Daddy's Day Out with Baby	Mixed	N/A
Wendy's Kid's Meal	Competitive Dad	Yes	No
Whirlpool	Best Dad	Mixed	N/A

Since the analysis focuses on representations of fathers doing carework, the vast majority of the ads show only paternal carework. However, there are ads included in the sample that also show mothers doing carework. Out of the sixty ads in the sample, fourteen (23 percent) include representations of maternal carework. Among the ads representing mothers, two (14 percent) show moms doing carework that is exclusively leisure based; six (43 percent) show moms doing a mix of leisure-based and non-leisure-based carework; and six (43 percent) show moms doing only non-leisure-based carework.

These data reveal that representations of paternal carework in recent television advertising strongly privilege leisure-based activities. Ads that show men only doing tasks such as laundry, cleaning, or meal preparation are few and far between when compared to ads that show men playing, having fun, and engaging in entertainment activities with children. The opposite is true for those ads that also include women. For ads that include representations of material carework, the vast majority show women doing tasks that care for children indirectly by doing more traditional housekeeping activities related to food prep and maintenance of the domestic sphere. Taken together, these representations show that the leisure gap between mothers and fathers is reflected in contemporary advertising. These texts favor traditional parenting practices of dads tending toward play and moms tending to household chores.

DISCUSSION

Advertising representations of carework offer a way to understand shared values of what constitutes acceptable household work for fathers and mothers. The following three subsections investigate particular advertisements that speak to the larger messages found in the sample pertaining to the leisure gap. The first subsection, the "privilege of play," takes a closer look at the primary finding of this study, proving the point that leisure-based carework is emphasized in the tasks men perform in the ads analyzed. Next, the subsection "exceptions that prove the rule," explains how ads that show men doing non-leisure-based carework tasks are represented as a deviation from the so-called normal division of household labor. The third subsection, "paternal carework as a branding strategy," probes the affective dimensions of fatherhood advertising to reveal how the privilege of play is used to reinforce brand identity and to get dads to participate in the marketing of a product in ways that deflect from the leisure gap.

Privilege of Play

Play is privileged in representations of fatherhood for television commercials such as Nissan's "With Dad," an ad that received significant viewership.[19] It is a coming-of-age family tale that focuses on the relationship between a Nascar driving father and his son. Via montage, the commercial establishes a family with a delivery scene during which a teary man holds what is presumably his son. This scene is intercut with images of the man in full racing gear driving on a Nascar track. As the man is shown driving, the woman is shown caring for the child with scenes of her testing the temperature of milk from a bottle and her applauding the staggering steps of a toddler. There are other shots of carework, such as the man and woman cuddling in a bed with the child, and the boy, now school age, being read to by the man. However, it's established that the dad is largely absent from the boy's life, as represented by shots of the boy looking mournful while watching the father leave home in a taxi. The mother and son watch on television one of the dad's races where he gets into a serious crash. The crash is followed by images of the father's life flashing before his eyes, shots of playtime activities with the father and son. One such shot shows the duo laughing as they dive backward into a swimming pool. Another shot shows father and son driving a boat together. As the child ages into adolescence, the son engages in racing activities with go-karts and other daredevil stunts to further link father and son. The commercial ends with the father picking up the son, now high school age, and the two share a tender hug with the dad behind the wheel of a Nissan.

The commercial "With Dad" is notable for the prevalent representation of carework during which a dad is shown largely responsible for playtime. Even his career as a race car driver further establishes the link between play and the father's identity. At the same time, the mom is shown as the person primarily responsible for non-leisure-based carework. Using #withdad, Nissan links a range of cross-platform content such as a series of videos like "Playtime With Dad." This two-minute promotional video begins in a verite style to mimic home movies with a point of view shot from what is later revealed to be a father playing with his son. The duo engage in playing catch with base-balls, playing the game Rock 'em Sock 'em Robots, and with the son having imaginative play with toys while the father drives. Each of these activities are integrated with sophisticated computer-generated action that adds to the fun. The video ends with the dad speaking into the camera promoting the use of #withdad and thanking Nissan for their sponsorship. The video calls for other fathers to upload videos of playtime with their kids to use the Nissan-inspired hashtag. The video works as a model for fathers to participate in the brand, and Nissan aligns itself as validating fatherhood in general and carework in particular. However, this validation emphasizes leisure-based carework that privileges play.

"Daddy Day Care," a commercial for the Little Movers style of Huggies diapers, offers a similar representation of fatherhood in that paternal care-work is primarily leisure based. The ad begins with five smiling men play-ing with babies in what appears to be a traditional day-care setting. These babies are carefully shot to show that they are wearing Huggies diapers. The voiceover establishes the scene. "To prove new Huggies diapers can stay in place no matter what, we asked real dads to put them to the test with their own babies during a no holds barred playtime session." The images offer a quick sequence of men having fun with the babies. There's toy xylophone fun, tickling, wrestling, and a wide array of other play-based activities. The commercial concludes with the five dads lifting up their babies presumably to show that the product passed the test of having the diapers stay in place. "Daddy Day Care" offers another glimpse of the ways paternal carework is represented as leisure based. It's of particular interest that a commercial about the functionality of diapers shows no shots of men actually changing a diaper. The commercial instead privileges father-baby play instead of the most com-mon carework activity one associates with such a product. The commercial trades on the cultural bias that men are more physically active than women by having an only male caretaking team; however, the only caretaking shown consist entirely of play.

An Allegra commercial, "Dad," further demonstrates the way play is privi-leged for paternal carework. The ad begins in black and white with a father blowing his nose while watching a young boy, presumably his son, leave through the front door. Text on the screen reads, "Before Allegra." The commercial then cuts to a shot sequence in color where the same father/son duo run, jump, and play in a grassy field. The text changes to "After Allegra." The voiceover states, "Before Allegra, allergies kept me from being the fun dad. After Allegra, I'm non-stop entertainment." From the images and voiceover, one can infer that a father was kept from reaching full fatherhood potential without pharmaceutical intervention.

For argument purposes it's worth noting that the ad values "non-stop entertainment" as an admirable trait for fathers. One would hope that there would be a time and place for both parents to provide entertainment and a time and place for both parents to do dishes or scrub the toilet. Allegra's "Dad" commercial invites discussion of how the product itself might shape the type of activities represented. In other words, an Allegra ad is going to show people battling allergens and winning the fight, hence "Dad" depicts outdoor fun. It remains true that there was no "Mom" corollary commercial for Allegra during the time frame analyzed. Still, the father figure could have been represented battling allergens while doing other kinds of carework (mowing the lawn, for example, or scrubbing mold from the grout in a bathroom shower). In other words, the lopsided carework representation in these ads do not necessarily follow from the type of products advertised. Choices were made to position fathers in ways that privilege leisure-based activities. The product promises to make dads more productive caregivers, not by facilitating completion of household chores, but by given them more time to play.

Even the consuming of prepackaged food can be represented as a leisure-based activity in contemporary commercial representations of fatherhood. In a recent advertising campaign for Kellogg's Frosted Flakes, a father shares cereal with a child in ways that blend with leisure-based activities. In "T-I-G-E-R," a father and daughter play a game of basketball to determine who will get to eat the remaining Frosted Flakes. The ad begins with the duo sitting down at a breakfast nook to find that their cereal supply is limited, and they look back to a basketball hoop visible in the background of the frame. The dad and daughter play the game typically known as "H-O-R-S-E" where contestants attempt to make baskets from particular locations (in the commercial the two play T-I-G-E-R because it matches the mascot for Frosted Flakes). At the end of the ad, the father and daughter decide to split the remaining amount of cereal evenly though the dad prevailed in the contest.

In a commercial similar to T-I-G-E-R, a father and son play football in a yard next to a single family home. The boy and his dad continue their game of football into the house, but the box of Frosted Flakes and then the bowls of the cereal itself become extensions of the football. As the two eat their cereal, the father's banter offers a ceaseless array of proper football playing tips. In both of these Frosted Flakes advertisements, fathers are asserted as figures

for play. Even mealtime presents nothing more than extended opportunities
for leisure. The fathers aren't shown shopping for the product or cleaning up
following the meal. Instead, the household work around the eating of Frosted
Flakes is completely removed from the scene. Carework, as shown in these
two ads, appears as a fun, effortless, entertaining way for men to be fathers
with no chores attached.

Extra Spearmint gum trades on a pathos appeal with its recent commercial
"Origami" that further demonstrates how leisure-based paternal carework is
emphasized in ads. In another coming-of-age tale, a sequence of shots feature
a father and daughter through the years. In the first scene, a school-age girl
and her dad share gum while riding a train. The father makes a small origami
bird out of the wrapper and hands it to the daughter. In the next scene the
daughter, now several years older, is at a baseball game with the father where
the same gum wrapper origami ritual occurs, and then the ritual happens yet
again at the beach. Now, the daughter appears almost adult and is crying in
a bedroom where the father gives her another gum wrapper origami bird.
The next shot shows that the family is packing to take the daughter away to
college. As the dad loads boxes into the back of a station wagon, one falls
and opens to reveal dozens of gum wrapper origami birds, presumably collected through the years of daddy-daughter moments during which Extra gum
played a pivotal part. This commercial underscores the value that a child's
memory of her father should come from moments of leisure. At the beach,
at a baseball game, on a trip, these activities privilege the playtime part of
carework. Yet it's important to note that not all representations of fathers
exclusively privilege play. The next section examines representations of
fathers doing non-leisure-based carework.

Exceptions that Prove the Rule

Some commercials show dads doing household chores, nevertheless a closer
look at these ads further support the notion that paternal carework is represented as play based. Even commercial images of men doing domestic
labor can help assert the value of women as the primary keeper of the house.
Often when men are running errands, cleaning, packing lunch, or doing other
non-leisure-based care, this labor is established as unusual within the commercial's narrative. Take, for example, a recent GoGurt advertising campaign
that focuses primarily on fathers. In "Dad's Way," a father and son talk while
the former is packing a lunch. The following dialogue ensues:

Son: "Mom usually puts a GoGurt in there."

Father: "Well Mom's not here today so we're doing things Dad's way."

Son: "Which means I get . . ."

Father and Son (in unison): "Two!"

The dad and son then have an impromptu dance party during which they both chant "snack time and lunch." The commercial establishes that mom is the default maker of the lunch, with the son having to remind the dad what usually gets packed. Not only that, but when the dad takes on the task of packing a lunch, it's a state of exception. The son gets double the usual sugary treat, and even the packing of the lunch becomes a play-based activity. Non-leisure-based carework is reshaped into play when it's a father doing the work. Much like in the aforementioned Frosted Flakes ad campaign, mundane domestic tasks take on shadings of leisure only when fathers are represented.

In a similar vein, the GoGurt commercial "Sticky Notes" supports the idea that it's exceptional for dads to do domestic work that doesn't involve play. A man stands in a kitchen and looks at an empty lunchbox with a note that reads, "Hon—Don't forget the GoGurt." The man then opens a cabinet with another GoGurt reminder. In the next shot he opens the refrigerator where there's a series of notes, the first of which reads "dad" with subsequent notes showing arrows that point to a box of GoGurt. A young boy then passes through the kitchen, grabs the now packed lunch, and asks, "GoGurt?" To which the man replies, "Yep." The commercial's tagline is delivered via voiceover and text on the screen that reads, "Dad's who get it, get GoGurt."

These sticky notes serve two purposes. First, the notes assert the importance of GoGurt from the perspective of the mom (presumably author of the first note) and that of the son (presumably author of the notes in the refrigerator). Second, the mere presence of the notes points to the fact that dad is not the regular lunch packer for the household. Furthermore, the commercial represents dads as in need of tremendous assistance from the rest of the household to make sure he meets expectations for the work. To "get it," then refers to meeting a standard for domestic labor, and a dad can only reach this standard via help. Taken together these GoGurt ads show that dads can only do everyday carework when it turns into play. If no play is involved, dads are represented as morons who require relentless signage to do a simple domestic task correctly.

"Daddy's Day Out With Baby," a commercial that promotes mobile banking features for Wells Fargo, offers another example of how non-leisure-based paternal carework is represented as a deviation from the norm. In the ad, a man wears a baby in a carrier while accomplishing a series of errands. Periodically the man talks on the phone, presumably to the mom, and asserts "I got this." He also has to assuage the fears that he's making mistakes with the errands, such as when he speaks into the phone while exiting the grocery store and says, "Yes, honey, everything all natural . . . done!" At the end of the commercial, the man remembers a check he forgot to deposit, but thanks to Wells Fargo mobile banking he accomplishes that task as well, thereby delivering on the promise that he is able to accomplish the errands with aplomb.

As with the GoGurt ads, the Wells Fargo commercial shows that men doing household chores is unusual, given the fact that he must constantly reassure a person, presumably a woman, who is regularly responsible for these tasks. In addition, the man is shown as only able to complete all the errands thanks to the product being advertised. In other words, the normal state of affairs shows a man who rarely does these types of errands and is not able to do them correctly without special assistance. This commercial also demonstrates how play is often incorporated into representations of paternal carework. In between the bank and the grocery store, the man takes time to have lunch and a beer at a bar while he cheers on a sports team. The commercial, therefore, goes out of its way to assure audiences that this dad also gets to play while he does these regular chores. The baby, too, gets into the playful spirit when the man holds up the baby's hand while cheering on the team. Even normal errands become play-based bonding when paternal carework is represented.

Paternal Carework as a Branding Strategy

The emphasis on play in these ads sheds light on contemporary notions of fatherhood as they relate to current branding practices. A look at a recent Dove campaign, Dove Men + Care, attests to the larger trend identified in this analysis, namely that when dads are shown doing carework, it tends to focus on leisure-based activities. Take, for example, the commercial "Stronger Skin" that promotes body wash in the Dove Men + Care line. The ad shows a dad and his daughter playing in what looks to be a suburban backyard. The dad and daughter smile as she hangs from the dad's arm as he lifts her from the ground. A close-up of the arm reveals the dad's smooth skin, presumably from the regular use of Dove body wash. As seen in many of the other ads described above, dads do carework while having fun. At the same time as the campaign supports the privilege of play hypothesis, it also reflects how the emotional resonance of leisure-based activities function in relation to brand culture.

Banet-Weiser writes about the history of Dove marketing, arguing that recent Dove campaigns are built around notions of improving self-esteem for consumers that work to brand consumer citizens.[20] The Dove campaign for Real Beauty has been hugely successful for the company, and by extension for its parent company Unilever. The Real Beauty campaign ostensibly challenged the unrealistic beauty norms perpetuated in cosmetic advertising with its focus on nontraditional models, and the recent Dove Men + Care campaign, and its attendant #realstrength promotional tag, builds on previous branding efforts to build influence with consumers interested in superficial interrogation of gender norms. As Banet-Weiser asserts, the Real Beauty campaign is "about creating and supporting a shifted manifestation of the citizen consumer, one who is critical of marketing and its unrealistic norms and is invited to develop this narrative in conjunction with corporate culture (and alongside the buying of a beauty product)."[21] And we see similar actions at work with this latest iteration of Dove marketing, this time focused on dads.[22] Dove justifies the focus on paternal carework and its push for #realstrength on empirical data. "Dove hired Edelman Berland to interview 1,000 fathers ages 25–54. 'Three-quarters of dads say they are responsible for their child's emotional well-being,' said Rob Candelino, marketing vice president and general manager, Unilever's skin care. 'But only 20 percent see that in media.'"[23] The quote suggests that Dove is seeking to make up for the lack of carework representation of fathers out of the goodness of their collective hearts. Yet the depiction of dad's responsibility of a child's emotional well-being is part and parcel of its branding efforts.

It's true that play is privileged in the paternal carework of the Dove campaign, but in the representations of play, there is a sophisticated mobilization of emotions that reflects contemporary brand culture built on affective relationships between consumers and products. When play-based carework is privileged there is a wider range of emotions shown than one might commonly associate with play. In addition to excitement, happiness, and delight, these ads often show other emotions such as love, fear, sadness, etc. In other words, there is an affective cluster around these ads that speaks to contemporary branding strategies that work to develop relationships with consumers by establishing authenticity and sincerity. These sophisticated emotional representations invite viewers to live the brand, and this emotional investment is a part of the discourse for the ad campaign.

Companies like Dove incite sophisticated emotional responses to build brand identity and trade on conventional masculine values.[24] For example, "Real Strength," a part of the Dove Men + Care campaign, is another of the fatherhood ads broadcast during the 2015 Super Bowl. The commercial's tagline, "Care makes a man stronger," is established via a montage of father-parent interactions. In each shot, the child says, "Dad" or "Daddy." The scenes range from mealtime to playground and pool fun to weddings and holidays. The shots are interspersed with two title cards the first of which reads, "What makes a man stronger?" The second card reads, "Showing that he cares." And the commercial concludes with an image of Dove products with a voiceover and text on the screen that states, "Dove Men + Care. Care makes a man stronger." While it's true that the majority of the activities represented in the ad are play based, a closer look at the emotional resonance of the clips tell a richer story of what's going on here.

Many of the shots in "Real Strength" offer play-based fun with excitement, happiness, and delight represented. However, some shots depict other emotions. Take, for example, a shot sequence with a boy dangling from monkey bars. A child appears to be in a precarious situation, and when he calls out "Dad!" it's with an anxious, terrified tone. In the next shot we see a man, presumably the dad, come to the rescue and gently take the boy into his arms. The final shot of the sequence shows the man and boy share a tender kiss and hug. The fear depicted in the beginning of the sequence turns to love.

The wide range of emotions represented in ads such as "Real Strength" attests to the use of sincerity to build brand relationships, and these connections do more than merely inspire dads to purchase products. In addition, these pathos appeals invite dads to participate in the marketing of the product. Dove encourages fathers to take to social media and integrate the marketing campaign into their virtual life thereby living the brand with tags such as #realdadmoments or #realstrength. A similar strategy described above was also seen via Nissan and its #withdad campaign. As Nissan invites dads to create their own promotional content and upload it using #withdad, Dove does the same with #realdadmoments. In fact, the appeal to dads to participate in these lifestyle branding initiatives is quite common. In addition to efforts by Nissan and Dove, there's #swifferdad, Toyota's #oneboldchoice, and many others.

Play-based activities offer a particularly effective means of building a sincere, authentic relationship with a brand. It's easier to marshal a range of emotions with depictions of playground fun than it is with depictions of cleaning a toilet. And while ads like those of the aforementioned GoGurt campaign show men as largely incompetent with household chores, campaigns such as Dove Men + Care show men as expert caretakers when doing affective labor with kids for play-based activities. When play is privileged for paternal carework, men are shown as effective parents who provide emotional support for their children, but the opposite is true when men are shown doing household chores. The leisure gap remains in representations of fathers doing carework. In short, these ads tell us that good dads connect with children during play, and good dads need not bother with the other aspects of carework. The value of play works to reinforce brand strategies that inspire dads to participate with a brand, not to inspire dads to participate equally in the second shift.

CONCLUSION

The privilege of play in contemporary television advertising reflects the fact that certain types of carework still tend to be identified as "women's work."

Fathers in the United States have more leisure time than mothers, and ads depict dads as having more fun when caring for their kids. A useful corollary to this study would be to analyze ads that feature maternal carework to see how leisure-based activities are represented. Nevertheless, the analysis above shows that advertising depictions of fathers are changing in ways that show a broader range of what a father can be. One of the reasons why dads don't always take on an equal share of the second shift is that men sometimes have a limited idea of what "fatherhood" means.[25] Many of the ads described above add an emotional richness to the range of fatherhood representations previously available. Hochschild asserts that to foster stronger emotional connections between dads and their kids is a vital part of closing the leisure gap. She states that "at the very root of a successful gender revolution is, I believe, a deep value on care—making loving meals, doing projects with kids, emotionally engaging family and friends."[26] At the level of advertising and cultural representations of fatherhood, there is an increasing attention toward showing dads as emotionally engaged caretakers. However, changes in the depictions of fathers will not be enough to close the leisure gap and therefore take us a step toward finishing the unfinished feminist revolution.

When one watches the leisure gap in contemporary advertising one sees that paternal caretaking is being colonized by current marketing initiatives. Representations of the emotional bond between dads and kids are now fodder for lifestyle branding and an impetus for user-generated promotional content. These economic imperatives embedded in the changing depictions of paternal carework reflects the fact that cultural change and structural change go hand in hand. If one only looks to fatherhood representations, then the burden lies on fathers as individual agents of change to pick up the second shift slack. Yet as demonstrated above, the depiction of dads in advertising rarely shows the full range of parental carework required to maintain a productive household. Furthermore, significant structural problems remain that inhibit the progress of equitable divisions of domestic labor. "Compared to other postindustrial nations, the United States lags woefully behind in the supports it offers families. Of the twenty-one richest countries in the world, only the United States and Australia do not mandate paid parental leave, and among the industrialized Western nations, only the United States does not mandate paid vacations."[27] In other words, federal policies add pressure to contemporary working families, and there has yet to be a structural equivalent to the cultural changes seen in representations of dads in advertising.

The answer to the question of how to close the leisure gap is not as simple as just getting dads to have less leisure time. And the ads described above deflect from the fact that the quantity of leisure time is a problem to begin with. Contemporary television commercials perpetuate a mythology of bountiful leisure that runs contrary to the real world where our economic system demands that people increasingly forego non-productive leisure-based activities. It remains true that contemporary men tend to not share the second shift equally, and the resilience of the patriarchy burdens mothers unfairly. The means to redress these inequalities will need larger structural shifts that favor more parent-friendly work policies and a greater respect for time spent at home, away from productive tasks. The ultimate goal should be making the home an equitable space where there is plenty of leisure time for dads and moms alike because play only appears as a privilege when viewed through the inverted lens of capitalism.

NOTES

1. Parker, Kim and Wendy Wang, *Modern Parenthood: Roles of Moms and Dads Converge as They Balance Work and Family* (Pew Research Center, 2013). http://www.pewsocialtrends.org/2013/03/14/modern-parenthood-roles-of-moms-and-dads-converge-as-they-balance-work-and-family.

2. Hochschild, Arlie with Anne Machung, *The Second Shift: Working Families and the Revolution at Home, Revised Edition* (London: Penguin Books, 1989/2012), 11–12.

3. Neff, Jack, "Move Over, Mom, It's Dad's Turn In Ads," *Advertising Age,* January 27, 2015, http://adage.com/article/news/nissan-toyota-dove-put-dad-super-bowl/296786.

4. Neff, "Move Over, Mom."

5. Heine, Christopher, "Dove's New Ad Shows What Dads Really Do Besides Resenting Gender Stereotypes," *AdWeek,* June 8, 2014, http://www.adweek.com/news/advertising-branding/doves-new-ad-shows-what-dads-really-do-158181; and on notions of equality in the private sphere, see Gerson, Kathleen, *The Unfinished Revolution: Coming of Age in a New Era of Gender, Work, and Family* (Oxford: Oxford University Press, 2010), 225.

6. Szalai, Alexander, ed, *The Use of Time: Daily Activities of Urban and Suburban Populations in Twelve Countries,* (The Hauge, Mounton, 1972).

7. Hochschild, Arlie with Anne Machung, *The Second Shift: Working Families and the Revolution at Home, Revised Edition* (London: Penguin Books, 1989/2012), 4.

8. Belkin, Lisa. "When Mom and Dad Share It All." *The New York Times Magazine,* June 15, 2008, http://www.nytimes.com/2008/06/15/magazine/15parenting-t.html?pagewanted=all&_r=0.

9. Gerson, *Unfinished Revolution,* 5–6.

10. Ibid., 217.

11. Zimmerman, Mary K.; Litt, Jacquelyn S.; and Bose, Christine E., eds, *Global Dimensions of Gender and Carework,* (Stanford: Stanford University Press, 2006), 3–4.

12. Ibid., 4.

13. Carework, both play based and otherwise, is often devalued relative to other types of labor. For an examination of this perspective, see England, Paula. "Emerging Theories of Care Work," *Annual Review of Sociology* 31 (2005): 382.

14. Zimmerman, Litt, and Bose, *Global Dimensions of Gender and Carework*, 4.

15. Fowles, Jib, *Advertising and Popular Culture*, (Thousand Oaks, CA: Sage, 1996), 26–50; for more on the mythology of advertising see Williams, Raymond, "Advertising: the Magic System" In *Culture and Materialism: Selected Essays, 2nd ed.*, (London: Verso, 1995).

16. Banet-Weiser, Sarah, *AuthenticTM: The Politics of Ambivalence in a Brand Culture,* (New York: New York University Press, 2012), 4.

17. Ibid., 37.

18. Zimmerman, Litt, and Bose, *Global Dimensions of Gender and Carework,* 4.

19. "With Dad" was first broadcast during the 2015 Super Bowl, and it received the highest online ratings in the weeks following the event with more than 22 million online views, see *Business Wire*, "Nissan's 'With Dad' Super Bowl Commercial Wins YouTube's AdBlitz 2015," February 16, 2015, http://finance.yahoo.com/news/nissan-dad-super-bowl-commercial-164500691.html. Furthermore, the commercial won YouTube's AdBlitz competition for which viewers vote for their favorites.

20. Banet-Weiser, *Authentic^{TM}*, 42.

21. Ibid.

22. For more on how Dove uses parent participation see Barak-Brandes, Sigal and Einat Lachover, "Branding Relations: Mother–Daughter Discourse on Beauty and Body in an Israeli Campaign by Dove," *Communication, Culture & Critique*, doi: 10.1111/cccr.12111.

23. Heine, Christopher, "Dove's New Ad Shows What Dads Really Do Besides Resenting Gender Stereotypes," *AdWeek*, June 8, 2014, http://www.adweek.com/news/advertising-branding/doves-new-ad-shows-what-dads-really-do-158181.

24. Dove Men + Care builds on traditional notions of physical strength as a way to appropriate emotional strength. To foster an emotional connection with a child can be seen as a hallmark of recession-era America where men need to take care of themselves as a neoliberal mandate in a prolonged recession America, see Banet-Weiser, Sarah, "'We Are All Workers': Economic Crisis, Masculinity, and the American Working Class," In *Gendering the Recession: Media and Culture in an Age of Austerity*, edited by Diane Negra and Yvonne Tasker, (Durham, NC: Duke University Press, 2014), 83. These men are shown caring for children as a therapeutic endeavor that is simultaneously tied to consumption. Only through the purchase of Dove products, can a dad have #realstrength.

25. Hochschild with Machung, *The Second Shift*, 224.

26. Ibid., 269.

27. Gerson, *Unfinished Revolution*, 222.

BIBLIOGRAPHY

Banet-Weiser, Sarah. "'We Are All Workers': Economic Crisis, Masculinity, and the American Working Class." In *Gendering the Recession: Media and Culture in an Age of Austerity,* edited by Diane Negra and Yvonne Tasker, 81-106. Durham, NC: Duke University Press, 2014.

Banet-Weiser, Sarah. *Authentic^{TM}: The Politics of Ambivalence in a Brand Culture.* New York: New York University Press, 2012.

Barak-Brandes, Sigal and Einat Lachover. "Branding Relations: Mother–Daughter Discourse on Beauty and Body in an Israeli Campaign by Dove." *Communication, Culture & Critique* (2015) doi: 10.1111/cccr.12111.

Belkin, Lisa. "When Mom and Dad Share It All." *The New York Times Magazine,* June 15, 2008 http://www.nytimes.com/2008/06/15/magazine/15parenting-t.html?pagewanted=all&_r=0.

Business Wire. "Nissan's 'With Dad' Super Bowl Commercial Wins YouTube's AdBlitz 2015." February 16, 2015. http://finance.yahoo.com/news/nissan-dad-super-bowl-commercial-164500691.html.

England, Paula. "Emerging Theories of Care Work." *Annual Review of Sociology* 31 (2005): 381–399.

Fowles, Jib. *Advertising and Popular Culture.* Thousand Oaks, CA: Sage, 1996.

Gerson, Kathleen. *The Unfinished Revolution: Coming of Age in a New Era of Gender, Work, and Family.* Oxford: Oxford University Press, 2010.

Heine, Christopher. "Dove's New Ad Shows What Dads Really Do Besides Resenting Gender Stereotypes. *AdWeek.* June 8, 2014. http://www.adweek.com/news/advertising-branding/doves-new-ad-shows-what-dads-really-do-158181.

Hochschild, Arlie with Anne Machung. *The Second Shift: Working Families and the Revolution at Home, Revised Edition.* London: Penguin Books, 1989/2012.

Neff, Jack. "Move Over, Mom, It's Dad's Turn In Ads." *Advertising Age.* January 27, 2015. http://adage.com/article/news/nissan-toyota-dove-put-dad-super-bowl/296786.

Parker, Kim and Wendy Wang. *Modern Parenthood: Roles of Moms and Dads Converge as They Balance Work and Family.* Pew Research Center, 2013. http://www.pewsocialtrends.org/2013/03/14/modern-parenthood-roles-of-moms-and-dads-converge-as-they-balance-work-and-family.

Szalai, Alexander, ed. *The Use of Time: Daily Activities of Urban and Suburban Populations in Twelve Countries.* The Hauge: Mounton, 1972.

Williams, Raymond. "Advertising: the Magic System" In *Culture and Materialism: Selected Essays, 2nd ed.* London: Verso, 1995.

Zimmerman, Mary K.; Litt, Jacquelyn S.; and Bose, Christine E., eds. *Global Dimensions of Gender and Carework.* Stanford: Stanford University Press, 2006.

Chapter 6

Detecting Fatherhood

The "New" Masculinity in Prime-time Crime Dramas

Sarah Kornfield

The crime genre is a long-standing staple of the entertainment industry and typically features male detectives as private eyes, frontier lawmen, armchair detectives, buddy cops, or FBI agents. Through these portrayals, the crime genre participates in normalizing authority, rationality, violence, and virility as key characteristics of masculinity.[1] For example, *Magnum PI* aired for eight years (1980–1988) on CBS, during which the lead actor, Tom Selleck, was asked to "boost [his] macho output" while portraying Thomas Magnum.[2]

Recently, however, prime-time broadcast networks began airing crime dramas in which the male detectives seemingly share little in common with Thomas Magnum. Instead, *Bones* (2005–), *Fringe* (2008–2013), *The Mentalist* (2008–2015), and *Castle* (2009–) prominently characterize their male detective as a nurturing father. These men are deeply invested in their families and characterized through the traditionally feminine trait of caring for children and the elderly. Indeed, television reviews welcomed these detectives as gender "reversed" characters who are "in touch" with their "feminine nature" since they love their children, understand emotions, and follow their intuitions while solving crimes.[3] Indeed, even these fathers' romantic pursuits are framed as part of their nurturing, feminine nature. While these series avoid storylines in which the single fathers search for "substitute mothers" for their children, they nonetheless feature the male detectives as men who think about sex "like women," prioritizing romance, commitment, and monogamy while wooing their partners.

Seemingly, these series portray a new twist on the familiar TV genre of crime dramas by transforming the traditionally rational, logical, evidence-based male detective who eschews emotions and domesticity into a playful, intuitive, emotionally attuned father who also solves crimes. This is hardly the first time that TV crime dramas have tampered with the generic formula in order to revitalize the genre; nor is it the first time a crime drama has altered its gendered portrayals to stand apart from other popular crime series. For example, in 1981, *Cagney & Lacey* debuted on the CBS network, adding a new twist to the classic crime genre: unlike its contemporaries, *Starsky & Hutch* (1975–1979) and *Chips* (1977–1983), *Cagney & Lacey* engaged a "feminist consciousness" by portraying two women as the "buddy cops."[4] In 1993, *The X-Files* continued this trend of "feminist consciousness" as it too tested the boundaries of crime dramas, this time by partnering a man and woman together and turning "buddy cops" into a slow-moving romance.[5] *Bones*, *Fringe*, *The Mentalist*, and *Castle* build on the crime drama's historical template while using their portrayals of the male detective to renew the genre; as Andrew Marlowe—*Castle's* creator and executive producer—stated, his goal was to take a familiar genre and "blow it up."[6]

However, *Bones*, *Fringe*, *The Mentalist*, and *Castle* have not "blown up" the gendered norms for masculinity. Instead of embodying gender reversals, these male detectives simultaneously perform traditionally masculine and feminine traits, without troubling the binary. That is, these male characters perform "feminine" traits rather than de-gendering behaviors such as raising children. Specifically, these male detectives combine gendered traits so that they are 1) both domestically and career oriented, and 2) relationally committed and monogamous while also being sexually experienced and promiscuous.

By analyzing *Bones*, *Fringe*, *The Mentalist*, and *Castle's* contradictory combinations in their portrayals of fatherhood, I argue two specific points. First, although these male detectives are popularly understood as gender-reversed characters, they are ultimately the same patriarchal detectives routinely featured in crime programming. Essentially, the shifts toward nurturing and fun-fatherhood in these series are merely feints, gestures without substance. Second, this lip-service is richly rewarded within the narrative structures of *Bones*, *Fringe*, *The Mentalist*, and *Castle*: when men and women perform the same traditionally feminine characteristics—for example, raising children—the men are rewarded and the women are punished within these series. Although these series are heralded for their new masculinity and gender equality, these crime dramas reproduce patriarchy in a smoke-and-mirrors façade. Television functions as a public forum, airing "important cultural topics"; by analyzing how fatherhood functions on *Bones*, *Fringe*, *The Mentalist*, and *Castle* this research works to shed light on the "various mechanisms" through which US culture makes sense of masculinity and fatherhood.[7]

OVERVIEW OF SERIES

Following in the generic footsteps of series such as *Get Smart* (1965–1970), *Remington Steele* (1982–1987), *Hart to Hart* (1979–1984), and *The X-Files*

(1993–2002), these series pair together male and female detective partners and develop a romance between the partners. Unlike their predecessors, however, in each of these new pairings one partner is not employed by a law-enforcement agency—creating a mismatched pairing between one "standard-issue" cop and one "sleuth-with-something-extra."[8] *Bones* debuted in 2005 on the Fox network, partnering FBI Agent Seeley Booth with Temperance Brennan, who works as a civilian forensic anthropologist and is nicknamed "Bones." After *Bones* had proven itself with strong ratings into its third season, Fox introduced another crime drama, *Fringe*. *Fringe* positioned their female detective, Olivia Dunham, as the FBI agent and partnered her with a former con-man, Peter Bishop. Like *The X-Files*, *Fringe* also added science-fiction elements into the crime drama, including a parallel universe, futuristic technology, and Peter Bishop's father, Walter, who is a mad-scientist. The CBS network then launched *The Mentalist*, again positioning the female detective as the law-enforcement officer: Teresa Lisbon is a head detective in the California Bureau of Investigation (CBI) where she works with Patrick Jane. Formerly a charlatan psychic, Jane joined the CBI after a serial killer, Red John, murdered his family. Finally, the ABC network introduced *Castle*, creating perhaps the most farfetched partnership: NYPD Detective Kate Beckett is partnered with a novelist, Richard Castle, so that he can observe her detective work—thereby gathering research for his new book series.

These series are not inconsequential. The United States Bureau of Labor Statistics reports that the average U.S. citizen over the age of 15 self-reported spending 2.8 hours per day watching television in 2013.[9] Averaging close to 20 hours per week, this makes television the number one leisure activity for U.S. citizens, with socializing as a distant second at slightly over 5 hours per week.[10] Television is a major U.S. culture industry in which these series have enjoyed longevity and sizable audiences. *Bones* averaged between approximately 8.9 and 11.57 million viewers over the last nine seasons and is airing its tenth season.[11] *Fringe*—which aired primarily on Friday nights—averaged between approximately 4.22 and 10 million viewers, concluding after five seasons.[12] Throughout its seven seasons, *The Mentalist* consistently had strong ratings, averaging between 11.82 and 17.52 million viewers.[13] Finally, *Castle's* first six seasons averaged between approximately 10.19 and 12.26 million viewers, and it is currently airing a seventh season.[14] Each week, viewers are tuning in to watch these detectives solve murders, examine grisly corpses, and banter flirtatiously with each other while supposedly embodying gender-reversed characteristics.

In reviewing and critiquing these series, popular newspaper and TV guides focused on the gendered portrayals, often celebrating these series' use of feelings-oriented male detectives and the prominent displays of fatherhood.[15] For example, Sean Mitchell described *Bones* in the *New York Times*, stating, "In some ways the traditional male-female roles are reversed in *Bones*, with Brennan, the scientist, cast as the stolid, lonely careerist, while Mr. Boreanaz's character [Agent Booth] is, by contrast, emotional and caring, an unmarried father who is seeking redemption for his past as an Army sniper."[16] Similarly, *Fringe*, *The Mentalist*, and *Castle* all feature the female detectives as "masculine" through their use of science and emotional detachment while the male detectives are domesticated by their families and "feminized" through their emotional intuition.

MASCULINIZING FATHERHOOD

As gender theorists have amply demonstrated, gender is something we do rather than something we are: gender is performance, not biology.[17] As such, masculinity is "a social construction" and therefore subject to change.[18] Moreover, masculinity can be performed differently: individuals can be more or less masculine and correspondingly, more or less powerful.[19] While these concepts are rigorously fleshed out in gender theory, they are also deployed in a common sense and often pejorative fashion throughout popular culture. This is perhaps best exemplified through Arnold Schwarzenegger's term "girlie-men," which originated in his 1988 *Saturday Night Live* skit and was resurrected in his political rhetoric as he labeled Democrats, economic pessimists (or realists), and a variety of other political opponents as "girlie-men."[20] Rightly criticized as sexist, homophobic, and sensationalist, Schwarzenegger's term, "girlie-men," reveals that within U.S. culture masculinity is not a static, biological category but a social hierarchy replete with its own catalog of gender performances, nuances, options, and contradictions.[21] Schwarzenegger's phrase not only demonstrates that our culture recognizes different types of masculinity as more or less powerful but also highlights that feminine contamination lessens masculine power. That is, to be "girlie-men" is necessarily less powerful than being "men" in Schwarzenegger's—and U.S. culture's—discursive logic.

Media representation plays an "integral part" in masculinity's social construction as popular entertainment and news discourses extend, constrain, and promote "particular ideals as appropriately masculine."[22] Analyzing TV news coverage of stay-at-home fathers in the 1990s, Mary Vavrus noted that "nurturance" was being sutured into a masculine ideal. Essentially, the media coverage surrounding "Mr. Moms" framed stay-at-home fathers as being experts at nurturing children.[23] That is, just as being a gourmet chef at a five-star restaurant is an appropriately masculine career but cooking dinner for a family of four is a feminized activity in U.S. culture, the media framed these fathers as masculine because—in part—they had mastered the art of nurturing children.[24] The crime dramas *Bones*, *Fringe*, *The Mentalist*, and *Castle* build on this expanded definition of masculinity. The male detectives are portrayed as naturally nurturing to the extent that their emotional acumen transfers into their careers, making them consummate detectives. By focusing on nurturing fathers who work outside the home these series close a loop, creating narratives that use men's expertise at traditionally feminized traits to reinforce *traditional* masculinity. That is, in a maddening twist, these crime dramas portray men's nurturing and emotional expertise as character traits that make them virile, rich, successful, and powerful outside the home.

These crime dramas not only altered the male detectives' characteristics, they also changed the female detectives' gendered characteristics. As Judith Bulter theorized and Bonnie Dow chronicled, one "cannot alter definitions or expectations for one gender without affecting the other."[25] Beyond featuring the female detectives as "masculine" through their use of science and emotional detachment, in these narratives sexism ended long ago: the women are at the top of their respective fields and face little if any backlash from their male colleagues and subordinates. By featuring a world without overt sexism and thereby suggesting that feminism is unnecessary, these series engage in postfeminist discourse.[26] Indeed, these series explicitly portray their "co-ed" detective partnerships as equitable. For example, the networks promote these series by featuring the detective partners side by side and the characters themselves regularly describe their partnerships as equal. For instance, on *The Mentalist*, Patrick Jane explains that he is neither "above nor below" his partner, but "to the side."[27] In these series' equitable frameworks, all a woman needs is "the right man," and these series serve him up on a platter.[28] Postfeminist entertainment often portrays male characters as the "prize," and these series follow suit.[29] By portraying the male detectives as nurturing fathers who pursue monogamous romances, these series offer the female detectives (and the audience) idealized, postfeminist men.

However, rather than eschewing traditional masculinity, these series combine nurturance, emotional acumen, and monogamy with traditional masculinity. As such, the male detectives on *Bones*, *Fringe*, *The Mentalist*, and *Castle* can be applauded as "gender reversed" in popular TV reviews without risking effeminacy: these detectives are not "girlie-men." Rather, these male detectives turn traits that are liabilities for female characters into attractive, positive characteristics while also performing a dominant, virile version of masculinity on these programs. In contrast, these series portray the women's "masculine" traits, such as being logical, unemotional, and caring more about their careers than their romantic relationships, as personality defects. However, as postfeminist heroes, the male detectives' love cures their female partners of their unfeminine characteristics. Indeed, through the courtship process the male detectives ultimately teach each female detective to prioritize her relationship above her career, to express her own emotions and recognize others', and to adopt gentler, more caring social behaviors.

PATERNAL WORKAHOLICS

The male detectives on *Bones*, *Fringe*, *The Mentalist*, and *Castle* are all parental figures, performing the traditionally feminine trait of taking care of children and/or ailing parents. This domesticates the male detectives, making them ideal family-men, since they are—without exception—good men who express love, care, and support to their dependents. For example, on *Bones*, Seeley Booth is an exemplary father to his children, Parker and Christine, even as he blends his family together. For instance, when his daughter is born in the seventh season, Booth's fathering skills are portrayed as so exceptional that—rather than being insecure or resentful of his new half-sister—Parker is secure enough in his father's love that he creates a special mobile to welcome his half-sister, Christine.[30] On *Fringe*, Peter Bishop takes care of his elderly father, Walter, throughout the series. As such, he maintains the house, calms Walter's unreasonable fears, copes with Walter's outbreaks and demands, and even occasionally feeds and clothes Walter. Once in a relationship with Olivia Dunham, he is the one excited about children and the series portrays him as the more emotionally attached parent to their daughter, Henrietta. On *The Mentalist*, Patrick Jane's family has been murdered, but the series carefully constructs Jane as a caring and devoted father through flashbacks, Jane's reminiscing, and the way Jane interacts with other children. Finally, on *Castle*, Richard Castle is a caring single father, raising a remarkably mature teenage daughter, Alexis, and providing for (and housing) his out-of-work mother. These home-lives domesticate the male detectives on these series. This focus is visually emphasized on *Castle* and *Fringe* as these series regularly stage scenes in the male detectives' homes.

Not only are these male detectives domesticated through the series' focus on their familial relationships, but the series feature these men as exemplary caretakers. These are not average fathers; rather, these men have mastered fatherhood. For example, on *Castle*, Richard Castle has a caring, open relationship with his daughter, Alexis: they regularly seek each others' advice, divulge intimate stories with each other, and fondly reminisce on her childhood and his parental choices. This frames Castle as a conscientious but playful and accessible father. For instance, in the episode "Nanny McDead" from the first season, when Castle returns home from the precinct, he joins Alexis in clearing the after-dinner dishes and they begin discussing Castle's case, in which a young nanny was murdered. As they discuss who could have murdered the nanny while scrubbing plates, Alexis asks, "How come we never had a nanny?" Castle jokingly responds, "Well, your mother and I decided that if someone was going to screw you up, we wanted it to be me. Only, you managed to turn out fine somehow anyway."[31] Castle then takes a call from his partner, Beckett, and decides to return to the precinct. The episode revisits this conversation, however, in its conclusion. After solving the crime, Castle is working late in his office writing his latest novel when Alexis comes in to say good night. After some light-hearted banter, in which Castle compliments his daughter by stating that he is constantly surprised by her maturity, Alexis kisses him goodnight and then pauses to say, "thanks for being my nanny," to which Castle replies, "no sweat, kiddo."[32] These conversations are typical as *Castle* portrays its father-daughter relationship as dynamic and fun while clearly positioning Castle as an exemplary father. Although he briefly mentions Alexis' mother in this episode, it is clear from the conversation that Castle was responsible for raising Alexis, and returning viewers know that Alexis' mother is a flighty, irresponsible woman who left Castle and Alexis shortly after Alexis' birth.

All four of the male detectives are positioned as emotionally attuned, domesticated men who take care of those around them. Even before Peter Bishop has a child, *Fringe* painstakingly frames him as a caretaker by featuring him nursing his ailing father, Walter. Indeed, Bishop is recruited by the FBI in the pilot episode, not for his detective skills, but to be Walter's caretaker. Olivia Dunham needs Walter's expertise to solve complicated technological crimes, but she cannot manage the mad-scientist; as such, she partners with Bishop—who has the authority to check Walter out of his insane asylum and the ability to take care of him during their cases.

Similarly, although Patrick Jane's daughter was murdered, leaving him childless, *The Mentalist* carefully frames him as a father. His decision to become a detective is motivated by his need to avenge his family's death at the hands of the serial killer Red John. Moreover, the series goes to considerable lengths to portray him in fatherly contexts. For instance in the fifth season, Jane spends most of an episode in a dream state in which he is visited by his daughter's ghost and they solve a crime together.[33] Yet the series does not need to portray Jane with his own daughter to demonstrate his fatherly instincts, nearly any child will do. For example, during the first season of *The Mentalist*, Jane and Lisbon are working a case in which a young woman was murdered. Using his fatherly instincts, Jane recognizes that the evidence the other detectives assumed was cocaine is actually baby formula. He then single handedly locates the missing infant, rescuing the baby from a locked car. Unlike Lisbon who never even touches the infant, Jane is delighted by the baby and is naturally good at soothing and comforting the little one. When social services come to collect the infant, Lisbon is unmoved, but Jane is reluctant, concerned for the baby's future. Over the course of the investigation, Jane locates the baby's grandparents and the episode concludes with him removing the child from social services and placing her into her grandmother's arms.[34]

These four men are consistently portrayed as emotionally available, exemplary caretakers who are closely tied to the domestic sphere. Yet, each man is also career oriented and quite successful at his chosen profession. Booth is a rising FBI agent with a large corner office, full autonomy in the later seasons, and a background as an elite army sniper. Peter Bishop was a successful con-artist/entrepreneur who faked a doctorate in physics and worked at MIT, publishing original research until his duplicity was discovered. When the series opens, Bishop has just successfully brokered an important—if shady—business deal when Olivia Dunham recruits him to nurse his father. After joining the FBI's Fringe Division and partnering with Dunham, Bishop proves that he is a gifted scientist and detective in his own right, becoming an integral team member. Before his family's death, Patrick Jane was a consummate con-artist, successfully posing as a psychic in Los Angeles, where he had TV appearances, helped the local police departments with cases, and owned a mansion and an antique car collection. After joining the CBI and becoming Teresa Lisbon's partner, Jane makes a name for himself as a man who can close cases. Indeed his detective skills are unparalleled, to the extent that the CBI tolerates his childish-but-charming behavior and even copes with his refusal to wait for warrants. Finally, Castle is a famous crime novelist whose success has led to a celebrity status in New York City. Although he originally joins the NYPD to shadow Kate Beckett, he quickly becomes one of their most valued consultants and Beckett's partner since his outside-the-box thinking closes cases. At the outset of these narratives, the male characters are in thriving careers and as the stories progress these men only become more successful—despite radical career changes for Peter Bishop, Patrick Jane, and Richard Castle.

As such, these series add nurturance and exemplary fatherhood into the traditionally masculine traits of professional, financial, and sociopolitical success. However, rather than integrating familial and career goals, these series celebrate masculine domesticity without requiring the male detectives to engage in substantive domestic labor. Indeed, despite their popular acclaim, these are not "gender-reversed" characters: they are not feminine characters, stay-at-home fathers, or househusbands, nor do they actually do housework or spend time child-rearing. They have the joys of home and family without the responsibilities. They are professionally and financially successful men who spend all of their time working. To achieve this level of success, any real-world individual would certainly be consumed in work—and these male detectives are too, but this goes almost unnoticed within the machinations of these stories.

For example, consider the *Castle* episode described above in which Richard Castle bonds with his daughter over being her "nanny." Castle has returned home late—he has missed dinner. While discussing his work, he briefly begins to help with the dishes, but then he is called back to work. In the touching conclusion when Alexis thanks him for being her "nanny," Castle is still working as he types away at his new novel. Similarly, the other male detectives almost never engage in the labor of caretaking. Booth's ex-girlfriend has primary custody of their son: she performs the childcare labor off-screen while Booth enjoys touching father-son scenes on-screen. Since Jane's daughter has died, Jane has no caretaking responsibilities. Of the male detectives, Bishop performs the most domestic labor as he cares for his father; yet since the father is an adult, Bishop does not need reliable or affordable day care and can easily rush off to join Dunham on a case. Moreover, Dunham's assistant, Astrid Farnsworth, becomes Walter's unpaid caretaker as the series progresses. Despite framing these men as exemplary fathers, they perform almost no household or caretaking labor. These are not familymen. These are workaholics who have impossibly good relationships with kind family members. Moreover, they interact with their family members by primarily discussing their work—the current murder mystery.

Each of these series portrays male detectives who embody an irreconcilable juxtaposition of unparalleled professional success and domesticity. These male detectives are exemplary fathers *and* workaholics. Although emphatically positioned as caretakers by the series' narratives, these men spend virtually no screen-time taking care of their dependents. Their domesticity is simply a new layer of paint on the crime drama's classic masculine character. Moreover, these men's domesticity is rewarded within the narratives while the female detectives' is not. For example, both Seeley Booth on *Bones* and Olivia Dunham on *Fringe* want to spend time with the children in their lives—Booth with his son, Parker, and Dunham with her niece, Ella. In both series, the detectives plan special days to spend with these children who are clearly very important to them. Booth's plans succeed while Dunham's inevitably fail. In "The Man in the Fallout Shelter," Booth plans to celebrate Christmas with Parker; his plan gets jeopardized when he and the other characters are quarantined due to exposure to a dangerous substance during the course of their investigation. Booth spends his time in quarantine quite happily stoned as a side effect of prescribed medication, and—after solving the murder case and resolving the quarantine issue—Booth celebrates Christmas, as planned, with his son.[35]

Likewise on *Fringe*, Olivia Dunham plans a vacation day to take her niece, who currently lives with her, to an amusement park. However, work intrudes, forcing Dunham to cancel her vacation day and disappointing her niece by abandoning her and rushing off to solve the latest crime. This episode concludes by granting Dunham a couple hours to spend with Ella at the amusement park, but even this happy scene is spoiled by two ominous characters who watch them from afar—stalking Dunham—as they remark, "Look how happy she is. It's a shame things are about to get so hard for her."[36] Essentially, the *Bones* episode was designed to return Booth to his son, enabling them to happily celebrate Christmas together, as Booth remarked, "I'm the coolest dad this Christmas!"[37] However, the *Fringe* episode is designed to take Dunham away from her niece. Booth's fathering is rewarded, but Dunham's involvement in her niece's life is not.

Bones, Fringe, The Mentalist, and *Castle* consistently position the male detectives as capable of navigating successful domestic lives and careers while the women suffer under a second shift when they try to have both a personal and professional life. Analyzing women's labor, feminist scholars characterize women's professional labor as a "first shift" and their household labor as a "second shift," emphasizing the idea that women work two shifts back-to-back rather than working one shift and then primarily resting as men traditionally do.[38] These crime series normalize this representation of a gendered "second shift": the women face a second shift but the male detectives have time to develop and maintain ongoing, dynamic, healthy relationships with their family members in addition to their careers.

Bones, Fringe, The Mentalist, and *Castle* position their male detectives as good father figures without considering the time these relationships require, creating impossible combinations of personal and professional achievements. In and of itself, this is not necessarily negative: television airs many impossibilities each day. Rather, the problem is that these male detectives engage in virtually no domestic labor while being framed as domestic: Castle missed dinner, barely helped with the dishes, and rushed back out to work instead of spending the evening at home, while being framed by the narrative, blocking (Castle and his daughter are physically comfortable and affectionate with each other on-screen), and dialogue as a loving, caring, and exemplary father. Moreover, the male detectives can achieve this impossibly happy combination of familial bliss and career success but the women cannot. The women do not have the time to date, raise children, or interact with their family members, and it becomes a crisis for the women when they try to enjoy family. These series are all too cognizant of the second shift when it comes to women, reminding viewers that women cannot have it all while portraying male detectives who do.

ROMANTIC DADS AND SEXY PLAYERS

Just as the male detectives are simultaneously workaholics and domestic gurus, they also have bifurcated characteristics when it comes to romance

and sexuality. When interacting with women other than their detective partners, the male detectives adopt a promiscuous approach, displaying a virile
masculinity as they casually seduce a variety of women. Essentially, these
men act like "players" when interacting with most women. However, when
interacting with their detective partners, these men monogamously pursue
them, building stable, romantic relationships with their partners. Here, these
male detectives operate as fathers. For example, these male detectives ensure
that their current family members—especially their children—approve of
the female detective as a romantic choice before pursuing her; they follow
traditional courtship rituals—proposing to, marrying, and settling down in
stable, nuclear family homes; and the male detectives on *Bones*, *Fringe*, and
The Mentalist all father children with their spouses. As such, these series
bifurcate the male detectives' sexuality, creating male characters that are
simultaneously "sexy players" who can bed the women of their choosing and
"romantic dads" who prioritize their current children, romance their partners,
and function within family-oriented relationships. Throughout the vast majority of these series' episodes—prior to the detectives' marriages—these narratives combine and sustain these seemingly incompatible personas of "sexy
player" and "romantic dad" in their male detectives. In so doing, these series
create a space in which the male detectives can demonstrate their masculinity
by sexually pursuing random women without disrupting their fatherly roles,
which include the romantic pursuit of their detective partner.

These series accomplish this contradictory combination through their episodic narrative structure and the slow-moving nature of the primary romance.
In their pilot episodes, *Bones*, *Fringe*, *The Mentalist*, and *Castle* all hint
at a romance between their detective partners as the characters interact in
romantically charged scenes. Commenting on these burgeoning romances,
TV reviews cited the detectives' witty dialogue, lingering glances, and sexual
chemistry as evidence of the programs' assured "slow-burning" romances.[39]
From their opening scenes, these series created a *telos*, or end-goal, for their
detective partners: the relationships are designed to culminate in romantic,
committed, monogamous love. All four series eventually made good on this
promise of romance: in the ninth season on *Bones*, Brennan and Booth are
married with a daughter; when *Fringe* concluded, Dunham and Bishop were
also happily married with a daughter; in *Castle's* seventh season, Castle and
Beckett got married; and the detectives on *The Mentalist* married each other
and became pregnant in the series' finale.

Although these series began romantically uniting the detectives in the pilot
episodes, they drew out this process, keeping the characters primarily in a
stage of flirtatious bickering and/or a one sided, unrequited love throughout at
least the first four seasons. This delayed romance is deliberate. For example,
Nathan Fillion—who plays Richard Castle—stated in an interview that his
series had "learned a valuable lesson from *Moonlighting*" and that while

sparks may fly between the detectives the series would "keep them separated" for a considerable time.[40] By invoking the *"Moonlighting* Curse," Fillion alludes to Cybil Shepherd's and Bruce Willis' hit show's precipitous ratings decline after the central characters slept with each other. Fearing the same fate, series that depend upon a "will they or won't they" romantic tension tend to postpone coupling their characters for "as long as humanly possible," fearing that romantic resolution "spells doom" for the series' ratings.[41]

The slow-burning romances between the detective partners structure these narratives, adding tension to the story lines and marking the characters' development. However, despite the presence of these central romances, all four crime dramas feature episodes in which the male detectives sexually pursue other women—even though they know they are in love with their detective partners. Essentially, these series destine the men for committed, monogamous relationships with their partners, but cannot consummate those relationships during the early seasons lest the series lose their romantic tension and suffer the *"Moonlighting* Curse." As such, in order to portray the male detectives' sexual proficiency, these series feature brief, casual sex through which the male characters assert their sexual prowess.

These romantic conquests are not central to the ongoing plotlines nor are they carefully developed. All four of these crime dramas are episodic serials, combining the episodic approach (in which each episode features a discrete story) and the serial approach (in which the narrative spills from one episode into the next).[42] As such, some story lines (such as tracking down serial killers or romantically pairing the detectives) develop over the course of several seasons while each individual episode in those seasons has an open-and-shut case. The majority of the male detectives' sexual conquests are featured as an episodic element: these women are rarely recurring characters and even more rarely part of an ongoing story arc. Rather, these scenarios appear almost at random, demonstrating that the male detective has a sex drive, is sexually attractive, and is capable of seducing the women of his choosing. For example, in *The Mentalist's* fourth episode, "Ladies in Red," Jane decides—at a funeral—to seduce the new widow. This decision is part of a bet with Agent Wayne Rigsby: when Rigsby cannot figure out how to ask their colleague, Agent Grace Van Pelt, out on a date, Jane remarks that by showing a woman "love and affection" a man can seduce any woman. Rigsby then bets Jane one hundred dollars that Jane cannot seduce the widow—a bet Rigsby loses. The episode is salvaged from tawdriness, when Jane decides not to sleep with the widow and instead reveals her as a murderer.[43]

While the other series are perhaps less outrageous, their machinations are just as contrived. For example, the sixth episode of *Castle*, "Always Buy Retail," opens to Castle making love to his first wife, Alexis' mother, and then her unexpected announcement that she is returning to New York to find a job.[44] She then, unbeknownst to Castle, pulls Alexis out of school to go on a shopping spree, and when Castle gets home the ever responsible Alexis states that her life is better when her mother does not live in New York City. Castle then calls in a favor and has a friend offer his ex-wife a terrific job across the country—a job she accepts.[45] While this story line adds tension to the episode as Castle worries about how to get his ex-wife to leave New York City while sifting through murder clues with Beckett, the scenario is nicely designed to demonstrate Castle's sexual prowess *and* his parental nature, which ought to be at odds in this episode but, instead, work together seamlessly. His sexual encounter with his ex-wife does not complicate his relationship with her or with their daughter: instead of being mad or confused that Castle slept with her semi-estranged mother, Alexis is grateful that she lives with her father, prefers him as a parent, and despite his dalliance (which would complicate any real family) Castle is portrayed as the mature adult figure in this episode. Through these sexual conquests, these series portray the male detectives as sexually proficient and desirable while entirely disconnecting these sex-acts from these men's fatherly roles. These sex-acts bolster the male detectives' masculinity without affecting their children or their romantic pursuit of the female detectives.

In case these sexual exploits from the early seasons are forgotten, the series throw in unconsummated flirtations and seductions later on—after the male detectives have committed themselves to pursuing exclusive romantic relationships with their partners. For example, after confessing his love for Beckett in the third season finale, Castle flirts shamelessly with a non-recurring character in "Eye of the Beholder."[46] More pointedly, on *Fringe*, Peter Bishop becomes distraught after learning that Walter is not actually his biological father; instead of seeking comfort from Dunham, who he has been romantically pursuing, Bishop goes on a road trip and seduces a waitress—who conveniently dies before Bishop can sleep with her.[47] Both instances demonstrate these series' penchant for exhibiting the male detectives' sexual proficiency and attractiveness without actually disrupting the romantic relationships they have been pursuing with their partners. These men know they are in love with their partners, yet seduce other women. Again, the clear contrivance is staggering: these series create scenarios—such as sending Bishop off on a road trip—in which the men can encounter beautiful, unattached women to seduce, thereby proving the men's sexual proficiency.

The recurring presence of these casual, episodic love interests for the male detectives across all four series suggests that within these TV narratives the fatherly characteristics of nurturance, commitment, monogamy, and domesticity were insufficiently masculine. As such, while maintaining these fatherly personas for the male detectives, the series added the components of virility, sexual adventurousness, and sexual proficiency. Essentially, these series bulked up the fathers' masculinity by having them seduce random women. David Boreanaz, who plays Booth on *Bones*, commented to this extent in an interview. When asked, "So you'll get a love interest [in season two]?" Boreanaz replied, "Yeah. There's going to be more than one love interest . . . I think my relationship with Bones will always be there, but hey, a man's got to do what a man's got to do."[48] These exhibitions of sexual prowess are typically episodic: they do not affect the story arcs, disrupt the men's portrayals of fatherhood, or create ongoing tensions or jealousies between the detective partners. Rather, these sexual encounters occur and are forgotten within the narratives of *Bones*, *Fringe*, *The Mentalist*, and *Castle*. This creates a strange contradiction in which the men are simultaneously players and yet are believably responsible fathers who are committed to monogamous relationships with their partners. With the partial exception of Castle who purposefully cultivates the rakish celebrity persona, these series do not frame their male detectives as playboys who need to be reformed, tamed, or somehow "settled down." The female detectives do not "catch" their partners. Rather, within these narratives, the men are already good, already father-material, already commitment-types, and already serious about their partners. These fathers are simply (in Boreanaz's words) doing what a "man's got to do."

Not only do these male detectives exhibit these contradictory traits of romantic dads and sexy players, their sexual encounters are framed very differently from the female detectives' sexual encounters. There are five prominent differences between how the male and female detectives' sex lives are represented on *Bones*, *Fringe*, *The Mentalist*, and *Castle*. First, the men simply have more sexual partners than the women. Second, the male detectives are more often portrayed in the act of love-making than the female detectives are. Third, the male detectives often engage in casual sex, while the women are more likely to have sex with committed partners. Fourth, the women are more likely to be punished for their sexual encounters (committed or otherwise) than the men are. And finally, the women's sexual relationships are more likely to be serialized—to contribute to ongoing plotlines and/or character development within the series—than the male detective's sexual conquests.

For example, on *Castle*, Kate Beckett has two brief boyfriends over the course of the first three seasons (i.e., three years within the story world). Beckett is never portrayed in bed with either of her significant others, and her two boyfriends serve to make Castle jealous, which actually moves Castle and Beckett's relationship forward as he recognizes that he is jealous and then realizes that he has strong feelings for Beckett. Finally, Beckett is punished for her relationships: in the third season finale, the series reinterprets her previous two boyfriends as emotional crutches or coping mechanisms, suggesting that Beckett was too emotionally damaged during childhood by her mother's mysterious death to create meaningful bonds with her romantic partners. Castle confronts Beckett, stating "I know you hide there . . . you hide in these nowhere relationships with men you don't love."[49] This is a shaming statement that clearly frames Beckett's sexual relationships not as fun, comforting, mutually supportive, and/or exciting, but as a negative, unhealthy behavior that needs to end. Fascinatingly, Castle delivers this line without a hint of irony and the series itself in no way recognizes the enormous incongruity of having Castle—the celebrity rake—chide Beckett for having loveless sex. Moreover, since this narrative has already tipped its hand, implying from the pilot episode that Castle and Beckett are destined for each other, this scene suggests that Castle is the only man she can have a meaningful romantic relationship with, further implying that Castle tames Beckett, healing her of her crippled romantic behavior and rescuing her from a "wild-oats" stage by bringing her into a mature relationship.

Despite the clearly patriarchal influences structuring the way sexuality is portrayed in these series, *Bones* and *The Mentalist* both attempt to frame their female detectives as progressive female characters by having them engage in casual sex—as if casual sex is a benchmark of gender equality. For example, during the early seasons of *Bones*, Brennan talks about sex in clinical, scientific terms, eschews love as a chemical reaction, and believes that sex is primarily concerned with physical gratification. By representing these female characters as women who can have sex "like a man," these series tighten the links between casual sexuality and masculinity while distancing sex from procreation and fatherhood. Yet just as these female detectives are caught in a "second shift" in their labor, they face a double standard in their sexual activity. For example, despite being carefully portrayed as a progressive woman who enjoys sexual pleasures, Brennan cannot escape the system of punishment and monogamy these series create for their female detectives. For instance, in "The Man in the Outhouse," an early episode in the fourth season, Booth barges into Brennan's apartment at 6:30 a.m. and is surprised to see a man there, prompting the following conversation with Brennan:

Brennan: It would be good if you called first.

Booth: Well, who knew you were even dating?

Brennan: Well, I wouldn't call it dating. We occasionally make arrangements to spend time together.

Booth: I'm just surprised you're not more picky.

Brennan: My relationship with Mark is purely physical, and I am very satisfied with him in that area. Did you see his chest and thighs?

Booth: Bones. What [are you doing]?

Brennan: Haven't you chosen someone because they were satisfying sexually?

Booth: There has to be more than sex.[50]

In this scene, Booth is shocked that Brennan has had sex recently. While clearly an over-reaction, his surprise is warranted by how little Brennan has dated over the course of this series' past four years. Later in the episode, Booth is upset to learn that Brennan is going out on a date with a different man and assumes she has stopped seeing Mark.

> *Booth:* Oh I get it. You dumped Mark. *[Sarcastically]* It's too bad, I kinda liked the guy.
>
> *Brennan:* No, I didn't dump Mark, I'm seeing both of them.
>
> *Booth:* At the same time?
>
> *Brennan:* Mark and I have a physical connection. The botanist, while brilliant and fascinating, just . . . just doesn't appeal to me in that way.
>
> *Booth:* Okay, so all that stuff about monogamy being unnatural, you're just making excuses.
>
> *Brennan:* I do not make excuses. Only people who are ashamed make excuses.
>
> *Booth:* Bones, two guys at the same time, it's not right. I mean, that's why they invented dueling.[51]

At first glance, the dialogue in these two conversations frames Brennan as progressive with a casual approach to sex and Booth as the champion of monogamy and committed relationships, thereby demonstrating their "reversed gender" characteristics: that is, she is having sex like a man and he thinks about sex like a woman. However, as the series has amply demonstrated, Booth is no stranger to one-night-stands, casual sex, and friends-with-benefits. Booth's problem is not with casual sex, it is with the idea of Brennan having casual sex. For example, in this same episode, when asked how his sex life is, Booth brags, "I do fine." Moreover, the tension in this episode centers on Brennan's apparently controversial decision to have two boyfriends, but she is only sleeping with one of them: this is hardly the polygamous crisis Booth thinks it is.

Moreover, Booth's dialogue throughout the episode is meant to punish Brennan, bringing her back in line with sexual standards he himself does not maintain. This punishment is completed in the final scene of the episode, where Brennan reveals that both men have broken up with her. Finally, Brennan's interactions with these men served to make Booth blatantly jealous and the episode concludes with Booth taking Brennan out for dinner and consoling her with the obviously hinting statement, "There is someone for everyone.

Someone you're meant to spend the rest of your life with. All right? You just have to be open enough to see it."[52]

Although the episode frames Brennan as a sexually progressive character who approaches sex casually enough to date two men simultaneously, the narrative structure hems her into a much more conservative stance by the end of the episode. Moreover, Brennan's original approach to sexuality in this episode is hardly progressive: it was rare for her to have a sexual partner, she only had one sexual partner, she only wanted one sexual partner, and she recants from even this when punished at the end of the episode. Yet Booth's "feminized" approach to sexuality causes him to shame Brennan during the episode, espousing a sexual standard he eschews in his own behaviors throughout the series.

Throughout *Bones*, *Fringe*, *The Mentalist*, and *Castle*, the men are consistently portrayed as responsible fathers who pursue committed, family-oriented relationships with their partners. Simultaneously—and without complicating their roles as fathers and monogamous romantics—these series portray the male detectives as sexually promiscuous men who "do fine" and can seduce the women of their choosing. These are loving, dedicated fathers and hounddogs: the series very pointedly develop both sides of these men's characters, creating this irreconcilable contradiction of monogamy and promiscuity. Meanwhile, the female detectives have sex less frequently, are almost never pictured in bed, usually cultivate sexual relations only within committed, long-standing relationships with men who further the plot and/or character developments, and the female detectives are typically punished for having sex by shaming from the other characters and through plot machinations.

CONCLUSION

This new iteration of the crime drama portrays the male detectives as nurturing fathers, but they engage in almost no caretaking labor while enjoying unparalleled career success. Similarly, they are framed as monogamously responsible parents while they seduce strangers. These male characters are being celebrated in TV reviews and rewarded within these series' narratives for these traditionally feminine traits (domesticity and monogamy), yet they are only part of these men's characters—the rest of which feature traditionally masculine components such as earning career acclaim and causally bedding women along the way. Moreover, these traditionally feminine traits of domesticity and monogamy are only celebrated when men perform them. In these series, the female detectives are unable to engage in domesticity due to the second shift (which does not affect the men) and the concept of romantic monogamy is used to shame the women's sexual behaviors.

This is deeply problematic. Feminists' efforts toward equity—equal pay, equal rights, equal opportunities, equal representation, and the end of domestic and sexual violence—largely depend upon the recognition that gender roles (i.e., traits and behaviors associated with masculinity and femininity) are culturally constructed and therefore have no biological impetus or inherent value. However, these series' portrayals largely affirm traditional gender roles. Herein lies the crux of the issue: by referring to the male detectives as "gender reversed" when they perform domestically and monogamously, these traits continue to be marked as feminine within public discourse. As such, these male detectives embody a "new" masculinity that replicates traditional masculinity. Indeed, these male detectives appear as experts at feminine traits without having to engage in the corresponding relational and physical labor and without curtailing their traditionally masculine behaviors. Ultimately, this new masculinity is the old masculinity, except it also shames women as incompetent at femininity since these male detectives outperform them as parents and spouses.

NOTES

1. See James Inciardi and Juliet Dee, "From the Keystone Cops to *Miami Vice* Images of Policing in American Popular Culture," *Journal of Popular Culture* 21 (1987): 84–102; Erica Scharrer, "Tough Guys: The Portrayal of Hypermasculinity and Aggression in Televised Police Dramas," *Journal of Broadcasting & Electronic Media,* 45 (2001): 615–634.

2. Susan Faludi, *Backlash: The Undeclared War Against American Women* (New York: Anchor Books Doubleday, 1991).

3. See Robert Bianco, "The Stars Flesh Out *Bones,*" *USA Today,* September 13, 2005, accessed January 22, 2013, http://usatoday30.usatoday.com/life/television/reviews/2005–09–12-bones_x.htm; Angel Cohn, "*Bones'* Booth gets his Sexy On," *TV Guide,* August 30, 2006, accessed February 15, 2015, http://www.tvguide.com/news/Bones-booth-gets-37492.aspx; Doug Elfman, "*Bones* Star is One Strange Agent," *Chicago Sun-Times,* September 13, 2005, accessed February 28, 2013, http://infoweb.newsbank.com.ezaccess.libraries.psu.edu/iwsearch/we/InfoWeb?p_product=AWNB&p_theme=aggregated5&p_action=doc&p_docid=10D32AD92AEB1750&p_docnum=3&p_queryname=8; David Hinckley, "Tweaks could make *Castle* Rock-Solid," *Daily News,* March 8, 2009, accessed February 15, 2015, http://www.nydailynews.com/entertainment/tv-movies/tweaks-castle-rock-solid-article-1.369213; Sean Mitchell, "Ex-Vampire Turns into Regular Guy," *The New York Times,* December 27, 2006, accessed February 15, 2015, http://www.nytimes.com/2006/12/27/arts/television/27bore.html; Rob Owen, "TV Preview: Ex-*Guardian* Baker Lightens Up as *The Mentalist,*" *Post-Gazette,* September 23, 2008, accessed February 28, 2013, http://www.post-gazette.com/pg008267/914216–42.stm; and Molly Willow, "Pair Sure to Heat Up Morgue," *Columbus Dispatch,* September

13, 2005, accessed January 22, 2013, http://infoweb.newsbank.com.ezaccess.libraries.psu.edu/iwsearch/we/InfoWeb?p_product=AWNB&p_theme=aggregated5&p_action=doc&p_docid=10C9BF4BF6630CC8&p_docnum=5&p_queryname=9.

4. Julie D'Acci, *Defining Women: Television and the Case of* Cagney & Lacey (Chapel Hill, NC: The University of North Carolina Press, 1994), 4.

5. Linda Badley, "Scully Hits the Glass Ceiling: Postmodernism, Postfeminism, Posthumanism and *The X-Files*," in *Fantasy Girls: Gender in the New Universe of Science Fiction and Fantasy Television*, ed. E. Helford (Lanham: Rowman & Littlefield Publishers, 2000), 61–90.

6. Philiana Ng, "*Castle* Creator Talks Season 4, Future of the Castle-Beckett Relationship and the New Captain (Q&A)," *Hollywood Reporter*, September 19, 2011, accessed March 20, 2015, http://www.hollywoodreporter.com/live-feed/Castle-creator-talks-season-4-237181.

7. For a discussion of television as a cultural forum, see Horace Newcomb and Paul Hirsch, "Television as a Cultural Forum: Implications for Research," *Quarterly Review of Film Studies* 8 (1983): 48; the phrase "various mechanisms" is quoted from Bonnie Dow, "*Ellen*, Television, and the Politics of Gay and Lesbian Visibility," *Critical Studies in Media Communication* 18 (2001): 124.

8. Mary McNamara, "*Castle*," *Los Angeles Times*, March 9, 2009, accessed March 20, 2015, http://www.latimes.com/entertainment/tv/la-et-castle9–2009mar09-story.html.

9. "Economic News Release: American Time Use Survey Summary," United States Department of Labor, last modified June 18, 2014, http://www.bls.gov/news.release/atus.nr0.htm.

10. "Economic News Release: American Time Use Survey Summary."

11. "Ranking Report: 2008," ABC MediaNet, http://www.abcmedianet.com/web/dnr/dispDNR.aspx?id=052008_06; Bill Gorman, "2010–11 Season Broadcast prime-time Show Viewership Averages," *TV By the Numbers*, June 1, 2011, accessed March 20, 2015, http://tvbythenumbers.zap2it.com/2011/06/01/2010–11-season-broadcast-primetime-show-viewership-averages/94407/; Kate Stanhope, "*Bones* Renewed for Tenth Season, Reclaims Monday Timeslot in March," *TV Guide.com*, January 29, 2014, accessed March 20, 2015, http://www.tvguide.com/news/bones-renewed-season10–1076961.aspx.

12. "Ranking Report: 2009," ABC MediaNet, http://abcmedianet.com/web/dnr/dispDNR.aspx?id=060209_05; Bill Gorman, "Complete List of 2011–12 Season TV Show Viewership: *Sunday Night Football* Tops, Followed by *American Idol, NCIS & Dancing with the Stars*," *TV by the Numbers*, May 24, 2012, accessed March 20, 2015, http://tvbythenumbers.zap2it.com/2012/05/24/complete-list-of-2011–12-season-tv-show-viewership-sunday-night-football-tops-followed-by-american-idol-ncis-dancing-with-the-stars/135785/.

13. "Ranking Report: 2009"; Sara Bibel, "Complete List of 2012–13 Season TV Show Viewership: *Sunday Night Football* Tops, Followed by *NCIS, The Big Bang Theory* & *NCIS: Los Angeles*," *TV by the Numbers*, May 29, 2013, accessed March 20, 2015, http://tvbythenumbers.zap2it.com/2013/05/29/complete-list-of-2012–13-season-tv-show-viewership-sunday-night-football-tops-followed-by-ncis-the-big-bang-theory-ncis-los-angeles/184781/.

14. "Ranking Report: 2009"; Bibel, "Complete List of 2012–13 Season TV Show Viewership."

15. Bianco, "The Stars Flesh Out *Bones*"; Cohn, "*Bones'* Booth gets his Sexy On"; Elfman, "*Bones* Star is One Strange Agent," Hinckley, "Tweaks could make *Castle* Rock-Solid"; Robert Laurence, "Fox Throws *Bones* onto that Heaping Pile of *CSI* Imitators," *San Diego Union-Tribune*, September 13, 2005, accessed March 20, 2015, http://www.utsandiego.com/uniontrib/20050913/news_lz1c13remote.html; Mitchell, "Ex-Vampire Turns into Regular Guy"; Owen, "TV Preview: Ex-*Guardian* Baker Lightens Up as *The Mentalist*"; Amy Robinson, "The Idiot Box: *Castle* Just Another Ho-Hum Crime Procedural," *Charleston Gazette*, March 12, 2009, accessed March 20, 2015, http://www.highbeam.com/doc/1P2-19984730.html; and Willow, "Pair Sure to Heat Up Morgue."

16. Mitchell, "Ex-Vampire Turns into Regular Guy."

17. Judith Butler, *Gender Trouble: Feminism and the Subversion of Identity* (New York, NY: Routledge, 1990); John Sloop, *Disciplining Gender: Rhetorics of Sex Identity in Contemporary U.S. Culture* (Amherst, MA: University of Massachusetts, 2004).

18. Mary Vavrus, "Domesticating Patriarchy: Hegemonic Masculinity and Television's 'Mr. Mom,'" *Critical Studies in Media Communication* 19 (2002): 353.

19. Alan Petersen, *Unmasking the Masculine: "Men" and "Identity" in a Skeptical Age* (London: Sage Publications, 1998).

20. Peter Nicholas, "Schwarzenegger Deems Opponents 'Girlie-Men'—Twice," *Los Angeles Times*, July 18, 2004, accessed March 20, 2015, http://www.sfgate.com/cgi-bin/article.cgi?file=/chronicle/archive/2004/07/18/MNGH57NKAF1.DTL.

21. Dan Walters, "Schwarzenegger's Budget Vows Hit Immovable Political Wall," *Sacramento Bee*, July 20, 2004, accessed March 20, 2015, http://www.calstate.edu/pa/clips2004/july/20july/wall.shtml.

22. Vavrus, "Domesticating Patriarchy," 353.

23. Vavrus, "Domesticating Patriarchy."

24. Rebecca Swenson, "Domestic Divo? Televised Treatment of Masculinity, Femininity and Food," *Critical Studies in Media Communication* 26 (2009): 36–53; and Vavrus, "Domesticating Patriarchy."

25. Butler, *Gender Trouble*; Bonnie Dow, "Conversation and Commentary: The Traffic in Men and the *Fatal Attraction* of Postfeminist Masculinity," *Women's Studies in Communication* 29 (2006): 127.

26. For a discussion of postfeminism, see Bonnie Dow, *Prime-Time Feminism: Television, Media Culture, and the Women's Movement Since 1970* (Philadelphia: University of Pennsylvania Press, 1996); and Angela McRobbie, *The Aftermath of Feminism: Gender, Culture and Social Change* (Los Angeles, CA: Sage Publications, 2009).

27. *The Mentalist*, "Red Alert," episode no. 13, Season 3, first broadcast February 3, 2011, by CBS, directed by Guy Ferland and written by Jordan Harper.

28. Sherryl Vint, "The New Backlash: Popular Culture's "Marriage" with Feminism, Or Love Is All You Need," *Journal of Popular Film and Television* 34 (2007): 163.

29. Dow, "Conversation and Commentary," 126.

30. *Bones*, "The Warrior in the Wuss," episode no. 10, Season 7, first broadcast April 23, 2012, by Fox, directed by Chad Lowe and written by Dean Lopata and Michael Peterson.

31. *Castle*, "Nanny McDead," episode no. 2, Season 1, first broadcast March 16, 2009, by ABC, directed by John Terlesky and written by Barry Schindel.

32. *Castle*, "Nanny McDead."

33. *The Mentalist*, "Devil's Cherry," episode no. 2, Season 5, first broadcast October 7, 2012, by CBS, directed by Randy Zisk and written by Daniel Cerone.

34. *The Mentalist*, "The Thin Red Line," episode no. 8, Season 1, first broadcast November 25, 2008, by CBS, directed by Matt Earl Beesley and written by Ken Woodruff.

35. *Bones*, "The Man from the Fallout Shelter," episode no. 9, Season 1, first broadcast December 13, 2005, by Fox, directed by Greg Yaitanes and written by Hart Hanson.

36. *Fringe*, "August," episode no. 8, Season 2, first broadcast November 19, 2009, Directed by Dennis Smith and written by J.H. Whyman and Jeff Pinkner.

37. *Bones*, "The Man from the Fallout Shelter."

38. Shari Dworkin and Faye Linda Wachs, "'Getting Your Body Back': Postindustrial Fit Motherhood in *Shape Fit Pregnancy* magazine," *Gender and Society* 18 (2004): 616.

39. Cohn, "*Bones*' Booth Gets his Sexy On"; Cristina Kinon, "J.J. Abrams illuminates Dark Science with *Fringe*," *Daily News*, September 7, 2008, accessed March 20, 2015, http://articles.nydailynews.com/2008–09–08/entertainment/17905842_1_abrams-anna-torv-Fringe; Brian Lowry, "*Bones*: TV Review," *Variety*, September 13, 2005, accessed March 20, 2015, http://www.variety.com/review/VE1117928109/; Mitchell, "Ex-Vampire Turns into Regular Guy"; Ng, "*Castle* Creator Talks Season 4"; Robinson, "The Idiot Box: *Castle*."

40. John Crook, "Fillion's Bad Boy Charm Makes Him King of ABC's *Castle*," *ReadingEagle.com*, March 5, 2009, accessed March 20, 2015, http://www2.readingeagle.com/article.aspx?id=128430.

41. Tiffany Vogt, "From *Castle* to *Bones*: Is the *Moonlighting* Curse Still Relevant Today?" *TheTVAddict.com*, April 10, 2012, accessed March 20, 2015, http://www.thetvaddict.com/2012/04/10/from-castle-to-bones-is-the-moonlighting-curse-still-relevant-today/.

42. Jason Mittell, "Narrative Complexity in Contemporary American Television," *The Velvet Light Trap* 58 (2006): 29–40.

43. *The Mentalist*, "Ladies in Red," episode no. 4, Season 1, first broadcast October 21, 2008, by CBS, directed by Chris Long and written by Gary Glasberg.

44. *Castle*, "Always Buy Retail," episode no. 6, Season 1, first broadcast April 13, 2009, by ABC, directed by Jamie Babbit and written by Gabrielle Stanton and Harry Werksman.

45. *Castle*, "Always Buy Retail."

46. *Castle*, "Eye of the Beholder," episode no. 5, Season 4, first broadcast October 17, 2011, by ABC, directed by John Terlesky and written by Shalisha Francis.

47. *Fringe*, "Northwest Passage," episode no. 21, Season 2, first broadcast May 6, 2010, by Fox, directed by Joe Chappelle and written by Ashley Edward Miller, Zack Stentz, Nora Zuckerman, and Lilla Zuckerman.

48. Cohn, *"Bones'* Booth Gets His Sexy On."
49. *Castle*, "Knockout," episode no. 24, Season 3, first broadcast May 16, 2011, by ABC, directed by Rob Bowman and written by Will Beall.
50. *Bones*, "The Man in the Outhouse," episode no. 3, Season 4, first broadcast September 17, 2008, by Fox, directed by Steven DePaul and written by Carla Kettner and Mark Lisson.
51. *Bones*, "The Man in the Outhouse."
52. *Bones*, "The Man in the Outhouse."

BIBLIOGRAPHY

Badley, Linda. "Scully Hits the Glass Ceiling: Postmodernism, Postfeminism, Posthumanism and *The X-Files*." In *Fantasy Girls: Gender in the New Universe of Science Fiction and Fantasy Television*, ed. E. Helford. Lanham: Rowman & Littlefield Publishers, 2000. 61–90.

Bianco, Robert. "The Stars Flesh Out *Bones*." *USA Today,* September 13, 2005. Accessed January 22, 2013, http://usatoday30.usatoday.com/life/television/reviews/2005–09-12-bones_x.htm.

Bibel, Sara. "Complete List of 2012–13 Season TV Show Viewership: *Sunday Night Football* Tops, Followed by *NCIS*, *The Big Bang Theory* & *NCIS: Los Angeles*." *TV by the Numbers*, May 29, 2013, Accessed March 20, 2015, http://tvbythenumbers.zap2it.com/2013/05/29/complete-list-of-2012–13-season-tv-show-viewership-sunday-night-football-tops-followed-by-ncis-the-big-bang-theory-ncis-los-angeles/184781/.

Bones. "The Man from the Fallout Shelter." Episode no. 9, Season 1. Directed by Greg Yaitanes. Written by Hart Hanson. 20th Century Fox. Original broadcast December 13, 2005.

Bones. "The Man in the Outhouse." Episode no. 3, Season 4. Directed by Steven DePaul. Written by Carla Kettner and Mark Lisson. 20th Century Fox. Original broadcast September 17, 2008.

Bones. "The Warrior in the Wuss." Episode no. 10, Season 7. Directed by Chad Lowe. Written by Dean Lopata and Michael Peterson. 20th Century Fox. Original broadcast April 23, 2012.

Butler, Judith. *Gender Trouble: Feminism and the Subversion of Identity*. New York, NY: Routledge, 1990.

Castle. "Always Buy Retail." Episode no. 6, Season 1. Directed by Jamie Babbit. Written by Gabrielle Stanton and Harry Werksman. ABC. Original broadcast April 13, 2009.

Castle. "Eye of the Beholder." Episode no. 5, Season 4. Directed by John Terlesky. Written by Shalisha Francis. ABC. Original broadcast October 17, 2011.

Castle. "Knockout." Episode no. 24, Season 3. Directed by Rob Bowman. Written by Will Beall. ABC. Original broadcast May 16, 2011.

Castle. "Nanny McDead." Episode no. 2, Season 1. Directed by John Terlesky. Written by Barry Schindel. ABC. Original broadcast March 16, 2009.

Cohn, Angel. "*Bones'* Booth gets his Sexy On." *TV Guide*, August 30, 2006. Accessed February 15, 2015, http://www.tvguide.com/news/Bones-booth-gets-37492.aspx.

Crook, John. "Fillion's Bad Boy Charm Makes Him King of ABC's *Castle*." *ReadingEagle.com*, March 5, 2009. Accessed March 20, 2015. http://www2.readingeagle.com/article.aspx?id=128430.

D'Acci, Julie. *Defining Women: Television and the Case of* Cagney & Lacey. Chapel Hill, NC: The University of North Carolina Press, 1994.

Dow, Bonnie. "Conversation and Commentary: The Traffic in Men and the *Fatal Attraction* of Postfeminist Masculinity." *Women's Studies in Communication* 29 (2006): 113–131.

Dow, Bonnie. "*Ellen*, Television, and the Politics of Gay and Lesbian Visibility." *Critical Studies in Media Communication* 18 (2001): 123–140.

Dow, Bonnie. *Prime-Time Feminism: Television, Media Culture, and the Women's Movement Since 1970*. Philadelphia: University of Pennsylvania Press, 1996.

Dworkin, Shari and Faye Linda Wachs. "'Getting Your Body Back': Postindustrial Fit Motherhood in *Shape Fit Pregnancy* magazine." *Gender and Society* 18 (2004): 610–624.

Economic News Release: American Time Use Survey Summary." United States Department of Labor. Last modified June 18, 2014. http://www.bls.gov/news.release/atus.nr0.htm.

Elfman, Doug. "*Bones* Star is One Strange Agent." *Chicago Sun-Times*, September 13, 2005. Accessed February 28, 2013. http://infoweb.newsbank.com.ezaccess.libraries.psu.edu/iwsearch/we/InfoWeb?p_product=AWNB&p_theme=aggregated5&p_action=doc&p_docid=10D32AD92AEB1750&p_docnum=3&p_queryname=8.

Faludi, Susan. *Backlash: The Undeclared War Against American Women*. New York: Anchor Books Doubleday, 1991.

Fringe. "August." Episode no. 8, Season 2. Directed by Dennis Smith. Written by J.H. Whyman and Jeff Pinkner. 20th Century Fox. Original broadcast November 19, 2009.

Fringe. "Northwest Passage." Episode no. 21, Season 2. Directed by Joe Chappelle. Written by Ashley Edward Miller, Zack Stentz, Nora Zuckerman, and Lilla Zuckerman. 20th Century Fox. Original broadcast May 6, 2010. 20th

Gorman, Bill. "2010–11 Season Broadcast primetime Show Viewership Averages." *TV By the Numbers*, June 1, 2011. Accessed March 20, 2015. http://tvbythenumbers.zap2it.com/2011/06/01/2010–11-season-broadcast-primetime-show-viewership-averages/94407/

Gorman, Bill. "Complete List of 2011–12 Season TV Show Viewership: *Sunday Night Football* Tops, Followed by *American Idol, NCIS & Dancing with the Stars*." *TV by the Numbers*, May 24, 2012. Accessed March 20, 2015. http://tvbythenumbers.zap2it.com/2012/05/24/complete-list-of-2011–12-season-tv-show-viewership-sunday-night-football-tops-followed-by-american-idol-ncis-dancing-with-the-stars/135785/.

Hinckley, David. "Tweaks could make *Castle* Rock-Solid." *Daily News*, March 8, 2009. Accessed February 15, 2015. http://www.nydailynews.com/entertainment/tv-movies/tweaks-castle-rock-solid-article-1.369213.

Inciardi, James and Juliet Dee. "From the Keystone Cops to *Miami Vice* Images of Policing in American Popular Culture." *Journal of Popular Culture* 21 (1987): 84–102.

Kinon, Cristina. "J.J. Abrams illuminates Dark Science with *Fringe*." *Daily News*, September 7, 2008. Accessed March 20, 2015. http://articles.nydailynews.com/2008–09-08/entertainment/17905842_1_abrams-anna-torv-Fringe

Laurence, Robert. "Fox Throws *Bones* onto that Heaping Pile of *CSI* Imitators." *San Diego Union-Tribune*, September 13, 2005. Accessed March 20, 2015. http://www.utsandiego.com/uniontrib/20050913/news_lz1c13remote.html.

Lowry, Brian. "*Bones*: TV Review." *Variety*, September 13, 2005. Accessed March 20, 2015. http://www.variety.com/review/VE1117928109/

McNamara, Mary. "*Castle*." *Los Angeles Times*, March 9, 2009. Accessed March 20, 2015. http://www.latimes.com/entertainment/tv/la-et-castle9–2009mar09-story.html.

McRobbie, Angela. *The Aftermath of Feminism: Gender, Culture and Social Change.* Los Angeles, CA: Sage Publications, 2009.

The Mentalist. "Red Alert." Episode no. 13, Season 3. Directed by Guy Ferland. Written by Jordan Harper. CBS. Original broadcast February 3, 2011.

The Mentalist. "Ladies in Red." Episode no. 4, Season 1. Directed by Chris Long. Written by Gary Glasberg. CBS. Original broadcast October 21, 2008.

The Mentalist. "Devil's Cherry." Episode no. 2, Season 5. Directed by Randy Zisk. Written by Daniel Cerone. CBS. Original broadcast October 7, 2012.

The Mentalist. "The Thin Red Line." Episode no. 8, Season 1. Directed by Matt Earl Beesley. Written by Ken Woodruff. CBS. Original broadcast November 25, 2008.

Mitchell, Sean. "Ex-Vampire Turns into Regular Guy." *The New York Times*, December 27, 2006. Accessed February 15, 2015. http://www.nytimes.com/2006/12/27/arts/television/27bore.html.

Mittell, Jason. "Narrative Complexity in Contemporary American Television." *The Velvet Light Trap* 58 (2006): 29–40.

Newcomb, Horace and Paul Hirsch. "Television as a Cultural Forum: Implications for Research." *Quarterly Review of Film Studies* 8. Issue 3. (1983): 45–55.

Ng, Philiana. "*Castle* Creator Talks Season 4, Future of the Castle-Beckett Relationship and the New Captain (Q&A)." *Hollywood Reporter*, September 19, 2011. Accessed March 20, 2015. http://www.hollywoodreporter.com/live-feed/Castle-creator-talks-season-4–237181.

Nicholas, Peter. "Schwarzenegger Deems Opponents 'Girlie-Men'—Twice." *Los Angeles Times*, July 18, 2004. Accessed March 20, 2015. http://www.sfgate.com/cgi-bin/article.cgi?file=/chronicle/archive/2004/07/18/MNGH57NKAF1.DTL.

Owen, Rob. "TV Preview: Ex-*Guardian* Baker Lightens Up as *The Mentalist*." *Post-Gazette*, September 23, 2008. Accessed February 28, 2013. http://www.post-gazette.com/pg008267/914216–42.stm

Petersen, Alan. *Unmasking the Masculine: "Men" and "Identity" in a Skeptical Age.* London: Sage Publications, 1998.

"Ranking Report: 2008." ABC MediaNet. http://www.abcmedianet.com/web/dnr/dispDNR.aspx?id=052008_06

"Ranking Report: 2009." ABC MediaNet. http://abcmedianet.com/web/dnr/disp-DNR.aspx?id=060209_05

Robinson, Amy. "The Idiot Box: *Castle* Just Another Ho-Hum Crime Procedural." *Charleston Gazette*, March 12, 2009. Accessed March 20, 2015. http://www.highbeam.com/doc/1P2-19984730.html.

Scharrer, Erica. "Tough Guys: The Portrayal of Hypermasculinity and Aggression in Televised Police Dramas." *Journal of Broadcasting & Electronic Media* 45 (2001): 615-634.

Sloop, John. *Disciplining Gender: Rhetorics of Sex Identity in Contemporary U.S. Culture.* Amherst, MA: University of Massachusetts, 2004.

Stanhope, Kate. "*Bones* Renewed for Tenth Season, Reclaims Monday Timeslot in March." *TV Guide.com*, January 29, 2014. Accessed March 20, 2015. http://www.tvguide.com/news/bones-renewed-season10-1076961.aspx.

Swenson, Rebecca. "Domestic Divo? Televised Treatment of Masculinity, Femininity and Food." *Critical Studies in Media Communication* 26 (2009): 36-53.

Vavrus, Mary. "Domesticating Patriarchy: Hegemonic Masculinity and Television's 'Mr. Mom.'" *Critical Studies in Media Communication* 19. Issue 3. (2002): 352-375.

Vint, Sherryl. "The New Backlash: Popular Culture's "Marriage" with Feminism, Or Love Is All You Need." *Journal of Popular Film and Television* 34. Issue 3. (2007): 160-169.

Vogt, Tiffany. "From *Castle* to *Bones*: Is the *Moonlighting* Curse Still Relevant Today?" *TheTVAddict.com*, April 10, 2012. Accessed March 20, 2015. http://www.thetvaddict.com/2012/04/10/from-castle-to-bones-is-the-moonlighting-curse-still-relevant-today/.

Walters, Dan. "Schwarzenegger's Budget Vows Hit Immovable Political Wall." *Sacramento Bee*, July 20, 2004. Accessed March 20, 2015. http://www.calstate.edu/pa/clips2004/july/20july/wall.shtml.

Willow, Molly. "Pair Sure to Heat Up Morgue." *Columbus Dispatch*, September 13, 2005. Accessed January 22, 2013. http://infoweb.newsbank.com.ezaccess.libraries.psu.edu/iwsearch/we/InfoWeb?p_product=AWNB&p_theme=aggregated5&p_action=doc&p_docid=10C9BF4BF6630CC8&p_docnum=5&p_queryname=9.

Chapter 7

Magazine Depictions of Fathers' Involvement in Children's Health

A Content Analysis

Justin J. Hendricks, Heidi Steinour, William Marsiglio, and Deepika Kulkarni

Fatherhood scholarship has begun to pay more attention to how fathers nurture their children and negotiate co-parenting, a shift away from predominantly focusing on men's financial contributions.[1] Indeed, scholars have increasingly championed efforts to promote fathers' involvement in family life and to make sure that family policies recognize the importance of men's positive involvement in their children's lives.[2] One aspect of this shift has been exploring depictions of fatherhood in popular culture and everyday life. These studies reveal cultural narratives about how men presumably interact with their own children and are situated within their communities. Researchers have studied fatherhood representations in diverse ways, including studies of: comic strips,[3] parenting magazines,[4] newspapers,[5] television commercials,[6] and how public portrayals of fathers have changed over time.[7] The cultural backdrop for these studies includes changing ideas about gender, especially what parenting means for men and women.[8] Studies of parenting magazines and parenting sections of newspapers suggest that these sources help define the discourses that shape how men experience fatherhood.[9] Although these analyses have generated valuable insights about public perceptions and media depictions of fathering in recent eras, they do not advance understandings of how men are portrayed in more specific contexts, including areas typically associated with women (e.g., child health or education). Research on children's health suggests that men are becoming more involved, but we suspect that these changes may not be represented in popular media portrayals. As a result, the purpose of this study is to explore media portrayals of fathers compared to mothers in parenting and health-related magazines, with an eye toward assessing images of fathers within the context of child health and human development. We focus on the extent to which men compared to women are portrayed as being attentive to their children's health as well as the ways parenting and health magazines frame images of fathers when they are portrayed.

FATHERS AND CHILDREN'S HEALTH

Much of the research discussing father involvement in children's health focuses on whether or not the father lives with his children and his relationship with the mother. Some individual studies, both in the early 90s and more recently, have suggested that children living with biological fathers fare the best in terms of health and well-being.[10] However, there is some disagreement about whether or not this positive benefit is based on where the father resides or the father's level of engagement.[11] Indeed, a later review of longitudinal research concluded that father engagement, regardless of living arrangements, predicts the best health and development outcomes.[12] Thus, it is reasonable to conclude that engaged fathers are likely to have healthier children, and fathers living at home may be less likely to have barriers preventing them from being actively involved with their children.

Still, while research indicates that fathers can improve their children's health the mechanisms associated with this benefit are unclear and most studies suggest a gender normative view of father involvement. For example, in a study of families with children who have a long-term illness or medical condition, mothers were more concerned with establishing relationships with professionals and being attentive to current clinical issues such as managing appointments and transporting the child while fathers were more focused on their children's long-term outcomes and acting as protectors.[13] This notion of "father as protector" is a common idea in health research.[14] This literature suggests that men acting as protectors can help children explore risk-taking opportunities and grow personally within a safe environment, which allows them to make their own decisions.[15] Brussoni and Olsen use the dimensions of risk engagement and protection to develop a fourfold typology for fathers' actions: heightened protector (low risk engagement, high protection), prepared adventurer (high risk engagement, high protection), less involved (low risk engagement, low protection), and inconsistent (high risk engagement, low protection).[16]

Aside from protecting their children, we contend that fathers are capable of supporting their children's health and development in other ways. For example, they can manage and schedule doctor and dental appointments, plan and cook healthy meals, purchase cognitive development materials, encourage healthy emotional expression, and so on. Quirke suggests that according to popular parenting magazines, parenting has become a more deliberate task with a greater focus on healthy child development as compared to fun and play.[17] In this climate we might expect that media representations of fathers would also be focused on the health and development of children. However, there is some doubt as to whether or not this has occurred.[18] As a result, part of our purpose is to determine if fathers in popular health and parenting magazines are being depicted as deliberate agents engaged in their children's health and development or if they continue to be portrayed as playmates.

FATHERHOOD IN MEDIA

Many studies of fathers in popular media suggest significant changes over time.[19] Scholars first began to notice these shifts in the 80s when media began to leave behind the distant, traditional fathers that were popular in the 50s and 60s in exchange for the fathers who were more commonly seen in the home and involved in sports/play.[20] However, while these early studies found that the number of father depictions were increasing, including depictions of single and stay-at-home fathers and fathers spending one-on-one time with children,[21] women still remained the parent associated with childcare and household activities.[22]

More recent articles continue to suggest that while men are more frequently portrayed in family matters, these portrayals still situate fathers as less involved than mothers, and differ by type of media.[23] For instance, while a few recent television programs have begun to depict men as stay-at-home dads or primary caregivers,[24] television commercials tend to feature fathers and children involved in sports and outdoor play.[25] Additionally, analyses of parenting magazines have found that articles and images directed at mothers far outweigh those targeting fathers;[26] although discussions of fathers have increased over the past century.[27] Magazine portrayals often show fathers as engaged in sports or active play while mothers are seen as taking care of the house and other child-related activities.

These studies contribute to Sunderland's argument that parenting texts perpetuate a part-time father and full-time mother discourse.[28] She discusses how this discourse positions mothers as the primary care providers and fathers as the "mother's helper." Media's reliance on this discourse tends to normalize childcare, cooking, cleaning, and household maintenance as the mother's responsibility. As a result, Sunderland argues, these texts exclude fathers from childcare responsibilities and give men the impression that being involved in their children's lives is not essential to their children's healthy development. Wall & Arnold also note that depictions of fathers in a parenting column of a newspaper position men as passive parents, rather than active fathers with a great deal of influence in their children's lives.[29]

The tendency for media to frame men as uninvolved fathers undermines the importance of men's roles as fathers and the importance of fathering on childhood development. Many academics have argued that the quality of time men spend with their children can increase father involvement and is positively associated with children's educational outcomes, emotional development, social competence, and cognitive development.[30] Research suggests that children develop autonomy, independence, and the confidence to take risks when fathers are actively and positively involved in their lives.[31] As such, we argue that media representations of fathers as mother's helpers, child entertainers, or uninvolved parents are not productive in encouraging men to become more directly involved in their children's lives. Therefore, we move the field forward by examining how fathers are depicted and what contributions they can make in child health contexts.

CULTIVATION THEORY AND CONSTRAINED CHOICES

Theories of media and behavior suggest that media influences behavior. The cultural indicators project of the mid-to late twentieth century found evidence that media, specifically television, influenced viewers because those who watch more television are more likely to view the world in the way that television portrays it.[32] This resulted in the idea of *cultivation*—media consumers use media to cultivate a perceived and lived reality. Reviewing several decades' worth of research, Gerbner and colleagues find a great deal of support for this idea.[33] Although this line of research focuses primarily on TV, other media sources could provide a similar effect. In light of recent research, we assume that magazines, especially parenting and health magazines, can alter or at least reinforce how individuals construct their orientation toward parenting and health.[34]

Cultivation theory asserts that limited portrayals of behavior restrict individuals' opportunities to see themselves performing certain tasks or engaging in certain behaviors. Consequently, we assume that fewer media representations of fathers may result in a limited number of perceived options for paternal behavior.[35] Similarly, Bird and Rieker suggest that a father's commitment to managing his child's health is constrained by a gendered landscape that influences how a typical father and mother raise their child and orient themselves toward their child's health.[36] Media can work to reinforce a father's behavior by depicting and reinforcing popular gender and parenting discourses. At the same time popular media stands uniquely poised to offer new alternatives and discourses by representing men as nurturing, involved, and active agents in their children's health and development.

Our study explores how fathers and mothers are specifically portrayed in children's physical, social/behavioral, and cognitive health and development. Additionally, we examine how depictions of fathers differ from those referencing mothers. Informed by previous scholarship in the health and media literatures, we pose several research questions:

How often are fathers portrayed in our sample of four magazines compared to mothers?

Are some magazines more likely than others to portray fathers?

How do portrayals differ by health/development domain or context?

Considering the previous literature we expect that fathers will be portrayed less often than mothers in areas concerning children's health across all magazines. We also expect that most portrayals of fathers will be traditionally gendered. In other words, dads will be portrayed as playing with children, providing financial assistance for them, or protecting them. Thus we anticipate fathers to be more likely to appear in physical health settings, such as sports, play, and safety. Finally, we expect that advertisements will depict mothers more often rather than fathers because research suggests that women are more likely to purchase items for their children and homes.[37]

Method

In order to determine how fathers are depicted relative to their children's health and development, we reviewed a year's worth of text and images from issues of *Runner's World*, *Parents*, *Men's Health*, and *Shape* starting with May 2014 and working backward. A total of 44 issues were analyzed. Most of the magazines were comparable in size with approximately 190 pages per issue, however, *Runner's World* had a significantly lower mean number of pages per issue with 126. These magazines were chosen for their ability to facilitate strategic comparisons based on male and female readership and attention to health-related matters. Table 7.1 details the readership of the four magazines. According to Mediamark Research & Intelligence as of spring 2014 men make up 83% of *Men's Health* readers, 15% of *Parents*, 49% of *Runner's World*, and 11% of *Shape*. Considering the readership of the magazines and assuming that advertisers, authors, and editors will tailor their content to their readers we would expect *Men's Health* to target men, *Shape* to target women, *Parents* to target women, and *Runner's World* to appeal to men and women. This sample gives us the ability to see how fathers are portrayed in magazines that are likely to be gendered in different ways.

We base our analysis on the World Health Organization's (WHO) definition of health: "a state of complete physical, mental and social well-being

Table 7.1   Magazine Readership

	Total Readership	Men	Women	Percent Men
Men's Health	13,187,000	10,954,000	2,232,000	83.0%
Parents	13,411,000	2,019,000	11,392,000	15.0%
Runner's World	3,128,000	1,536,000	1,592,000	49.1%
Shape	5,783,000	645,000	5,139,000	11.2%

and not merely the absence of disease or infirmity."[38] Our approach to health also includes child development. Any article or advertisement that directly or indirectly referenced children's health was coded for analysis. For example, we include advertisements for packaged food, articles on child brain development, and discussions about children's emotional responses during a tragedy. Therefore, we chose to focus solely on cases that addressed all aspects of children's health (physical, social, and behavioral), while taking note of where and how mothers, fathers, and parents were present in each context.

CODING AND ANALYSIS

For coding purposes, units of analysis were specified as one individual text or image relating to children's health that was at least one-fourth of a page in length or size. This allowed for a comprehensive analysis of all cases with a focus on the gendered nature of health and parenting. In total we analyzed 737 individual cases (646 referencing both parents, or mothers or fathers independent of each other; and 91 with only children being portrayed). We derived our coding method from the content analysis method described by.[39] After consulting literature and reviewing prior issues of the magazines we developed a codebook that detailed coding steps for our analysis. Additionally, we conducted a qualitative analysis of all of the images where fathers were explicitly and implicitly mentioned. We treat this section of the project as a kind of extreme case analysis.[40] The results of this analysis suggest how men are being portrayed across these magazines in relation to children's health.

PARENT PORTRAYAL

Our dependent variable *Parent Portrayal* documented any advertisement, image, or article that referenced children's health. This variable was initially coded using six categories depending on which parent was present in each case. This gave us a coding scheme of no parents, explicitly mothers, implicitly mothers, both parents, implicitly fathers, explicitly fathers. Portrayals were coded as explicit when a textual reference was made to mothers or fathers, for example, "Choosy Moms choose Jiff." References were coded as implicit if images of mothers or fathers were present or in a few select cases where the text indirectly referred to mothers or fathers. After data collection and coding we realized that separate categories for "no parents" and "both parents" would be better represented as a gender neutral posturing by content producers. As a result, we collapsed these two variables into a "neutral" category that was used to represent cases where implicit or explicit gendered depictions of parents were not present.

HEALTH

Independent variables included health divided into categories, codes, and sub-codes; type of content (either advertisement or article); and magazine type (*Men's Health*, *Women's Health*, etc.). *Health* was defined as a reference to any dimension of children's health or development, using the WHO definition referenced above. We divided health into three main categories, each of which was comprised of codes and these codes were comprised of sub-codes. *Physical Health* was defined as cases that involved physical development or movement, physical impairments, diseases, and cardiovascular or other related activities. Physical health also included physical nutrition such as food, drinks, vitamins, and baby formula. *Cognitive Health* focused on the mind and associated mental functions, different forms of mental illness/prevention such as ADHD, cognitive and development, academic development, games, and reading books. *Social/Behavioral Health* examined behavioral health issues, social interaction, group work, social isolation, and pretend play.

Our list of sub-codes included 35 different health-related products or topics. The categories for sub-codes included safety (car, outdoor, sleep, toys), food (products, items, cooking, drinks, vitamins), medicines (first aid, hygiene, supplements, allergies), and play (running, walking, sports, equipment, playgrounds). We also coded references to mental games (books, reading, learning games, flashcards); behavioral disorders such as autism, ADHD, and learning disorders; and discipline-related content such as rebellion, tantrums, and bullying. In the case that multiple codes applied we coded at the next level up leaving out the more specific code, which resulted in a general health category for cases that described more than one health category in a given case.

Results

In total 737 cases were coded. Of these cases, 453 were advertisements and 281 were articles. Advertisements ranged from a quarter page to six pages

Table 7.2   Parent Portrayal

	Frequency	Percent	Valid Percent	Cumulative Percent
Kids Only	442	60.0	60.0	60.0
Explicitly Mothers	85	11.5	11.5	71.5
Implicitly Mothers	101	13.7	13.7	85.2
Both Parents	83	11.3	11.3	96.5
Implicitly Fathers	18	2.4	2.4	98.9
Explicitly Fathers	8	1.1	1.1	100.0
Total	737	100.0	100.0	

with an average of 1.13 pages and a standard deviation of .61 while articles ranged from a quarter to about eight pages with a mean of 1.32 and a standard deviation of 1.59. The distribution of cases by magazine were as follows: *Parents* magazine had the most cases referencing children's health (677); *Shape* had the next largest number (26); *Men's Health* (18); and *Runner's World* (16). Table 7.2 shows the differences in parent portrayals.

Mothers were represented in 186 of the health cases, while fathers were referenced in 26 instances, and 525 cases are considered neutral. Further breakdown of these categories reveals that 85 of the cases containing mothers were explicitly focused on mothers and 101 implicitly focused on mothers. This is in sharp contrast to depictions of fathers who are only explicitly referenced 8 times and implicitly referenced 18 times. We found that overall references to health were primarily focused on physical health (580 cases): 14 cases dealt with general health, 80 cases described social/behavioral issues, 63 portrayed cognitive health.

Tables 7.3 and 7.4 provides cross-tabulations showing parenting portrayals by magazine and health. Table 7.3 indicates that *Men's Health* and *Parents* magazine are the most likely places where depictions of fathers can be found.

Men's Health contains 18 cases of child health and development, 13 of which reference fathers, five of which are explicit. Mothers are not represented other than in neutral cases. *Parents* contains 677 total cases with nine references to fathers, two of which are explicit. In contrast mothers appear 174 times with 82 explicit references, and 494 neutral cases. *Runner's World* contains one reference to fathers and *Shape* contains three.

Tables 7.4 highlights the differences in parent portrayals by health context. While mothers are portrayed much more than fathers in all health categories, both mothers and fathers are represented in physical health contexts more often than any other context.

Of the physical health cases, 19 reference fathers while mothers are represented 158 times. Further analysis by health code suggests that of the 19 incidents referencing fathers, nine are related to health care and five are related to feeding children, all of which are advertisements for prepackaged food, while

Table 7.3   Magazine Name * Portrayal Crosstabulation

Count

	Portrayal					
	Explicitly Mothers	Implicitly Mothers	Neutral	Implicitly Fathers	Explicitly Fathers	Total
Men's Health	0	0	5	8	5	18
Parents	82	92	494	7	2	677
Runner's World	0	3	12	0	1	16
Shape	3	6	14	3	0	26
Total	85	101	525	18	8	737

Table 7.4   Category * Portrayal Crosstabulation

Count

	Audience					
	Explicitly Mothers	Implicitly Mothers	Neutral	Implicitly Fathers	Explicitly Fathers	Total
Cognitive	1	5	54	0	3	63
General	1	2	10	0	1	14
Physical	77	81	403	17	2	580
Social/Behavioral	6	13	58	1	2	80
Total	85	101	525	18	8	737

three and two are related to safety and exercise respectively. Mothers are also well represented in physical health contexts and largely within health-care (42) and feeding (40) situations. Compared to fathers, however, mothers are more often represented in packaged food references (13) as well as infant feeding (17) an area in which fathers are not represented. While fathers are represented in general health-care cases (9) mothers are represented in more specific dental (11) and medicine (16) contexts. Mothers are also well represented in hygiene contexts (55), an area composed mainly of diaper and soap/shampoo advertisements, and one in which fathers are not represented. Both fathers and mothers are represented in additional specific health contexts, but there were so few cases as to make comparisons meaningless.

FRAMING OF FATHERS

Our qualitative analysis provides a more nuanced way to understand and explain how men are being portrayed within child health and development contexts and how these portrayals are framed. As noted above, we found that there are very few cases of father depictions in child health and development contexts (26). Overall, the main fathering discourse in these magazines situates men as entertainers, providers, and protectors. It is evident that mothers are present more often in health-related matters, specifically in *Parents* magazine. However, we find that a few select cases present fathers in ways that differ from narratives of the father as provider or entertainer.

Among the four magazines there are 14 visual images of fathers with children in a health-related context. Sunderland suggests that, "the paucity of visual representations of fathers may be less important than the visuals themselves."[41] Therefore, we analyzed the content of each visual to see how men are framed in fathering contexts across these representations. We found that images of fathers usually portray men in the background of advertisements for food products, stem cell/blood cord research, cell phones, and allergy medications. Almost all of these images directly depict fathers engaging in playful activities with their children. Fathers are shown playing with their children, chasing them, attending baseball games, and playing "dress-up" in their homes. These images tend to reinforce previous research that suggests magazines depict men in traditionally masculine roles that encourage outdoor play, sports, and physical protection.[42]

Among the four magazines, *Men's Health* has the most implicit and explicit references to fathers. Most of these references are framed in a stereotypically masculine way. For example, men are portrayed as protectors in articles that discuss their concern for child well-being and safety. Men are also characterized as financial providers in a few articles that discuss funding a child's college education. One article advises fathers on the variety of ways they can financially provide an environment that stimulates their child's intellectual development. Furthermore, there was an article discussing positive ways to handle fights on the playing field and another written by a father discussing his concern with the physical safety of his family. From these texts, we find that fathers, while active in some of the conversations, are still being framed within the dominant discourse of fathering that situate men as providers and protectors.

One of the more surprising findings was the limited number of explicit references to men as parents, especially involved, nurturing parents. Throughout the texts of these magazines there are only eight explicit portrayals of fathers whereas there are 84 explicit portrayals of mothers. Within these eight references there are a few instances where men are framed within a traditional, fathering context that places them as providers, protectors, and playmates in their child's lives. For instance, fathers are encouraged to stimulate active play or participate in outdoor sports with their children. There are also advertisements directly placing men in outdoor activities (such as biking) with their children.

In contrast to fathering portrayals, mothers are often represented in advertisements and images for medication, toothpastes, shampoos, diapers, formula, Tylenol, and baby wash. Additionally, many of these advertisements directly depict moms saying such as things as: "Mom's knows best" or "Hey Mom, you are the best!" This comparison shows that mothers are still framed as the main parents who attend to daily activities, physical health and hygiene, and the overall well-being of their children, whereas fathers are absent from these activities. Moreover, the direct mentioning of mothers (and not fathers) implies that mothers make most of the health-related decisions for their children. This may discourage men from taking an active role in health-related decisions on their child's behalf.

Although most of the representations of fathers rely on traditional stereotypes documented by previous research, we find a few representations of fathers actively monitoring their child's health. For example, an article in *Men's Health* discussed the role men can play helping their children develop appropriate social behavior. In this case fathers are encouraged to set an example for their children, one that promotes positive social interactions and communication skills. This article encourages men to consider their behavior and its effects on their child's behavioral activities. A second representation was found in *Parents* magazines in an article titled, "Rising to The Occasion." The article addresses long-term and short-term ways men can care for a child with disabilities, encourages fathers to seek out medical attention, research doctors, prioritize their schedules, and join a support group to help raise money and awareness for the condition their child is battling. These two representations are distinct from the traditional messages about fathering because they encourage men to become actively involved in their child's social, emotional, and physical health.

Notwithstanding a few portrayals of active father engagement most references to fathering contain elements of dominant discourses that position fathers as providers, entertainers, and part-time parents. These discourses are being drawn on repeatedly to position mothers and fathers in their respective stereotypical gendered parenting roles. Although we find that a majority of parenting references in these magazines are framed using the language "parents," research suggests that parents, often times, equates to mothers.[43] Therefore, we find that all four magazines do little to represent fathers in general, and are remiss in providing images and stories that might encourage fathers to maintain and actively promote their children's health.

DISCUSSION

The results indicate that men and women are portrayed in different, gendered ways when it comes to children's health representations in health and parenting magazines. In general the results support our hypotheses. Additionally, several findings from this study are consistent with previous research. First, women are more likely to be portrayed in children's health-related matters than men. Second, women are more likely to be framed as primary parents than men. Third, when men are represented, they are more likely to be engaged in sports, play, and outdoor activities as well as situated as financial providers and protectors of families. We also see a gendered difference in advertisements with women more often being depicted in advertisements for hygiene, first aid, diapering, and formula products.

While research has found that fathers can be effective in promoting children's health and well-being,[44] we contend that men may be constrained in how they are able to involve themselves in their children's health care.[45] Using Gerbner's cultivation theory we suggest that these constraints are partly a reflection of gendered media representations that perpetuate a narrow, gendered image of men's experiences with children's health issues.[46] We hypothesized from this that: fathers will be less often portrayed in health contexts than mothers, men are more likely to be portrayed in physical health contexts in (i.e., sports, play, safety), and advertisements are more likely to target mothers.

The data support our first hypothesis because compared to men, women are referenced roughly seven times more often in health-related instances (186 to 26). This finding is consistent with previous research on parenting magazines,[47] and other parenting texts.[48] The second hypothesis is also supported because mothers are included more often than fathers in the majority of the health-related advertisements. This finding is consistent with previous research on fathers and men in advertising.[49] The third hypothesis received partial support. Fathers are portrayed most often in physical health settings, but most of these cases (34.6%) are focused on general health care. Additionally, there are five depictions (19.2%) involving prepackaged food, three depictions (11.5%) involving safety, and two (7.7%) for exercise. The qualitative portion of our study revealed, however, that even in these cases men are being portrayed in ways that are not necessarily related to the product or article content. For example, fathers may be holding a child in the background or playing with a child in an advertisement for allergy medication. As such our findings are consistent with previous research indicating that fathers are typically depicted as the "part-time parent,"[50] or passive parent,[51] and that they are often portrayed as playmates or entertainers.[52]

LIMITATIONS

Our analyses cover a relatively short time span for the magazines. One year did not provide many cases for most of the magazines besides *Parents* thus our analysis techniques were constrained. Although we could have expanded the number of issues, we chose to look at the recent issues in greater depth to provide a snapshot for 2013–2014. The neutral category is also potentially problematic. We assume a category is neutral because of genderless pronouns, portrayals of both parents, and leaving parents out, but magazine readership is clearly gendered. As a result, even when using genderless pronouns or gender-neutral images, the content provider likely recognizes the makeup of his or her audience. However, if this were true it would only reinforce the idea that women are more likely to be targeted, especially in *Parents* magazine.

CONCLUSION

We contend that studying media content is an important aspect of fathering research as it provides an opportunity to bring to light the lack of portrayals or models available to fathers while also highlighting the portrayals that do exist. There are few cases of fathers operating outside of gendered norms, but most portray fathers as playing with their children. However, this should not be interpreted as particularly troublesome considering that fathers' play with their children is important for child health and development.[53] Ginsburg suggests that children have lost much of their exploration and free play time to overscheduling and structured activities.[54] Thus, fathers can make an important contribution by simply doing what is depicted in these magazines: playing with their children. Additionally, fathers could take the lead in freeing children's schedules so as to provide time for important free-play activities.

At the same time, mothers and fathers could both benefit from fathers operating in capacities outside of being an entertainer. If magazines portrayed fathers more frequently in nontraditional ways those messages might directly encourage fathers to become more involved in monitoring their children's health, especially in administrative functions such as scheduling appointments with doctors, keeping track of immunizations, and so on. More progressive media images of fathers might also indirectly affect fathers by generating co-parental support from mothers for an engaged, nurturing style of fathering. Additionally, magazines, at least the ones we reviewed, seemingly do not portray fathers in safety contexts in the way that is reported in the literature.[55,56] This is surprising because public discourses tend to project fathers as having an important protective role in families. In one case we did find a discussion about fathers getting involved in their children's long-term health conditions, encouraging fathers to become actively involved in all aspects of caring for their child's health including managing clinical matters, caring for the child, and learning about the ailment. This case reflects promising future possibilities in popular media. It also offers a counterexample to previous research indicating that fathers' attention to long-term health concerns is mainly focused on outcomes and the physical safety of their children.[57]

Future research could look further into passive and active displays of involvement in managing children's health, both with fathers and mothers. A historical analysis of depictions of fathers in health contexts could help document any changes over time. It may be that there were periods when fathers were focused on independent of mothers, but that they have since been replaced by depictions either involving both parents or neither parent. These neutral depictions may also warrant further study. In depictions involving both mothers and fathers, researchers could ask questions about the positioning of parents in images or the ways in which the text references each parent. It may be that neutral references are more gendered than may be initially expected.

Overall fathers can make a strong contribution to their children's health, but popular media does not adequately represent the various ways fathers can involve themselves. Magazines, especially men's magazines, are poised to represent fathers in more diverse ways, but their unwillingness to do so works against men cultivating more inclusive forms of masculinities that celebrate a broad range of acceptable behaviors.[58] Unfortunately, there have been few real incentives for magazines to include advertisements or other content that would portray fathers in more diverse ways. Gentry and Harrison suggest that advertisements in particular prevent social change in terms of limiting men's options and possibilities for greater active involvement in their children's lives by creating confusion between changing discourses and traditional media depictions.[59] However, there are potential ways that fathers could be engaged and portrayed in more active ways. For example, one interesting finding includes the several instances in which fathers are writing their own content that is addressed to other men/fathers. In these cases we see men actively engaging other men in conversations about child protection, overcoming disabilities, positive social behaviors, and the importance of exercise. These examples highlight the possibilities that may exist if more fathers are employed to write about active father engagement in health-related activities.

At the same time, we are also encouraged by exciting grass roots efforts like the Dad 2.0 Summit, a conference organizing online dads who want to transform public images of fatherhood and hold the commercial sector accountable for their stale advertising images of how fathers think and what they do with their children.[60] Bloggers have already shown their effectiveness in altering negative portrayals of dads in Huggies' diaper ads. If more progressive dads are successfully mobilized as a consumer block for children's products and services, media images of fathers in advertising and other venues may be altered to align more closely with the nurturing dad ethos. Ultimately, the challenge for stakeholders interested in child health and development, as well as those interested in promoting a more nurturing style of fathering, is to develop strategies to motivate and incentivize those who control the media to represent fathers in more progressive ways.

NOTES

1. William Marsiglio and Kevin Roy, *Nurturing Dads: Social Initiatives for Contemporary Fatherhood* (New York: Russell Sage Foundation, 2012).

2. Richard Warshak, "Social Science and Parenting Plans for Young Children: A Consensus Report," *Psychology, Public Policy, and Law* 20, no. 1 (2014): 46.

3. Ralph LaRossa, Charles Jaret, Malati Gadgil, and G. Robert Wynn, "The Changing Culture of Fatherhood in Comic-Strip Families: A Six-Decade Analysis," *Journal of Marriage and Family* 62, no. 2 (2000): 375–387.

4. Jane Sunderland, "'Parenting' or 'Mothering'? The Case of Modern Childcare Magazines," *Discourse and Society* 17, no. 4 (2006): 503–527.

5. Jane Sunderland, "Baby Entertainer, Bumbling Assistant and Line Manager: Discourses of Fatherhood in Parentcraft Texts," *Discourse and Society* 11, no. 2 (2000): 249–274.

6. Scott Coltrane and Kenneth Allan, "'New' Fathers and Old Stereotypes: Representations of Masculinity in 1980s Television Advertising," *Masculinities* 2, no. 4 (1994): 43–66; Gayle Kaufman, "The Portrayal of Men's Family Roles in Television Commercials," *Sex Roles* 41, no. 5–6 (1999): 439–458.

7. Maxine Atkinson and Stephen P. Blackwelder, "Fathering in the 20th Century," *Journal of Marriage and the Family* 55, no. 4 (1993): 975–986; Ralph LaRossa, *The Modernization of Fatherhood: A Social and Political History* (Chicago: University of Chicago Press, 1997); LaRossa et al., "The Changing Culture," 375–387.

8. Elizabeth Francis-Connolly, "Constructing Parenthood: Portrayals of Motherhood and Fatherhood in Popular American Magazines," *Journal of the Motherhood Initiative for Research and Community Involvement* 5, no. 1 (2003): 179–185.

9. Sunderland, "Baby Entertainer, Bumbling Assistant and Line Manager: Discourses of Fatherhood in Parentcraft Texts," 249–274; Sunderland, "'Parenting' or 'Mothering'?," 503–527.

10. Deborah Dawson, "Family Structure and Children's Health and Well-being: Data from the 1988 National Health Interview Survey on Child Health," *Journal of Marriage and the Family* 53, no. 3 (1991): 573–584; Kathleen Ziol-Guest and Rachel E. Dunifon, "Complex Living Arrangements and Child Health: Examining Family Structure Linkages with Children's Health Outcomes," *Family Relations* 63, no. 3 (2014): 424–437.

11. Paul Amato and Joan G. Gilbreth, "Nonresident Fathers and Children's Well-being: A Meta-analysis," *Journal of Marriage and the Family* 61, no. 3 (1999): 557–573.

12. Anna Sarkadi, Robert Kristiansson, Frank Oberklaid, and Sven Bremberg, "Fathers' Involvement and Children's Developmental Outcomes: A Systematic Review of Longitudinal Studies," *Acta Paediatrica* 97, no. 2 (2008): 153–158.

13. Veronica Swallow, Heather Lambert, Sheila Santacroce, and Ann Macfadyen, "Fathers and Mothers Developing Skills in Managing Children's Long-term Medical Conditions: How do their Qualitative Accounts Compare?," *Child: Care, Health and Development* 37, no. 4 (2011): 512–523.

14. Vincent Arockiasamy, Liisa Holsti, and Susan Albersheim, "Fathers' Experiences in the Neonatal Intensive Care Unit: A Search for Control," *Pediatrics* 121, no. 2 (2008): 215–222; Dubowitz, Howard, "Fathers' Role in Protecting Children," *Journal of Developmental & Behavioral Pediatrics* 32, no. 7 (2011): 546–547.

15. Ibid., 546–547.

16. Mariana Brussoni and Lise Olsen, "Striking a Balance between Risk and Protection: Fathers' Attitudes and Practices toward Child Injury Prevention," *Journal of Developmental & Behavioral Pediatrics* 32, no. 7 (2011): 491–498.

17. Linda Quirke, "'Keeping Young Minds Sharp'": Children's Cognitive Stimulation and the Rise of Parenting Magazines, 1959–2003," *Canadian Review of Sociology/Revue Canadienne de Sociologie* 43, no. 4 (2006): 387–406.

18. William Marsiglio, "Healthy Dads, Healthy Kids," *Contexts* 8, no. 4 (2009): 22–27.

19. Daniel Bretl and Joanne Cantor, "The Portrayal of Men and Women in US Television Commercials: A Recent Content Analysis and Trends over 15 Years," *Sex Roles* 18, no. 9–10 (1988): 595–609; LaRossa, *The Modernization of Fatherhood*; LaRossa et al., *Journal of Marriage and Family*, 375–387; Melissa Milkie and Kathleen E. Denny, "Changes in the Cultural Model of Father Involvement Descriptions of Benefits to Fathers, Children, and Mothers in Parents' Magazine, 1926–2006," *Journal of Family Issues* 35, no. 2 (2014): 223–253.

20. Bretl and Cantor, "The Portrayal of Men and Women," 595–609; Coltrane and Allan, "'New' Fathers and Old Stereotypes," 43–66.

21. Janice Drakich, "In Search of the Better Parent: The Social Construction of Ideologies of Fatherhood," *Canadian Journal of Women and the Law* 3 (1989): 69.

22. Coltrane and Allan, "'New' Fathers and Old Stereotypes," 43–66.

23. Atkinson and Blackwelder, *Journal of Marriage and the Family*, 975–986; Francis-Connolly, "Constructing Parenthood", 179–185; Glenda Wall and Stephanie Arnold, "How Involved is Involved Fathering?: An Exploration of the Contemporary Culture of Fatherhood," *Gender & Society* 21 (2007): 508–527; Kaufman, "The Portrayal of Men's Family Roles," 439–458; Sunderland, "Baby Entertainer, Bumbling Assistant and Line Manager: Discourses of Fatherhood in Parentcraft Texts," 249–274; Sunderland, "'Parenting' or 'Mothering'? The Case of Modern Childcare Magazines," 503–527; Melissa Martinson, Amanda Hinnant, and Barbara E. Martinson, "Visual Depictions of Gender in Parenting Magazines," *Media Report to Women* 36, no. 4 (2008): 12–20.

24. Jenna Goudreau, "Changing Roles of TV Fathers," *Today*, Last modified June 24, 2010, http://today.msnbc.msn.com/id/37758834/ns/today-entertainment/t/changing-roles-tv-fathers/.

25. Kaufman, "The Portrayal of Men's Family Roles," 439–458; Wan-Hsiu Tsai and Moses Shumow, "Representing Fatherhood and Male Domesticity in American Advertising," *Interdisciplinary Journal of Research in Business* 1, no. 8 (2011): 38–48.

26. Francis-Connolly, "Constructing Parenthood," 179–185.

27. Milkie and Denny, "Changes in the Cultural Model of Father Involvement," 223–253.

28. Sunderland, "Baby Entertainer, Bumbling Assistant," 249–274.

29. Wall and Arnold, "How Involved is Involved Fathering?," 508–527.

30. Michael Lamb, "Fathers and Child Development: An Introductory Overview and Guide," in *The Role of the Father in Child Development*, ed. Michael Lamb (New York: Wiley, 1997) 1–18; Ross Parke, *Fatherhood* (Cambridge, MA: Harvard University Press, 1996); Natasha Cabrera, Catherine S. Tamis-LeMonda, Robert H. Bradley, Sandra Hofferth, and Michael E. Lamb, "Fatherhood in the Twenty-first Century," *Child Development* 71, no. 1 (2000): 127–136; Amato and Gilbreth, "Nonresident Fathers and Children's Well-being," 557–573.

31. Brussoni and Olsen, "Striking a Balance," 491–498; Dubowitz, "Fathers' Role in Protecting Children," 546–547.

32. George Gerbner, "Cultivation Analysis: An Overview," *Mass Communication and Society* 1, no. 3–4 (1998): 175–194; George Gerbner, Larry Gross, Michael Morgan, Nancy Signorielli, and James Shanahan, "Growing Up with Television: Cultivation Processes," *Media Effects: Advances in Theory and Research* 2 (2002): 43–67.

33. Gerbner et al., "Growing Up With Television," 43–67.

34. Salvatore Giorgianni and Jennifer Cooper, "Comparison of Print Media Health Advertising to Men and Boys Compared to Women and Girls," Presentation at the annual meeting of the American Public Health Association, San Francisco, CA, October 30, 2012; Quirke, "Keeping Young Minds Sharp," 387–406.

35. Gerbner et al., "Growing Up With Television", 43–67.

36. Chloe Bird and Patricia Rieker, *Gender and Health: The Effects of Constrained Choices and Social Policies* (Cambridge, UK: Cambridge University Press, 2008).

37. "Women Call the Shots at Home: Public Mixed on Gender Roles in Jobs," *Pew Research Center*, Last modified September 25, 2008. http://www.pewsocialtrends.org/2008/09/25/women-call-the-shots-at-home-public-mixed-on-gender-roles-in-jobs/.

38. "Preamble to the Constitution of the World Health Organization as adopted by the International Health Conference," *Official Records of the World Health Organization* 2 (1946): 100.

39. Klaus Krippendorff, *Content Analysis: An Introduction to its Methodology* (Thousand Oaks: Sage, 2012).

40. Markku Jahnukainen, "Extreme Cases," In *Encyclopedia of Case Study Research,* edited by Albert J. Mills, Gabrielle Durepos, and Eiden Wiebe (Thousand Oaks, CA: Sage, 2010), 379–381.

41. Sunderland, "'Parenting' or 'Mothering'?," 517.

42. Ibid., 503–527; Kaufman, "The Portrayal of Men's Family Roles," 439–458.

43. Francis-Connolly, "Constructing Parenthood," 179–185.

44. Eirini Flouri and Ann Buchanan, "The Role of Father Involvement in Children's later Mental Health," *Journal of Adolescence* 26, no. 1 (2003): 63–78; William Marsiglio, Dads, Kids, and Fitness: A Father's Guide to Family Health (New Brunswick, NJ: Rutgers University Press, Forthcoming); Morgan et al., "The 'Healthy Dads, Healthy Kids' Randomized Controlled Trial: Efficacy of a Healthy Lifestyle Program for Overweight Fathers and their Children," *International Journal of Obesity*

35, no. 3 (2011): 436–447; Sarkadi et al., "Fathers' Involvement and Children's Developmental Outcomes," 153–158.

45. Marsiglio, "Healthy Dads, Healthy Kids," 22–27; Bird and Rieker, *Gender and Health*.

46. Gerbner, "Cultivation Analysis: An Overview," 175–194.

47. Francis-Connolly, "Constructing Parenthood," 179–185.

48. Sunderland, "Baby Entertainer, Bumbling Assistant," *Discourse and Society*, 249–274.

49. James Gentry and Robert Harrison, "Is Advertising a Barrier to Male Movement Toward Gender Change?," *Marketing Theory* 10, no. 1 (2010): 74–96; Tsai and Shumow, "Representing Fatherhood and Male Domesticity," 38–48.

50. Sunderland, "Baby Entertainer, Bumbling Assistant," *Discourse and Society*, 249–274.

51. Wall and Arnold, "How Involved is Involved Fathering?," 508–527.

52. Coltrane and Allan, "'New' Fathers and Old Stereotypes," 43–66; Francis-Connolly, "Constructing Parenthood," 179–185.

53. Jaak Panksepp and Eric L. Scott, "Reflections on Rough and Tumble Play, Social Development, and Attention-deficit Hyperactivity Disorders," in *Physical Activity across the Lifespan*, eds. Aleta L. Meyer and Thomas. P. Gullotta (New York: Springer, 2012): 23–40.

54. Kenneth R. Ginsburg, "The Importance of Play in Promoting Healthy Child Development and Maintaining Strong Parent-child Bonds," *Pediatrics* 119, no. 1 (2007): 182–191.

55. Brussoni and Olsen, "Striking a Balance," 491–498.

56. Dubowitz, "Fathers' Role in Protecting Children," 546–547.

57. Swallow et al., "Fathers and Mothers Developing Skills," 512–523.

58. Eric Anderson, *Inclusive Masculinity: The Changing Nature of Masculinities* (New York: Routledge, 2009).

59. Gentry and Harrison, "Is Advertising a Barrier to Male Movement," 74–96.

60. http://www.dad2summit.com

BIBLIOGRAPHY

Arockiasamy, Vincent, Liisa Holsti, and Susan Albersheim. "Fathers' Experiences in the Neonatal Intensive Care Unit: A Search for Control." *Pediatrics* 121, no. 2 (2008): 215–222.

Atkinson, Maxine P., and Stephen P. Blackwelder. "Fathering in the 20th Century." *Journal of Marriage and the Family* 55, no. 4 (1993): 975–986.

Amato, Paul R., and Joan G. Gilbreth. "Nonresident Fathers and Children's Well-being: A Meta-analysis." *Journal of Marriage and the Family* 61, no. 3 (1999): 557–573.

Anderson, Eric. *Inclusive Masculinity: The Changing Nature of Masculinities.* New York: Routledge, 2009.

Bird, Chloe E., and Patricia P. Rieker. *Gender and Health: The Effects of Constrained Choices and Social Policies.* Cambridge, UK: Cambridge University Press, 2008.

Bretl, Daniel J., and Joanne Cantor. "The Portrayal of Men and Women in US Television Commercials: A Recent Content Analysis and Trends over 15 Years." *Sex Roles* 18, no. 9–10 (1988): 595–609.

Brussoni, Mariana, and Lise Olsen. "Striking a Balance between Risk and Protection: Fathers' Attitudes and Practices toward Child Injury Prevention." *Journal of Developmental & Behavioral Pediatrics* 32, no. 7 (2011): 491–498.

Cabrera, Natasha J., Catherine S. Tamis-LeMonda, Robert H. Bradley, Sandra Hofferth, and Michael E. Lamb. "Fatherhood in the Twenty-first Century." *Child Development* 71, no. 1 (2000): 127–136.

Coltrane, Scott, and Kenneth Allan. "New" Fathers and Old Stereotypes: Representations of Masculinity in 1980s Television Advertising." *Masculinities* 2, no. 4 (1994): 43–66.

Dawson, Deborah A. "Family Structure and Children's Health and Well-being: Data from the 1988 National Health Interview Survey on Child Health." *Journal of Marriage and the Family* 53, no. 3 (1991): 573–584.

Drakich, Janice. "In Search of the Better Parent: The Social Construction of Ideologies of Fatherhood." *Canadian Journal of Women and the Law* 3, (1989): 69.

Dubowitz, Howard. "Fathers' Role in Protecting Children." *Journal of Developmental & Behavioral Pediatrics* 32, no. 7 (2011): 546–547.

Flouri, Eirini, and Ann Buchanan. "The Role of Father Involvement in Children's later Mental Health." *Journal of Adolescence* 26, no. 1 (2003): 63–78.

Francis-Connolly, Elizabeth. "Constructing Parenthood: Portrayals of Motherhood and Fatherhood in Popular American Magazines." *Journal of the Motherhood Initiative for Research and Community Involvement* 5, no. 1 (2003): 179–185.

Gerbner, George. "Cultivation Analysis: An Overview." *Mass Communication and Society* 1, no. 3–4 (1998): 175–194.

Gerbner, George, Larry Gross, Michael Morgan, Nancy Signorielli, and James Shanahan. "Growing Up with Television: Cultivation Processes." *Media Effects: Advances in Theory and Research* 2, (2002): 43–67.

Gentry, James, and Robert Harrison. "Is Advertising a Barrier to Male Movement Toward Gender Change?" *Marketing Theory* 10, no. 1 (2010): 74–96.

Ginsburg, Kenneth R. "The Importance of Play in Promoting Healthy Child Development and Maintaining Strong Parent-child Bonds." *Pediatrics* 119, no. 1 (2007): 182–191.

Giorgianni, Salvatore J. Jr., and Jennifer Cooper. "Comparison of Print Media Health Advertising to Men and Boys Compared to Women and Girls." Presentation at the annual meeting of the American Public Health Association, San Francisco, CA, October 30, 2012.

Goudreau, Jenna. "Changing Roles of TV Fathers." *Today*. Last modified June 24, 2010. http://today.msnbc.msn.com/id/37758834/ns/today-entertainment/t/changing-roles-tv-fathers/.

Jahnukainen, Markku. "Extreme Cases." In *Encyclopedia of Case Study Research,* edited by Albert J. Mills, Gabrielle Durepos, and Eiden Wiebe, 379–381. Thousand Oaks, CA: Sage, 2010.

Kaufman, Gayle. "The Portrayal of Men's Family Roles in Television Commercials." *Sex Roles* 41, no. 5–6 (1999): 439–458.

Krippendorff, Klaus. *Content Analysis: An Introduction to its Methodology.* Sage, 2012.

Lamb, Michael E. "Fathers and Child Development: An Introductory Overview and Guide." In *The Role of the Father in Child Development* 3, 1–18. New York: Wiley, 1997.

LaRossa, Ralph. *The Modernization of Fatherhood: A Social and Political History.* Chicago: University of Chicago Press, 1997.

LaRossa, Ralph, Charles Jaret, Malati Gadgil, and G. Robert Wynn. "The Changing Culture of Fatherhood in Comic-Strip Families: A Six-Decade Analysis." *Journal of Marriage and Family* 62, no. 2 (2000): 375–387.

Martinson, Melissa, Amanda Hinnant, and Barbara E. Martinson. "Visual Depictions of Gender in Parenting Magazines." *Media Report to Women* 36, no. 4 (2008): 12–20.

Marsiglio, William. "Healthy Dads, Healthy Kids." *Contexts* 8, no. 4 (2009): 22–27.

Marsiglio, William, and Kevin Roy. *Nurturing Dads: Social Initiatives for Contemporary Fatherhood.* New York: Russell Sage Foundation, 2012.

Marsiglio, William. The Health Matrix: Dads, Kids, and Fitness: A Father's Guide to Family Health (New Brunswick, NJ: Rutgers University Press, Forthcoming).

Milkie, Melissa A., and Kathleen E. Denny. "Changes in the Cultural Model of Father Involvement Descriptions of Benefits to Fathers, Children, and Mothers in Parents' Magazine, 1926–2006." *Journal of Family Issues* 35, no. 2 (2014): 223–253.

Morgan, Philip J., D. R. Lubans, Robin Callister, Anthony D. Okely, T. L. Burrows, R. Fletcher, and C. E. Collins. "The 'Healthy Dads, Healthy Kids' Randomized Controlled Trial: Efficacy of a Healthy Lifestyle Program for Overweight Fathers and their Children." *International Journal of Obesity* 35, no. 3 (2011): 436–447.

Quirke, Linda. "Keeping Young Minds Sharp: Children's Cognitive Stimulation and the Rise of Parenting Magazines, 1959–2003." *Canadian Review of Sociology/ Revue Canadienne de Sociologie* 43, no. 4 (2006): 387–406.

Panksepp, Jaak, and Eric L. Scott. "Reflections on Rough and Tumble Play, Social Development, and Attention-deficit Hyperactivity Disorders." In *Physical Activity across the Lifespan*, edited by Aleta L. Meyer and Thomas. P. Gullotta, 23–40. New York: Springer, 2012.

Parke, Ross. *Fatherhood.* Cambridge, MA: Harvard University Press, 1996.

"Preamble to the Constitution of the World Health Organization as adopted by the International Health Conference." *Official Records of the World Health Organization* 2, (1946): 100.

Sarkadi, Anna, Robert Kristiansson, Frank Oberklaid, and Sven Bremberg. "Fathers' Involvement and Children's Developmental Outcomes: A Systematic Review of Longitudinal Studies." *Acta Paediatrica* 97, no. 2 (2008): 153–158.

Sunderland, Jane. "Baby Entertainer, Bumbling Assistant and Line Manager: Discourses of Fatherhood in Parentcraft Texts." *Discourse and Society* 11, no. 2 (2000): 249–74.

Sunderland, Jane. "'Parenting' or 'Mothering'? The Case of Modern Childcare Magazines." *Discourse and Society* 17, no. 4 (2006): 503–527.

Swallow, Veronica, Heather Lambert, Sheila Santacroce, and Ann Macfadyen. "Fathers and Mothers Developing Skills in Managing Children's Long-term Medical Conditions: How do their Qualitative Accounts Compare?" *Child: Care, Health and Development* 37, no. 4 (2011): 512–523.

Tsai, Wan-Hsiu Sunny and Moses Shumow. "Representing Fatherhood and Male Domesticity in American Advertising." *Interdisciplinary Journal of Research in Business* 1, no. 8 (2011): 38–48.

Wall, Glenda, and Stephanie Arnold. "How Involved is Involved Fathering?: An Exploration of the Contemporary Culture of Fatherhood." *Gender & Society* 21, (2007): 508–527.

"Women Call the Shots at Home: Public Mixed on Gender Roles in Jobs." *Pew Research Center*. Last modified September 25, 2008.

http://www.pewsocialtrends.org/2008/09/25/women-call-the-shots-at-home-public-mixed-on-gender-roles-in-jobs/

Warshak, Richard A. "Social Science and Parenting Plans for Young Children: A Consensus Report." *Psychology, Public Policy, and Law* 20, no. 1 (2014): 46.

Ziol-Guest, Kathleen M., and Rachel E. Dunifon. "Complex Living Arrangements and Child Health: Examining Family Structure Linkages with Children's Health Outcomes." *Family Relations* 63, no. 3 (2014): 424–437.

Chapter 8

New Paternal Anxieties in Contemporary Horror Cinema

Protecting the Family Against (Supernatural) External Attacks

Fernando Gabriel Pagnoni Berns
and Canela Ailen Rodriguez Fontao

SOCIAL CRISIS AND NURTURING: FATHER'S NEW ROLE

The presence of fathers in horror cinema has been historically very limited. Only with the coming of the new millennium and with a strong boost to the American horror film, have fathers begun to appear as heroes and anti-heroes. However, this presence increased largely in recent years: *Insidious* (2010) and *The conjuring* (2012), both from James Wan, *The mist* (Frank Darabont, 2007), *Dark skies* (Scott Stewart, 2013), the remake of *The Amityville horror* (Andrew Douglas, 2005), *The New Daughter* (Luiso Berdejo, 2009), *Sinister* (Scott Derrickson, 2012), *We Are What We Are* (Jim Mickle, 2013) or *The purge* (James DeMonaco, 2013) are just some of the popular films that have the common feature of having father figures as main characters.[1] These films have us think about why in the last years the recurrent image of the father (a figure that had never interested that much to horror cinema before) is suddenly so interesting. What changes have occurred in recent years to the father image to gain the interest of the horror industry? How do these films reflect those changes?

First, there have been changes in the research about fatherhood and its anxieties,[2] since the father figure now goes beyond being just financial support to the family to actively raising children. Fathers as an integral part of the upbringing were unthinkable just some years ago, but now there are two opposing trends in fatherhood: "the 'good father' as the new nurturing father who is taking more direct responsibility for child care. The 'bad father' is the emotionally distant father who is absent and spends little time or no time with his child."[3] Years ago, that "bad father" was the only conception of fatherhood since upbringing children was one of the "essential" characteristics of womanhood in the division of labors.[4]

Economic crisis and its effects in fatherhood are tied to the idea of nurturing. Fathers, in the classical conception of fatherhood, keep emotive distance from their children. That was explained because fathers were the breadwinners of the household. Now, this responsibility is shared with the mother in many homes. Moreover, economic crisis represented by the threat of unemployment destabilizes the solid figure of the father as the one in charge of granting (better) futures to their children. Since they cannot guarantee the futures of their sons and daughters, they supplanted this failure with nurture. Fathers now share the upbringing of children because it is their way of compensating them as the possibility of securing the children's future, once part of the father's responsibility, is becoming less and less possible as unemployment increases.[5]

On the other hand, Hannah Hamad argues that the 9/11 attacks led to the fact that masculinity has to be rebuilt into what could be called "protective paternalism"[6] in which the father must protect his family from external threats, in horror films metaphorized into supernatural threats.

If since 9/11, a previously unfashionable paradigm of protectorate masculinity has returned to the representational fore of popular film",[7] we believe that the proliferation of ineffectual fathers on current horror cinema stems from the widespread disorientation originated due to two matrices: changes associated with the raising of children as integral part of fatherhood and on the other hand, the social crises that destabilizes both masculinity and the father image. Currently, the image of fatherhood is filled with contradictions[8] in our era post-9/11, dominated by the "precariousness of life."[9]

Leaving aside the terrorists attacks of 9/11, another crisis framed current America: the bankruptcy of Lehman Brothers. Lehman borrowed significant amounts to fund its investing in the years leading to its bankruptcy in 2008. A significant portion of this investing was in housing-related assets, which were very strong in the nineties,[10] making it vulnerable to a downturn in that market. Between 1993 and 1999, more than two million of American citizens became new homeowners since banks were "making thousands of loans without any cash-down deposits whatsoever, an unprecedented situation."[11] In those years, "it was easier to finance a new house than it was to finance a new car. In fact, it was cheaper to buy a house than rent an apartment."[12] In 2008, Lehman faced an unprecedented loss due to the continuing subprime mortgage crisis. In August 2008, Lehman reported that it intended to release 6% of its work force—1,500 people—and filled bankruptcy later that year, generating one of the most terrible crises of capitalism in history and ending the credit/real estate market bubble in America.

The default of Lehman Brothers was totally unexpected. Families were roughly shaken in their economies and suddenly, fathers and mothers found out that they could not keep their houses. But in the popular imaginary, keeping the house was a male-related task since men are those in charge of providing security to their families. Then, in the new millennium, fathers could not protect their families against the external attack of terrorism and economic crisis.

Both matrices unite in a new reconfiguration of fatherhood in the twenty-first century: a father that shares the responsibility of nurturing with the mother and in some cases, takes care of his children alone, united with the anxieties provoked by the unstable context of a global world whose frontiers and boundaries are permeated to radical attacks, to which family is the main target, while a depowered head of the family sees himself "feminized" at the threat of unemployment[13] and in the act of nurturing.[14]

This reconfiguration of paternity goes through the social discourses of popular culture, including one of the most popular cinematographic genres, the horror film. Then, following Robin Wood (2004) and his theory that horror cinema reflects the social anxieties of the sociohistorical context,[15] it is interesting to see how this complicated amalgam composed by the new anxieties provoked by this "feminization" of the father, now in his new role of man upbringing children in a context of post-9/11, that asks for radicalization of manliness and conservative paternalistic attitudes while unemployment is at the turn of the corner, is mirrored in the structures of a genre recognizable for working with the dark side of daily life.

FAILED STATE, FAILED FATHERHOOD

First, we must establish what we mean when we speak of failed fathers. Masculinity has always needed a way to exert control over femininity building a domestic perimeter on the reproductive power of women. Marriage works as an exercise of power by which the female body and subjectivity remain under the guardianship of the male, the husband in hegemonic masculinity, which is the "configuration of gender practice which embodies the currently accepted answer to the problem of the legitimacy of patriarchy, which guarantees (or is taken to guarantee) the dominant position of men and the subordination of women."[16] One of the strategies to keep this domination was to present both femininity and masculinity as stable and fixed features. Any slight deviation of the norm, every turn from what was expected from a man, even a display of emotions, was considered what Kaja Silverman calls "deviant masculinities,"[17] which deviates not from a moral idea, but from stereotypes or naturalized social discourses about manhood, promoted, valorized and validated through endless reiteration.

One of the forms of control that patriarchy has had since its inception is to keep women within the private sphere, giving the upbringing matters exclusively to mothers because it is supposed that only in motherhood and nurture will women find complete realization.[18] Thus, women end up confined to the home, while the man, the husband/father is the provider of security. Traditionally, since the father is the link between the outside and the inside because he is the figure that moves from home to abroad, he is responsible for the creation of a sort of moral bubble and security that prevents the entry of harmful agents within the home under the guise of thoughts, ideas or undesirable persons.

However, during World War II, with 10 million working-age men into the armed services, a marked shift took place in America with respect to gender. Following the demands of wartime economy, women entered the labor force in record numbers. During the postwar period, America was framed in part through rhetoric of "failed masculinity"[19] in which the conservative role of men as the sole breadwinner was then falling apart. Even if in declining, the breadwinner role has been considered one of the most important, if not the most important, measurement of masculinity, and this image undergoes a slight restoration after 9/11. As Elaine Tyler May convincingly argues, traditional male roles, in the twenty-first century, hardly can make a comeback. Still, the crisis of 9/11 brought forth images of strong, competent men rescuing weak citizens,[20] producing a slight restoration of previous roles of the father figure as the ideological/intellectual/moral matrix of the family. Contradictorily, the collapse of finances frames current lives into uncertainty. It is this intercrossing of contradictory images that prompt new anxieties about the roles of fathers. When external and harmful elements enter the house and the father cannot safeguard the family, we find an ineffective man, a failed father. In this sense it is very interesting that the Western world has increasingly involved "the state and its networks of power, in the definition, construction and control of fathers and fatherhood"[21] with the gendering of nation as masculine because of its role as protection of the families against external threats. This phenomenon, as already discussed, increased after 9/11. But since state has failed in protect the citizens against foreign terrorism, thus fathers fail to protect their families.

The increasing of "militarized" fathers can be observed in two horror films: *The purge* (James DeMonaco, 2013), and the British film *28 weeks later* (Juan Carlos Fresnadillo, 2005) present fathers whose inability to protect the family mirrored the inability of state-nations (again, structured around masculine values) in ensuring proper protection. Furthermore, these fathers are in charge of the security of the nation and by inclusion, of their families, but fails in both accounts.

In the futuristic America of *The Purge*, a wealthy family is held hostage for harboring the target of a murderous mob during the Purge, a 12-hour "carnivalesque" period in which any and all crime is legalized as a way to prevent social scale of violence. Of course, at this juncture those who are most vulnerable are those homeless living on the streets, while families who own homes have a certain guaranteed security. And the more technologized the house is (i.e., upper class), the safer it is. This situation strongly resembles America after 9/11 when budgetary priorities in security against external attacks left largely outside low-income families.[22]

James Sandin (Ethan Hawke) belongs to that upper class. He gains his high income precisely by devising various technologies aimed at maintaining the safety of houses. He is a family man who has become rich keeping safe all the families in the neighborhood. By extension, he should be considered the *ultimate* father. Keeping all America safe, he can be read as a representation of the state, which is called within the film, "Founding Fathers," a term that had always gendered the roots of the nation.[23] State, fatherhood and James are equalized in this scenario through the use of protective power. James is a man in charge of "militarizing" America against foreign threats. Indeed, his home is filled with cameras that constantly watch and control the dangerous "outside." James is a "hypermasculine" father who protects whole families.

The new paradigm of fatherhood requires, as already mentioned, a complex and not resolved interaction between paternalistic attitudes that reinforces the figure of the father as a counter-terrorist who must resort to violence (i.e., exaggerated manliness) to protect his family, at the time that the father must feminize himself in the nurture of his children. If he even fails in just one of these two matrices he implicitly fails as a father and, in horror cinema, at least, this result in the annihilation of the paternal figure.

Another example of militarized father can be seen in *28 weeks later*. Don (Robert Carlyle) is a military chief in a zone knows a District 1, situated in a little island within London. The island had fortified itself, with the help of the US Army, against the external attacks of a zombie pandemic. In this highly militarized city, everyone is safe from the unsafe exterior, including Don's kids, Andy (Mackintosh Muggleton) and his older sister Tammy (Imogen Poots). Like in *The purge*, citizens are under constant surveillance of hit-men with snipers, always ready to shoot any "suspect" of being a carrier of the virus that turns people into zombies. Don has secured his two sons in a safe place, with the promise that in two months they all will move to a nonmilitarized home. Don is the prototype of the hypermasculine[24] new father post-9/11: he takes care of his children, even when the cost is losing some civil rights. Cut out human rights in name of defense was, of course, one of the practices that U.S. standardizes after the 9/11. People lose privacy (in both films, citizens are constantly under surveillance) and mobility in the name of national or communal security in the new highly paternalistic order. Both James and Don are in charge of national/familiar protection through militarization, which is commonly gendered as masculine,[25] while the increase in surveillance is typical in times of national crisis.[26]

However, in the same way that a state can fail in protecting its citizens from foreign terrorism, both men fail in protecting their families. James tries to marry his position as the ultimate neoliberal capitalist who only takes care of himself and his family, with the role of the new nurturing father. The dinner scene is very telling: James is dinning with his family and asks for everyone to tell about their days to comply with the role of communicative fatherhood. Even so, at the end, it is all about his capitalist success as the best salesman of security devices. His news of the day is that he "did it" and he is "on top" since his division sold the most upgraded security systems. There is no real communication between him and his children, and it is from this failed attribute that the horror begins. Both, his son Charlie (Max Burkholder) and her daughter Zoey (Adelaide Kane), allows the access of strangers within the house during the purge. Charlie lets in within the house a stranger (Edwin Hodge) hunted by a horde of citizens while Zoey hides his boyfriend (Tony Oller), who carries murderous intentions. James has failed in communicating to his son a comprehensible reason behind the purge day. He has failed in effective communication, which any manual of father/son relationship establishes as "the cornerstone to their later desirable man-to-man relationship."[27] Meanwhile, he has neglected his daughter and her relationship with her boyfriend. When arriving home, James' wife Mary (Lena Headey) asks him to help his daughter, who has problems with her boyfriend. He simply walks away, considering that his adolescent daughter is old enough to resolve her own problems and that those are not that important anyway ("She's just gonna have to sulk. She'll get over it"). Then, the failure in his highly calculated security system is related with his status as a father rather than with technology. No one enters the house because the sophisticated system of alarms has failed: the access of strangers within the household is led by the children.

In *28 weeks later*, Don has secrets of his own which, if they come to the light, will produce a rupture of his fabric of hypermasculinity. Don had done nothing to save his wife Alice (Catherine McCormack) when she, months ago, was attacked in London by a horde of zombies. Now, to keep both his masculinity and his father image intact, he narrates a story to Tammy and Andy that obliterates the truth. Like James, Don fails in sustaining proper communication with his children, a communication that will really convince them about the risks involved in disobeying. Tammy and Andy will escape the military facility and take to the London streets to go to their old family home to get some stuff that connects them with their past, and there they will find their mother alive, who is swiftly conducted to the military facility where she will be a threat to Don's hypermasculinity. After Alice's arrival and with her, the shattering of the paternal image, the family falls apart. Don will fail as a husband (he left his wife behind) and as father (he is unable to control his children, who go to London in search of images of her mother. Clearly, Don alone cannot supply for his wife's absence[28]) and for that, he is doubly punished by his family. His wife will bite him and contaminate him with the plague and Tammy will shoot him dead in the film climax when he attempts to murder both his kids. After been bitten by his wife, Don turns into a monster who ignites the spreading of the plague within the island. Just minutes after Don's conversion, the entire island is not secure anymore. Then, his failure as father is extended in his failure as protective state.

The families of *The purge* and *28 weeks later* eventually will survive but both with a loss: the death of the father. This death is necessary because it is he who commits the various errors that lead to the ordeal. In *28 weeks later* the father is turned into a zombie who seems to finds an extra pleasure in attacking his own children. This action has the symbolic motive of erasing the only witnesses of Don's failure as a hypermasculine father, his own children. But it will be Tammy and Andy who kill their father since he, same as James, has been unable to carry the family to a good end. In *The purge*, James, even if Hawke is top billed, dies long before the film's resolution. It is the rest of the family, with the help of the intruder, who manage to contain the citizens who insist on taking that home as their hunting zone. The death of James does not even have the form of final heroic sacrifice. There is no one who is saved with his murder but rather, his family is left all on its own. There is a clear relation between nation-states and fatherhood as forms of traditional patriarchies that must take charge of the members of the family,[29] and here, James and Don failures signals both the failure of fathers and state to protect the families during times of terrorism or economic crisis.

WHEN FATHERS KILL THEIR CHILDREN
(OR AT LEAST THEY TRY TO)

"It is the society that is condemned through the act of a parent murdering a child."[30]

Filicide is understood as the murder of a child by his or her parents. Art history has given multiple representations of this issue spanning not only different periods but also different artistic media and genres. From the ancient Greek and Roman culture, to movies and modern literature, characters as Agamemnon sacrificing his daughter Iphigenia or Jack Torrance (Jack Nicholson) chasing his young son in *The Shining* (Stanley Kubrick, 1980) realize that "at all times and in all places, child homicide was also a constant reminder of the fragility of the prevailing moral order."[31] We consider the problem of filicide "involve not only the crime, but also the social and economic environments that spawn the despair and insensitivity that make such acts possible."[32]

Here, filicide is related with the anxieties created by the new role of fathers as nurturing actors. In both *Hide and Seek* (John Polson, 2005) and *The New Daughter*, the loss of the mother left men in charge of children, a situation that obliged them to make a shift in their lives previously framed into traditional roles as breadwinners. The films address the changing policies toward fatherhood around nurture in a society in which traditional paradigms of fatherhood as emotional distance and economic support still survive. The father of *Hide and Seek* is psychologist David Callaway (Robert De Niro) who, after the suicide of his wife (Amy Irving), decides to move to the suburbs of New York with his young daughter Emily (Dakota Fanning), with the purpose of improving the stagnant relationship that he has with her, who has become emotionally distant. The father of *The New Daughter* is John James (Kevin Costner), a recently divorced man who must assume, like David in *Hide and Seek*, a paternal role for which he is not ready because he had never exercised it before. Like David, he moves to the suburbs with his teenage daughter Louisa (Ivana Baquero) and soon enough, the relationship starts to deteriorate. It must be pointed that both films begin with the premise of fathers[33] moving far from the city as a passage of sorts to another stage in their lives. If in the cities they were the ones in charge of economic support, in the suburbs, with little or no neighbors, they are obliged to pass more time with their daughters. It is interesting also that both fathers have to toil with troublesome daughters rather than sons (even if John has an unproblematic son), which widened the gap between them.

The first scenes of both films establish the tone and the failure of fathers to accomplish what the mother could do. *Hide and Seek* show how the family dynamic is established in relation to the interactions between both parents and daughter. The active nature of the mother in the upbringing of Emily (they share games, codes, gestures), contrast with the father's passive character (limited in the gain of income for the family, while staying out of upbringing). The subsequent suicide of the mother requires the abandonment of passivity on the part of David and the need to be, as he himself points out, a full-time father.

The move involves a kind of mutation in David's functions as father. Now it is he who cooks, cleans, educates, plays and even interacts with the neighbors. These tasks are far from easy, showing that the distance between him and his daughter needs to be shortened. In this regard, we understand that the fulfillment of these tasks involves David's feminization since, as already noted, the (modern) father has now to fulfill functions that were considered previously as female-only. David tries to take the place of the mother. He repeats the same games, the same phrases ("I love you more than anything in the world"), and the same gestures. These attempts are uncomfortable for

Emily, who becomes more and more introverted in her feelings since all those gestures fit awkwardly with her father for the simple reason that those were *uncommon,* and thus forced, in him. Certainly, David fails as father the whole time: the first thing that he does when arriving in town is losing his daughter from sight, he is incapable of opening a window to air Emily's bedroom, and everyone in town seems to doubt his capabilities as a father. Also, it is insinuated that he has been incapable of sexually satisfying his wife. The latter is a diminishing of masculinity that connects him with John. In this respect, in *The New Daughter*, Louisa reproaches that her father as has done nothing in particular to retain his wife, so the mother abandoning the children is due to the lack of properly masculine actions. This represents a contradictory movement: David and John are not male enough to retain their wives while not soft enough to comply with their new role of upbringing fathers. For example, John must face the reality that in the process of moving he has forgotten to buy very necessary items such as milk or cat food and more important, food for the children. As Louisa tells it, fatherhood is a practice that requires experience and John clearly lacks the knowledge to do it properly.

Over the days, the father-daughter relationships begin to get more strained, to the point that both girls start to look outside for the understanding that they do not find within the home. Louisa visits a haunted mound in the woods which increasingly affirms a supernatural grip upon the girl, while Emily acquires an imaginary friend, whom she calls "Charlie."

From this point on, the horror begins for both parents. The fears of David about his daughter's brooding mood seem to dissipate with the distance consultations held with Katherine (Famke Janssen), Emily's psychiatrist, who thinks that Charlie can be a useful tool to build a father-daughter bond. If at first, Charlie's arrival is an improvement in the relationship between them, visible through an increased father-daughter interaction, soon it will become a threat to the father figure when a series of creepy acts, as the recreation of the mother's suicide in the bathroom, take place, always committed, according to Emily, by her imaginary friend Charlie.

Nightmares, threats (inscriptions that allude to David's responsibility in the suicide of his wife, menacing neighbors), fears (represented by Emily's mental instability) and even murder (a neighbor, a policeman), acquire meaning for the audience when it is revealed the true identity of Charlie who turns to be, surprisingly, David Callaway himself.

David's split personality is due to the fact that he had discovered his wife in an act of infidelity. From there, his masculinity and, by extension, his role as father becomes unstable. David displaces his emotions through fantasies. Charlie's creation allows him to connect with his daughter from another place where infantile games, in this case the "hide and seek" of the title, takes central stage. This is evident not only literally, but also in the way in which the split personality of David is constructed: when Charlie comes out, the father hides; when Davis is present, Charlie sleeps.

Charlie, contrary to David, will be built with characteristics similar to those of the deceased mother, fulfilling what should be an active and softer father. According to Emily, "Charlie is fun, just like Mom." As a father, Charlie succeeds where David fails. With a foot firmly in the traditional role, to comply as a new father, David must split in two: David is the male role since he is unsuccessful in his attempts to replace the mother in "feminine" tasks such as play with children, while Charlie fulfills the nurturing role. David only can fulfill the new role of nurturing by getting lost within his mind. David metaphorizes in his schizophrenia the abrupt changes that the concept of fatherhood as a paradigm faces in our current times. As scholars about fatherhood and masculinities argue, "for some fathers, particularly among those who have been socialized to be detached emotionally from their children, male socialization and the changing role expectations of fathers are difficult and painful and may interfere with their generative fathering ability and motivation to be an involved father." Furthermore, "this difficulty reveals the conflict some fathers face as they find the new expectation of fatherhood freeing and fulfilling, yet the reality of meeting these expectations (. . .) can be changeling."[34] David is a distant father (canonical figure of fatherhood) who cannot stand the doubly disappearance of his wife (both as a "good" wife and psychically) and thus, comes into a crisis. He has been not man enough as a husband and as a father. With the wife dead, David must face a new concept of fatherhood, but he is too unprepared to do it and retreats into madness as a way of escape of this new role. To comply as father, he must dissociate of himself, illustrating the current ambivalence and hesitance in embracing the softer side of masculinity,[35] while the traditional role becomes increasingly more outdated and reprehensible.

In his mind, Charlie is constructed as a nemesis. He can embrace what David cannot: being a new father. Paradoxically, it is because of this dislocation that Emily can relate to her father and when Charlie begins to feel threatened by this new bond, he seems to wonder about what the worst thing is to do to a father to hurt him: kill his child.

Although David tries to fight Charlie believing him an external threat, once the truth comes out to the light, David, as father, hides within himself and is Charlie the one who takes control. It will be Katherine, a maternal figure, who saves Emily from David/Charlie. At the death of the mother, David had to face a new fatherly role. Since he cannot do it, the (surrogate) mother has to come to the rescue. David had failed in embracing the new paternal figure.

Meanwhile, *The New Daughter* culminates with a father actually killing his child. John, like David, must fulfill a paternal role for which he is not ready because he had never exercised it before. A sign that he cannot properly exercise it as a father is the fact that John, as the (only) authority figure in the house, fails in keep Louisa away from the mound. As days pass, the influence exercised by the mound upon the girl grows up while the rebellion of the girl upon his father increases. Even if a supernatural film, *The New Daughter* recurrently utilizes images which can relate with everyday frustrations and fears of parents. John's lackluster role is symbolized in the act that his son plays with a loaded gun, risking the whole family. The paradigmatic union of the images of hungry and very unsafe children conform an imaginary that paints John as an incapable father.

The supernatural elements of the film illustrate the challenges involved in establishing a relationship between a divorced man and his teenage daughter. The more John insists on penetrating his daughter's world, the more resistance he finds. Louisa's antisocial behavior in school just adds another layer to the impotence that John feels as a father against her daughter's sudden mood swings.

So strong is his feeling of bad-performing in fatherhood that John comes to the rather pathetic level of finding ways to communicate with his child using the Internet as a resource. John hopes to find online tools which enable him to establish a healthy father daughter bond. Such is his degree of helplessness that in the online search engine he types in the phrase "crappy father," thus self-referencing as such.

Already with Louisa definitely taken by supernatural forces, John will decide not only to sacrifice himself but also his daughter by causing a large explosion on the mound, in which both die. Interestingly, what the supernatural forces wanted from the girl was bred in her (thus creating the "new daughter" of the title). Therefore, John has lost control over the sexuality of his daughter, who has gone through the typical teenage alienation toward parents. Now with his daughter turned into some "Other" because she is now a reproductive menace,[36] John decides to eliminate her since he was unable to prevent his daughter from becoming involved with "bad company." He was indeed a "crappy father" and punishes himself and his daughter killing them both.

These films refer to the changes of fathers as family patriarchs, and the anxieties created by men in domestic space. Nurturing is increasingly commonplace in American society. But "for many fathers, however, taking on sole care of their children might well be confusing, frustrating, and difficult. The day will expose their lack of competence, without direction or understanding of what to do; it might even be terrifying, fearsome."[37] These terms perfectly fit into horror cinema, which is the perfect vehicle to illustrate these new social anxieties about the status of fatherhood in current times.

WHEN CHILDREN KILL THE PARENTS

In 2010 opens the Mexican horror film *Somos lo que hay* (Jorge Michel Grau). The film tells about the whereabouts of a Mexican family whose father dies, leaving the family in distress. The mother (Carmen Beato) and her two sons and daughter are now in charge of following the paternal mandate of consumption of human flesh as an annual rite of cannibalism.

This Mexican film had its U.S. remake in 2013, *We Are What We Are* (Jim Mickle). Interestingly, the remake changes the sex of the main characters and in this version, the one who dies is the mother (Kassie Parker). Now, it is the father, Frank Parker (Bill Sage) who must take charge not only of the cannibalistic ritual, but also of the nurture of three kids, his two daughters, Rose and Iris (Julia Garner and Ambyr Childers) and a little son, Rory (Jack Gore).

In both versions, then, it is possible to find different anxieties about paternity. While the Mexican film channels the anxieties about the lacking in the household of the father figure, the remake works with the impossibility of the father to carry the family to a good end. The father of the U.S. version is clearly set in the past (hence his insistence in old rites), so he is unworried about new roles of fatherhood. The change about the gender of the parental figure who dies in the opening of the two films supports the idea that the U.S. version seems to be obsessed with the idea of fathers and their inability to manage correctly their families.

If in the Mexican film the diverse tensions within the family comes to light when the father disappears, in *We Are What We Are* the problems appears because the father is now alone conducting the household. Rose and Iris continually complain about the ritual and the sacrifices of human beings. Both girls make plans to end the rite "the following year" and it seems that it is the absence of the mother that ignites this rebellion. Before that, both are enthusiastic about the preparations for the rite, but after the news of their mother death, they become gloomy and critical about the reasons and necessity of continuing the ritual. They challenge the patriarchal axiom and prepare a future rebellion against the father.

This rite has its roots in centuries ago, when the Parker lineage were just beginning. In a period of serious famine, the Parkers, lost in the deep of a forest, face sure death if they are not able to get some food. The patriarch, Mathias Parker, takes a drastic decision: he kills his brother to ensure food to his family, through the consumption of human flesh. This doing resembles the mandate that the ultimate act of fathers is to provide food to his wife and children. If not, he fails both as a man and as a father. Since Frank fails to grant a continuation to the cannibalistic ritual, which acts as a remembrance to what extent a father comes to feed his family, he symbolically fails in feeding his children. The wife, the home's true foundation, has died and Frank is unable to support the family. The constant invasion in the house of a good-natured neighbor, Marge (Kelly McGillis), serves to remind him that a home without a female adult's presence cannot work properly. Indicative of this is that Frank kills Marge in the climax, since is his way to prove that he can manage the family alone, even if this means poisoning his children as a way of obliterate his own inability to carry on his shoulders the chore of a family, as an extreme way of bending their daughters' will.

Finally, the only way in which Iris and Rose can get away with their idea of ending the ritual is by practicing cannibalism in their father's flesh. The oppressive patriarchal mandate only ends with the killing of the father performed by the two daughters. Only in parricide the kids obtains the freedom that they desire so much.[38] In both, the Mexican film and the remake, kids seem to obtain what they desire only with the death of the father, but in the U.S. version it is the father who fails to maintain the family united. In *Somos lo que hay*, however, the children never have doubts about the ritual. It must go on. The mother's presence is strong enough to avoid any doubt. Frank, in the other hand, sees how all his family comes apart when his wife dies. His presence is not strong enough to keep the family together since he is clearly and proudly steeped in old versions of fatherhood.

The failure of the father as an assurance of food and as keeper of family junction strongly resonates in *Sinister*, another film in which children chastise paternal failure through murder. Here, the food is replaced by the means to obtain it: money. Ellison Oswalt (Ethan Hawke) is the father of a family who move on to a suburban house in which, years ago, a hideous crime was committed. Ellison's goal is to investigate the crime and write a book about the case, a book that make him come back to the top of the best-seller list, a place from which he fell a decade ago, since his posterior books never achieve the same level of success of that his first book. To do this, Ellison must face a lot of challenges: the authorities of the town do not want him there and besides, he must lie to his family about the house's true nature. But the hardest challenge that Ellison must overcome is himself: he passes the days remembering the years of money and fame of old. It is his wife, Tracy (Juliet Rylance) who economically supports their home, so that her husband can work to finish his new book, which may or may not be successful enough to cover all the family's debts.

Ellison fails as a father in a doubly way: he is not the financial supporter of the home, a role that his wife fulfills. This situation resembles the reality of many men that, by choice or by unemployment, are "househusbands" while their wives are the breadwinners. But Ellison fails too in the nurture of his two sons, Trevor (Michael Hall D'addario) and Ashley (Clare Foley) since he occupies all his free time in a book that he is not, in fact, writing and ignoring his children. One scene illustrates this: Ashley takes the morning cup of coffee to her father, who is working in his studio. The little girl knocks the door and Ellison answers, grateful for the coffee, but close the door without more exchange of words with her daughter than a simple "thanks." While Ashley wants some quality time with her father, Ellison is too immersed in his work to notice that he is neglecting his children. Furthermore, Trevor's sleep disorders and nocturnal terrors are making its come back because, the audience knows, the evil specter visiting the house. But it is Ellison who insists in keeping the family under the roof of that sinister house even when he knows that something more horrid than a past single murder is going on. He spends the nights watching home videos which display whole families being slaughtered and a supernatural presence is present in all the recordings, but he is willing to sacrifice his family if this means another best-seller. As his family disintegrates before his eyes, much eager is Ellison to recover his place as the true breadwinner of the house, a place that he lost at his wife's hands.

Only too late Ellison will understand that his whole family is in serious danger and all of them must leave the house. By this time, his daughter would be already "contaminated" by the evil supernatural being that reaches children through the use of images, the Bughuul (Nick King) and, same as had happened with other families, the Oswalts will be murdered by the younger kid in the family.

It is interesting that Bughuul comes to the children through the media. Ashley and presumably the other children leave their home because they felt the evil being closer than their parents. It can be argued that *Sinister*, among other things, makes a call of attention about who is really educating children: are the parents or the media, especially television? The film speaks about the anxieties and fears that our current times brings about children been educated and "trapped" by media because their parents are not in home to keep an eye on them.[39] Since Tracy works to sustain the family, this job of watch over the children fells upon Ellison, who, as father, fails in both, grant money and takes care of the children.

Unlike the fathers of the last section, both parents of *We Are What We Are* and *Sinister* sit in the past, indicating a shared nostalgic desire to return to older values. None of them are interested in the new role of nurturing, but rather in the old practices of breadwinners as the sole locus of fatherhood. This is what prompted their destruction, since they cannot see that their families are asking more of them.

CONCLUSIONS

The new millennium has brought terrorist attacks that put state security into a precarious balance and economic global crisis that showcase the fragility of social structures. All these paradigmatic changes are related to fatherhood, as seen in the equaling of a failed nationhood and failed fatherhood seen in the fathers of *The Purge* and *28 Weeks Later*. However, fathers are now increasingly involved in the upbringing of children, and society expects them to embrace this new scenario, while downplaying the traditional roles of emotional detachment. Still, it is not an easy transition from one paradigm to another, especially considering that the previous one still survives strongly in today's society. The fathers of *Hide and seek* and *The New Daughter* try to fit into this new role, but fail, collapsing under the weight of their own shortcomings. Meanwhile, the fathers who sit upon the old conceptions of parenthood, such as in *We Are What We Are* and *Sinister* are blind to the path of self-destruction that they undertook and their demise at the hands of their children, as an act of releasing from stagnant patriarchy, is unavoidable.

As can be seen, the current images of fatherhood are traversed by many contradictions rather than a fixed paradigm, and these conflictive politics are illustrated by one of the best vehicles in staging social anxieties: the horror genre.

NOTES

1. *Insidious*, directed by James Wan (2010; Culver City, CA: Sony Pictures Home Entertainment, 2011), DVD; *The Conjuring*, directed by James Wan (2013; Burbank, CA: Warner Home Video, 2013), DVD; *The Mist*, directed by Frank Darabont (2007; New York: The Weinstein Company, 2007), DVD; *Dark Skies*, directed by Scott Stewart (2013; Beverly Hills, CA: Anchor Bay Entertainment, 2013), DVD; *The Amityville Horror*, directed by Andrew Douglas (2005; Santa Monica, Calif.: MGM Home Entertainment, 2010), DVD; *The New Daughter*, directed by Luiso Berdejo (2009; Beverly Hills, CA: Anchor Bay Entertainment, 2010), DVD; *Sinister*, directed by Scott Derrickson (2012; Universal City, Calif: Summit Home Entertainment, 2013), DVD; *We Are What We Are*, directed by Jim Mickle (2013; Toronto: Entertainment One, 2014), DVD; *The Purge*, directed by James DeMonaco (2013; Universal City, Calif: Universal Studios Home Entertainment, 2013), DVD.

2. Peter Gray and Kermyt Anderson, *Fatherhood: Evolution and Human Paternal Behavior* (Cambridge:Harvard University Press, 2010).

3. Jay Fagan and Glen Palm, *Fathers and Early Childhood Programs* (Clifton Park, NY: Delmar Learning, 2004), 68.

4. Riki Wilchins, *Queer Theory, Gender Theory: An Instant Primer* (Los Angeles: Alyson Books, 2004), 128.

5. Mike Donaldson, "What is hegemonic masculinity?," *Theory and Society*, vol. 22, no. 5, Special Issue: Masculinities (1993): 651.

6. Hannah Hamad, *Postfeminism and Paternity in Contemporary U.S. Film: Framing Fatherhood* (New York: Routledge, 2013), 52.

7. Sarah Godfrey and Hannah Hamad, "Save the Cheerleader, Save the Males: Resurgent Protective Paternalism in Popular Film and Television After 9/11," in *The Handbook of Gender, Sex and Media*, ed. Karen Ross (Malden, MA: Wiley-Blackwell, 2012), 170.

8. Margret Fine-Davis, Jeanne Fagnani, Dino Giovannini, Lis Højgaard, and Hilary Clarke, *Fathers and Mothers: Dilemmas of the Work-Life Balance* (Dordrecht, NL: Kluwer Academic Publishers, 2004), 38.

9. David Greven, *Manhood in Hollywood: From Bush to Bush* (Austin, TX: University of Texas Press, 2009), 43.

10. Lawrence McDonald and Patrick Robinson, *A Colossal Failure of Common Sense: The Inside Story of the Collapse of Lehman Brothers* (New York: Random House, 2009), 4.

11. Ibid.

12. McDonald and Robinson, *A Colossal Failure*, 115.

13. Mirra Komarovsky, *The Effect of Unemployment Upon the Unemployed Man and His Family* (Walnut Creek, CA: Altamira Press, 2004), 1.

14. Nancy Dowd, *Redefining Fatherhood* (New York: New York University Press, 2000), 172.

15. Robin Wood, "An introduction to the American horror film," in *Planks of Reason: Essays on the Horror Film*, ed. Barry Keith Grant (Lanham, MD: Scarecrow Press, 2004), 109.

16. Raewyn Connell, *Masculinities* (Berkeley: University of California Press, 1995), 77.

17. Kaja Silverman, *Male Subjectivity at the Margins* (New York and London: Routledge, 1992), 185.

18. Wilchins, *Queer Theory*, 6.

19. Miriam Reumann, *American Sexual character: Sex, Gender, and National Identity in the Kinsey Reports* (Berkeley and Los Angeles: University of California Press, 2005), 70.

20. Elaine Tyler May, *Homeward Bound: American Families in the Cold War Era* (New York: Basic Books, 2008), 226.

21. Jeff Hearn, "Men, Fathers and the State: National and Global Relations," in *Making Men into Fathers: Men, Masculinities and the Social Politics of Fatherhood*, ed. Barbara Hobson (New York: Cambridge University Press, 2004), 270.

22. Kenneth Neubeck, *When Welfare Disappears: The Case for Economic Human Rights* (New York: Routledge, 2006), 154.

23. Andrew Schocket, *Fighting Over the Founders: How We Remember the American Revolution* (New York: New York University Press, 2015), 30.

24. Anna Agathangelou, "Powers, Borders, Security, Wealth: Lessons Of Violence and Desire From September 11," *International Studies Quarterly* 48 (2004): 519.

25. Hearn, "Men, Fathers and the State," 265.

26. Mark Sidel, *More Secure, Less Free? Antiterrorism Policy & Civil Liberties after September 11* (Ann Arbor: The University of Michigan Press, 2004), 4.

27. Lewis Yablonsky, *Fathers and Sons* (Lincoln, NE: iUniverse, 2000), 190.

28. It is interesting to note that Tammy and Andy both survive the plague because they were far from the family, in a sleepaway camp. Only with them far from the family are they kept safe.

29. Hearn, "Men, Fathers and the State," 246.

30. Lita Linzer Schwartz and Natalie Isser, *Child Homicide: Parents Who Kill* (Boca Raton, FL: Taylor and Francis, 2007), 17.

31. Schwartz and Isser, *Child Homicide*, 2.

32. Schwartz and Isser, *Child Homicide*, 4.

33. Characters performed by actors old enough to be credibly anchored in previous paradigms of fatherhood.

34. Chen Oren et al., "Counseling Fathers from a Strength-Based Perspective," in *Counseling Fathers*, ed., Chen Oren and Dora Chase Oren (New York: Routledge, 2010), 33.

35. Donald Unger, *Men Can: The Changing Image and Reality of Fatherhood in America* (Philadelphia: Temple University Press, 2010), 176.

36. Barbara Creed, "Kristeva, Femininity, Abjection," in *The Horror Reader*, ed., Ken Gelder (New York: Routledge, 2000), 70.

37. Dowd, *Redefining*, 21.

38. Judith Van Herik, *Freud on Femininity and Faith* (Berkeley: University of California Press, 1982), 78.

39. Scot MacDonald, *Public Education and Our Government Schools: An Expose* (Mustang, OK:Tate Publishing, 2011), 48.

BIBLIOGRAPHY

Agathangelou, Anna. "Powers, borders, security, wealth: lessons of violence and desire from September 11." *International Studies Quarterly* 48 (2004): 517–538.

The Amityville Horror. Directed by Andrew Douglas. 2005. Santa Monica, Calif.: MGM Home Entertainment, 2010. DVD.

The Conjuring. Directed by James Wan. 2013. Burbank, CA: Warner Home Video, 2013. DVD.

Connell, R.W. *Masculinities.* Berkeley: University of California Press, 1995.

Creed, Barbara. "Kristeva, Femininity, Abjection." In *The Horror Reader*, edited by Ken Gelder, 64-70. New York: Routledge, 2000.

Dark Skies. Directed by Scott Stewart. 2013. Beverly Hills, CA: Anchor Bay Entertainment, 2013. DVD.

Donaldson, Mike. "What is hegemonic masculinity? *Theory and Society*, vol. 22, no. 5, Special Issue: Masculinities, (1993): 643–657.

Dowd, Nancy, *Redefining Fatherhood.* New York: New York University Press, 2000.

Fagan, Jay and Glen Palm, *Fathers and Early Childhood Programs.* Clifton Park, NY: Delmar Learning, 2004.

Fine-Davis, Margret et al, *Fathers and Mothers: Dilemmas of the Work-Life Balance.* Dordrecht: Kluwer Academic Publishers, 2004.

Godfrey, Sarah, and Hannah Hamad. "Save the cheerleader, save the males: resurgent protective paternalism in popular film and television after 9/11." In *The Handbook of Gender, Sex and Media*, edited by Karen Ross, 157–173. Malden, MA: Wiley-Blackwell, 2012.

Gray, Peter, and Kermyt Anderson. *Fatherhood. Evolution and Human Paternal Behavior.* Harvard University Press, 2010.

Greven, David. *Manhood in Hollywood: From Bush to Bush.* Austin: University of Texas Press, 2009.

Hamad, Hannah. *Postfeminism and Paternity in Contemporary U.S. Film: Framing Fatherhood.* New York: Routledge, 2013.

Hearn, Jeff. "Men, Fathers and the State: National and Global Relations." In *Making Men into Fathers: Men, Masculinities and the Social Politics of Fatherhood*, edited by Barbara Hobson, 245-272. New York: Cambridge University Press, 2004.

Insidious. Directed by James Wan. 2010. Culver City, CA: Sony Pictures Home Entertainment, 2011. DVD.

Komarovsky, Mirra. *The Effect of Unemployment Upon the Unemployed Man and His Family.* Walnut Creek, CA: Altamira Press, 2004.

McDonald, Lawrence and Patrick Robinson. *A Colossal Failure of Common Sense: The Inside Story of the Collapse of Lehman Brothers.* New York: Random House, 2009.

MacDonald, Scot. *Public Education and Our Government Schools: An Expose.* Oklahoma, Tate Publishing, 2011.

The Mist. Directed by Frank Darabont. 2007. New York: The Weinstein Company, 2007. DVD.

The New Daughter. Directed by Luiso Berdejo. 2009. Beverly Hills, CA: Anchor Bay Entertainment, 2010. DVD.

Elaine Tyler May, *Homeward Bound: American Families in the Cold War Era* (New York: Basic Books, 2008), 226.

Neubeck, Kenneth. *When Welfare Disappears: The Case for Economic Human Rights.* New York: Routledge, 2006.

Oren, Chen, et al. "Counseling Fathers from a Strength-Based Perspective." In *Counseling Fathers*, edited by Chen Oren and Dora Chase Oren, 23-48. New York: Routledge, 2010.

The Purge. Directed by James DeMonaco. 2013. Universal City, Calif.: Universal Studios Home Entertainment, 2013. DVD.

Reumann, Miriam. *American Sexual character: Sex, Gender, and National Identity in the Kinsey Reports.* London: University of California Press, 2005.

Schocket, Andrew. *Fighting Over the Founders: How We Remember the American Revolution.* New York: New York University Press, 2015.

Schwartz, Lita Linzer and Natalie Isser. *Child Homicide: Parents Who Kill.* Boca Raton, FL: Taylor and Francis Group, 2007.

Sidel, Mark. *More Secure, Less Free? Antiterrorism Policy & Civil Liberties after September 11.* Ann Arbor: The University of Michigan Press, 2004.

Silverman, Kaja. *Male Subjectivity at the Margins.* New York and London: Routledge, 1992.

Sinister. Directed by Scott Derrickson. 2012. Universal City, Calif.: Summit Home Entertainment, 2013. DVD.

Tyler May, Elaine. *Homeward Bound: American Families in the Cold War Era.* New York: Basic Books, 2008.

Unger, Donald. *Men Can: The Changing Image and Reality of Fatherhood in America*. Philadelphia: Temple University Press, 2010.

Van Herik, Judith. *Freud on Femininity and Faith*. Berkeley: University of California Press, 1982.

We Are What We Are. Directed by Jim Mickle. 2013. Toronto: Entertainment One, 2014. DVD.

Wilchins, Riki. *Queer Theory, Gender Theory: An Instant Primer*. Los Angeles: Alyson Books, 2004.

Wood, Robin. "An introduction to the American horror film." In *Planks of Reason: Essays on the Horror Film*, edited by Barry Keith Grant, 107-139. Maryland: Scarecrow Press, 2004.

Yablonsky, Lewis. *Fathers and Sons*. Lincoln, NE: iUniverse, 2000.

Section III

REPRESENTING DADS

Chapter 9

From *Good Times* to *Blackish*

Media Portrayals of African American Fathers

Shirley A. Hill and Janice Kelly

INTRODUCTION

Fathers have always been important members of families, but our social expectations and images of them have evolved over time. Changing notions of what it means to be a good father are largely driven by economic transitions, which tend to produce new attitudes and ideologies. In colonial America, for example, fathers were expected to train their children occupationally and spiritually, and they were often depicted as stern disciplinarians and emotionally distant. The modern era, ushered in by the rise of the industrial economy, separated the home and workplace and led to a new breadwinner-homemaker ideology. In this era, being a good father was mostly defined as being a good breadwinner. The current information and services economy, or the postindustrial economy, has eroded the wage-earning abilities of men, and drawn more women into the labor force, making dual-income families the norm. Most married women, including those with young children, are now in the labor force, and fathers are expected to share equally in caring for children.

The media and social science research have historically captured or focused on dominant societal images of fathers, which usually reflect a middle-class bias.[1] Television portrayals of fathers tend to associate competent fathering with socioeconomic status, with those in the higher classes seen as more competent.[2] This was evident in early television shows, such as *Leave it to Beaver*.[3] The show featured the Cleaver family, a white, middle-class, suburban, breadwinner-homemaker family. Ward Cleaver (Hugh Beaumont) personified the image of the breadwinner father: He spent his days at work and earned a good living for his family and, while removed from the everyday

work of child-rearing, consulted with his wife on the best strategies for dealing with their sons.

Social science research reflected a similar middle-class bias: Prior to the
1960s, scholars idealized the breadwinner-homemaker family model as inherently superior to all other family models.[4] However, shows like *Leave it to
Beaver* soon became the linchpin for criticism of research and media images
that neglected racial and social class diversity among families and portrayed
women in marginal, stereotypical roles.[5] In fact men, especially fathers, were
also depicted in a limited fashion. Black men, on the rare occasions that they
were seen on television, were often subjected to denigrating stereotypes. The
most popular example is the *Amos n' Andy Show*[6], which began in the 1920s
as a minstrel-type radio show that was voiced by two white actors and later
moved to television. *Amos n' Andy* reinforced white stereotypes of African
American men as ignorant buffoons, and all but ignored their family roles.
During the civil rights, the *Pittsburgh Courier*[7] and the NAACP[8] began to
protest these racist depictions, which led to more diverse media images of
African Americans. In the 1970s, Norman Lear produced several television
sitcoms that featured black men in prominent roles, such as *Sanford and Son*[9],
The Jeffersons[10], and *Good Times*[11] (1974).

THE CURRENT STUDY

This paper analyzes the images and roles of African American fathers as portrayed in popular television sitcoms. We situate their experiences in historic
and contemporary context, highlighting differences in how black and white
families evolved as well as how their family patterns have converged over
time. Our overarching theme is that the economy tends to shape dominant
expectations about fatherhood, but the ability of men to conform to those
expectations is shaped by their racial and social class position. Centuries of
slavery and racial inequality have undoubtedly shaped African American
families, at times making it nearly impossible for fathers to effectively
train, discipline, provide for, or bond with their children. In recent decades,
black men have made significant socioeconomic progress, but they remain
overrepresented among the poor, incarcerated, the unemployed, and the
unmarried—all factors that shape their relationships with their children. Thus,
we explore how social class shapes television sitcoms' portrayals of African
American fathers.[12]

The media and scholarly research have contributed to the dominant image
of African American fathers as missing from their families. Prior to the
civil rights era, research on black families was scarce, but tended to focus
on single-mother families and describe black fathers as missing, weak, or

ineffectual.[13] Some early television shows seemed to follow their lead. One of the first black family shows was *Julia*[14], which premiered in 1968 and featured a widowed black mother who worked outside of the home but was raising her son. Later shows of the 1970s, like *That's My Mama*[15] and *What's Happening*[16] also normalized the missing black father by offering little to no explanation for their absence from the family. But scholars are now looking more closely at the ways African American men, even those who do not reside with their children, contribute to their well-being. Similarly, black fathers are now featured in a variety of television sitcoms and socioeconomic contexts.

We contend that the media images of African American men have important implications for how they are perceived in the broader society. As noted by McLuhan in his seminal 1964 book, *Understanding Media: The Extensions of Man* the media do not simply spread ideas, but they also influence how people think and—perhaps even more significant—the media subconsciously influence behavior.[17] The mediated experience of television becomes incorporated into our repertoire of norms, values and behaviors of the viewers. For example, despite new technologies such as the mobile phones or computers, television is still the primary medium for influencing the behavior of the public, sometimes in prosocial ways. Therefore, it attempts to promote ethnic or racial tolerance by showing minority groups in positive roles can contribute to racial harmony and acceptance or the acceptance of new forms of gender identity.[18] Neil Postman stated that televised images and messages of what is normal are imbedded into our subconscious mind, and we then strive, as unrealistic as it may be, to role model such behavior.[19] For example, according to Donna Bassin's work mothers repeatedly compared themselves to television mothers like June Cleaver and Claire Huxtable.[20]

Our research paper takes the media images of black fathers as its focus, acknowledging that these images can have real-life consequences. How are African American fathers presented in television sitcoms, and how do images of them vary based on social class? To answer these questions, we analyze six popular television sitcoms featuring black families, ranging from the 1970s to the current time. For upper- and upper-middle-class black families, we analyze *The Cosby Show*[21] and a more recent television sitcom, *blackish*.[22] Both shows feature dual-career, professional families where both parents are college educated and employed. Our analysis of *My Wife and Kids*[23] and *The Jeffersons* focuses on middle- and lower-middle-class black families. In both shows, the families have the money to qualify as middle class; however, neither parent in these shows has a college education, nor do they have the cultural capital or social manners of the upper-middle class. Our analysis of the black working- and lower-class families is drawn from *Good Times* and *Everybody Hates Chris*.[24] These fathers have low-status work and their wives are full-time homemakers. All of these shows are currently running on syndi-cated cable channels, which show their continued popularity.

FAMILIES IN TRANSITION

Dominant societal ideologies about the roles of fathers have changed sig-nificantly over the course of history. The rise of the industrial economy, for example, produced the notion that families should conform to a breadwinner-homemaker structure, with mothers responsible for most of the housework and child-rearing and fathers responsible for earning sufficient wages to support the family. The male wage earner ideology was supported by paying men the "family wage," or wages sufficient to meet the needs of the entire family.[25] The breadwinner-homemaker family headed by a male wage earner became the dominant societal expectation although many families, especially working-class families and families of color, we're unable to conform to this expectation.

African American men were especially in a limited position to fulfill the male provider role for most of the nineteenth century, as the vast majority of them were still enslaved. Slavery forbade legal marriages among black people and sometimes even defined black families in mother and child units, failing to acknowledge black fathers.[26] Black children, who were already the property of slave owners, usually entered the slave labor system at age 6,[27] further diluting the power of fathers to influence their lives. Emancipation did little to change this, as most black people moved from slavery into share-cropping, a labor system that not only insured poverty, but also demanded the labor of entire black families—women and children included. Black men not only did not earn a "family wage," but were often penalized for trying to conform to the breadwinner-homemaker family model, as they were seen as inappropriately imitating white families.[28]

Nevertheless, family scholarship of the early twentieth century idealized the breadwinner-homemaker ideology and focused almost exclusively on white, middle-class families as models for this ideology. Some scholars argued that, given the economic prosperity of American society, most fami-lies that were not middle class were on their way to achieving that status. An exception was made for African American families, as they were seen as capable of achieving such success.[29] The few studies that focused on black families highlighted the fact that so many of them were headed by single-mothers, which was seen as inherently pathological.[30] The dominant perspective on African American families was that they had essentially been destroyed by centuries of slavery; thus, was born the deficit approach to viewing black families.[31]

As African Americans began to migrate from the South to the North and social unrest over racial inequality escalated, the single-mother family structure gained greater scrutiny. Thus, at the height of the civil rights movement, African Americans' demand for racial justice was met by the now infamous Moynihan Report,[32] which suggested that the "matriarchal" family structure prevalent among African Americans was largely responsible for their lack of socioeconomic progress.[33] Published in 1965 and produced for the U.S. Department of Labor's Office of Planning and Policy Research, Senator Moynihan's[34] report and growing racial protest ignited a controversy that became a turning point in how black families were viewed by scholars and depicted in the media. The deficit approach was challenged by a strengths perspective that emphasized the diversity, resilience, and cultural distinctiveness of black families.[35]

The women's movement also challenged the legitimacy of the breadwinner-homemaker, as women were increasingly entering the labor market and demanding that their male partners become more involved in the domestic arena. Most married women hold full-time jobs, and only about 7 percent of families consist of married couples with dependent children and a male-breadwinner/female-homemaker family structure.[36] According to Hodge and Lundeen, since 1965, the percentage of American married women working outside the home have increased from 47% to 66%.[37] Participation in the labor force and dual-income families have always been the norm for African American women; in fact, Bart Landry describes black women as pioneers in the creation of such families and more equitable relationships between spouse.[38] The participation of mothers in the labor force has resulted in a growing demand that fathers take on more of the responsibility for caring for and socializing children. Family sociologist Philip N. Cohen has described the transition in fathering expectations as moving from the male provider ideal to the involved father ideal; that is, a father is expected to be "an emotional, nurturing companion who bonds with his children as well as providing for them."[39]

FATHERHOOD IN CONTEMPORARY SOCIETY

Despite this new expectation, the family revolutions of the latter twentieth century often seemed to create more distance between fathers and their children. The divorce rate skyrocketed as more women entered the labor market, and by the 1970s it exceeded the marriage rate.[40] Today 19% of white households and 53% of black households are headed by single parents—about 85% of them single-mothers. Black single-parent households are largely the result of a decline in marriage: In 2010, only 54% of black women had ever married, compared to 76% of white women.[41] The Moynihan Report[42] decried the fact that nearly one-third of black children were born to single-mothers.[43] However, by 1970 that figure had risen to 38% of black children, and it now stands at 70%.[44] Stepfamilies and nonmarital co-habitation have also increased significantly, and today men are increasingly expected to participate in the care of children who are not their biological offspring. All of these factors have distanced fathers from their children, creating a crisis in fatherhood. In 1998, the federal government issued an executive order directing more research and strategies to focus on how to encourage active fathering.[45]

Scholars have responded to the crisis in fatherhood with more research on understanding how fathers define their roles and contribute to the lives of their children. Several studies have confirmed that the involved father ideal has become dominant in American culture: for example, one study found that 64% of fathers living with their own infant children said showing the child love and affection was their top goal, compared to 6% who ranked taking care of the child financially as their top goal.[46] This fathering ideology has led to an increase in the amount of one-on-one time married fathers spend with their child, which has doubled since the 1960s. Researchers have found that there are emotional and marital benefits for fathers who become more involved in child-rearing and those fathers tend to make unique contributions to the development of their children. They engage in more recreational activities with children and teach children instrumental skills, such as problem solving, goal setting, and independence.[47]

Fathers who are married and living with their children are in the best position to become involved in their care. Jacobsen and Edmondson analyzed data from the National Survey of Families and Households and found that, among married fathers, African American, Hispanic, and white fathers are equally involved with their children.[48] Gender ideologies intersect with race in affecting how fathers divide their time between work and family life. When white married men with traditional gender ideologies become fathers they spend even more time at work, but fathers with egalitarian gender ideologies spend less time at work.[49] This study found that black married fathers, regardless of their gender ideology, adopted more egalitarian work-family arrangements when they became fathers.

The crisis in fatherhood theme, however, has focused mostly on men who are separated from their children, especially African American men. Being a non residential father was equated with being absent from the lives of children, but studies show that this is not the case. Fathers who do not live with their children also embrace the involved father ideal, and today are more likely to see their children every week than they were in the 1970s.[50] Other researchers have found that the actual amount of time fathers spend with their children is less important than their child-rearing style and how much responsibility they assume for childcare.[51] Most nonresidential fathers (65%) pay at least some child support and many single fathers have custody of their children.[52] In 1980, there were 690,000 single-father families, but the figure has now risen to 1.8 million.[53] Recent studies have also documented the participation of low-income and nonresidential black fathers in the lives of their children, challenging the myth of the missing black father.[54]

SOCIAL CLASS DIVERSITY AND FATHERHOOD

The ability of fathers to participate in the lives of their children, how they interact with their children, and their child-rearing strategies are strongly shaped by their social class position. Social class has been found to be the major factor predicting parental ideologies and child-rearing strategies although these studies have focused more on mothers than fathers.[55] As modernization unfolded in the early twentieth century, ideologies about how children should be reared changed, as parents (mostly mothers) were supposed to invest more intently in the emotional and psychological well-being of their children. The focus on strict obedience and physical punishment was waning and, while parents were still in control, they were more likely to negotiate decisions with their children. But to what extent were American parents actually embracing these new modern values? Melvin Kohn explored that question and found that social class shaped child-rearing strategies more than any other factor.[56] Lower- and working-class parents expected obedience and conformity from their children; they were not very verbally expressive with their children and tended to discipline them physically. Middle-class parents embraced the new modern values: They valued curiosity and autonomy in their children and engaged verbally with their children. Children were allowed and encouraged to speak up and, while parents were in control, they negotiated more decisions with their children.

These findings have been updated in a more recent study, *Unequal Childhoods*. Published in 2011 by Annette Lareau, the study found that social class—even more than race—shaped how parents socialized their children. Middle-class parents engaged in what she called *concerted cultivation*: They reasoned and negotiated with their children, taught them to speak up (even to authority figures), and invested heavily in activities that fostered their children's talents and intellectual growth.[57] The child-rearing strategy of lower- and working-class parents was described as *accomplishment through natural growth*. They emphasized the subordinate status of their children, issued more directives, taught their children to distrust institutions and authorities outside of the family, cultivated kin relationships, and pretty much left their children to entertain themselves playing in the neighborhood. These studies by Kohn and Lareau reflect Baumrind's distinction between authoritarian parenting (a strict, controlling child-rearing strategy that often lacks warmth and support) and authoritative parenting (a blend of social control, warmth, and support).[58]

How the intersection of race and social class influences fathering, however, has not been a topic of much scholarly research. It is still common for research on black fathers to focus on low-income, unmarried, and nonresidential fathers and neglect the class diversity among Blacks that currently exists. Prior to the 1960s, few African Americans were college educated or held professional jobs. Since then, however, blacks have experienced considerable educational and career gains. Today, nearly one-fourth (24%) of African Americans who are employed and over the age of 25 have attained at least a bachelor's degree. The Bureau of Labor Statistics shows that in 2010, 34% of black women and 24% of black men hold jobs in the top occupational category, professional and managerial workers. These educational and professional gains are reflected in higher earning for African Americans: in 2012, more than one-third (38%) of African Americans earned between $35,000 and $100,00 annually, which places them in the middle or upper-middle class. Still, it's worth noting that Black people (15%) remain overrepresented among the poor.[59]

MEDIA MESSAGES AND AFRICAN AMERICAN FATHERS

Although scholars have often neglected to consider how social class matters in fathering, the media have begun to show a more class-diverse image of fathers. Television portrayals implicitly suggest that social class shapes the fathering work and ideologies of men.[60] Too often, the role of father is predicated on the ability to provide material support for the family. Fathers, like mothers, struggle to find a balance between the world of work and family life. The demands of work may explain why married college-educated fathers actually spend less time with their preschool children than less educated fathers.[61]

Television is believed to affect the way in which people think about the American family. It tells us who we are as a society and how we define the family. Brown and Bryant's research indicates that television modifies children's attitudes about the proper behavior by parents and siblings.[62] Yet, as one African American young man said when he called into a talk radio show to announce the news that he was going to be a father for the first time, he stated he will borrow from the images of those TV fathers he grew up with since he did not have a male role model as a child.

Programming can establish an ideological notion of what fathers ought to be. African American men once played marginal and stereotypical roles on television, and were relegated to the status of sub-characters, their concerns as subplots on various shows. This began to change in the 1970s, when Norman Lear created domestic situational televised comedy shows which featured African American men in prominent roles. Some media critics questioned Lear's[63] comedies as too progressive, but one thing was clear: The programs cracked the glass ceiling and opened the door to expose black family life to many viewers. Lear's comedies focused on themes of poverty, race relations, and racial inequality.[64] As Thomas and Callahan stated in *Allocating Happiness: TV Families and Social Class*, the problem with many working-class shows was that they concluded with bittersweet endings.[65]

OUR SOCIAL CLASS ANALYSIS OF
BLACK FATHERS IN SITCOMS

The number of social classes identified by social scientists can range from two (as was the case in classical Marxist theory) to six social classes.[66] For convenience, those six classes are often lumped into three broad groups—For example, the privileged classes, the middle classes, and the lower classes. We follow a similar convention in our analysis by grouping the social classes into three groups: The upper and upper-middle class, the middle and lower-middle class, and the working class and poor.

Lower-Class and Working-Class Fathers

Good Times[67] and *Everybody Hates Chris*[68] offer examples of fathers in the lower and working classes, where African American men are still overrepresented. We analyze these two classes together, although there are some distinctions between them. People in the lower class typically have less than a high school diploma, few marketable skills, and a marginal attachment to the labor market. Their jobs rarely pay livable wages or offer benefits and they experience bouts of poverty, leaving them struggling to survive. Such was the case in the television sitcom *Good Times*, featuring the Evans family, a nuclear family of five composed of two parents and three children. John Amos ("James") and Estelle Rolle ("Florida") played the parents. Both had rural, southern roots and less than a high school education. Both quit high school for financial reasons; James after his father abandoned the family and Florida to help the family survive. The Evans, like thousands of African Americans, migrated north in search of greater opportunity, and moved to live in the Chicago public housing. Their struggle to survive was the key theme of the show.

The life circumstances of people in the working class are often better. People in the working class often have earned a high school diploma and often have additional vocational training. They have varying levels of skills—from manual laborers to those in the skilled trades, such as plumbing. Although the designation is used less today, they usually hold "blue-collar jobs"—they receive hourly wages, perform physical work, and have little job autonomy. It's unclear exactly what Julius the father figure in *Everybody Hates Chris* does for a living, but he fits the working-class image. He is nearly always depicted in a work uniform and carrying a lunchbox. The show revolved around the experiences of teenage, "Chris," who was growing up in the early-to-mid-1980s as part of a five-member nuclear family that lived in Bedford-Stuyvesant, Brooklyn, New York.

Both *Good Times* and *Everybody Hates Chris* depict economically marginal families, although economic survival is more prominent in the former. James Evans, a low-level mechanic, brought few skills to the labor market, other than a willingness to work hard. Despite his best efforts, he was chronically out of work, but continually optimistic about job prospects that never seem to pan out. Their struggle to survive is a theme for the very first episode, when they were short of rent money and every family member had to find a way to contribute to it. In the best circumstances, James is at best a marginal provider. They had sufficient food, but a restricted variety. In one episode, for example, James peeped into a pot of greens on the stove and, disappointed, notes that they usually had meat on Sundays.[69] This contrasts with the working-class family depicted in *Everybody Hates Chris*, where the father (though quite frugal) was a workaholic who held two jobs. Food was never an issue for this stable working-class family. In fact, the mother devoted considerable time to cooking and setting out rather lavish family meals.

James defies scholarly research that implicitly characterizes low-income black fathers as absent from their families. Abandoning the family is never an issue and, despite his lack of job skills and bouts of unemployment, he believes in the traditional family structure. James struggled constantly to conform to the ideology of male as sole wage earner, often at great cost since his wife Florida could have made a significant economic contribution. In one episode, Florida pleaded with James to allow her to return to school, complete her high school degree, and get a job, but he adamantly refused, asking who would do the cooking and cleaning if she went to work.[70] Florida managed to cajole James into some concessions, but he had the final say. James admitted he feared that if she got more education, it would create an imbalance in their relationship—or even marital separation. But James later relented, encouraged her to go to school and announced that he was going to take some classes with her. What is evident in this episode and the series is despite their many challenges their ability to communicate is one of their strongest assets.

Although James is loyal to his family, he is depicted as an angry and hostile patriarch, mostly because of his frustrated struggle to provide for his family. His parenting style matches the working- or lower-class authoritarian model described earlier, as he expects subordination and obedience from his children. He routinely swore at the children and threatened bodily harm to people who offended him. In one episode, his son Michael was so afraid of his father, he feared what he might do that he hid the family gun.[71] Yet, one could also argue that James was frustrated and exhausted which made him appear angry. He never felt like he could get ahead.

Everybody Hates Chris also depicts a traditional breadwinner-homemaker family, but in this case the working-class father, Julius, provides adequately for his family. In fact, he works two jobs, but beyond the satisfaction of taking care of his family, there is no indication that he finds his jobs gratifying. In one episode he is diagnosed with high blood pressure and the doctor prescribes more rest and a better diet.[72] His wife, however, cannot imagine how a man with *two good jobs* and a nice family can be under stress. Nevertheless, his ability to full-time wage earner role allows him to embrace a softer patriarchy and to bend gender roles. His wife is far from the submissive domestic: She is smart, loud, and opinionated and rules her domain with a tight fist, practically barking commands and threats at her children. The father, however, is soft spoken and willing to help with the children. In one episode the two youngest children had the chicken pox and he took care of them, forfeiting an night out with his wife and encouraging her to give his ticket to one of her girlfriends.[73]

These sitcoms also offer differing images of how fathers help their children survive in their neighborhoods and navigate their school environment. Both families lived in apartments and in neighborhoods that are predominantly black, but the quality of their homes and environments differed. The Evans lived in publically subsidized housing project, while Julius had moved his family from public housing to a brownstone. In both cases the children (mostly the sons) faced some bullying, but in *Good Times* that spilled over into criminal activity. In *Everybody Hates Chris,* Chris faced multiple problems, from being bullied and teased for being rejected by girls. He relied on the men in the neighborhood for advice more than his father. His father rarely has good advice about the problems he faced. In one episode, Chris ran for class president and found himself in a lot of trouble.[74] The father blamed him for the problem and told him to figure out how to fix it. On the other hand, in *Good Times*, when Junior (the son) gets in trouble on the streets James is determined to handle it in a manly way—to respond with physical violence.[75]

Research has shown that African American families have high educational aspirations for their children, although they often lack the wherewithal to help their children excel at school.

In *Good Times*, James and Florida have no particular educational goals for their two oldest children (although one of them had college aspirations), but they hang their hopes of their youngest son, who is already excelling in school. This son tried not to disappoint, but his parents simply did not know how to help him achieve academic success: They did not encourage him to study, help him with homework, or consult with his teachers. In *Everybody Hates Chris*, Chris is selected to attend a predominately white school, where the teacher subtle use of racism knows no bounds.[76] There is a tacit implication that he is going to a "better" school and therefore is likely to succeed.

In sum, both of these shows challenged the dominant stereotype about low-income African-American families—that is, that they were single-mother/father absent families. These fathers are present and doing their best to financially support their families and conform to the dominant breadwinner-homemaker family model. Their fathering style leans more toward an authoritarian model, especially with their sons: They expect obedience to the rules and the threat of corporal punishment is often implied, although not actually shown in these sitcoms. Their child-rearing also reflects Lareau's *accomplishment by natural growth*: Their children do not play organized sports or take music or dance lessons, and they are pretty much expected to organize their own leisure time activities.[77]

These families model a certain amount of gender traditionalism, and pass these norms on to their children. In both shows, fathers are allowed to be more nurturing to their daughters than their sons. In *Everybody Hates Chris*, Chris is often reminded that a man must have money to attract women. In one *Good Times* episode, "Insane James," James erupted in an absolute rage after failing to get hired as a window washer, yet was completely dismissive of a job opportunity that was available to his teenage daughter because if she took it she would be out too late. They are proud of their children and their accomplishments, but do not seem to see themselves as very instrumental in their success. Never did these fathers visit their children's schools or teachers, play sports with their children, or take them to football games or other events.

Good Times also calls into question the ideology of the American Dream, the notion that anyone who is willing to work hard in this nation can succeed. James is willing to take on nearly any kind of work, yet he meets with nothing by racial and social class barriers. Still, the family members share a strong sense of solidarity. Both fathers believe their primary job is to keep their family together, whatever the challenges. As stated previously, often times network television promotes the notion that a father's level of respect and self-worth is correlated to his monetary value, but this is not the case for working-class African American television fathers. It wasn't monetary value that gave James or Julius respect among their children, but their ability to keep their family "intact" as they struggle to survive. In obvious and subtle ways these shows present images of low- and working-class African American fathers that challenge the Moynihan Report and most recent scholarly literature that focuses on their absence from families.[78]

The Middle and Lower-Middle Class

America is known as a middle-class society, but the middle class is a large amorphous group that can include a broad range of incomes, occupations, and lifestyles. Today, about 40% of all African American households are in the middle class, as defined by having an annual income of between $35,000 and $100,000.[79] Those in the middle class usually have stable jobs, a college education, and a certain amount of occupational autonomy. Those who were born into the middle class also have the social graces, manners, and cultural capital associated with being middle class. The two television sitcoms we have chosen to analyze in our discussion of fathers in the middle class, *The Jeffersons* and *My Wife and Kids*, have achieved middle-class status in their own lifetime by becoming successful entrepreneurs. They have acquired the economic resources and established the material lifestyles that enable them to claim middle-class status, but neither father has a college degree or many of the values associated with being middle class. In fact, scholars usually define small business owners as being in the "lower-middle class."[80]

The Jeffersons was one of the longest running sitcoms in television history.[81] It premiered in 1975 and ran eleven seasons. Sherman Helmsley ("George Jefferson") and Isabel Sanford (who played Louise, or "Weezie" were the parents of one teenage son, Lionel. These characters were introduced in Lear's popular *All in the Family* sitcom as the working-class neighbors of Archie and Edith Bunker.[82] In *The Jeffersons*, George was the owner of several dry cleaning businesses, which he was able to purchase after suing a bus company for rear-ending his car. That the family is "moving on up" into a higher class is a key theme of the first episode, as they leave their working-class neighborhood for a "deluxe high rise apartment in the sky" in New York City. George, in fact, is moving away from the support of his community and must rely on his own wits and resources to sustain his family. Power and privilege are associated with his new status, but as a black man George finds that difficult to attain.

In comparison, *My Wife and Kids*[83] featured Damon Wayans ("Michael Kyle") as a loving husband and father of three children which ran five seasons, from 2001 to 2005. Michael married "Jay," played by Tisha Campbell Martin, after he impregnated her at the age of seventeen. Despite this very rough beginning, he went on to own a successful trucking company, and has moved his family into a spacious suburban home in Stanford, Connecticut.

Both families conform to the breadwinner-homemaker family model, with the women in charge of the domestic arena. Although they had only one son, who was already a teenager, and Louise was a full-time housewife, George insisted they hire a maid, "Florence," as evidence of their new status. Florence is a major character in the sitcom and appeared in all episodes—even more than their son Lionel. One TV critic stated it was Florence, who kept George grounded and made him remember his roots, more than Louise.

George has made it, but he is not content to rest on his laurels. He was nearly always shown dressed in a suit and tie, forever trying to advance his business or persona. As a result, he was perpetually stressed out. George's business does not leave much time for him to spend with his son, Lionel. When he does interact with him, it is in an authoritarian manner: He expects his teenage and, later, even college student son to do what he is told. Lionel, however, has more progressive ideas about life than his father and they are often at odds. Lionel rarely backs down; for example, he dates and eventually marries an interracial woman, and in one episode insists that he is going to quit college, regardless of what his father has to say.[84] Despite his resources, George's efforts to control his son are often futile.

George's own personality is one of the limitations he faces in being a more effective father. The struggles he has had achieving success in a predominantly white society seem to have left deep scars: Historian Henry Louis Gates described George's character as "short, feisty, rich, racist, and vulgar."[85] He maintains the bee-bop walk characteristic of his working-class roots and, absorbed in work, devotes little time to cultural pursuits, such as the arts. George also lacks the social graces and manners of the middle class: He lives in a predominantly white high-rise apartment, but routinely call his white neighbors "honkies" and refers to Lionel's interracial girlfriend as a "zebra." He slams the door in people's faces and makes it clear that it is his way or the highway. His brutish ways often leave him at odds with his wife and son. They respect his success, but they challenge the way he relates to family and friends.

In *My Wife and Kid*, Michael is a much more laid back business owner—always dressed in casual clothes and appearing rather carefree. Premiering 15 years later than *The Jeffersons*, the show suggests that business success comes easily to at least some African American men. As a father, Michael is young, cool, and hip. Michael's plans hinge on making sure his children do well in life and that they do not make the same mistakes he did, for example, early marriage and parenthood. Michael exemplifies the involved father model. He pampers his youngest daughter and is protective of the sexual purity of his oldest daughter, in some cases being deliberately threatening to the boys she tries to date. Michael constantly talks to his son about career decisions and tries to make him strive for higher things. Gender shapes his child-rearing patterns and the way he treats his children, although the gender distinctions are not rigid. For example, he doesn't mind thumping Junior's head to make a point, but does not behave similarly with his daughters.

Gender may influence his expectations for his children. He wants to protect them all from early pregnancy and childbearing, but while abstinence is the standard for his daughter, it appears that protection is the advice for his son. Despite their best efforts, their son tells them that he is going to be a father. Instead of throwing his son out of the house, he pulls him in and embraces him and tells him "we're not going to let you fall apart and have a rough start the way we did" so he had the son's girlfriend move in to live with them creating an extended family.[86]

In sum, these shows highlight how social class mobility starts to redefine the fathering roles and strategies of these men. In both *The Jeffersons* and *My Wife and Kids*, the fathers are successful in being the sole wage earner for their families, which lessens the threat to their masculinity. In a sense they are able to ease away from an authoritarian parenting style, to negotiate decisions with their children, and to respect their individuality. In the case of *The Jeffersons*, George has little choice as Lionel actively resists being controlled by his father. The younger children featured in *My Wife and Kids*, however, simply have a more loving relationship with their parents. Still, the shows do not depict their child-rearing styles as *concerted cultivation*, as there is little evidence that the parents are building their children's cultural capital by exposing them to arts, museums, and organized leisure time activities.

Upper-Middle-Class Fathers

The Cosby Show the first African-American upper-class family on prime-time television, premiered in the fall of 1985 and had nine successful seasons.[87] The show starred Bill Cosby as "Heathcliff (Cliff) Huxtable" and Phylicia Rashad ("Clare Huxtable") as parenting a family of five children, ranging in age from grade school to a college undergraduate at Princeton. Their occupations–Clare is a successful lawyer and Cliff an obstetrician—and the fact that they live in an upscale neighborhood in Brooklyn Heights, New York places them in the upper-middle class. Their social class origins are unclear, but when the parents of Cliff or Clare appear on the show, they are depicted as solidly middle class. The show's themes are drawn largely from comedian Bill Cosby's stand-up routines, which often focus on the challenges of child-rearing. On the show, Cliff and Clare have a collaborative form of parenting, but the show, especially, features how Cliff deals with his children. Although he enjoys lapsing into traditional black cultural parenting humor ("I brought you into this world, and I can take you out of it!"), he has an authoritative style of parenting. He does not try to exercise unilateral authority in making family decisions and he relies on family meetings, communication, and collaboration.

Blackish is the most recent sitcom featuring an upper-middle class, affluent black family. The show stars Anthony Anderson ("Dre Johnson") and Tracee Ellis Ross ("Rainbow—"Bow"—Johnson") as the parents of four children, who range in age from 16 to twins who are 6 years old. Laurence Fishburne ("Earl "Pops" Johnson") appears in most episodes as Dre's father, who lives with the family. Dre is the senior vice president of the New Urban Division of an advertising agency and his wife, Bow, is a physician. Their college education, professional careers, and life style place them in the upper-middle class, although the show often suggests that there is some level of class tension between Dre and Bow. Bow, a mixed race daughter of hippies, is firmly entrenched in upper-middle class values, including when it comes to child-rearing. Dre, on the other hand, blends traditional black cultural norms—often associated with the lower class—with the expectations of his new class status. Thus, Dre is a complex character. He wants to be the dad with "swagger." He has a walk-in closet lined with dozens of sneakers and rarely is he seen wearing a business suit to work to display his wealth and ease to his viewers. His parenting style is more intrusive, but it is also thoughtful and authoritative. Dre provides his children with all of the comforts of upper-middle-class life, but wants them to understand black cultural traditions.

Both Dre and Cliff take fathering seriously and engage in the lives of their children. They use humor and pranks as part of their disciplinary style and focus on allowing their children to learn life lessons. In one episode, for example, Cliff challenges his son Theo's mediocre school performance and insistence that, unlike his professional, college-educated parents, he just wants to be like "ordinary people" with a hands-on and comedic lesson about finances. Dre is eager to teach his son life lessons, such as dealing with bullies at school by playing the dozens rather than physical violence. He wants his son to be successful in the larger society as well as in his own community.

One of the differences between Cliff and Dre in their fathering roles emerges from their class backgrounds: Cliff is from middle-class roots and, while often frustrated with his children, more confident in his ability to deal with them. Dre, on the other hand, is evolving in his role as father, as seen in an episode where he is torn apart over a decision of whether or not to spank his 6-year-old son.[88] What is most interesting about Andre's character is that he was comfortable self-disclosing his fears or problems as a parent to his colleagues. At his workplace he has created a male parenting support system, which is comprised of a racially diverse group. He talks about his childhood, parenting and marital mistakes or racial dilemmas. It is refreshing to see Andre opening up about his marriage and parenting and revealing he's not perfect in either one. As one media critic said, "The producers of blackish are comfortable not following Cosby's model of perfection as a father."[89] The producers suggest that part of parenthood is making mistakes, the only difference is the Johnsons have enough support and resources not to get caught up in them.

Of the six black sitcoms analyzed in this paper, *The Cosby Show* and *blackish* are best at showing that most African American parents engage in the racial socialization of their children. Racial socialization includes a broad range of behaviors, from instilling in black children a sense of pride to teaching them how to survive in a predominantly white society. *The Cosby Show* has been criticized for not dealing with racial issues, yet is it replete with subtle and sometimes open affirmations of the black experience. The parents are graduates of historically black universities, their home displays black art, their children meet successful black celebrities, and episodes end by recalling events such as the March on Washington.[90] Cliff's goal is not only to provide material items or money to his children, but to transfer a strong sense of culture by exposing them to jazz, the arts, historical black colleges, and various historical traditions. He sees education as the key to success and is disappointed when one of his daughters drops out of college.

Racial socialization is the Johnson household, as depicted in *blackish*, comes mostly from Dre and is often unconventional. For example, he wants to celebrate Martin Luther King Day not by attending a rally or church services, but by taking his children on a skiing trip and staying in an upscale lodge—something Blacks could not do prior to the civil rights movement. Dre, aided by his father Pop, wants to teach his 13-year-old son African American cultural signifiers such as "The Nod" and "Playing the Dozens," which also represent a form of black masculinity.[91] Thomas Garner describes the dozens as a game to use language to ridicule and vilify an opponent.[92] The nod is a subtle lowering of a man's head to acknowledge each other's existence in a primarily white environment and to show ethnic solidarity.

On a broader level, these shows also highlight the strong intergenerational family ties that are characteristic of African American families. In lower-income families, these ties are often more obligatory and based on financial hardship, but among more affluent families that tend to be voluntary and mutually satisfying, although not completely without strains. On *The Cosby Show* both Cliff and Claire are close to their own parents, who often appear on the show. They are doting grandparents, but are not depended on for babysitting or financial help, and they rarely interfere with child-rearing decisions. In *blackish* the family structure is extended, as Dre's father ("Pops") lives with the family. Here again we see subtle differences in the roles of grandparents, with this leaning more toward the traditional model. Pops sees himself as somewhat the family patriarch who questions his son's parenting style and imparts life lessons to his grandson. But Dre is open to improvement and change, willing to do things differently than his own parents.

In sum, *blackish* and *The Cosby Show* makes upper-class family life seem attainable for African American families. At the same time, they tacitly promote a heterosexual ideology and the notion that marriage promotes wealth and family stability, and they tacitly associate success, power, and privilege with middle-class values. They demonstrate the involved fathering model by being actively involved in the daily activities and the lives of their children; they also exemplify authoritative parenting, which means being supportive, establishing limits, providing assistance, and noncoercive discipline. Their children are well dressed, attractive and well behaved and void of serious social problems that some children living in the city experience. According to most social theorists, authoritative parenting predicts academic success, lower levels of the externalizing behavior problems and internalizing problems, and positive social behavior. Parke claims "fathers who remembered their childhood attachment experiences, including both, positive and negative feelings, and who were open and nondefensive about their recollections continued to be better fathers as their children developed."[93]

We are starting to see more affluent African American families on television. These are household with the annual earning of $350,000 and above. For the past decade, several representatives of upper-class families have aired on cable network television, instead of prime-time network television, with a growing number of shows as reality programming. These reality television shows feature personalities drawn from the entertainment and sports world who display their wealth, family dynamics and extreme lifestyle.

IMPLICATIONS

Televised family sitcoms are comedic takes on how families handle situations that, for the most part, are easily resolvable. Most feature middle-class white families; thus, *Good Times* broke new ground by featuring a poor, black family. The show was often criticized, but research has found that many men can relate to the father ("James Evans") in this show. According to one study, 87% of young working-class urban males viewed James stronger and more masculine than Cliff Huxtable, the father in *The Cosby Show*, who was seen as effeminate and weak.[94] As Cazenave states "there are differences in how black and white men see their world and the appropriate strategies for operating within it."[95]

When working-class white families are depicted in sitcoms (e.g., *All in the Family*, *The Simpsons*, *Roseanne*), the show makes clear that they are neither normative American families nor representative of the American Dream.[96] In fact, over the past 50 years there has been a plethora of research, analyzing network television's portrayal of working-class families, and much of it is criticizing the portrayal of working-class men as clowns, buffoons and ineffective dads. *Everybody Hates Chris*, however, offers a positive portrayal of a black working-class family. "Julius" is not depicted as a clown, buffoon, or irresponsible father; rather, he works two jobs and, when needed, is willing to pitch in around the house. His relationship with his children is somewhat detached, but mostly due to his own inability to instill in them middle-class norms. Middle-class African American fathers, depicted in *The Jeffersons* and *My Wife and Kids*, have provided their children with sufficient material resources, and they work hard to make sure they will take advantage of them.

Finally, *The Cosbys* and *Blackish* represent black men as having a highly involved and hands-on approach to childbearing. Both embrace an authoritative model of parenting, although the father ("Dre") in *blackish* struggles to keep some black traditions and release others. He wants children who can effectively navigate white and black environment, and is torn on issues such as whether children should be spanked. These shows represented the American dream in which middle-class fathers are comfortable socializing with their neighbors and have time to spend at home with their children, providing them with a sense of safety and security. What was lost from these shows were the ability to tell unique stories about their struggles and experiences.

CONCLUSION

We have argued that media images are powerful; they shape attitudes and even behaviors. For most of U.S. history, the lives of African Americans have been constrained by either slavery or racial segregation, both of which were justified by theories of biological inferiority and racist stereotypes. Thus, television sitcoms that depict African Americans in a demeaning fashion have always been especially objectionable, as they can perpetuate racist attitudes and behaviors. On the other hand, sitcoms that present black families as merely darker versions of white families can also be criticized for suggesting that race no longer matters in American society. The variety of sitcoms now being aired, however, characterize African American fathers in ways that offer a further rebuff to the Moynihan Report.[97] These shows also illustrate that there is no single "black family"—instead, African American families are evolving, diverse, and increasingly shaped by social class.

206 *Shirley A. Hill and Janice Kelly*

NOTES

1. Richard Butsch, "Class and Gender in Four Decades of Television Situation Comedy," *Critical Studies in Mass Communication,* 9, no. 4, (1992): 387–399.

2. Jake Harwood and Karen Anderson, "Social Change Membership and Family Involvement on Prime-Time Television," *The Electronic Journal of Communication,* 11, no. 1 (2001): 11–28.

3. *Leave it to Beaver,* CBS-TV, October 4, 1957–June 20, 1963.

4. Talcott Parsons, "Family Structure and the Socialization of the Child," in *The Ecology of Human Development: Experiments by Nature and Design,* ed. Urie Bronfenbrenner (Cambridge: Harvard University Press, 1979), 238–248.

5. Barbara Risman, *Gender Vertigo: American Families in Transition* (New Haven: Yale University Press, 1998).

6. *Amos n Andy Show,* NBC-TV, November 1951–May 1953.

7. *Pittsburgh Courier Newspaper,* Established 1910–1966.

8. NAACP, established in Baltimore, MC, February 12, 1979.

9. *Sanford and Son,* NBC-TV, January 14, 1972–March 25, 1979.

10. *The Jeffersons,* CBS-TV, January 18, 1975–July 2, 1985.

11. *Good Times,* CBS-TV, February 8, 1974–August 1, 1979.

12. Barbara Laslett and Barrie Thorne, "Life Histories of a Movement: An Introduction," in *Feminist Sociology: Life Histories of a Movement,* eds. Barbara Laslett and Barrie Thorne (New Brunswick, NJ: Rutgers University Press, 1997).

13. Donna L. Franklin, *Ensuring Inequality: The Structural Transformation of the African American Family* (New York: Oxford University Press, 1997); Edward Franklin Frazier, *The Negro in the United States* (New York: MacMillan, 1949).

14. *Julia,* NBC-TV, September 17, 1968–March 23, 1971.

15. *That's My Mama,* ABC-TV, September 4, 1974–December 24, 1975.

16. *What's Happening!!,* ABC-TV, August 5, 1976–April 28, 1979.

17. Marshall McLuhan, *Understanding Media: the Extensions of Man* (New York: McGraw-Hill, 1964).

18. Leslie B. Inniss and Joe. R. Feagin. "*The Cosby Show*: The View from the Black Middle Class," *Journal of Black Studies,* 25, no. 6 (1995): 692–671.

19. Neil Postman, *Amusing Ourselves to Death: Public Discourse in the Age of Show Business* (New York: Viking 1985).

20. Donna Bassin, Margaret Honey, and Meryle M. Kaplan, *Representation of Motherhood* (New Haven: Yale University Press, 1996).

21. *Cosby Show,* NBC-TV, September 20, 1984–April 30, 1992.

22. *Blackish,* ABC-TV, September 24, 2014–Present.

23. *My Wife and Kids,* ABC-TV, September 24, 2001–April 26, 2005.

24. *Everybody Hates Chris,* UPN-TV, September 22, 2005–May 8, 2006.

25. Marie Osmond and Thorne Barrie, "Feminist Theories: The Social Construction of Gender in Families and Society," in *Sourcebook on Family Theories and Methods: A Contextual Approach,* ed. Pauline Boss, William J. Doherty, Ralph LaRossa, Walter R. Schumn and Suzanne K. Steinmetz (New York: Plenum, 1993), 591–622.

26. John W. Blassingame, *The Slave Community: Plantation Life in the Antebellum South, 1750–1925* (New York: Oxford University Press, 1972).

27. Steven Mintz and Susan Kellogg, *Domestic Relations: A Social History of American Family Life* (Cambridge: Belknap Press of Harvard University Press, 1988).

28. Bonnie Thornton Dill, "Our Mothers' Grief: Racial Ethnic Women and the Maintenance of Families," *Journal of Family History,* 13, no. 4 (1988): 415–431.

29. Andrew G. Truxal and Francis E. Merrill, *The Family in American Culture* (New York: Prentice-Hall, 1947).

30. Franklin, *Ensuring Inequality;* Frazier, *The Negro in the United States.*

31. Shirley A. Hill, *Black Intimacies: A Gender Perspective on Families and Relationships*, (Walnut Creek, CA: AltaMira Press, 2005).

32. Daniel Patrick Moynihan, *The Negro Family: The Case for National Action*, (Washington DC: Office of Policy Planning and Research, 1965).

33. Ibid.

34. Ibid.

35. Robert B. Hill, *The Strengths of Black Families*, (New York: McGraw-Hill, 1972); Andrew Billingsley, *Black Families in White America* (Englewood Cliffs, NJ: Prentice Hall, 1968).

36. Philip N. Cohen, *The Family: Diversity, Inequality, and Social Change* (New York: W.W. Norton & Company, 2015).

37. Scott Hodge and Andrew Lundeen, "America Has Become a Nation of Dual-income Working Couples," Last modified November 21 2013. http:www.taxfoundation.org. Accessed August 13, 2015.

38. Bart Landry, *Black Working Wives: Pioneers of the American Family Revolution* (Berkeley: University of California Press, 2000).

39. Cohen, *The Family: Diversity, Inequality.*

40. Andrew J. Cherlin, *Marriage, Divorce, Remarriage* (Cambridge: Harvard University Press, 1992).

41. Frank Avenilla, Emily Rosenthal and Pete Tice, *Fathers of U.S. Children Born in 2001: Findings From Childhood Longitudinal Study, Birth Cohort* (Washington, D.C.: U.S. Department of Education, 2006).

42. Moynihan, *The Negro Family.*

43. Ibid.

44. Cherlin, *Marriage, Divorce, Remarriage.*

45. William Marsiglio, Paul Amato, Randal D. Day and Michael E. Lamb, "Scholarship on Fatherhood in the 1990s and Beyond," *Journal of Marriage and Family* 62, no. 4 (2000): 1173–1191.

46. Avenilla, *Fathers of U.S. Children.*

47. Richard Spoth, Cleve Redmon, Chungyeol Shin, and Kari Azevedo, "Brief Family Intervention Effects on Adolescent Substance Initiation: School Level Growth Curve Analyses 6 Years Following Baseline," *Journal of Consult Clinical Psychology*, 72, no. 3 (2004): 535–542.

48. Linda Jacobsen and Brad Edmondson, "Father Figures," *Demographics* 15, no. 8 (1993): 22–29.

49. Rebecca Glauber and Kristi L. Gozjolko. "Do Traditional Fathers Always Work More?" *Journal of Marriage and Family* 73, no. 5 (2011): 1133–1148.

50. William Marsiglio et al., "Scholarship on Fatherhood," 1173–1192.

51. Ronald Palkovitz, "Involved Fathering and Child Development: Understanding our Understanding of Good Fathers," in *Handbook of Father Involvement: Multidiscpinary Perspectives*, ed. Catherine. S. Tamis-LeMonda and Natasha Cabera (Mahwah, NJ: Lawrence Erlbaum Associates, 2002), 119–140.

52. Linda Jacobsen and Brad Edmondson, "Father Figures," *Demographics* 15, no. 8 (1993): 22–29.

53. Cherlin, *Marriage, Divorce, Remarriage.*

54. Robert L. Coles, "Black Single Fathers: Choosing to Parent Full-Time," *Journal of Contemporary Ethnography* 31, no. 4 (2002): 411–440; Jennifer Hamer, "What It Means To Be A Daddy: Fatherhood For Black Men Living Away From Their Children," in *Shifting the Center: Understanding Contemporary Families,* ed. Susan J. Ferguson. (New York: McGraw-Hill, 2010), 334–348.

55. Annette Lareau, *Unequal Childhoods: Class, Race, and Family Life* (Berkeley: University of California Press, 2006); Melvin L. Kohn, "Social-Class and Parent-Child Relationships," *American Journal of Sociology* 68, no. 4 (1963): 471–480.

56. Kohn, "Social-Class and Parent-Child Relationships."

57. Lareau, *Unequal Childhoods: Class, Race.*

58. Diane Baumrind, "Effects of Authoritative Parental Control on Child Behavior." *Child Development* 37 (1966): 62–86.

59. Ibid.

60. Jake Harwood and Karen Andersen, "The Presence and Portrayal of Social Groups on Prime-time Television," *Communication Reports*, 15 (2002): 81–97.

61. Ibid.

62. Dan Brown and Jennings Bryant, "Effects of Television on Family Values and Selected Attitudes and Behaviors," in *Television and the American Family*, ed. Jennings Bryant (Hillsdale, NJ: Lawrence Erlbaum Publishers, 1990), 253–274.

63. *Leave it to Beaver*, CBS-TV, October 4, 1957–June 20, 1963.

64. Ella Taylor, *Prime-time Families: Television Culture in Postwar America* (Oakland, CA: University of California Press, 1989).

65. Sari Thomas and Brian P. Callahan, "Allocating Happiness: TV Families and Social Class," *Journal of Communication*, 32 (1982): 184–190.

66. Dennis Gilbert, *The American Class Structure in an Age of Growing Inequality* (Thousand Oaks, CA: Sage Publication, 2011)

67. *Good Times*, CBS-TV, February 8, 1974–August 1, 1979

68. *Everybody Hates Chris*, UPN-TV, September 22, 2005–May 8, 2005.

69. *Good Times,* Season, 1, episode 3.

70. *Good Times,* Season, 2, episode 15.

71. *Good Times,* Season 3, episode 2.

72. *Everybody Hates Chris*, Season 1, episode 16.

73. *Everybody Hates Chris*, Season 1, episode 21.

74. *Everybody Hates* Chris, Season 2, episode 2.

75. *Good Times*, season 2, episode 9.

76. Martin N. Marger, *Social Inequality: Patterns and Processes* (New York: McGraw-Hill, 2008).

77. Baumrind, "Effects of Authoritative Parental Control."

78. Moynihan, *The Negro Family.*

79. Gilbert, *The American Class Structure.*

80. Marger, *Social Inequality: Patterns and Processes.*

81. *The Jeffersons*, CBS-TV, January 18, 1975–July 2, 1985.

82. *All in the Family*, CBS-TV, January 12, 1971–April 18, 1979.

83. *My Wife and Kids*, ABC-TV, September 24, 2001–April 26, 2005.

84. *The Jeffersons*, season 1, episode 4.

85. Henry Louis Gates, "TV's Black World Turns—But Stay Unreal," *New York Times*, November 12, 1989, accessed August 8, 2015, http://www.nytimes.com/all&src=pm.html.

86. *Wife and Kids*, season 4, episode 1.

87. *Cosby Show*, NBC-TV, September 20, 1984–April 30, 1992.

88. *Blackish*, Season 1, episode 5.

89. Debra Smith, "Critiquing Reality-based Televised Black Fatherhood: A Critical Analysis of Run's House & Snoop Dogg," *Critical Studies in Media Communication*, 25, no. 4 (2008): 393–412.

90. *The Cosby Show*, season 3, episode 6.

91. *Blackish*, Season 1, episode 3; *Blackish*, Season 1, episode 15.

92. Thomas Garner, "Playing the Dozens: Folklore as Strategies for Living," in *African American Communication & Identities*, ed. Ronald L. Jackson (Thousand Oaks, CA: Sage Publications, 2004), 80–88.

93. Ross Parke. "Father Involvement: A development Perspective." *Journal of Marriage and Family Review*, 29 (2009), 43–58.

94. Anne Chen, "Bill Cosby: America's Father," in *Black Fathers: An Invisible Presence in America*, eds. Michael E. Connors and Joseph White (New York: Routledge, 2006).

95. Noel A.Cazenave, "Middle-Income Black Father: An Analysis of the Provider Role: The Family Coordinator," *Journal of Men's Roles in the Family*, 28, no. 4 (1979): 583–593.

96. *The Simpsons*, FOX-TV, December 17, 1989–Present; *Roseanne* ABC-TV, October 18, 1988–May 20, 1997.

97. Moynihan, *The Negro Family.*

BIBLIOGRAPHY

Amos n Andy Show. NBC-TV. November 1951–May 1953.

Avenilla, Frank, Emily Rosenthal, and Pete Tice. *Fathers of U.S. Children Born in 2001: Findings From Childhood Longitudinal Study, Birth Cohort*. Washington, DC: U.S. Department of Education, 2006.

Bassin, Donna, Margaret Honey, and Meryle M. Kaplan. *Representation of Motherhood*. New Haven: Yale University Press, 1996.

Baumrind, Diane. "Effects of Authoritative Parental Control on Child Behavior." *Child Development* 37 (1966): 62–86.

Billingsley, Andrew. *Black Families in White America.* Englewood Cliffs, NJ: Prentice Hall, 1968.

Blackish. ABC-TV, 2014–Present.

Blassingame, John W. *The Slave Community: Plantation Life in the Antebellum South, 1750–1925.* New York: Oxford University Press, 1972.

Brown, Dan, and Jennings Bryant. "Effects of Television on Family Values and Selected Attitudes and Behaviors." In *Television and the American Family*, edited by Jennings Bryant, 253–274. Hillsdale, NY: Lawrence Erlbaum Publishers, 1990.

Butsch, Richard. "Class and Gender in Four Decades of Television Situation Comedy." *Critical Studies in Mass Communication*, 1992: 387–399.

Cazenave, Noel A. "Middle-Income Black Father: An Analysis of the Provider Role: The Family Coordinator." *Journal of Men's Roles in the Family,* 28, no. 4 (1979): 583–593.

Chen, Anne. "Bill Cosby: America's Father." In *Black Fathers: An Invisible Presence in America*, edited by Michael E. Connors and Joseph White. New York: Routledge, 2006.

Cherlin, Andrew J. *Marriage, Divorce, Remarriage.* Cambridge: Harvard University Press, 1992.

Cohen, Philip N. *The Family: Diversity, Inequality, and Social Change.* New York: W.W. Norton & Company, 2015.

Coles, Robert L. "Black Single Fathers: Choosing to Parent Full-Time." *Journal of Contemporary Ethnography* 31, no. 4 (2002): 411–440.

Cosby Show, The. NBC-TV, 1984–1992.

Dil, Bonnie Thornton. "Our Mothers' Grief: Racial Ethnic Women and the Maintenance of Families." *Journal of Family History* 13, no. 4 (1988): 415–431.

Everybody Hates Chris. UPN-TV, 2005–2006.

Franklin, Donna L. *Ensuring Inequality: The Structural Transformation of the African American Family.* New York: Oxford University Press, 1997.

Frazier, Franklin Edward. *The Negro in the United States.* New York: MacMillan, 1949.

Garner, Thomas. "Playing the Dozens: Folklore as Strategies for Lliving." In *African American Communication & Identities*, edited by Ronald L. Jackson, 80–88. Thousand Oaks, CA: Sage Publications, 2004.

Gates, Henry Louis. "TV's Black World Turns—But Stay Unreal." *NY Times.* November 12, 1989. http://www.nytimes.com/all&src=pm.html. (accessed August 8, 2015).

Gilbert, Dennis. *The American Class Structure in an Age of Growing Inequality.* Thousand Oaks, CA: Sage Publication, 2011.

Glauber, Rebecca, and Kristi L. Gozjolko. "Do Traditional Fathers Always Work More? Gender Ideology, Race, and Parenthood." *Journal of Marriage and Family* 73, no. 5 (2011): 1133–1148.

Good Times. CBS-TV, 1974–1979.

Hamer, Jennifer. "What It Means To Be A Daddy: Fatherhood For Black Men Living Away From Their Children." In *Shifting the Center: Understanding Contemporary Families*, edited by Susan J. Ferguson, 334–248. New York: McGraw-Hill, 2010.

Harwood, Jake, and Karen Anderson. "Social Change Membership and Family Involvement on Prime-time Television." *The Electronic Journal of Communication* 11, no. 1 (2001): 11–28.

Harwood, Jake, and Karen Anderson. "The Presence and Portrayal of Social Groups on Prime-time Television." *Communications Reports* 15 (2002): 91–97.

Hill, Robert B. *The Strengths of Black Families*. New York: McGraw-Hill, 1972.

Hill, Shirley A. *Black Intimacies: A Gender Perspective on Families and Relationships*. Walnut Creek, CA: AltaMira Press, 2005.

Hodge, Scott, and Andrew Lundeen. "America Has Become a Nation of Dual-income Working Couples." *taxfoundation.org*. November 21, 2013. http:www.taxfoundation.org (accessed August 13, 2015).

Inniss, Leslie B., and Joe R. Feagin. "The Cosby Show: The View from the Black Middle Class." *Journal of Black Studies* 25, no. 6 (1995): 692–711.

Jeffersons, The. CBS-TV, 1975–1985.

Jacobsen, Linda, and Brad Edmondson. "Father Figures." *Demographics* 15, no. 8 (1993): 22–29.

Julia. NBC-TV, 1968–1971.

Kohn, Melvin L. "Social-Class and Parent-Child Relationships." *American Journal of Sociology* 68, no. 4 (1963): 471–480.

Landry, Bart. *Black Working Wives: Pioneers of the American Family Revolution*. Berkeley: University of California Press, 2000.

Lareau, Annette. *Unequal Childhoods: Class, Race, and Family Life*. Berkeley: University of California Press, 2006.

Leave it to Beaver. CBS-TV, 1957–1963.

Marger, Martin N. *Social Inequality: Patterns and Processes*. New York: McGraw-Hill, 2008.

Marsiglio, William, Paul Amato, Randal D. Day, and Michael E. Lamb. "Scholarship on Fatherhood in the 1990s and Beyond." *Journal of Marriage and Family* 61, no. 4 (2000): 1173–1191.

McLuhan, Marshall. *Understanding Media: The Extensions of Man*. New York: McGraw-Hill, 1964.

Mintz, Steve, and Steven Kellogg. *Domestic Relations: A Social History of American Family Life*. Cambridge: Belknap Press of Harvard University Press, 1988.

Moynihan, Daniel Patrick. *The Negro Family: The Case for National Action*. Washington, DC: Office of Policy Planning and Research, 1965.

My Wife and Kids. ABC-TV, 2001–2005.

Osmond, Marie, and Barrie Thorne. "Feminist Theories: the Social Construction of Gender in Families and Society." In *Sourcebook on Family Theories and Methods: A Contextual Approach*, edited by Pauline Boss, William J Doherty, Ralph LaRossa, Walter R. Schumm and Suzanne K. Steinmetz, 591–622. New York: Plenum, 1993.

212 *Shirley A. Hill and Janice Kelly*

Palkovitz, Ronald. "Involved Fathering and Child Development: Understanding our Understanding of Good Fathers." In *Handbook of Father Involvement: Multidisciplinary Perspectives*, 119–140. Mahwah, NJ: Lawrence Erlbaum Associates, 2002.

Parke, Ross. "Father Involvement: A Development Perspective." *Journal of Marriage and Family Review* 29 (2009): 43–58.

Parsons, Talcott. "Family Structure and the Socialization of the Child." In *The Ecology of Human Development: Experiments by Nature and Design*, edited by Urie Bronfenbrenner, 238–248. Cambridge: Harvard University Press, 1979.

Postman, Neil. *Amusing Ourselves to Death: Public Discourse in the Age of Show Business*. New York: Penguin Books, 1985.

Risman, Barbara. *Gender Vertigo: American Families in Transition*. New Haven: Yale University Press, 1988.

Roseanne. ABC-TV, 1988–1997.

Sanford and Son. NBC-TV, 1972–1979.

Simpsons, The. FOX-TV, 1988–Present.

Smith, Debra. "Critiquing Reality-based Televised Black Fatherhood: A Critical Analysis of Run's House & Snoop Dogg." *Critical Studies in Media Communication* 25, no. 4 (2008): 393–412.

Spoth, Richard, Cleve Redmon, Chungyeol Shin, and Kari Azevedo. "Brief Family Intervention Effects on Adolescent Substance Initiation: School Level Growth Curve Analyses 6 Years Following Baseline." *Journal of Consult Clinical Psychology* 72, no. 3 (2004): 535–542.

Taylor, Ella. *Ella Taylor, Prime-time Families: Television Culture in Postwar America*. Oakland, CA: University of California Press, 1989.

That's My Mama. ABC-TV, 1974–1975.

Thomas, Sari, and Brian P. Callahan. "Allocating Happiness: TV Families and Social Class." *Journal of Communication* 32 (1982): 184–190.

Thorne, Barrie, and Barbara Laslett. "Life Histories of a Movement: An Introduction." In *Feminist Sociology: Life Histories of a Movement*, edited by Barbara Laslett and Barrie Thorne. New Brunswick, NJ: Rutgers University Press, 1997.

Truxal, Andrew G., and Francis E. Merrill. *The Family in American Culture*. New York: Prentice-Hall, 1947.

What's Happening!! ABC-TV, 1976–1979.

Chapter 10

Queering Daddy or Adopting Homonormative Fatherhood?

Lynda Goldstein

REPRESENTING GAY DADS ON PRIME-TIME TELEVISION SITUATION COMEDIES

Coaching a son in his ring-bearing duties only to have him back out on the wedding. Teaching a son the fine art of embalming a body so he can assume the family business. Bribing a son with Cheerios to lie about your age, then twenty years later smiling at the idea he is marrying your best friend's daughter. These moments portray gay fatherhood as poignant, nurturing, and amusing milestones in a gay man's life. Indeed, linked as they are to marriage and inheritance, they also mark inevitable milestones (from a traditional perspective) in a gay couple's relationship. Each occurred in the final episodes of three television shows—*Queer as Folk*, *Six Feet Under*, and *Will & Grace*—making 2005–2006 a watershed year for representing a very different kind of identity for gay men in the culture.[1] In the wake of the AIDS crisis in the gay community, liberalized surrogacy and adoption laws, and the Lawrence v. Texas decision,[2] social, legal, and public policy changes[3] that accommodated the idea of—even the desire for—gay fatherhood became cultural realities reflected by prime-time cable and network television shows. Previously considered incompatible and unimaginable, both in society and on television,[4] the combination of gay identity and fatherhood was ready for prime time in 2005–2006 as a coherent and stable identity. The gay dad—at least in the final episodes of these long-running series[5]—was presented as a reasonable identity, although with limited narrative development or attention drawn to its importance as a cultural phenomenon. Yet the gay dad as a *continuing* television character would appear thereafter with increasing frequency and nuance on other shows, culminating most recently in its most "normalized" representations on two prime-time network situation comedies: ABC's *Modern Family* (2009–Present) and NBC's *The New Normal* (2012–2013).

Understanding how these representations of gay fatherhood ply the contours of normalization—in its most common sense meaning of "average" or "like everyone else"—necessitates tracing the historical context of representing gay dads on television and a consideration of the extent to which these representations have reflected or challenged some of the complexities and realities of gay fathers in the world.[6] As well, it requires examining the possibilities and constraints posed by genre and various distribution systems on cable or network television. Finally, it means considering the cultural context in which these representations are both made and watched. Read within an already existing (yet changeable) interpretive framework, televisual representations most immediately impact viewers, yet have a ripple effect on the larger culture. A crucial question for what these normalized televisual representations of gay fatherhood mean in and for contemporary American society is whether they "queer" the notion of what it means to be a dad or, as some critics allege, recuperate gay men into a homonormative narrative of fatherhood that compromises their queerness as a positively imagined marginal status.[7]

Certainly, one of the constitutive factors in "normalizing" the gay dad for audiences is how the character occupies the narrative and imaginative space of a television show. Does the narrative *lead* to gay fatherhood as a sign of a maturing relationship—whether represented with some nuance or reductively presented as a plot device—or is it *premised* (as are *Modern Family* and *The New Normal*) on de facto gay fatherhood? The latter is far more "normalizing" of the gay dad for audiences, because fatherhood is conceived as the social precondition for an adult male. Moreover, privileging gay dads as main characters (in ensemble or with a supporting cast) rather than positioning them as regular supporting or recurring characters signals a shift toward mainstreaming, rather than marginalizing, the representational status of gay dads.[8] Another factor contributing to normalization is genre and viewer access. The situation comedy has some of the most constraining genre elements, tending toward limiting character development and narrative trajectory. Any "normalization" that accrues to a previously marginalized character in one of the most popular television formats can only do so because the genre simultaneously reinforces and innovates its characterizations and narrative form, and it does so within cultural, social, and political contexts that are in flux. Putting the representations of gay dads in *Modern Family* and *The New Normal* into this rich context reveals the extent to which the social realities of gay fatherhood are being reconceptualized and renegotiated.

On one level, the constraints on character development offered by genre and distribution, particularly for shows packaged by the television industry for consumption by similarly interested audiences,[9] mean that audience expectations for what is possible are carefully calibrated. Thus, a darkly comic drama on cable television will have fewer constraints on character development and narrative complexity than a situation comedy on network television and each will have an audience calibrated to those differences. *Queer as Folk* and *Six Feet Under* have the genre flexibility and small, dedicated audiences typical of subscriber cable channels to represent the difficulties of negotiating queer professional identities or interracial relationships (between dads Keith and David and between David and the adopted boys) and of negotiating extended family systems as well as those governing foster care and adoption. On the other hand, *Will & Grace* as a network sitcom addressed to a mass audience can only *refer* to the alternative means (surrogacy) of becoming parents and only *refer* to Will and Vince as parents—at least in 2006, and this opacity may satisfy a mass audience while frustrating an audience more invested in the representation of gay fatherhood or more desirous of character complexity. On another level, the constraints of social realities and theoretical imaginings of what it means to be gay, to be a father, and to be queer at a particular moment in history will also influence what representations of gay dads mean. Clearly, there are political and existential consequences for society at large, as well as the broader LGBTQ community, so how these representations are theoretically framed is not simply a matter of academic debate. Televisual representations of characters that belong to any group considered outside the mainstream matter deeply to members of those groups because of the ways that viewers—both in and outside of those groups—tend to reduce those representations to stereotypes that they imagine characterize all group members.[10] This reductive framing is often dichotomous; for our discussion, these either/or formulations have historically divided the identities (and representations) of "gay" from "father" and separated "queer" from "homonormative gay parents." Ultimately, such polarized framing needs to be shifted. It is possible—it is necessary—to transcend or transform how we think about the "normalization" of gay dads, in their televisual and real social worlds, without also fostering a "normative" identity that punitively impacts other LGBTQ identities.

A HISTORY OF REPRESENTING GAY DADS ON TV: CHANGING CONTEXTS AND MEANINGS

Fleshing out the televisual history of gay fatherhood will accomplish two things: provide a context for understanding the significance of *premising Modern Family* and *The New Normal* on the notions of *becoming* and *being* gay dads in a specific narrative and cultural moment and provide a context for an analysis of two types of narrative movement—toward openness or closure, toward messy possibilities or tidy integrations. Historicizing these two narrative possibilities for representing gay dads on television—open to the future and closed within present constraints—provide the starting point for our discussion of *Modern Family* and *The New Normal*. So, we return to our watershed trio of television shows. When Michael and Ben officially adopted Hunter, an HIV-positive teenager, in the season finale of *Queer as Folk*, their action represented a distinct shift in depictions of gay men on TV. From the Showtime cable program's inception, the focus had been on the intersecting lives of several gay and lesbian friends in Pittsburgh as they negotiated love, sex, careers, and lifestyle choices (ranging from clubbing/drugging to home ownership and tenure). Arguably, at its heart was the question of what it might look like (on television) to be queer, to live as gay and lesbian and bisexual people in an urban community with the social and business infrastructure to support those identities. Pitting club star Brian (the "essential gay") against his friend Michael (the "conformist gay" who will move to a house with Ben, get married, and adopt Hunter), the drama imagined the range of desires for gay men: free from the encumbrances of normative family life or embracing those benchmarks of normative adult identity.

That Brian and Michael both are also fathers—each donating sperm to one half of a lesbian couple (Brian to Lindsay, resulting in Gus and Michael to Melanie, resulting in Jenny)—with varying degrees of interest and parental activity over the five seasons of the show's run is important to note. The depiction of gay fatherhood here is at its most reductive a sperm donation to lesbian moms who perform all of the active parenting[11] and at its most participatory an occasion to manipulate one or more of the friends into some selfishly motivated action (such as not moving to Canada). While Brian has his ring-bearer moment with Gus and Michael and Ben nurture their foster son Hunter as much as an independently minded teen will allow, the show is not concerned with showcasing how gay men exercise their good parenting skills. It is, however, concerned with the messy entanglements of queerness, gayness, coupling/uncoupling, and notions of family that are ultimately defined in Kath Weston's terms as "families we choose."[12] In the final scene of the series, Michael and Brian recapture their free and open dance club lives at Babylon (fire-bombed and burned to the ground). While Babylon may no longer be a physical reality, its presence—relived in memories—is meant to convey the *essential* characteristic of their gay male identities. Their status as gay dads is not, not even for the more ostensibly "normative" Michael who is married with two children.

In sharp contrast, subscribers to HBO watched David Fisher and Keith Charles finally stabilize their relationship, then adopt Anthony and Durrell, two African American brothers whom they were fostering in Season 5 of the dark comedy, *Six Feet Under*. As fathers, they struggled to determine the right balance of discipline and affection for two boys with trust and anger issues caused by their previous foster care experiences. These moments of engaged parenting provided viewers with sustained representations of two gay men as dads, intertwined with other events in the couple's life (such as David's nightmarish memories of a horrifying attack in Season 4) and all of the other extended family members' life events and entanglements. In other words, their parenting was imagined as no more or less significant than any of the other characters' activities, playing out as part of the entire interwoven narrative fabric of the Fisher family's lives together. In the show's finale, David and Keith become the proprietors of the family's funeral home, Fisher & Sons, and in the montage sequence of flash forward, we see Anthony carry on their same-sex affections while Durrell takes over the legacy of the family business. The projection of David and Keith's family into the future makes logical narrative sense having been prepared for by representations of their active, nurturing parenting in earlier episodes of the final season. As with all of the other narrative threads in *Six Feet Under*, the results of their parenting are represented in the flash-forward montage as culminating events of their lives together as a couple and as members of the extended Fisher family.

Less than a year later, the NBC network hit situation comedy *Will & Grace* reprised this flash-forwarding technique, ending its series run by projecting the narrative twenty years into the future after best friends Will and Grace had become estranged. Pregnant in the previous episode, we see Grace reunited with Leo and raising their daughter Lila together.[13] Meanwhile, we learn that Will and his partner Vince have used in vitro fertilization and surrogacy to have their own son, Ben. But the narrative thrust of the finale, as with the entire eight-year run, centers on the relationship between Will and Grace, not on anyone's parenting abilities. Simply *identified* as de facto parents in this final episode, Will and Vince are represented at the end-life of their hands-on parenting years (and, to be fair, the same could be said of Grace and Leo). Unlike *Six Feet Under*, there is no representation of the struggles, and little in the way of the joys, of becoming or being supportive parents to Ben, who has fallen in love with Lila while at college and whose marriage to one another will ultimately serve as the occasion for mending the rift between the friends. That Will and Grace has each pursued a romance and parenthood separate from one another is the ostensible cause of the rift in the first place, so having their offspring bring closure to their split and to the series is narratively neat. Indeed, such closure marks a significant way in which the use of the fast-forwarding technique differs on *Will & Grace* from *Six Feet Under*. While the latter opens up the narrative, taking us into an imaginative space that emphasizes continuity even as parents die off, the former closes the narrative, returning us to the imaginative space of the friends' younger selves.

In other words, the flash-forward over twenty years of disaffection followed by a flashback to their younger selves in *Will & Grace* allows the show to slickly sidestep any representation of the couple *behaving* as gay dads. Where *Six Feet Under* represented some of the difficulties of *becoming* and *being* adoptive parents, leading to a future image of success as parents, *Will & Grace* merely presents parenthood as an accomplished fact that works in the service of enabling the friends' relationship to come full circle. Of course, this full circle imagining is communicated through the flashback to the friends' twenty-something selves. As a nostalgic turn it is quite different in tone and meaning from the sequence that ends with Brian dancing in an imaginatively resurrected Babylon in *Queer as Folk*. In this case, there is a "set piece" quality about the image, as first Michael and Brian, then Brian alone, are returned to a moment that the audience imagine actually happened. They are simultaneously present in the burned shell of Babylon and transported to the energy—but not the imagery—of their younger, queerer (non-dad) selves. There is a frisson of possibility and openness in being those queer men *and* these current men who also happen to be fathers with varying levels of involvement in their kids' lives. *Will & Grace*, on the other hand, communicates a "that was then, this is now" moment in reverse, portraying fatherhood as a distinctively separate phase in Will's life and friendship configurations.

While fatherhood may have been an option for couples that were *already* gay in the 2005–2006 time period during which *Queer as Folk*, *Six Feet Under* and *Will & Grace* aired, it was also a reasonably difficult journey for individual couples, requiring the negotiation of challenging cultural and/or emotional issues as well as the financial and bureaucratic obstacles presented by foster care, adoption, and surrogacy.[14] It is this demanding cultural moment of *becoming* gay dads, as well as some sense of *being* gay dads in very different ways, that cable dramas such as *Queer as Folk* and *Six Feet Under* attempted to represent while the network sitcom *Will & Grace* elided the difficulty, unable to represent grappling with becoming, or the realities of being, gay dads (aside from exhibiting pride in their offspring, Ben). Both cable shows explored the messiness of becoming fathers—negotiating with lesbian friends/primary parents around sperm donation and (co)parental rights and responsibilities or haggling with foster care and adoption systems—and the attendant difficulties of being fathers in an extended family formation or an interracial relationship or when combatting one's own traumatic issues.

However much *Will & Grace* avoids representing what everyday gay fathering might look like by flash forwarding to a future sometime in the mid-2020s, it does suggest that gay fatherhood is quite unremarkable. If it evades a normalized and quotidian "watch me while I (gay) parent" depiction, it certainly joins *Queer as Folk* and *Six Feet Under* in representing the banal *fact* of gay fatherhood. If we were to flashback to five years before, when Fox Network viewers in 2000 might have seen John Goodman portray "Butch" Gamble, who returns to his hometown of Normal, Ohio after running off to Los Angeles in order to "be gay,"[15] we would have seen a still remarkable representation of gay fatherhood—remarkable not because of Butch's fathering abilities or lack thereof, but because of the gayness of the main character. The backstory here is that Butch's coming out precipitates his divorce from his wife as well as any active parental role to Charlie, who is a college-aged adult son in the pilot episode. Fatherhood in this case precedes "gayness," the discovery of which necessitates a move to the coast away from, rather than into, family. Thus, the show deploys a spatial metaphor of separation between gayness and fatherhood by locating gayness in Los Angeles and fatherhood in Normal, such that Butch's return to Normal—an attempt to reconcile these two nominally irreconcilable categories of being—is conceived more as an opportunity to represent the comic inconsistencies of a football loving bear of a man who breaks into show tunes than as an occasion to explore—even humorously—what a gay father might look like in the act of actually parenting.[16] In part, this occurs by making Charlie an adult who is no longer in need of active parenting, which is not to say that the show overlooks the damage divorce and absent fathers can visit on a child. But Charlie's emotional hurt at being abandoned by his father's coming out is smoothed away between the pilot and second episode with a speed and superficiality beyond the usual sitcom flightiness. The friction simply evaporates, as does any possibility that fatherhood and gayness might be reconcilable notions, let alone have a different temporal relationship to one another (gay first, dad second).

Canceled after eight episodes aired, *Normal, Ohio* represented gay fatherhood through the most common scenario in the culture at the time: having become fathers men within (typically earlier) heterosexual relationships, they often struggled to be fathers postdivorce because of court-ordered non-custodial agreements. By 2005 the cultural landscape for gay dads had changed dramatically, as seen in *Queer as Folk*, *Six Feet Under* and *Will & Grace*. Yet substantial narratives about gay fatherhood in these shows were not sustainable. One has to wonder whether these shows end with gay fatherhood because the idea poses an idyllic possibility whose representation exceeds the shows' more constrained narrative trajectories or because gay fatherhood somehow makes these characters no longer representable, functioning as more sophisticated extensions of the social norm that gayness and fatherhood are irreconcilable, more simplistically presented in *Normal, Ohio*. Adoptions by single men and women or gay men and lesbians had gained increasing acceptance; reproductive technologies had become more widely available and affordable, and surrogacy had become a legal and financially viable option for all sorts of individuals and couples desiring children. Still, these remained relatively abstract for most mainstream Americans so that representations of gay parents on American network television programs remained limited to special topic, made-for-TV movies or singular appearances of characters on otherwise heterosexually oriented programs with the exception of the short-lived portrayals mentioned above.[17]

Not until the 2007–2008 television season did gay dads become featured as regular or recurring characters on scripted prime-time network shows. That year, *Gossip Girl* introduced Blair's estranged father, Harold, who returned from Europe with his lover, although his was an infrequent appearance. Two years later Kevin Walker, a principal character in the family drama, *Brothers & Sisters* and out in his personal and professional lives from the show's premiere in 2006, began a search for a surrogate with partner Scotty during the fourth season. Similarly, *Desperate Housewives* regulars Bob and Lee were reunited as a couple and became adoptive fathers to Jenny in 2011 during the seventh season. The following year during the fourth season of *Glee*, Rachel had a parental history literally fleshed out when gay dads Leroy and Hiram, initially represented only in a photo in the first season, appeared in a few episodes. And, most recently in 2014 on *Marry Me*, Annie's dads Kevin 1 and Kevin 2 were prominently featured.[18] Despite these five examples in eight years, one could hardly say that prime-time television became overrun with gay fathers, but they have been somewhat consistently represented among various family formations and television genres. And that it has been gay dads, rather than lesbian moms on television screens,[19] say as much about the production process of television as it does about contemporary attitudes regarding fatherhood generally and gay fatherhood in particular.[20] That is, it reflects both the inequity of gender representation on television—according to a GLAAD Report, "Women continue to lose visibility on broadcast primetime, making up just 40% of series regulars"[21] in the 2014–2015 season—so that the over-representation of gay dads (relative to lesbian mothers) on broadcast prime-time shows is an extension of the over-representation of men in general on television, as well as the inequity of women employed behind the scenes as producers, creators, and writers.[22] So if more men behind the scenes of prime-time network TV programs accounts (at least in part) for more men *on* our TV screens, the sheer numbers of gay dads with regular or recurring roles in prime-time is reasonably easy to understand.

But *how* gay dads are represented on network television, particularly on *Modern Family* and *The New Normal* requires keeping the following rough history in mind. *Normal, Ohio*, *Gossip Girl*, and *Glee* comprise a first stage of representation: fathers who come out as gay (so that "gay" and *dad* are mutually exclusive, uneasily managed or very marginalized). *Desperate Housewives* and *Brothers & Sisters* represent the second stage: gay men who eventually couple and overcome obstacles to become parents (so that the narrative traces a movement of the gay man into coupledom and fatherhood with the clear suggestion that fatherhood conveys maturation lacking in the gay man who is not a father). Their more substantial gay dad storylines are fitted into the larger narrative trajectory either by introducing recurring gay characters such as Bob and Lee, who become fathers into an already established series or by having already present characters such as Kevin and Scotty struggle through relationship difficulties and soap operatic twists to finally have two children by the final season. The third stage of representation occurs in *Modern Family, The New Normal,* and *Marry Me*: gay couples who simply become or be are gay dads (so that their desire for fatherhood is already normalized rather than a signifier of their character development). But there is a distinct difference in the premises of these latter shows in terms of their "normalization" of gay fatherhood. In *Marry Me,* Annie's dads Kevin 1 and Kevin 2 are prominently featured from the pilot episode as regular characters, but the show is premised on daughter Annie's engagement to Jake, not on their parenting. The show does, however, take their fatherhood for granted; indeed, gay fatherhood is *responsible* for Annie's particularly dramatic personality. When Jake complains her outsized responses make him feel that "it's like marrying a drag queen," Annie not only agrees with his analogy but makes a distinctly biological-environmental claim for the genesis of her personality: "I'm the result of a lesbian surrogate my dads don't speak to and one of their sperms."[23] In other words, Annie believes—and the show is premised on—the idea that *who she is* as a person—and what that will mean for Jake who will marry her—is *determined* by having been raised by two gay dads.[24] More than anything, it is this narrative *premise* of gay fatherhood—and the implications for gay-parented offspring—that has allowed for increasingly normalized but not necessarily normative representations of gay dads since *Modern Family* premiered in 2009.

GENRE: WHAT'S SO FUNNY ABOUT GAY FATHERHOOD?

A network staple since the 1950s, the situation comedy has endured despite predictions of its demise[25] because, when executed well, the genre provides a narrative format for an intimate, character-driven, and often family-centered representation of American life in all of its broadly stereotypic comedy. Defined by some critics as a comic tone or comic approach to a narrative rather than a specific type of narrative structure,[26] the situation comedy is a fundamentally domestic, one might say domesticated, form of entertainment. Its primary focus on the family (or family-like groups, as in *The Office* or *Friends*) has meant that most critics see it as reflective rather than disruptive of contemporary social values, arguing it is conservative in nature.[27]

Others note that compared to British television, the American industry often shoots episodes a few weeks before airing, allowing it to incorporate current events.[28] Combined with a comic performance style "focused on excess, in which an over-the-top display of excessive emotional response or physical absurdity . . . constitutes the specific comic moment,"[29] the representation of these social issues through characters' narratives can be made more palatable. In this way, the conservative format of the sitcom may be articulated through more liberal leaning characters, creating a narrative dissonance for viewers to reflect upon. In addition, excessive performance styles call attention to the difference between the actor and character, reminding viewers of the performative nature of the character. Such a dissonance may carry over to what viewers think they know about a character—such as a gay dad—and how the character performs in a specific situation within the narrative. As reflected by the sitcom narrative and its comic performances, the social realities of gay dads (framed as a contemporary "social issue" for viewers without direct experience with gay dads) may normalize gay dads by representing them using the same conventions as for other kinds of dads while also using references to social issues from a gay perspective or the heightened performativity of its characterizations to distance the representations of gay dads from the normative.

By adopting the mock documentary style pioneered by *The Office* in 2005, *Modern Family* reinvigorates the character-driven nature of the situation comedy and fosters an intimacy between characters and viewers that might otherwise be difficult to achieve. Whether this is because of the sheer freshness of the approach, a general cultural disenchantment with or ironic distancing from the values associated with the traditional situation comedy, or because of a perceived gap in accepting culturally different characters is an open question, but the single-camera mockumentary style was an attempt to convey the "realness" of contemporary family life within the conventions of the situation comedy, as cocreator Steven Levitan stated in an interview.[30] Significant for the show's representation of its gay dads is that any cultural distance viewers might feel in relation to its two gay characters is persistently broken down through their directly addressing the camera and, by extension, viewers. Of course, the technique would break down distance between audience members and other characters in the show, in particular across ethnic/cultural (Gloria) or age distinctions (Jay), but the gayness of Cameron and Mitchell arguably represents for most mainstream viewers the least familiar family type. The impact of the technique, therefore, is greatest in cultivating familiarity with the gay dads and with common parental challenges. For example, in the episode "Do Not Push"[31] Cam and Mitch directly address viewers with their discovery that Lily feels left out of the prominently displayed portrait of her dads, which she has expressed by pasting a hand-drawn self-portrait between their images. Attempting to take a new family portrait, Lily's "forced smile" in shot after shot prompts Mitch to ask Claire for advice in capturing a more conventional smile. Instead, she informs him that weird grimacing is a normal phase for kids, so the narrative normalizes Lily's quirkiness and Cam and Mitch's difference as gay dads, resulting in a large version of the new family portrait.

Another way in which *Modern Family* normalizes its gay dads is through the ensemble performances and intertwined triple storyline format. They are never represented in isolation from the equally comic and complex representations of Jay and Gloria or Phil and Claire as parents. Indeed, the narratives are often tightly scripted to echo thematically, reinforcing the (potential) similarities among these related families. As Ken Tucker argues, it may be Jay's second-time around family that is "the trickiest job here,"[32] not only in terms of offering a fresh perspective on attempting to be a more present father than with daughter Claire and son Mitchell, but by having him do so in tandem with their attempts to raise their own families. Within the terms established by its version of the sitcom, then, all parenthood types—whether gay, May/December cross-cultural, or traditional (if neurotic and goofy)—and all character types are fraught with comic potential. And that potential is realized through witty dialogue, comic performances, absurd situations, and characters whose personal foibles and obsessions are put on display (often with a comic lack of self-knowledge) in direct address mockumentary confessionals that let viewers in on the joke.

Although *The New Normal* does not use a mockumentary style, it does use a single-camera setup and incorporate some innovative cinematic techniques in memory and fantasy sequences. At the level of character conception and performance, the show indulges in what Quinn Miller has described as "industrially organized, assembly-line-style" characters that are "unselfconsciously unconventional and exceedingly extreme."[33] Where historically, these "extreme" characters would have been the two gay dads-to-be, in *The New Normal,* they are represented by Rocky Rhoades, Bryan's loud African American assistant, the surrogate Goldie's dumb hunky boyfriend Clay, and her boorishly bigoted Republican grandmother, Jane. Of course, these are no less offensive than television's traditional reliance on campy/gay characters.[34] As Brett Mills notes in his survey of the sitcom, "for representations to be successful—and by successful, what is meant is easily understandable—they must conform to and utilize, normalized social conventions,"[35] and to the extent that these stock characters remain funny, they do so by embodying excessive attributes that some viewers may not themselves identify with.[36] Further, in the tradition of Norman Lear's 1970s situation comedies, that established the precedent for successfully conflating politics and humor,[37] the show privileges politically infused themes by attributing character motivations consistent with Bryan's and David's roles as dads-to-be to politicized contexts. This is not to say that *Modern Family* shies from political themes, but they tend to be defused rather than amplified as in *The New Normal*. For example, in the pilot episode,[38] Mitchell rants at fellow airline travelers in response to a remark made by one passenger to another about "that baby with those cream puffs," mistakenly thinking the comment is a homophobic judgment aimed at them as a gay couple with a baby. But as it turns out (and viewers see this coming because Cameron tries to interrupt Mitchell before he goes too far), baby Lily, unseen by Mitchell, is actually holding a cream puff pastry that plus-size Cameron (claiming "Daddy needed snacks") brought on board. In this case, the political content of Mitchell's shaming lecture is neutralized by seamlessly absorbing it into the comedy of the narrative and—pointedly—at Mitchell's expense.

While this classic use of misunderstanding and misdirection in *Modern Family* normalizes and constrains the political within the sitcom genre, a similar politically inflected rant by Bryan is less easily contained, arguably "queering" the narrative.[39] In "Baby Clothes,"[40] David and Bryan briefly kiss while clothes shopping for Shania (the daughter of their surrogate). Another dad witnesses the kiss and confronts the couple, stating "This is a family store—don't do that [kiss] in front of my kids," clearly establishing the authority of the traditional definition of "family" (oriented to parents *with* kids) and of "fatherhood" (physically and morally protective of children). Bryan's angry response—"Thank you for your intolerance . . . and your bigotry"—reveals a liberal sense of inclusiveness in contrast with more traditional values, but by itself does not give Bryan (and David) any access to definitions of "family" or "fatherhood." Without the presence of Shania or any other child to signal the possibility that fatherhood is attached to either/both of the men, Bryan's and David's identities are represented as "only" gay, an "anti-family" identity (in the traditional dad's view) that is literally "sealed with a kiss."

Later in the same episode as the couple prepares to sleep, Bryan remains visibly upset that such encounters could create an environment of intolerance with negative effects on their future child: "how are we supposed to protect our baby from hate?" That Bryan's remark to the dad in the store was neither funny in itself nor comically delivered, that the redefinition of "family" in this allegedly "new normal" moment in history must butt up against old definitions of "family" and their attendant privileges, that Bryan articulates a fatherly response ("protect our baby") equal to the traditional dad's protective demand, and that in the later scene David (and viewers) do not have an adequate, let alone comic, response to his concerns, all demonstrate the ways in which *The New Normal* not only refers to contemporary culture clashes around "the family" and "fatherhood," but does not neatly contain the messiness within the narrative. While the less even comic tone risks viewers' mirth (and coveted ratings), it suggests that there are limitations in the sitcom's representations of *gay* dads, especially in conveying upon them the same authority accorded to "traditional" dads. Yet it also suggests the conventions of the sitcom might be violated or expanded to open up the imaginative space needed for such a representation. In other words, it suggests how sitcoms representing gay dads might be "queered" out of their normative move to inclusion. What this scene represents, then, is the fraught place of the *potential* of gay fatherhood, an identity that will finally come into *being* by the final episode.

That is, because Bryan and David are not yet actually parents—but are in the stage of *becoming* gay dads—the show leverages their pre-fatherhood "gay identity" as the flag bearer for tolerance and inclusion, suggesting that once Brian and David *are* dads these values will be extended to the next generation of children. The episode, then, walks the line between two ways the sitcom historically represented fathers: as idealized, authority figures or as rather inept buffoons, the latter associated with either particularly immature fathers or working-class fathers, regardless of the race/ethnicity of the paternal figure.[41] That the white, middle-class father in the department store fits neatly into historical representations of an idealized, emotionally supportive and present father poses a problem in this interchange with Bryan and David. Both gay men are white; one is a television producer and the other a physician. By virtue of race, and more importantly class, they have a comparable status to the offended father. But they are not *yet* fathers, so it is their gayness that marks them as different from the other father, and Bryan uses this difference to challenge the status quo, rather than accede to it. That the encounter is not neatly resolved—there is no "snap" insult that trumps the father's angry request—but continues to trouble Bryan suggests that the challenge of gayness as "anti-family" remains a potent question for the larger culture, for the gay community, and for television genres. Bryan briefly internalizes this challenge, questioning whether they ought to become fathers. However, they persist in their pursuit of parenthood so that this moment opens up a speculative space for representation: will their race/class privilege grant them the historical authority accorded the traditional TV dad in contrast to representations of working-class buffoonery or will they be represented as somehow immature, overgrown boys incapable of responsible parenthood? That the show is unable to answer this beyond images of doting nurturance when Sawyer is born later in the season is not simply a matter of *The New Normal* having been canceled. It is also a matter of the network situation comedy (in its most conventional forms) not yet having the imaginative space to grant gay dads the authority role of positive, supportive parents while simultaneously resisting the impulse to position them in the default inept role or robbing them of their gay difference from other fathers.

So, to the question of whether there is something inherently funny about gay fatherhood, thereby requiring the situation comedy format, the answer appears to be yes to the extent that gay fatherhood *as a premise* is represented primarily as a comic situation. But the answer is also no, at least no more than about any other type of fatherhood or family structure in which dysfunction appears to be the norm. In *Modern Family,* Jay's tough-guy response to fatherhood is often undercut by a newly discovered sensitivity in his struggles to be a second dad to Manny and a biological dad to newborn, Joe, who is only a couple of years younger than his granddaughter, Lily (Cameron and Mitchell's adopted child from Vietnam). Phil's sometimes childish "I'm a cool dad" enthusiasm often conflicts with serious, "not fun," disciplinarian Claire's version of parenting with comic results, yet for all his silliness Phil is not an inadequate father. And Cameron and Mitchell, as gay fathers, are no more or less comically dysfunctional as their parenting styles come into conflict. Stay-at-home dad Cameron frets about Lily's progress relative to other children's development while Mitchell's bland demeanor turns nearly every encounter Lily has with other children into an embarrassing public display of his competitive nature. When these conflicting styles come into play with one another during the course of an episode, what it means to be a family has far more to do with negotiating *any* differences while also emphasizing the point to *be* a family together. Thus, extended family get-togethers, such as when Claire works to get the entire family to dress in white clothing and arrive on time for a group photo in the "Family Portrait" episode,[42] may quickly degenerate into literal and figurative mudslinging. But for all the shouting and mayhem the family members perpetrate on one another in the moments preceding the official portrait (of a mud-splattered but grinning family), the show's style remains consistently slapstick so that rancor is neutralized into self- and family-depreciating humor.

That *Modern Family* can represent Cameron and Mitchell as comparably beleaguered with the other parents in the show is not only a matter of its "just like us" worldview and the familial relationships among Jay, Claire, and Mitchell but also because all of the characters in *Modern Family* are *already* parents from the initial episode. "Coming out" as adoptive parents to the rest of the family condenses the transitional period of "being gay" to "being gay dads" in a matter of minutes. To their extended family members and the audience, Cameron and Mitchell are presumptively parental, whereas for Bryan and David in *The New Normal,* the narrative arc is in anticipation of fatherhood (which occurs in the midst of their wedding during the one-hour finale, neatly splitting it into two halves with fatherhood first and marriage second).[43] The comedy here is twofold: in the pre-emptive timing of the wedding and the disruptive timing of Sawyer Collins' birth. To put the show in context, the episode aired nearly three months before the U.S. Supreme

Court ruled on June 26, 2013 that California's Proposition 8 banning same-sex marriage was unconstitutional, but during the time period when marriage equality advocates knew the Justices were still writing their opinions on the case. This timing heightens the political dimension of the storyline while the timing of Goldie's water breaking—just before Bryan and David exchange vows during their over-produced wedding ceremony—heightens the comic component. Thus the political dimension emphasizes the "gay" in what it means to become gay dads while the comic delay of their wedding redirects the show toward the "dad" part which is dependent upon a surrogate who is now part of their "chosen" family.[44]

To be fair, virtually the entire season of *The New Normal* is focused on *becoming* rather than *being* fathers as it is in *Modern Family,* and it is on the joys and challenges of *becoming* gay fathers that the humor of the show is often predicated. Canceled after its first season of their anticipating parent-hood, the extent to which gay fatherhood—as situation or identity—might have been represented as funny could only have occurred in the storyline of a second season. Limited to a single network season, Bryan and David are only technically "gay dads" after Sawyer's birth and their second attempt at a wedding on the beach in the second half of the finale. Indeed, it is less than the birth of their son in the first half of the finale than their wedding consecra-tion ("I now pronounce you a family") by Father Michael in the second half that defines them as gay dads. While they are documented in the first half as dads—a series of shots with each holding newborn Sawyer, Bryan cooing "you can call me dad," and a soundtrack filled with John Lennon's *Beautiful Boy*—any representation of "dadness" as a performance—feeding, changing nappies, cuddling, bedtime reading—is deferred. The impromptu beach mar-riage ceremony in the second half occurs two weeks after Sawyer's birth. By pronouncing the couple a family that includes their son, as well as surrogate mother Goldie, her daughter Shania, Nana Jane and Rocky Rhodes, Bryan's assistant, not to mention the Catholic priest Father Michael who performed the ceremony, the show manages to redefine what it means to be gay dads even beyond the extended family configuration that Mitchell and Cameron inhabit. Premised upon the desire of *becoming* gay dads, *The New Normal* finale opens its narrative trajectory to embrace a queered and chosen family.

READING GAY DADS IN DOMESTIC TELEVISUAL SPACE

If *Father [Knew] Best* (1954–1960) during the Eisenhower years, televi-sion fathers in *Modern Family* and *The New Normal* during the Obama years exhibit anxiety about doing the right thing, a misguided sense of balance between creativity and discipline, and a general tendency toward over-indulgence.[45] Thus, the very definition of family and fatherhood in these two shows suggests not only a reconfiguration of who constitutes family members—from biological nuclear to blended, intergenerational, and chosen—but a reconfiguration of the power dynamics—from patriarchal to diffused, collaborative, and occasionally contentious—among its members.[46] Moreover, it suggests a shift from certainty to uncertainty and from knowledge to misunderstanding that result not from Cold War politics or nuclear armament but from shifting social patterns of and attitudes toward family formation and habits, as well as shifting habits of network television consumption. If the 1950s suburban family was centered in the living room with and by prime-time network television shows that reflected and shaped the preferred domestic configuration, the millennial family is more de-centered and (in *Modern Family* self-reflexively) multi-situated, which is further expanded at the level of viewership. For both shows, but particularly the long-running *Modern Family,* on-demand streaming, DVD sales, and syndication agreements with cable and HULU provide viewers access to what Michael Curtain has termed a "matrix medium" in which "distinctions between production and consumption blur" through time-shifted viewing, multiple platforms, and interactive and asynchronous social media.[47] All of this is to say that viewers make these shows their own in terms of multiple access points and in terms of how the narratives resonate with their own sensibilities. In other words, even as these two televisual gay families continue to reside in white and middle-class suburban neighborhoods, participating in the rituals of finding good schools, playing team sports or engaging in scouting activities—just like many of their viewers—they also introduce into this traditional domestic space a qualitative "gayness" that physically reimagines that space without making them "super queers."[48] And the multiple ways in which viewers can (repeatedly) access the shows can lead, as Needham has argued, to an experience of televisual time that is "fundamentally queer."[49] Spatially and temporally, then, the configurations and experiences of these televisual domestic spaces are not simplistically normative. Further, because "television programs continually use visual signifiers as tools to create symbolic value in the domestic space, which shapes the populist comprehension of home décor aesthetics,"[50] the representations of these gay dads' domestic spaces—and their noteworthy styles—contribute to imagining and reading them as simultaneously "gay" and "competent" parents.

The architectural and design choices of televisual homes not only reflect the consumer tastes of the families but convey how they see themselves and care to be seen by others. So foundational are these choices in establishing an identity as gay fathers that the pilot episode of *Modern Family* makes the decoration of Lily's room a crucial issue. After an on-camera interview with both dads seated side by side in their living room (Cameron admitting he "gained a few extra pounds while we were expecting"), there is a cut to the dads entering Lily's new room with luggage and baby in tow. Mitchell, holding Lily, turns toward the crib to discover that Cameron has commissioned a welcoming mural depicting her new fathers as protective angels. Including Lily in his complaint to Cam, he remarks, "We've taken you from everything you know, but don't worry, things are normal here, your fathers are floating fairies." [Addressing Cameron,] "Could you call Andre, have him paint something a little less . . . gay?" Clearly, Mitchell reads "fairies" as both sprites and gay men, but the overt "gayness" of the mural is a signifier for the real issue in (and comic thrust of) the story line. Mitchell, fearing criticism of their choice to become (gay) fathers has yet to inform his family that they've spent their vacation time in Vietnam adopting a daughter. Cameron, well aware of Mitchell's propensity to procrastinate informing others about important life events, has circumvented Mitchell's reluctance to come out as a gay dad to his family by explicitly displaying their status as fathers in Lily's room.

Moreover, Cameron sees gay fatherhood as an identity to be celebrated as a triumphant and "tribal"[51] moment later in the show. He interrupts yet another of Mitchell's chiding lectures (directed to his father, Jay) about respecting his gay relationship by entering the room with Lily held aloft in his silk-robed arms to dramatic lighting changes and the soundtrack of *The Lion King*. In so doing, Cam shifts the narrative (and arguably the entire series) away from a focus on *gay* men to gay *dads* without relinquishing gayness. Lily—and her fathers—are welcomed into the Pritchett-Delgado-Dunphy "tribe" as equal members in this "Circle of Life" pageant because of, not despite, Cameron's attention to (re)designing domestic space, in both Lily's bedroom and the living room. The change in the living room shifts the way we read the space and families in it from a closed set piece that defines the family in more traditional terms, as Lynn Spigel argued,[52] to one that opens it to a stage celebrating international adoption and gay fatherhood. And the mural design in Lily's bedroom suggests that "family" is informed, not limited, by her dads' gayness. Their status as gay fathers is as essential to Lily's well-being as the other adults in relation to their children. Indeed, the mural figures as such a talisman of parental protectiveness that Cam and Mitch give a similarly "angelic/fairy" mural to Jay and Gloria as a baby shower gift. Jay's initial (and predictable) consternation that his buff portrait is "too gay" is overridden by Gloria's gushing that "it looks just like you!"[53] so that "gay" design in/of domestic space is not only welcome but also transformative of notions of masculinity, fatherhood, and aesthetics.

Another episode in which the design of domestic space signifies a negotiation of what it means to be a gay dad occurs in an episode centered on the purchase of a white designer couch.[54] In this case, the show plays with both the stereotype of gay men having an innately superior interior design sense and the idea that stylish design is incompatible with children. Cam and Mitch debate whether they can upgrade from their practical couch (identifying them as "dads") to one that signifies their style (identifying them as "gay"). Anxious as to whether 6-year-old Lily is mature enough for them to make the transition, they frisk her for crayons and other childish contraband before allowing her anywhere near it, while their white cat Larry does not have to endure such indignities. "So," asks Lily, "Larry is allowed on the couch and I'm not?" to which Cameron responds, "Well, Larry is white." "Well, you chose me." Looking startled, Cameron responds, "That's not what I meant," shifting her interpretation of "whiteness" from a racial connotation to a merely descriptive one. Here the show subtly registers not only a comical send-up of the "incompatibility" of gayness and parenthood by dramatizing the ridiculous lengths to which Cam and Mitch attempt to keep Lily's messiness from their pristine designer couch but succinctly decenters the whiteness of the suburban family (as does Gloria's Latina persona with playful physical presence and language)—by having a 6-year-old point out their obvious racial/ethnic difference. Further, their anxiety about the couch is misplaced. It is not Lily's relationship with the couch that is problematic but the misguided notion of recapturing a "gay" sense of style. This is evident because it is their sloppily drunk overnight guest Brenda from Mitchell's office who is most dangerous to the couch (red wine, chocolate brownie, and sleep drool). At the end of the episode Cam and Mitch discover Lily reading a bedtime story to Brenda on the couch. It is her gesture that reconciles their gay interior design sense and fatherhood by virtue of its kindness (they take parental pride in her reading to their sad guest) and by virtue of its emulation of *their* good parenting, which has included nightly bedtime reading. Lily thus embodies a child chosen and raised by design, which is neither specific to "gay" nor incompatible with "dads."

Similarly, *The New Normal* uses interior design style signifying gayness to reimagine what the identity of a gay dad is. For example, in "Sofa's Choice" Bryan thinks Shania has scribbled on his leather couch—she did not—implying the sofa is a significant anchor to gay décor/identity, and the episode further amps up the "gay" quotient by having Bryan bond with Shania over the cult favorite, *Grey Gardens*.[55] But it is a later episode focused on David's uncritical love for and involvement in the Boy Scouts of America that the negotiation around design is more interesting. Where *Modern Family* heals the rift between identities and offers closure in its white couch episode, the fault in identities and narrative is left more open in *The New Normal*. In part, this openness is a function of location—Bryan and David live in the gay neighborhood of West Hollywood—with a less distinctively suburban feel than the West LA location of the *Modern Family* characters, so they are already marked as outside a normative "suburban" space (but not as far out as the urban NYC space of characters on *Will & Grace*). And, in part, it is a function of the show's inconsistent comic tone resulting from its deployment of politically inflected themes. Because activity around their as-yet-unborn son involves surrogate negotiations and nursery preparation rather than school projects and soccer games, David's spare time can be directed to other people's children. In "About a Boy Scout," an episode airing just two months before the national meeting to decide the question of allowing gays in the Boy Scouts of America, David is an Eagle Scout and exemplary leader.[56] After grappling with the implications of a letter revoking his Boy Scout membership for "homosexual conduct" the show depicts David's poignant sense of loss, ending with him packing away his treasured Boy Scout gear, signifying for him the best of masculine values.

How the narrative gets to his dismissal from the Boy Scouts is, not surprisingly, through design. That is, the episode opens with the more politically vocal Bryan calling out David for his involvement in the Boy Scouts: "Maybe you could earn your hypocrisy badge," he snipes. David responds, "I know that the Boy Scouts haven't exactly rolled out the red carpet for gay people, but this isn't about politics. It's about boys toasting marshmallows, hooking lanyards, and learning that when a black bear attacks, you play dead, and when a grizzly attacks, you stand up and fight." "And when a West Hollywood bear attacks," Bryan wryly quips, "you pretend to hate it." After dressing in his uniform and about to depart, David chides Bryan, "you don't always have to be so honest. Some things are better left unsaid." Whether David's gayness is better left unsaid to other Boy Scout fathers becomes the sticking point later in the narrative. The next day, Bryan's question about David's overnight camping trip is answered with a technically innovative split screen showing David the Eagle Scout outperforming all of the other less competent (heterosexual) dads. This splitting not only provides us with a visually efficient comparison of the dads (and gay dad-to-be) in relation to one another's performance as Scouts, but it makes clear that the use of space communicates more than taste. It communicates identity and value(s).

Bryan asks David if the other dads/troop leaders are supportive of him being gay and David responds, "Actually, it didn't come up," followed by a flashback to the previous night's conversation when one dad declaims, "I bet the old ball and chain in countin' down the days to that [the arrival of David's baby]." Clearly, the dad's characterization of David's partner as a "ball and chain," a not uncommon and derisive characterization of wives in some heterosexual marriages, suggests both that he has no inkling of David's sexuality and that it *did* in fact come up in conversation. David simply chose not to pursue the "unsaid." Bryan is unaware of this but no less persistent in prodding David to deal with the (institutional) homophobia within the

Boys Scouts. He subsequently suggests, "why don't you have the meeting here . . . with a man . . . who you take baths with." The explicit challenge of this suggestion is agreed to, and the following scene portrays David teaching a lesson on arachnids to the Scouts with one dad claiming, "You know everything, David. You should get a merit badge in just overall smartness. And your house should have one for tasteful decorating." Predictably, Bryan enters at that moment of gushing about home décor, and David is forced to introduce Bryan. After an awkward silence with an intercut to David imagining crazed Village People dancing—hello, gay signifier! —one dad responds, "Congratulations, Bryan, on landing an Eagle Scout." At the level of the personal, there seems not to be homophobia in the Boy Scouts, although we later learn that another of these dads who is insecure about his own parenting outs David to the national office, claiming he doesn't want David as a role model for his son Kyle. He wants his son "to be, you know, normal." That David has value and merit as a role model and potential father is as much communicated through his performance as "everything a Scout should be" as through their home décor: neat, tasteful, and reflective of two well-employed gay men. Moreover, it is conveyed through the inclusive living arrangements they have made with surrogate Goldie, who initially takes up residence with her daughter Shania in their guesthouse. For the couples in both shows, how they redefine domestic space—a staple of the network sitcom—with infusions of gayness *and* family-ness communicates their parenting abilities as protective, nurturing and supportive.

QUEERING DADDY OR ADOPTING HOMONORMATIVE FATHERHOOD?

In the final analysis, the representations of gay fatherhood in these two shows are neither simple nor reductively normative. While they may stretch the concept of fatherhood beyond the confines of its traditional definition (as do a number of unconventional postmodern family configurations),[57] it is certainly too much to say that they queer the concept of fatherhood and family. That territory is being more fruitfully explored in shows such as *Transparent* (February 6–September 26, 2014) on Amazon Prime and *Orange is the New Black* (July 11, 2013–June 11, 2015) on Netflix, both of which offer narratives about trans-dads (MTF Maura Pfefferman and MTF Sophia Burset) who struggle with coming out as transgendered and what that means for their status as biological dads to their children.[58] But neither are they confined by the hegemony of televisual domesticity to adopt homonormative fatherhood, thereby relinquishing any claim to gay street cred. Such has been the polarizing debate with a number of queer theorists dismissing these gay characters as sell-outs imitating the norms of heterosexual life while many viewers have argued with relief that there are shows that reflect their own lives with aspirations for social acceptance of their marriages and children *just like everybody else.*[59] Within the heteronormative worlds and suburban spaces in 1950s and early 1960s situation comedies, fathers were naturalized in terms of their expressions of masculinity and biological functions within the family. As shown in the discussion above, when gay dads enter these genre categories at this particular cultural moment they are no more comically represented than other dads. To the extent that contemporary fatherhood is humorously debunked of its authority yet also warmly accepted in its most participatory activities, gay dads who share this middle-class status also share in the same normalized/normalizing comedy.

And while the physical and cultural spaces of these white, mostly middle-class west coast gay male dads on *"Modern Family"* and *"The New Normal"* are specifically embedded in the normative domestic space created by television, as Lynn Spigel as argued in *Make Room for TV*, the narratives of gay fatherhood consistently oscillate against the confines of naturalized masculinity and function, opening up what Sara Ahmed terms "the contours of heterosexual space."[60] One obvious example of this is having Cam as likely to break out into a show tune as coach football. Moreover, while they share similar kinds of domestic spaces with conventional family situation comedies, they redesign or redefine the meanings attendant with those spaces. In this way, they are normalized while not being normatively represented. In other words, the genre conventions and the representational uses of domestic space may normalize gay dads by making them more familiar to mass audiences but they do not in themselves position these gay dads as the "new normative" identity of gay men. Granted, the lack of *other* kinds of LGBTQ characters on prime-time television shows raises legitimate concerns about stereotyping or the paucity of a wide range of character types, but this does not *necessarily* mean that any representation of gay dads on a network sitcom is de facto "normative" and demeaning of other types of LGBTQ lives.

For some critics, the adoption/surrogacy of children by the two gay male couples on *Modern Family* and *The New Normal* directly signals their adoption of homonormativity, making these gay dads acceptable to both their televisual worlds and to the audiences that watch them but unacceptable as representatives of a radical queer identity.[61] Proponents of assimilation who decades ago desired "a place at the table,"[62] as Bawer termed it, may have had corporate rather than kitchen tables in mind, but for televisual audiences who have long connected to domestic spaces in more intimate ways, the central trope of adopting heteronormative institutions and practices (marriage, raising children, living in the suburbs) has paralleled the dramatic acceptance of gay civil rights (including employment protection) among average

Americans in the last decade. Homonormativity, for all the anxiety that it may cause queer theorists who fear losing not only an essential "queer" identity proudly outside the mainstream but also the political will of the marginalized to make radical social change, is how many gay men (and lesbians) live—and have lived for decades ignored by queer theory. So inasmuch as these two ways of framing remain active, we ought not to think in terms of how some on one side or the other thinks about the issue (and what's at stake) but that they simultaneously exist and transform the closed narrative of each when they remain in dialogue with one another.[63]

Although specific to a discussion of the 2002 film *The Hours*, Julianne Pidduck raises an important critique concerning these theoretical framings, writing that "the antipathy toward the time of domesticity and family that marks a common theme in anti-relational queer theory has a misogynist edge, given the feminine connotations of domesticity,"[64] and while not suggesting that gay dads represent "the feminine," insofar as they *do* represent nurturing and caring kinds of fathers in these two shows, we must at least question the equation of queer with "outlaw" or "anti-family" and the "real" gay man as "hypermasculine" or "anti-child." Indeed, one of the hallmarks of what it means to be a gay dad in these two shows is the significance of their *yearning* for a child, one that is exemplified in both comic and poignant ways.[65] Bryan's biological clock is kicked into gear when he sees a baby while shopping (and David remarks that he can not return it to Barney's), a consumerist joke that points to Bryan's own superficiality, as well as cultural constructions of gay men as affluent and the troubling economy of surrogacy. But the show also presents an adult conversation between the two as they watch children in a playground, working through together what kind of commitment and changes to their lifestyle such a decision will mean.

Meanwhile, Cam and Mitch's sense of yearning is represented twice but well after they have already been raising Lily. Throughout the third season they have made various attempts to adopt another child, all of which fall through. In "Baby on Board,"[66] they have lost yet another chance (in a madcap *telenovela* sequence with Gloria translating) and Cam and Mitch lie crying under a starlit sky, finally giving up. At least, that is, until they confess to each other that he is ready for another child, justifying it as an opportunity to buy the entire duplex and expand their house/family when their elderly neighbor dies.[67] A day of babysitting nephew Joe, who trashes the treasured white couch in a way that Lily did not, comically squashes this yearning. That the desire is comically fulfilled or thwarted, as well as seriously considered and rendered, is how each show normalizes gay fatherhood. It is portrayed as consistent with heterosexual fathers' desires, and as much research shows,[68] their parenting is not only "just as good" as straight dads but indicates that gay fathers "put more energy into creating stable positive relationships with their children."[69] Not only do these moments of yearning echo with others in capturing the comic/seriousness of "buying" a baby through surrogacy or adopting a baby into a gay-designed household, but they render the focus on the child, a point that advocates of queer theory and homonormative realism overlook in making the discussion all and only about the dads.

A final example: when Mitchell confronts Cameron about taking Lily to a junior clown college behind his back, Mitchell responds, "Hey, I have been very upfront with you. You knew going in that I wanted to raise our child *as a clown*." Later he teams up with Lily to demonstrate to Mitchell that she's a "natural" clown because Cam is her dad, to which Mitchell responds, "She's adopted." The Fizbo and Lizbo[70] slapstick routine becomes increasingly violent, prompting Cam to suggest to Mitchell that if he had been more supportive of the clowning he loves and more supportive of Lily's performance she would not have resorted to "mean-spirited" gags to "turn [Mitchell] into Mr. McGiggles." Lily later confesses to Mitchell she hates being a clown but, not wanting to hurt Cam's feelings, tells him it is because she will never be as good as Fizbo. In his on-camera interview, Mitchell gloats, "coming up with a lie like that in the moment, that girl's no clown. She's going to be a lawyer." What happens in this episode of *Modern Family* reflects a decidedly normalized parental concern—even friendly competition—with the heritability of one's traits and interests by one's children—even when they are adopted and even when both fathers are gay while also representing a decidedly nonnormative desire. These two categories of gayness and fatherhood, previously assumed to preclude any discussion of inheritance, no longer do so. In large part, this is because notions of family relations are less constructed in terms of blood than in terms of nurturance, a category no longer exclusive to motherhood.

CONCLUSION

To the extent that gay dads may or may not "queer" domestic space/home on *Modern Family* and *The New Normal,* to the extent that their representation as dads is only possible through a certain denaturalization (surrogacy and adoption) of becoming fathers suggests a simultaneous dis/orientation of sexuality and masculinity of fatherhood in and from domestic space. In the end, these shows work to destabilize the representations of fatherhood from the 1950s to 1960s, sometimes in only the most superficial of ways and other times by redefining what is possible for all fathers. To expect more is perhaps too much to ask of network television sitcoms. That they provide us with access to representations of gay fatherhood that resonate in real and effective ways in relation to their televisual children and with audiences may close off our need for all representations to support the rigors of queer theory, but it may open up the constraints that have historically rendered gayness and fatherhood irreconcilable.

NOTES

1. *Queer as Folk*, "We Will Survive," episode no. 13, Season 5, first broadcast August 7, 2005, by Showtime, directed by Kelly Makin and written by Ron Cowen and Daniel Lipman; *Six Feet Under*, " Everyone's Waiting," episode no. 12, Season 5, first broadcast August 21, 2005, by HBO, directed and written by Alan Ball; *Will & Grace*, "The Finale," episode no. 23, Season 8, first broadcast May 18, 2006, by NBC, directed by James Burrows and written by David Kohan and Max Mutchnick.

2. The CDC reported the first substantial reduction in the number of deaths related to HIV infection occurred in 1996, see CDC, "Update: Trends in AIDS Incidence, Deaths, and Prevalence—United States, 1996," *MMWR Weekly* 46 (1997): 165–173, accessed May 13, 2015, http://www.cdc.gov/mmwr/preview/mmwrhtml/00046531. htm; in Lawrence v. Texas the Supreme Court overturned sodomy laws in 2003, see the opinion of the court at Cornell University Law School's website, accessed Jun 10, 2015, https://www.law.cornell.edu/supct/html/02–102.ZO.html.

3. For a brief history of activism in support of gay families, see Anthony Niedwiecki, "Save Our Children: Overcoming the Narrative that Gays and Lesbians Are Harmful to Children," *Duke Journal of Gender Law & Policy* 21 (2013): 149, accessed April 9, 2015, http://go.galegroup.com/ps/i.do?id=GALE%7CA36318828 9&v=2.1&u=car139591&it=r&p=LT &sw=w&asid=55bd0fe98610f122186e2c1805 2ea329. Single parent adoptions, particularly by gays and lesbians became increasingly common by the1990s while the American Academy of Pediatrics reported gay and lesbian parents were as fit as heterosexual parents. See The Adoption History Project, "Single Parent Adoptions," accessed July 17, 2015, http://pages.uoregon.edu/ adoption/topics/singleparentadoptions.htm; American Academy of Pediatrics, "Technical Report: Coparent or Second-Parent Adoption by Same Sex Parents." *Pediatrics* 109 (2002): 341–344, accessed May 9, 2015, http://pediatrics.aappublications.org/ content/109/2/341.full.

4. For discussions of the incompatibility of gayness and fatherhood as a social norm, see Robert L. Barret and Bryan E. Robinson, *Gay Fathers* (Lexington, MA: Lexington Books, 1990); Albert Joseph Sbordone, "Gay Men Choosing Fatherhood" (PhD diss., City University of New York, 1993); For discussions of American social codes equating fatherhood with masculinity and heterosexuality, see Robert L. Griswold, *Fatherhood in America: A History* (New York: Basic Books, 1993). So much was this code enforced that any "failure" in one's role as a man (such as the failure to reproduce) was considered tantamount to a declaration of homosexuality, which in turn was considered a condition insufficient for fatherhood. Griswold makes the further point that these social realities governing fatherhood were reflected in depictions of fathers in popular culture—especially television—during what has been termed the postwar "reproductive consensus," 190.

5. *Queer as Folk* (2000–2005) and *Six Feet Under* (2001–2005) each ran five seasons; *Will & Grace* (1998–2006) ran eight.

6. For an example of how actual gay dads and their children make use of these television representations, see Matt Briggs, *Television, Audiences and Everyday Life* (Berkshire, England: Open University Press, 2010), 105–106.

7. For a definition of homonormativity as a concern with acquiring the rights to marriage and military service, see Lisa Duggan, *The Twilight of Equality: Neo Liberalism, Cultural Politics, and the Attack on Democracy* (Boston: Beacon Press, 2003), 50; for a definition of queer as "unscripted by the conventions of family, inheritance, and child-rearing" see Judith Halberstam, *In a Queer Time and Place: Transgender Bodies, Subcultural Lives* (New York: New York University Press, 2005), 2.

8. For an early approach to representational studies concerned with numbers and types (main or marginal, nuanced or stereotypical) of gay, lesbian, bisexual, and transgender characters on TV, see Stephen Tropiano, *The Prime Time Closet: A History of Gays and Lesbians on TV* (New York: Applause Theatre & Cinema Books, 2002).

9. For a description of industry packaging processes, such as NBC's "Must See TV" for like-minded audiences, see Brett Mills, *Television Sitcom* (London: BFI, 2005), 5.

10. So much do these matter that monitoring agencies count the level, quality and accuracy of representations of ethnic/racial communities, such as Asians, Latinos, and African Americans, among others. GLAAD.org is one such organization for the LGBTQ community.

11. See Michael H. Popkin, accessed July 6, 2015, www.activeparenting.com for a theory of Active Parenting as a cognitive-behavioral approach based on Adlerian principles. I mean "active parenting" more generically as parenting that is attentive, nurturing, and participatory in a child's daily upbringing. Another way of thinking about this kind of active parenting is offered by Esther McDermott, *Intimate Fatherhood: A Sociological Analysis* (London: Routledge, 2008), who argues for a fatherhood-based intimacy "in terms of orientations and tasks; that is, what is being sought from and offered in a father-child relationship as an ideal and in terms of practical caring."

12. See Kath Weston, *Families We Choose: Lesbians, Gays, Kinship* (New York: Columbia University Press, 1997) for a discussion of the ways gays and lesbians form kinship relations outside of their biological families; Judith Butler, "Is Kinship Always Already Heterosexual?" in *Undoing Gender* (London: Routledge, 2004), 102–130.

13. *Will & Grace*, "Whatever Happened to Baby Gin," episode no. 22, Season 8, first broadcast May 11, 2006, by NBC, directed by James Burrows and written by Gary Janetti, Tracy Poust, and Jon Kinnally.

14. For a discussion of the difficulties, see Terry Boggis, "The Real Modern Family . . . Can Be Real Complicated," *Journal of Gay & Lesbian Mental Health* 16 (2012): 353–360; for a discussion of motivations for becoming a parent, see Thomas Poulos, "Gay Men's Motivations for Having Children: Gay Fathers and the Reconceptualization of Fatherhood and Homosexuality," *MJUR (Midwest Journal of Undergraduate Research)* (2011): 85–103, accessed May 22, 2014, http://research.monm.edu/mjur/files/2011/04/Gay_Fathers_2011.pdf.

15. *Normal, Ohio*, "Homecoming Queen," episode no. 1, Season 1, first broadcast November 1, 2000, by Fox, directed by Philip Charles MacKenzie and written by Bonnie Turner and Terry Turner. That fatherhood is equated with normalization while gayness is not abundantly clear from the name of Butch's hometown.

16. See Nancy E. Dowd, *Redefining Fatherhood* (New York: New York University Press, 2000) for an argument redefining fatherhood as nurturing behavior rather than simple biology or marital rights. In light of societal changes that increasingly acknowledge the existence of gay fathers, both the majority who come out as gay after fathering children in heterosexual relationships and the minority of gay men (singly or in couples) who choose to become fathers such a change could not only lead to less discrimination against such parents but also more attention to the needs of children, 191.

17. Tropiano, *The Prime Time Closet*, 109.

18. *Gossip Girl*, "Roman Holiday," episode no. 11, Season 1, first broadcast December 19, 2007, by The CW, directed by Josh Schwartz and written by Jessica Queller; *Brothers & Sisters*, "Last Tango in Pasadena," episode no. 5, Season 4, first broadcast October 25, 2009, by ABC, directed by Beth Rooney and written by Molly Newman and Jason Wilborn; *Desperate Housewives*, "I'm Still Here," episode no.13, Season 7, first broadcast January 16, 2011, by ABC, directed by Lonny Price and written by Josann McGibbon and Sara Patriott; *Glee*, "Heart," episode no. 13, Season 3, first broadcast February 14, 2012, by ABC, directed by Brad Falchuk and written by Ross Maxwell, Matthew Hodgson, and Ali Adler; *Marry Me*, "Pilot," episode no. 1, Season 1, first broadcast October 14, 2014, by NBC, directed by Seth Gordon and written by David Caspe.

19. The history of lesbian motherhood on TV is beyond the scope of this essay: "The Fosters," first broadcast June 3, 2013, by ABC Family, is an exception to television's gay dads' rule; it is also more dramatically driven in story development in contrast to the comedic treatments typical of the gay dads' shows.

20. See Hannah Hamad, "DAD TV-Postfeminism and the Paternalization of US Television Drama," *FlowTV* 11 (2009), accessed May 13, 2014, http://flowtv.org/2009/11/dad-tv-—-postfeminism-and-the-paternalization-of-us-television-drama-hannah-hamad-massey-university/.

21. GLAAD, *Where We Are on TV* (2014): 5, accessed February 14, 2015, http://www.glaad.org/files/GLAAD-2014-WWAT.pdf.

22. See Martha M. Lauzen, "Boxed In: Employment of Behind-the-Scenes and On-Screen Women in 2013–2014 Prime-time Television," *Center for the Study of Women in Television & Film* (2014): 1–5, accessed February 14, 2015, http://womenintvfilm.sdsu.edu/research.html; 27% of employees behind-the-scenes are women, with a decent 43% representation in production but only 19% as creators and 25% working as writers in 2013–14. Forty-four percent of all programs employed 4 or fewer women overall in behind-the-scenes roles while only 1% of programs employed as few men, 1.

23. *Marry Me*, "Pilot," October 14, 2014.

24. The extent to which the lesbian surrogate triples the queer quotient of Annie's parentage or tempers a double-whammy of showbiz-loving gay maleness with stereotypically no-nonsense lesbian practicality is left open.

25. Steve Lopez, "Death of a Sitcom," *Entertainment Weekly*, April 16, 1999, accessed October 10, 2014, http://www.ew.com/ew/article/0,,273101,00.html.

26. Brett Mills, *Television Sitcom* (London: BFI, 2005), 31.

27. Mills, *Television Sitcom*, 45.

28. Mills, *Television Sitcom*, 57.

29. Mills, *Television Sitcom*, 95.

30. Rob Salem, "Modern Family Worth Adopting," *The Toronto Star*, September 23, 2009, accessed March 31, 2015, www.lexisnexis.com/hottopics/Inacademic.

31. *Modern Family*, "Do Not Push," episode no. 2, Season 6, first broadcast October 1, 2014, by ABC, directed by Gail Mancuso and written by Megan Ganz.

32. Ken Tucker, "Modern Family," *Entertainment Weekly*, October 9, 2009: 49, accessed March 31, 2015, *Academic Search Complete*, EBSCOhost.

33. Quinn Miller, "Queer Recalibration," *Cinema Journal* (2014): 141.

34. Mills, *Television Sitcom*, 7.

35. Mills, *Television Sitcom*, 7.

36. Some viewers prefer more realism with their comedy: see Steve Tropiano, "Gaycoms in a Progressive Age? *Partners* and *The New Normal*," *FlowTV* 17 (2013), accessed April 3, 2014, http://flowtv.org/2013/06/flow-favorites-gaycoms-in-a-progressive-age/.

37. See *All in the Family*, CBS, January 12, 1971–April 8, 1979; *Maude*, CBS, September 12, 1972–April 23, 1978; and *The Jeffersons*, CBS, January 18, 1975–July 2, 1985.

38. *Modern Family*, "Pilot," episode no. 1, Season 1, first broadcast September 23, 2009, by ABC, directed by Jason Winer and written by Steven Levitan and Christopher Lloyd.

39. See Robyn Warhol and Susan S. Lanser, ed., *Narrative Theory Unbound: Queer and Feminist Interventions* (Columbus: The Ohio University Press, 2015) for essays exploring queer narrative theory; see Ron Becker, "Guy Love: A queer straight masculinity for a post-closet era," in *Queer TV: Theories, Histories,* Politics, ed. Glyn Davis and Gary Needham (London: Routledge, 2009), 121–140 for an exploration of how straight male TV characters can be "queered."

40. *The New Normal*, "Baby Clothes," episode no. 3, Season 1, first broadcast September 18, 2012, by NBC, directed and written by Ryan Murphy.

41. Timothy Allen Pehlke II and Charles B. Hennon, M. Elise Radina, and Katherine A. Kuvalanka, "Does Father Still Know Best? An Inductive Thematic Analysis of Popular TV Sitcoms," *Fathering* 7 (2009), 130–134.

42. *Modern Family*, "Family Portrait," episode no. 24, Season 1, first broadcast May 19, 2010, by ABC, directed by Jason Winer and written by Ilana Wernick.

43. *The New Normal*, "Finding Name-O," episode no. 21, Season 1, first broadcast April 2, 2013, by NBC, directed by Elodie Keene and written by Aaron Lee and Adam Barr; "The Big Day," episode no. 22, Season 1, first broadcast April 2, 2013, by NBC, directed by Max Winkler and written by Ali Adler and Ryan Murphy.

44. Weston, *Families We Choose*"; one might think this overt political dimension would unleash a backlash against *The New Normal* but that began before the show even aired. See "Andrew Rannells on 'The New Normal' Backlash, One Million Moms," *The Huffington Post*, August 28, 2012, accessed June 30, 2015, http://www.huffingtonpost.com/2012/08/28/andrew-rannells-new-normal-one-million-moms_n_1835963.html.

45. See, for example, William Marsiglio and Kevin Roy, *Nurturing Dads: Social Initiatives for Contemporary Fatherhood* (New York: Russell Sage Foundation, 2012); Jennifer Senior, *All Joy and No Fun* (New York: Ecco, 2014); and Judith Warner, *Perfect Madness: Motherhood in the Age of Anxiety* (New York: Riverhead Books, 2006).

46. For a discussion of our misremembering how fatherhood was represented in the 1950s, see Stephanie Coontz, *The Way We Never Were* (New York: Basic Books, 1993) and Ralph LaRossa, "The Culture of Fatherhood in the Fifties: A Closer Look" *Journal of Family History* 29 (2004): 47–70, DOI: 10.1177/0363199003261811; for a discussion of the redefinition of contemporary fatherhood, see McDermott, *Intimate Fatherhood*. For a discussion of gay fatherhood, see Ellen Lewin, *Gay Fatherhood: Narrative of Family and Citizenship in America* (Chicago: The University of Chicago Press, 2009).

47. Michael Curtain, "Matrix Media" in *Television Studies after TV: Understanding Television in the Post-Broadcast Era*, ed. Graeme Turner and Jinna Tay (London: Routledge, 2009), 19.

48. Kelly Kessler, "They should Suffer Like the Rest of Us: Queer Equality in Narrative Mediocrity," *Cinema Journal* 50 (2011): 143.

49. Gary Needham, "Scheduling Normativity: Television, the Family, and Queer Temporality" in *Queer TV: Theories, Histories, Politics*, ed. Glyn Davis and Gary Needham (London: Routledge, 2009), 143.

50. I. Styles Akira and Larry Ossei-Mensah, "The Construction of Taste: Television and American Home Décor" in *How Television Shapes Our Worldview: Media Representations of Social Trends and Change*, ed. Deborah A. Macey, Kathleen M. Ryan, and Noah J. Springer (Plymouth, UK: Lexington Books, 2014), 332.

51. The interpolation of Disney's interpretation of African tribal culture into a show with multiple ethnicities and sexualities is, of course, meant to be a humorous send-up of gay stereotypical fondness for musicals as well as white appropriations of other cultures.

52. See Lynn Spigel, *Make Room for TV* (Chicago: Chicago University Press, 1992).

53. *Modern Family*, "Mistery Date," episode no. 8, Season 4, first broadcast November 14, 2012, by ABC, directed by Beth McCarthy-Miller and written by Jeffrey Richman.

54. *Modern Family*, "Strangers in the Night," episode no. 9, Season 6, first broadcast December 3, 2014, by ABC, directed by Fred Savage and written by Chuck Tatham.

55. *The New Normal*, "Sofa's Choice," episode no. 2, Season 1, first broadcast September 11, 2012, by NBC, directed by Ryan Murphy and written by Ali Adler and Ryan Murphy.

56. *The New Normal*, "About a Boy Scout," episode no. 20, Season 1, first broadcast March 26, 2013, by NBC, directed by Scott Ellis and written by Mark Kunerth and Karey Dornetto; the Boy Scouts of America voted to accept gay members on May 27th, 2013. Two years after the show ended, the Boy Scouts of America voted to allow gay men to serve as leaders.

57. According to Population Reference Bureau, accessed March 31, 2015, only 7% of American households conform to the most traditional definition of family while heterosexual married and both employed couples with children raise the rate of "traditional" to only 23% of families. http://www.prb.org/Publications/Articles/2003/TraditionalFamiliesAccountforOnly7PercentofUSHouseholds.aspx.

58. A less successful attempt at queering the family was undertaken by *One Big Happy*, first broadcast March 17, 2015, by NBC, created by Liz Feldman. Canceled after 6 episodes, lesbian Lizzy and straight childhood best friend Luke agree to start a family together only to have it become more complicated when Luke's British fiancé Prudence makes it a threesome. Yes, it does sound like a *Three's Company* clone— only even less funny.

59. For examples, see Alysia Abbott, "TV's Disappointing Gay Dads" *The Atlantic Monthly*, October 31, 2012, accessed March 15, 2015, http://www.theatlantic.com/sexes/archive/2012/10/tvs-disappointing-gay-dads/264134/; Bill Keveney, "'Modern Family' Goes All Out for Cam and Mitchell." *USA Today* May 13, 2014, accessed April 2, 2015, http://www.usatoday.com/story/life/tv/2014/05/13/modern-family-big-mitchell-cam-wedding-on-set/8890595/; and Miller, "Queer Recalibration."

60. Sarah Ahmed, *Queer Phenomenology: Orientations, Objects, Others* (Durham, NC: Duke University Press, 2006), 172.

61. For a redefinition of "queer" representing "more narrowly pragmatic gay and lesbian identity and identity politics, the economic interest of neo liberalism and whiteness, and liberal political norms of inclusion" see David L. Eng, *The Feeling of Kinship: Queer Liberalism and the Racialization of Intimacy* (Durham, NC: Duke University Press), xi.

62. Bruce Bawer, *A Place at the Table: The Gay Individual in American Society* (New York: Simon & Schuster, 1994).

63. See Lynne Joyrich, "Queer Television Studies: Currents, Flows, and (Main) streams" *Cinema Studies* 53 (2014): 133–139 for a nuanced discussion of this debate for television studies.

64. Julianne Pidduck, "The Times of The Hours: Queer Melodrama and the Dilemma of Marriage" *Camera Obscura* 82 (2014), 61.

65. That Lily's first word is "mommy" not only reveals social concerns about gay dads of the "which of you is the father" variety, but of parental desire, which is traditionally associated with mothers rather than fathers (except where there is explicit desire for a boy child to carry on some idea of legacy).

66. *Modern Family*, "Baby on Board," episode no. 24, Season 3, first broadcast May 23, 2012, by ABC, directed by Steven Levitan and written by Abraham Higginbotham.

67. *Modern Family*, "Integrity," episode no. 21, Season 6, first broadcast April 29, 2015, by ABC, directed by Chris Koch and written by Stephen Lloyd and Chuck Tatham.

68. Dowd, *Redefining Fatherhood*, summarizes some of this research debunking the idea that gay parenting is de facto inferior, 77, pointing out that little of the research (yet) examines the qualities of gay parenting but some research suggests "gay fathers put more energy into creating stable positive relationships with their children . . . emphasiz[ing] nurture," 79.

69. Dowd, *Redefining Fatherhood*, 78–79.
70. *Modern Family*, "The Big Guns," episode no. 12, Season 6, first broadcast January 14, 2015, by ABC, directed by Jeffrey Walker and written by Vali Chandrasekaran. Mitchell remarks that Cam ought to work on that "Lizbo" name, implying through comic performance that it sounds too much like "lesbo" and is perhaps inappropriate as a queered stage name for a 7-year-old.

BIBLIOGRAPHY

Abbott, Alysia. "TV's Disappointing Gay Dads." *The Atlantic Monthly*, October 31, 2012. http://www.theatlantic.com/sexes/archive/2012/10/tvs-disappointing-gay-dads/264134/.

The Adoption History Project, "Single Parent Adoptions." Accessed July 17, 2015, http://pages.uoregon.edu/adoption/topics/singleparentadoptions.htm; American Academy of Pediatrics, "Technical Report: Coparent or Second-Parent Adoption by Same Sex Parents." *Pediatrics* 109 (2002): 341–344. Accessed May 9, 2015. http://pediatrics.aappublications.org/content/109/2/341.full.

Ahmed, Sarah. *Queer Phenomenology: Orientations, Objects, Others*. Durham, NC: Duke University Press, 2006.

Akira, I. Styles and Larry Ossei-Mensah. "The Construction of Taste: Television and American Home Décor." In *How Television Shapes Our Worldview: Media Representations of Social Trends and Change*, edited by Deborah A. Macey, Kathleen M. Ryan, and Noah J. Springer, 331–350. Plymouth, UK: Lexington Books, 2014.

All in the Family. Created by Norman Lear. CBS. Original broadcast January 12, 1971–April 8, 1979.

Barret, Robert L. and Bryan E. Robinson. *Gay Fathers*. Lexington, MA: Lexington Books, 1990.

Bawer, Bruce. *A Place at the Table: The Gay Individual in American Society*. New York: Simon & Schuster, 1994.

Boggis, Terry. "The *Real* Modern Family . . . Can Be Real Complicated." *Journal of Gay & Lesbian Mental Health* 16 (2012): 353–360.

Briggs, Matt. *Television, Audiences and Everyday Life*. Berkshire, England: Open University Press. 2010.

Curtain, Michael. "Matrix Media." In *Television Studies after TV: Understanding Television in the Post-Broadcast Era*, edited by Graeme Turner and Jinna Tay, 9–19. London: Routledge, 2009.

Desperate Housewives. Created by Marc Cherry. ABC. Original broadcast 2004–2012.

Dowd, Nancy E. *Redefining Fatherhood*. New York: New York University Press. 2000.

Duggan, Lisa. *The Twilight of Equality: Neoliberalism, Cultural Politics, and the Attack on Democracy*. Boston: Beacon Press. 2003.

Eng, David. L. *The Feeling of Kinship: Queer Liberalism and the Racialization of Intimacy*. Durham: Duke University Press. 2010.

The Fosters. Created by Brad Bredeweg and Peter Paige. ABC. Original broadcast 2013-present.

GLAAD, *Where We Are on TV Report* (2014). Accessed February 14, 2015. http://www.glaad.org/files/GLAAD-2014-WWAT.pdf.

Glee. Created by Ian Brennan, Brad Falchuk and Ryan Murphy. 20th Century Fox. Original broadcast 2009–2015.

Gossip Girl. Created by Stephanie Savage and Josh Schwartz. CW Network. Original broadcast 2007–2012.

Griswold, Robert L. *Fatherhood in America: A History*. New York: Basic Books, 1993.

Halberstam, Judith. *In a Queer Time and Place: Transgender Bodies, Subcultural Lives*. New York: New York University Press. 2005.

Hamad, Hannah. "DAD TV-Postfeminism and the Paternalization of US Television Drama." *FlowTV* 11 (2009). Accessed May 13, 2014. http://flowtv.org/2009/11/dad-tv-—-postfeminism-and-the-paternalization-of-us-television-drama-hannah-hamad-massey-university/.

Huffington Post. "Andrew Rannells on 'The New Normal' Backlash, One Million Moms." *The Huffington Post*, August 28, 2012. Accessed June 30, 2015. http://www.huffingtonpost.com/2012/08/28/andrew-rannells-new-normal-one-million-moms_n_1835963.html.

The Jeffersons. Created by Norman Lear, Don Nicholl, Michael Ross, and Bernard West. CBS. Original broadcast January 18, 1975-July 2, 1985.

Joyrich, Lynne. "Queer Television Studies: Currents, Flows, and (Main)streams." *Cinema Studies* 53 (2014): 133–139.

Kessler, Kelly. "They should Suffer Like the Rest of Us: Queer Equality in Narrative Mediocrity." *Cinema Journal* 50 (2011): 143.

Keveney, Bill. "'Modern Family' Goes All Out for Cam and Mitchell." *USA Today*. May 13, 2014. http://www.usatoday.com/story/life/tv/2014/05/13/modern-family-big-mitchell-cam-wedding-on-set/8890595/.

LaRossa, Ralph. "The Culture of Fatherhood in the Fifties: A Closer Look." *Journal of Family History* 29 (2004): 47–70. DOI: 10.1177/0363199003261811.

Lauzen, Martha M. "Boxed In: Employment of Behind-the-Scenes and On-Screen Women in 2013–2014 Prime-time Television." Center for the Study of Women in Television & Film http://womenintvfilm.sdsu.edu/research.html.

Lewin, Ellen. *Gay Fatherhood: Narrative of Family and Citizenship in America*. Chicago: The University of Chicago Press, 2009.

Lopez, Steve. "Death of a Sitcom." *Entertainment Weekly*, April 16, 1999. http://www.ew.com/ew/article/0,,273101,00.html.

Marry Me. Created by David Caspe. NBC Universal. Original broadcast 2014–2015.

Maude. Created by Norman Lear. CBS. Original broadcast September 12, 1972-April 23, 1978.

William Marsiglio and Kevin Roy, *Nurturing Dads: Social Initiatives for Contemporary Fatherhood* (New York: Russell Sage Foundation, 2012); Jennifer Senior, *All Joy and No Fun* (New York: Ecco, 2014).

McDermott, Esther. *Intimate Fatherhood: A Sociological Analysis*. London: Routledge, 2008.

Miller, Quinn. "Queer Recalibration." *Cinema Journal* 53 (2014): 140–144.

Mills, Brett. *Television Sitcom*. London: BFI, 2005.

Modern Family. Created by Steven Levitan and Christopher Lloyd. ABC. Original broadcast 2009-present.

Morreale, Joanne. "Television in the 1990s and Beyond." In *Critiquing the Sitcom*, edited by Joanne Morreale, 247–250. Syracuse, NY: Syracuse University Press, 2003.

Needham, Gary. "Scheduling Normativity: Television, the Family, and Queer Temporality" in *Queer TV: Theories, Histories, Politics*, ed. Glyn Davis and Gary Needham (London: Routledge, 2009), 143.

The New Normal. Created by Ali Adler, Ryan Murphy and Katherine Shaffer. NBC Universal. Original broadcast 2012–2013.

Niedwiecki, Anthony. "Save Our Children: Overcoming the Narrative that Gays and Lesbians Are Harmful to Children." *Duke Journal of Gender Law & Policy* 21 (2013): 149. Accessed April 9, 2015. http://go.galegroup.com/ps/i.do?id=GALE%7CA363188289&v=2.1&u=car139591&it=r&p=LT &sw=w&asid=55bd0fe98610f122186e2c18052ea329.

Normal, Ohio. Created by Bob Kushell, Bonnie Turner and Terry Turner. Produced by Carsey-Werner. FOX Network. Original broadcast 2000–2001.

Pehlke II, Timothy Allen and Charles B. Hennon, M. Elise Radina, and Katherine A. Kuvalanka. "Does Father Still Know Best? An Inductive Thematic Analysis of Popular TV Sitcoms." *Fathering* 7 (2009): 114–139.

Pidduck, Julianne. "The Times of *The Hours*: Queer Melodrama and the Dilemma of Marriage." *Camera Obscura* 82 (2014): 36–67.

Popkin, Michael H. Accessed July 6, 2015, www.activeparenting.com.

Population Reference Bureau. Accessed March 31, 2015. http://www.prb.org/Publications/Articles/2003/TraditionalFamiliesAccountforOnly7PercentofUSHouseholds.aspx.

Poulos, Thomas. "Gay Men's Motivations for Having Children: Gay Fathers and the Reconceptualization of Fatherhood and Homosexuality." *MJUR (Midwest Journal of Undergraduate Research)* (2011): 85–103. Accessed May 22, 2014. http://research.monm.edu/mjur/files/2011/04/Gay_Fathers_2011.pdf.

Queer as Folk. "We Will Survive." Episode no. 13, Season 5. Directed by Kelly Makin. Written by Ron Cowen and Daniel Lipman. Showtime. Original broadcast August 7, 2005.

Richardson, Justin and Peter Parnell. *And Tango Makes Three*. New York: Simon & Schuster Books For Young Readers. 2005.

Salem, Rob. "Modern Family Worth Adopting." *The Toronto Star*, September 23, 2009. Accessed March 31, 2015. www.lexisnexis.com/hottopics/Inacademic.

Sbordone, Albert Joseph. "Gay Men Choosing Fatherhood" (PhD diss., City University of New York, 1993.

Six Feet Under. Created by Alam Ball. HBO. Original broadcast 2001–2005.

Spigel, Lynn. *Make Room for TV*. Chicago: Chicago University Press, 1992.

Tropiano, Steve. "Gaycoms in a Progressive Age? *Partners* and *The New Normal*." *FlowTV* 17 (2013). Accessed April 3, 2014. http://flowtv.org/2013/06/flow-favorites-gaycoms-in-a-progressive-age/ - http://flowtv.org/2013/06/flow-favorites-gaycoms-in-a-progressive-age/.

Tucker, Ken. "Modern Family." *Entertainment Weekly*, October 9, 2009: 48–49 Accessed March 31, 2015. *Academic Search Complete*, EBSCOhost.

Warner, Judith. *Perfect Madness: Motherhood in the Age of Anxiety*. New York: Riverhead Books, 2006.

Weston, Kath. *Families We Choose: Lesbians, Gays, Kinship*. New York: Columbia University Press, 1997.

Will & Grace. Created by David Kohan and Max Mutchnick. NBC Universal. Original broadcast 1998–2006.

Chapter 11

Paternidad, Masculinidad, and Machismo

Evolving Representations of Mexican American Fathers in Film

Leandra H. Hernández

The Hispanic/Latino population is one of the fastest growing minorities in the United States. According to the Pew Research Center,[1] there were 54 million Hispanic/Latino people in the United States in 2013, comprising 17% of the total U.S. population, and it is estimated that this percentage will continue to increase in coming decades. Despite this population growth, Latino media and communication scholars such as Arlene Dávila[2] and Michelle A. Holling[3] note that representations of Latinos in the media are rare, and the representations that do exist create a negative presence for Latinos in the American consciousness because of the negative, demeaning, and sometimes offensive stereotypes that characterize these representations.

One of the most notable and significant representations—or lack thereof, according to Michelle A. Holling[4]—is the Latino family. It is estimated that Latino characters comprise a mere 1% of lead characters in top grossing, U.S. motion pictures.[5] Citing scholar Marco Portales'[6] work on representations of Mexican Americans in the public consciousness, Holling[7] asserts that "not only does the viewing public remain ignorant of Chicana/o families, Chicana/os themselves are not 'publicly represented as full-fledged Americans,' and that is an injustice to current and future generations." This notable mass media representation omission of the Latino family also manifests itself more specifically in one specific component of the Latino family: the Latino father. Situated within volatile debates about deadbeat fathers, Latino immigrant families that are heavily populating the United States, patriarchal family values, oppressive marital relationships, and many others, what it means to be a Latino father takes on very different meanings in different media contexts. To further explore what it means to be a Latino father in contemporary media, this chapter will conduct a critical media analysis of Mexican American fathers in popular films.

Although much research has explored representations of Latino families and masculinities in television shows,[8] there is a paucity of research that explores media representations of Mexican American fathers in film, the portrayals of Mexican masculinities as situated within larger representations of Mexican families, and the broader implications of these representations as they shape and affect the broader American consciousness. Thus, the research questions guiding this analysis are: 1) How are Mexican American fathers depicted in popular films, and 2) How is *masculinidad* depicted in these films, as related to the representations of Hispanic/Latino fatherhood? An analysis of films such as *Mi Familia, A Better Life, La Mission, Tortilla Soup* and *Quinceañera* suggests that while certain films do indeed provide representations of Mexican fathers as situated within positive characteristics of *machismo* and *paternidad*, such as providing for one's family and being a caring and loving father, a paradox exists in that these representations continue to reify pre-existing media stereotypes and tropes, thus leading one to question notions of authenticity and representation.

LATINO FAMILIES & MEDIA REPRESENTATIONS

Latino Families & Gender Norms: Machismo & Marianismo

Studies of Latino families and the gender norms that prevail, shape, and affect Latino marriages and relationships proliferate in many scholarly areas such as communication studies, Latina/o studies, women's and gender studies, and public health, among others. Historically, academic scholarship that studied Latino families more broadly and marriages more specifically operated under the notion of an "ideology of family," first coined by Patricia Zavella and later further examined by scholars such as Norma Wiliams.[9] In her germinal book, Patricia Zavella[10] noted that the "ideology of family" originated in social science, functionalist, and acculturation perspectives, which argued that Latino families were patriarchal, dominated by the father or head male family member, and operated under a strict and rigid gender-based family structure. Elaborating upon Zavella's observations, Norma Williams analyzed traditional social scientists' approaches to studying Mexican American families and described their ontological and methodological limitations, noting that these perceptions included how "Wives and daughters were perceived as passive and totally accepting of the husband's or father's authority. The man was characterized by his 'machismo,' or dominance over women."[11] Michelle A. Holling[12] details how sociological work advanced academic and popular conceptualizations of *la familia Mexicana* because it advocated for and advanced a characteristics-based approach that focused upon a more holistic and often positive manner of exploring the concept of family. According to Holling, "Characteristics included varying degrees of egalitarian relations among marital couples, a strong emphasis on family solidarity and extended relations, affectionate and close bonds, and celebrations of life-cycle rituals."[13] The family is the primary unit within Latino cultures and is a strong, if not the strongest, cultural value.[14] As such, important related concepts within the Mexican family specifically include *familismo* and *machismo*.

In many Mexican American families, there is much reliance upon family members and the family structure; as such, children stay at home longer than children of other races/ethnicities and extended family members often share the nurturing, raising, and disciplining of children, as well as financial responsibility and familial problem solving.[15] The notion of loyalty to both primary and extended family, even at the risk of the needs of the individual, is known as *familismo*. This concept places one's family and community relationships at the center of one's identity and is characterized by deep powerful bonds, loyalty, solidarity, and reciprocity within the immediate and extended family. The notion of a "familial self" is a useful concept for making sense of *familismo* within Mexican American families, as it suggests the internalization of family as an integral part of one's individual identity, thus contributing to family unity and family honor.[16] Both traditional and less-traditional *Mexicanos* who privilege and enact *familismo* value familial interdependence, encouragement, cooperation, and advice.[17]

Despite positive conceptualizations of *familismo* in academic literature and familial embodiment in everyday life, closely related concepts *machismo* and *marianismo* can sometimes be at odds with the notions of encouragement, egalitarianism, and cooperation. *Machismo* and *marianismo*, the Mexican male and female gender role performances respectively, govern Mexican intimate relationships and can have both positive and negative outcomes both in mass media representations of *la familia Mexicana* and in "real life." *Machismo*, the male gender performance, can have both positive and negative associations. Holling provides a succinct description of the historical origins of Chicano/Latino masculinity and the importance of viewing Latino masculinity as wholly descriptive or applicable to all Chicano/Latino men:

> Though cultural expectations of masculinity "carry over" from Mexico and are "rearticulated" in the U.S. (Delgado, 2005, p. 203), important to bear in mind are differences based on generation, national status, socioeconomics, and educational levels, among other factors, that influence the construction, performance, and representation of Chicano and Latino masculinities within the U.S. Within that context, Chicano masculinity is born from experiences of colonization, oppression, and resistance, as well as influenced by cultural attitudes of what constitutes a "man."[18]

According to Geri-Ann Galanti, positive aspects of *machismo* and what "constitutes a 'man'" include the pride of men to "behave valiantly to protect the honor and welfare of their families" and to provide for their family and live up to their male responsibilities.[19] *Machismo*, on one hand, is a strong work ethic and a man's dedication to his children and family's well-being.[20] On the other hand, Celia Jaes Falicov notes that the dark side of *machismo* can be defined as a strong or exaggerated sense of masculinity that stresses attributes such as physical courage, virility, aggressiveness, and domination of women. This aspect of *machismo* is a gender performance characterized by patriarchal dominance and authority. Chicana queer theorist and feminist Gloria Anzaldúa, however, notes that this construction of machismo is a "false machismo," which refers to the negative, stereotypical portrayal of the Mexican father.[21] Chicana feminist Ana Castillo elaborates upon "false machismo" by noting that it obscures the fact that machismo can also signify a man being a supportive father and husband. Many Chicana feminist scholars, including Anzaldúa and Castillo, argue that the negative, stereotypical representations of the "false machismo" Latino man and father abound in the mass media, which could have far-reaching implications.

Although stereotypical representations of Mexican fathers abound in pre-revisionist academic literature and the mass media, research that explores expectations of Mexican fathers and their gendered fatherhood performances tells a different story. Contrary to popular constructions of Mexican fathers as patriarchal, chauvinistic, anti-acculturational, and reluctant to embrace change, more contemporary research on Mexican fatherhood has redefined the term *machismo* and reconceptualized it to focus on positive cultural qualities such as honesty, respect, loyalty, trustworthiness, responsibility, and fairness.[22] Manifested within father-child relationships, this is embodied within actions such as providing for one's family, monitoring and interacting with children frequently, being involved with children's educational and recreational pursuits, and overall engaging in positive parenting situated within positive family values.[23] Research by Coltrane and colleagues found that Mexican fathers were more involved in interacting with their children when the family overall placed more emphasis on family values; moreover, in this study, counter to stereotypes about Mexican machismo, Mexican fathers happily supervised their children and even engaged in feminine activities like housework when their wives worked in spheres outside of the home.[24] Similarly, a study conducted by Cruz and colleagues found that Mexican fathers' positive machismo performances and attitudes were positively related to their children's perceptions of their fathers' involvement in their lives, thus suggesting a strong and important association between Mexican fathers' cultural values pertaining to fatherhood and paternal responsibility and their children's perceptions of positive fathering.[25]

Thus, given historical and academic conceptualizations of the Mexican American family, one could argue that it is not surprising to see stereotypical representations of Mexican American families in television shows, news stories, and films. What *is* surprising, however, is the perpetuation of these media representations, despite the fact that recent studies suggest that Hispanic/Latino marital relationships are increasingly being characterized by egalitarian relationships that reject archetypal marriage modes and embrace more positive parenting modes and involvement.[26] As Matthew C. Gutmann notes, the disparity between media representations of Hispanic/Latino families and cultural patterns in reality lies in the fact that "the conscious recognition of cultural patterns may lag behind actual changes in practice."[27] One of the possible explanations of this phenomenon lies in an exploration of racial/ethnic stereotyping.

Ethnic Stereotyping & Media Representations of Hispanic/Latino Families

Academic literature that explores and analyzes media effects more broadly and media representations of racial/ethnic minorities more specifically consistently concludes that media use plays a meaningful role in the development of audience members' racial/ethnic cognitions. Media effects scholar Dana Mastro explains that viewing media portrayals of various minority racial/ethnic groups is associated with evaluations of outgroup members' competence, group status, socioeconomic status, and judgments regarding stereotypes.[28]

Although Mastro[29] argues that few universals can be offered with regard to contemporary media representations of race/ethnicity, she also notes that there are typically a handful of media tropes that dominate media representations of various ethnic and racial groups. Hispanic/Latino people are largely underrepresented in American mass media; yet, when these representations do exist, these portrayals are often consistent with traditional stereotypes, whether it be via film or television.[30] For example, Mastro's research suggests that television representations of Latinos are typically confined to crime dramas and sitcoms, in which they emphasize the family unit and are often portrayed as being younger, lower in job authority, hot-tempered, less articulate than other racial/ethnic counterparts, less intelligent, and more likely to be characterized as domestic employees.[31] Political science scholar Stephanie Greco Larson elaborates upon Mastro's findings by positing that "Hispanics are presented in television entertainment and films in limited ways that simultaneously reinforces their inferior status while denying that it exists. This is done through the exclusion, stereotyping, and the system-supportive stories that are told about them."[32] Greco Larson further notes that this status of limited media representation overall occurs via mechanisms of criminalization, sexualization, and demeanment. However, one important media trope that differs from prime-time television representations and film representations is success via assimilation and the American Dream; in spite of this trope, Hispanic/Latino characters are continually represented in film both negatively and stereotypically.

Within a television context specifically, scant research has explored sitcom representations of Mexican families. The overall consensus is twofold: media representations of Hispanic/Latinos have increased, albeit still underrepresented, and depictions are becoming more positive. Heidi Denzel de Tirado's research showcases themes that characterize television sitcom representations of Mexican families, including *familismo* and family symbolism, positive male/father focal characters, and female agency and independence. Her analysis of television series including *The Brothers García*, *American Family: Journey of Dreams*, *The George Lopez Show*, and *Resurrection Boulevard* found two main themes pertaining to Mexican fatherhood: 1) fathers in these series were very family oriented in that they were loving, supportive, always available for their families, and even *mandilones*[33] in the sense that they took over maternal/feminine chores and responsibilities when necessary; and 2) there is a "coming-of-age tale" for the patriarch of the family, which details his journey to become a more flexible, patient, and tolerable parent.

Within a film context, the stereotypical and negative representations of Latino characters in film are situated within an industry that repeats, blends, and distorts these images. Scholar Christine List argues that "The three legacies which Hollywood passes on to Chicano feature filmmaking are its long history of negative stereotyping, its use of genre as a structuring device, and its power to generate popular myths."[34] Building upon earlier research findings on Hispanic/Latino representations in television shows, scholars such as Stephanie Greco Larson and Christine List note that the popular myths or stereotypes that accompany Hispanic/Latino male representations in film include the greaser, the buffoon, the Latin lover, the caballero, the gangster, the violent villain, the drug runner, and the delinquent.[35] Unsurprisingly, these stereotypes are situated within cultural, historical, and political contexts. Greco Larson, for example, notes that the "violent criminal/villain" and "bandit" stereotypes date back to propaganda during Texas' war of independence, and that these stereotypes transitioned to the "gang member" and "drug dealer" stereotypes found in present-day urban-violence films and television shows.[36]

What is missing from academic literature on film representations of Latino men, however, is an analysis of representations of Mexican American fathers. Given that the Latino population is the fastest growing minority in the United States *and* considering that Latino characters are drastically underrepresented in film, an analysis of film representations of Mexican American fathers can speak to the ways in which filmmakers conceptualize and discursively construct Latino families more broadly and Mexican American fathers more specifically. The scant research that has explored film representations of *la familia Mexicana* underscores the argument that contemporary films produced in the past 25 years offer little to no variance in the construction of *la familia* and the gender relations portrayed between and among family members. Holling, for example, notes that films such as *The Perez Family* portray the Puerto Rican family unit as firmly entrenched within patriarchal control.[37] Other films such as *Mi Familia* participate in what Rosa-Linda Fregoso refers to as "the Chicano familia romance" that is informed by cultural nationalism and entrenches *la familia* within conservative family values discourses[38]; moreover, the gender portrayals and relations in *Mi Familia* are problematic and relatively stagnant.

Thus, one can conclude that media representations of racial/ethnic minorities, especially Latino characters and families, are undoubtedly important because of the larger implications associated with their construction and deployment. Angharad N. Valdivia argues that "Representation, our presence in media content, speaks to issues of power, not of numbers."[39] The power lies in the discursive and symbolic power inherently located within films and television shows and the broader effects of these representations on the American imaginary. Furthermore, Valdivia notes that "[s]tudying representation is a crucially important component of Latina/o Media Studies as it speaks to the fulfillment of the democratic potential of communication practices and technologies, and the themes and messages that we and others use to make sense of the world."[40] Thus, this essay explores representations of Mexican American fathers in popular films to further understand how *Latinidad, paternidad,* and *masculinidad* operate in popular films through the lens of Mexican fatherhood. In an effort to explore the themes and gender performances of Latino fatherhood in film, this chapter asks the questions: 1) How are Latino fathers depicted in popular films, and 2) How is *masculinidad* depicted in these films, as related to and situated within representations of Latino fatherhood and *familia*?

A Critical Reading of Mi Familia, A Better Life, La Mission, Tortilla Soup, and Quinceañera

To answer the aforementioned research questions, a critical media analysis was conducted of the films *Mi Familia,*[41] *A Better Life,*[42] *La Mission,*[43] *Tortilla Soup,*[44] and *Quinceañera.*[45] These films were selected because this analysis sought to center upon fictional representations of Mexican families in recent film. An initial search of "films about Mexican families" was conducted to locate a preliminary list of films, and films such as *Selena* and *La Bamba* were excluded because they were based upon non-fictional families and musicians. Five films met the inclusion criteria: *Mi Familia, A Better Life, La Mission, Tortilla Soup,* and *Quinceañera.*[46] These films have many cinematic qualities in common: 1) the films detail the experiences of Mexican American families in California, which has a unique cultural, regional, and ethnic history as it pertains to one Mexican aspect of *Latinidad* (*Mi Familia, A Better Life, Tortilla Soup,* and *Quinceañera* in East Los Angeles and *La Mission* in San Francisco); 2) the films explore multigenerational Mexican American families and, in some cases, intergenerational *paternidad* and *masculinidad*; and 3) the films explore the struggles that the families confront in the face of racism, gang violence, police brutality, class issues, immigration, gentrification, and acculturation/assimilation, which results in an overarching grand narrative found in the films: the search for the American Dream and for a better life.

When conducting a critical reading of the films, an eye was kept to issues of gender relations, gender norms, fatherhood, the construction of the family unit, and the communication patterns and styles that occurred between fathers and sons and also fathers and spouses (if the spouses or relational partners were present in the film). First, the films will be analyzed individually and then discussed together in the discussion section.

PATERNIDAD, MASCULINIDAD, AND FAMILIA IN CHICANO FILMS

Positive Machismo & Paternidad in *Mi Familia*

Mi Familia tells the story of a Mexican American family with immigrant roots living in East Los Angeles. Narrated by Paco, James Edward Olmos' character and the oldest son, *Mi Familia* begins with the story of the family's grandfather and his journey from Mexico to Los Angeles. With scenery, music, and corn fields reminiscent of nostalgic Mexico, the film details first the relationship of José and María, the family's grandparents, and the growing of their family. Situated within traditional Mexican values such as *familismo* and *religiosidad*, José and María Sanchez (the first generation) have their first two children. Jose is a caring, loving, and dutiful father who provides for his family by gardening and working in the fields, jobs typically occupied by immigrant labor. In terms of *su paternidad*, José embodies the positive side of *machismo* as he cares for his family, shows them affection, and works tirelessly to provide for them. As the film progresses, José and María's family grows as they have more children, and José continues to be a supportive and loving father. One exemplar of the blending of positive machismo and *familismo* occurs when José and María's oldest daughter gets married. Instead of giving the toast alone, José calls his family members up the wedding table and toasts by saying, "The greatest riches a man can have in life are his familia."

As the film progresses, familial struggles and woes characterize the family's narrative. One such case occurs when Chucho, the third child, comes home with money and José questions where Chucho earned the money without having a job. An altercation ensues between Chucho and José, and the two have the following conversation before Chucho storms out of the house:

José: Where do you get this money?

Chucho: I just get it, that's all.

José: From where? Selling mota, is that it?

Chuco: What difference does it make?

José: The police called here tonight—la policía! I didn't raise my children to be sinverguenzas . . . delincuentes! When I think of all the years I struggled without complaining, like . . . like when I came here by walking all the way from Michoacan, and what your mother went through to bring you back when you were a baby so you'd grow up to be a man with respect! Don't you have any pride? Look at your sister Irene and your brother Paco—in the Navy! Pero tú, selling marijuana like some hoodlum! No tienes conciencia, no tienes dignidad!

Chucho: F*** dignidad! F*** it, and f*** your struggles! . . . I don't want to be like no Mexican. If you think for one minute I want to spend all f****** day pulling up weeds and mowing lawns, you got another thing coming. A la chingada con eso! I don't want to be like Irene. I don't want to be like Paco. Most of all, I don't want to be like you!

In this scene, José's fatherhood is tested as he struggles to reconcile his love for his son and his disdain for Chucho's *chuco* lifestyle and disobedience. Paco narrates this dissonance when he states in the next scene: "There was no communication at all between my father and my brother Chucho. They were from two different worlds. To my father, there was dignity in work. He crossed the bridges every morning to support his family. My father felt that he was right to throw Chucho out of the house, but deep down in his heart, he didn't feel so right." The significance of this narration is twofold: 1) it elaborates upon José's positive *machismo* as performed via his monetary and emotional support for his family, which is a key part of the overall film narrative, and 2) it elaborates upon his love for his son. It also foreshadows future trials and tribulations that the family encounters, such as Chucho's death at the hands of the police and Jimmy's incarceration (the youngest son), which could be inferred occurred as a result of witnessing Chucho's murder when he was a young boy.

As the film progresses, a new father emerges in the film: Jimmy, the youngest son. In the film, Jimmy robs a store after his wife dies in childbirth with their son, Carlitos, and is incarcerated shortly after his birth. When Jimmy returns home after a few years, he struggles severely while getting to know his son, who has been cared for by his parents throughout his incarceration. Here, we see a new fatherhood performance, one in which consistent perseverance characterizes his determination to build a relationship with his son, Carlitos. Although the bandido/thug stereotype appears in the film as evidenced in Chucho's and Jimmy's characters, Jimmy's incarceration is a more complex representation of this stereotype because it is situated within a larger web of police violence, retaliation, and trauma of witnessing his brother's murder. Carlitos repeatedly tells Jimmy, "You're not my father!" throughout the end of the movie, and Jimmy and José have a few heart-to-heart conversations where Jimmy tells his father that he wants nothing more than to be there for his son; as the movie comes to an end, Carlitos and Jimmy have a heartfelt moment where the two reconcile their differences and Carlitos becomes more affectionate toward him; in a closure of fatherhood, Jimmy finally has the opportunity to be the father he wanted to be.

Thus, in *Mi Familia*, José, the family patriarch, plays a positive central role throughout the familial and film narrative. His fatherhood and masculinity is performed throughout the film via his caring and supportive relationships with his wife María and his children and grandchildren and the constant reminder that he has wished for nothing more than to be a good provider and good father. It is no surprise that the entire family refers to José throughout the film as *jefe*, which literally translates to "boss" and can also colloquially signify "dad."

Positive Paternidad and Masculinidad in *A Better Life*

The film *A Better Life* chronicles the life of Carlos Galindo, a Mexican immigrant gardener and day laborer who works to provide for himself and his son, Luís. As opposed to *Mi Familia*, in which the viewer sees the parents, children, and eventually the grandchildren, Carlos and Luis are the only two family members showcased in this film. *A Better Life* is characterized by Carlos wishing for his son to follow the right path by going to school, getting an education, and getting a good job. In the first scene, the viewer sees Carlos and Luís eating breakfast together, and Luís asks his father for money. In a scene similar to the exchange between José and Chucho in *Mi Familia*, Luís tells his father that he needs money "to buy some stuff for school." Carlos responds with doubt, asking Luís, "Since when do you go to school?" With an angered tone, Luís tells his father, "Every day!" The exchange unfolds with Carlos telling his son that he does not want him to continue missing school, which incites the following fight:

Carlos: I don't want you to miss school no more. School's important. It's everything.

Luís: Sí, profesor?

Carlos: Sí, profesor. You wanna end up like me?

Luís: No. So, can I have the money or what?

Carlos: You want money? Come work. If you need money in this world, Luís, necesitas trabajar. You need to work. Get yourself an education.

In this scene, it becomes clear that Carlos cares very much for his son and wishes for him a life that he himself does not have. Carlos tries to instill work ethic and educational values in his son, which he hopes will translate into a brighter future for his son once he graduates from high school.

As the film's plot unfolds, Carlos has the opportunity to purchase his boss' truck. His boss, also a fellow immigrant and day laborer, tells Carlos that buying his truck will not only get him a new small business, but the American Dream as well. This purchase signifies the potential for Carlos to have upward mobility for himself and for Luís. The evening after he purchased the truck, Carlos tells Luís, "Listen, mijo. I'm gonna make something out of this business. I'll make it grow into something big, so we could move out of here and get you into a better school. And I'm not gonna work Sundays no more. We can do things, spend time together, if you want to, you know?" Startled by this statement, Luís tells Carlos that he is tired and wants to go to sleep. In this scene, however, it becomes apparent that Carlos' main goal throughout the movie is to do well for his family, provide for his son, and create a better life for them both. In terms of the multiple *machismo* stereotypes and archetypes evident in both academic literature and media representations of Latino men/Latino fathers, similar to the role of José in *Mi Familia*, Carlos' fatherhood and masculinity is characterized by positive *machismo* dimensions such as caring for his family and seeking to provide for his son at whatever the cost.

However, Carlos' luck quickly fades when a day laborer whom he hired steals his truck and his tools. This is a pivotal event in the film, as it signifies both a turning point in the plot and also in Carlos' relationship with his son. When Carlos comes home drunk in the middle of the night as a coping mechanism, Luís finally shows some interest in and compassion for his father, and the next day he vows to help his father find the day laborer who stole his truck. Carlos and Luís find the man who stole the truck. After locating the truck in an underground, black market shop, Carlos and Luís together steal the truck in hope of a chance to regrow the business and have future opportunities. This climactic scene soon takes a dark turn as Carlos is pulled over by a police offer and immediately sent to jail for deportation. Luís is sent to live with his Tía Anita, and in the final scene has a chance to say goodbye to his father before he is deported back to Mexico. Earlier in the film, Luís asks Carlos why so many poor people have children and, more specifically, why Carlos decided to have him. In this scene, Carlos finally answers Luís' question:

> You know, back in the village, you just did what any man would do. You found a novia, got married, and then headed north. And that's what I did 'cause I didn't know any different. So, we came here, and then we had you. Why? Because your mother and I loved each other very much. But then, people change, and things were different here. Your mother changed. She wanted more than I could give her, so she went away. And I was left alone with you. I didn't know how I was going to manage with a small boy, with no money and no regular job. I had a lot of anger inside of me. But the thing, the one thing that helped me to get over all of that was you. To be able to take care of you and to watch you grow, because I love you. You are the most important thing in this world to me, mijo. I wanted you to be able to be anything you wanted to be. That would make me feel worthy, if you became somebody. That's why I had you. For me, for me, for a reason to live.

In this critically important scene in the film, Carlos explains to Luís the reason he decided to have a child—for salvation, for worth, and out of love. Carlos fights through the trials and tribulations so that he can provide for his son and give him a better life, resulting in a strengthened relationship with his son and a foreshadowed return to the United States.

Paternidad in *Tortilla Soup*

Tortilla Soup opens with Martín, a master chef and the widowed family patriarch, cooking a large and elaborate dinner for himself and his three adult daughters. Martín is the former owner of an upscale Mexican restaurant and is described throughout the film by friends and family members as a "cultural purist:"[47] he prefers that his family members speak only English or only Spanish, not a mixture of the two, and he disdains the mixture of different cultural and ethnic ingredients in the food he cooks. This cultural purism translates to his parenting style, as well. Martín is a traditional first-generation immigrant Mexican father who exercises his fatherly power by expecting to be consulted before all of his daughters' major life decisions, despite the fact that they are all adults. In the film's first dinner scene, he lovingly scolds Maribel, his youngest daughter, for being late to dinner and then engages in a minor argument with Carmen, his middle daughter. Carmen tells Martín that she is planning on moving out of their home, and Martín expresses his disappointment that she did not consult with him beforehand to ask for his financial and parental advice. All three daughters live at home in traditional Mexican familial fashion, and in a telling, foreshadowing exchange between Martín and his restaurant partner, Martín paradoxically expresses that he wants his daughters to move out and live their lives, yet he also wants them to stay close to him.

Martín expresses his affection and love for his daughters not only through having raised them as a single father after his wife's passing fifteen years prior, but also through his cooking and his housework, two household spheres that are traditionally considered to be "women's work." In one scene, Martín is ironing Carmen's blouse and then scurrying about the house doing his daughters' laundry. He mentions to Hortensia, a breakfast guest and the mother of Leticia's friend, "A father's work never ends!" However, Martín also keeps a tight control grip on his daughters' actions, despite their age, which is evidence of the family being rooted within the patriarchal "Father knows best" mentality. For example, when Carmen, a Latin fusion aspiring chef, retaliates against Martín because he would not let her become a chef like him, he tells her, "I didn't send my daughter to graduate school so all she would do is make tortillas." In another scene, Maribel introduces her father and sisters to her new boyfriend and loudly announces that she wants to take a year off before she goes to college so that she can "find herself." In an expected manner, Martín tells her that she will go to college as planned because he "says so" in traditional parental fashion: "As long as you're living under my roof, you will do as I say!" Maribel retorts to everyone's surprise, especially her boyfriend, by stating that she is moving in with him. Highly offended, Martín asks how Maribel's boyfriend could sit at his dinner table and then offend him in such a manner.

As the film nears its conclusion, Carmen, Leticia, and Maribel make their own decisions, eventually with Martín's blessings. In one of *Tortilla Soup*'s final dinner scenes, Martín makes an announcement at dinner and states, "Leading our separate lives but under the same roof, worrying and caring about one another, it's that caring that makes us a familia."

Patriarchal Paternidad in *Quinceañera*

Quinceañera is a film that explores the intersection of religion, tradition, culture, and sexuality. In this film, Magdalena, the protagonist and a pastor's daughter, is approaching her 15th birthday. In Mexican culture, girls approaching their 15th birthday typically have a quinceañera, a birthday party that signals the young girl's transition to womanhood. As the film begins,

Magdalena is participating in her cousin Eileen's quinceañera. The scene transitions to Magdalena and Eileen's fathers talking, and Eileen's father asks Magdalena's father about her upcoming celebration. He tells Magdalena's father to prepare paying for it, and Magdalena's father responds, "You know what, though? Magdalena's won't be like that. She's different. She's a more traditional girl than Eileen." Eileen's father retorts, "Alright, Ernesto. If you say so."

Magdalena's father Ernesto is a spiritual man and traditional Mexican father who sees Magdalena's quinceañera as a major spiritual milestone, not necessarily a transition to womanhood. This is evidenced in multiple scenes, such as when he tells his wife that Magdalena's quinceañera should be about her relationship with God, not a Hummer and parties, and in one scene in particular when Ernesto and Magdalena are practicing the song she will sing during the church portion of her quinceañera. As the film progresses, the viewer sees Magdalena's relationship unfold with her boyfriend, Herman, and in a pivotal moment during the film, Magdalena tries on her quinceañera dress. When it fits too tightly, Magdalena's mother asks her if she has "had relations" with Herman. The scene cuts to an altercation between Magdalena's parents, more specifically Ernesto's rage when he discovers that Magdalena is pregnant. He tells his wife, "How could this happen? How could *you* let this happen?" Magdalena and Ernesto fight with each other, and Ernesto screams at Magdalena in Spanish, "How do you think your mother feels now? After the shame you've brought on this house? And on the church? You are so full of sin that you can't admit the truth, not even when your wickedness is there in front of you for the whole world to see!" This altercation prompted Magdalena to move in with her uncle Tomás, with whom her gay cousin Carlos lives. When Tomás visits Magdalena's parents in hopes of inspiring Ernesto to talk to Magdalena, Ernesto responds, "When she's ready to confess her sin, we'll talk. Not until then. I don't know her anymore. The girl I knew read the Bible at night and sang in my church. She didn't run around with boys and fornicate. She didn't lie to her father."

As the film progresses, Magdalena's mother takes her to the clinic, where the doctor informs her mother that the pregnancy is indeed an anomaly that was not caused by vaginal coitus. This realization prompts Ernesto to initiate contact with Magdalena at Tomás' funeral as he tells her, "The Lord works in mysterious ways." Magdalena tells him that her pregnancy was not God's work, to which he responds, "Everything is His doing." As the film nears its end, Ernesto asks Magdalena for her forgiveness and tells her, "I'll make it up to you." The film concludes with Magdalena's quinceañera and her father smiling at her as she walks down the aisle of their church.

In this film, Ernesto's character embodies both positive and negative characteristics of machismo. On the most positive end, he is a caring and loving father who works two jobs to provide for his family. Additionally, he is present and available for his family and children *until*, however, he discovers Magdalena's pregnancy. Firmly entrenched within a religious-based patriarchal worldview, it is difficult for him to separate his religious beliefs from his love for his daughter. He blames Magdalena's mother for the pregnancy because she did not tell him about Magdalena's relationship with Herman, and he also grounds his rage within religious attitudes about shame and disgrace. Moreover, he forgives Magdalena *only* when he learns that her status as a virgin has not been tainted.

Complex Machismo and Paternidad in *La Mission*

La Mission chronicles the life of Che Rivera, a recovering alcoholic and reformed prison inmate who is well known and well respected in his San Francisco neighborhood. Che embodies one version of Latino *masculinidad* in the film with his strength, masculinity, and role in the community. Not only is he well respected in his neighborhood and his community because of his strength, persona, and integral role in the community lowrider scene, but also because of his successful *paternidad*. When his wife passed away, he became the sole provider and role model for his only son, Jes, who excels in school, is well liked in the community, and is planning to attend UCLA. Che's fatherhood and *machismo* is questioned, however, when he finds pictures on Jes' nightstand of him and his boyfriend kissing at a nightclub. Che confronts Jes the next day about his pictures and about his sexuality, and then Che and Jes engage in a physical altercation, which makes its way to the front porch in front of the entire neighborhood. Jes leaves to spend some time with Che's best friend Rene, whereas Che spends time alone reflecting upon what happened between him and his son. When Jes returns to talk with Che, the two sit down to have a meal together. Jes tells Che that he has been gay for as long as he can remember, and, in typical patriarchal macho fashion, Che tells Jes that he "doesn't want [homosexuality] anywhere near [him]" and that Jes essentially has to choose between maintaining his relationship with his father or being true to himself and his sexuality.

As the film progresses, the strength of Che and Jes' relationship ebbs and flows. Although Che's friends and the community accept Jes regardless of his sexuality, Che continues to struggle with reconciling his homophobia, rooted in Catholicism and Mexican *machismo*, and his love for his son. For example, in one scene, Che asks Jes if he has evening plans, and Jes responds that he and a friend are going to study and then get dinner. Che asks with whom Jes has plans, and Jes said, "I thought you didn't want it anywhere near you, remember?" This statement ends the conversation and is the last interaction

Che and Jes have before Jes is shot that evening by a local gang member in a homophobic hate crime. Although it appears that this scene will be a pivotal moment in Che and Jes' relationship (the scene cuts to Che and his friends making a lowrider car as a graduation gift for Jes and then Che visiting Jes at the hospital frequently), this is short lived, given that Che verbally and physically threatens Jes' boyfriend Jordan when he sees him visiting Jes at the hospital. As a result, Jes checks himself out of the hospital and argues with Che when he arrives at Jordan's house to pick up Jes. Che orders Jes to pack his stuff to leave, and Jes refuses to leave with him:

Che: Look around you, boy. You think these people really give a s*** about you?

Jes: And you do?

Che: I'm all you got, remember?

Jes: I got a lot more than that. I got myself. If you can't accept me for what I am, for who I love, I think you should leave.

Che: Whose little speech is that—yours or theirs?

Jes: You humiliate me in front of the entire neighborhood, and then you threaten Jordan for visiting me in the hospital, and you can stand here and ask me that?

Che: Listen, I'm gonna give you one minute to get your ass in there and get your s*** together. If you ain't out by then, I'm gonna leave here without you. Me entiendes?

Jes: You still don't hear me, do you, Pop?

At the end of this scene, Che drives away alone, and the scene transitions to Jes' graduation. Jes sees his *padrinos* and his boyfriend in the crowd, and Che is drinking alcohol at home alone in his garage. After seeing a picture of him and Jes, Che grabs a wrench and starts slashing at the hood of his son's graduation gift, symbolically severing his relationship with his son. The scene cuts to Jes succeeding at UCLA and then to Che's apartment, the apartment in shambles and Che regressing into alcoholism and depression. Witnessing neighborhood Aztec dancers praying and dancing to a photo shrine with a picture of the young man who shot Jes prompts an intense moment of reflection and realization for Che, where he recognizes that he misses his son and should appreciate the fact that he still has his son. The film ends with Che driving Jes' car toward Los Angeles, foreshadowing a relational reconcilement between Che and Jes.

In terms of *paternidad* and *masculinidad*, Jes embodies both sides of the Mexican *machismo* dichotomy. On one hand, Che is a strong and powerful member of the community, both because of his role in reconstructing low-riders for community members and also because he is a hard worker and provider for his son, Jes. However, on the more negative end of the Mexican *machismo* dichotomoy, Che's *masculinidad* and *paternidad* is threatened to the point of him feeling like a failure as a father when he finds out his son Jes is gay. Rooted within Catholicism, homophobia, and the rigid patriarchal Mexican structure of the family, Che becomes a violent, aggressive, and insufferable father and community member as he spends the entire movie coming to terms with his son's sexuality and verbally and nonverbally abusing family and friends throughout the process.

DISCUSSION: *MACHISMO, PATERNIDAD,* AND *MASCULINIDAD* IN CHICANA/O CINEMA

Throughout the films, viewers are privy to seeing five different, yet very similar Mexican families experience daily struggles situated within family strength, family dissolution, deportation, gang violence, trauma, gentrification, and racism. At a broad level, in terms of the ways in which *la cultura Mexicana* is constructed in these films, traditional cinematic strategies reinforce traditional constructions of Mexican culture, such as with religious icons like statues of the Virgin Mary and rosaries adorning homes, altars, and cars; Spanish music as serving parts of the plots and also in the credits; the Spanglish and *pachuco* languages spoken between and among family members; and Mexican food staples such as rice, beans, salsa, and tortillas, especially in *Tortilla Soup*. In these ways, *Latinidad* is used to construct Mexican identity and authenticity and to serve as a platform for the "authentic identities" of the characters and families in the films.

At a more specific level, in terms of the ways in which Mexican fatherhood is constructed and performed throughout these films, two main representations of the Mexican masculinity archetypes emerge: that of positive *machismo/paternidad* and that of the negative, more aggressive *machismo/paternidad*. This conceptualization is not meant to provide a strict binary representation of Mexican fatherhood and masculinity, but rather to show the ways in which the characters' approaches to fatherhood ebb and flow throughout this gender performance spectrum, based upon the sociopolitical, sociocultural, and family structures within which they operate in the films. In *Mi Familia* and *A Better Life*, for example, José and Carlos (respectively) embody, at a base level, the immigrant filmic representation stereotype because they travel from Mexico to the United States for better opportunities for themselves and their families. Rooted within this family history is their approach to fatherhood, which is characterized by them putting their family's needs above their own at all needs and at all costs. Their families recognize, appreciate, and valorize their patriarchs' continued efforts to provide for the family, and their *paternidad* or *masculinidad* is characterized by what Anzaldúa, Castillo, and Galanti refer to as the more positive side of *machismo*, meaning their successful fatherhood is achieved via their provider status and their role as loving, caring fathers. Moreover, these characteristics are those found in research by scholars Coltrane and Cruz, suggesting that perhaps media representations of Mexican fathers are "catching up" to actual Mexican fatherhood in reality and in practice, despite the stereotypical contexts and tropes used throughout the films.

However, this is not appreciated by *all* family members and is even looked down upon, as evidenced within altercations between José and his son Chucho and Carlos and his son, Luís. In various scenes in both *Mi Familia* and *A Better Life*, Chucho and Luís make snide, rude, and disrespectful comments about their fathers' occupations and tell them in so many words that they do not aspire to be like them. This disrespect is partially motivated by the aspirations that Chucho and Luís have to assimilate and be more accepted by those around them. Their families' immigrant status and employment context are fundamentally at odds with these aspirations, which causes many of their altercations. Eventually, certain struggles and issues make Chucho and Luís realize that their fathers are good providers and compassionate, caring fathers, which acts as a relational catalyst and also a filmic plot catalyst in both films. These specific representations of Mexican American fathers are positive in that they disrupt dominant ideologies and representations of the abusive, aggressive Mexican American father and husband, yet this disruption is short lived, given that these representations are situated within dominant media tropes of Mexican men and fathers as immigrant day laborers, which carry with them broader implications pertaining to class, socioeconomic status, and education levels.

Falling more toward the middle of the spectrum are Ernesto and Martín, fathers in *Quinceañera* and *Tortilla Soup*, respectively. Although both fathers embody the more positive aspect of *machismo* as found in research by Coltrane and Cruz, such as being involved with their children's lives and providing for their families, their parenting styles are rooted within patriarchal control, perhaps because they have daughters. Ernesto's relationship with Magdalena is also influenced by his religious beliefs, which prompt him to ostracize her from the family when he learns of her unplanned pregnancy. Overall, these two films reaffirm hegemonic and patriarchal ideologies about Mexican Americans that obscure the potential for "offering nuanced, self-reflexive representations"[48] of Mexican families more broadly and Mexican fathers more specifically.

Leaning more toward the other end of the exaggerated Mexican *machismo/masculinidad* spectrum are Jimmy and Che, fathers in *Mi Familia* and *La*

Mission. These two characters have much in common: their masculinity is performed via their *pachuco* clothing styles and identities; they were both incarcerated, which plays a significant role in their character development and in the films' narratives; and they are both single fathers, as their wives passed away in both films. Their *pachuco* gender identities and performance significantly shape their approaches to fatherhood. Alfredo Mirandé details the history of the *pachuco* identity and notes that it is a masculine identity that is a symbol of heterosexuality, cultural identity, and *machismo*.[49] Moreover, the *pachuco* "is an instinctive rebel who struggles against the wrath vented toward Mexicans by American society."[50] This *pachucho* identity and rebellious nature is characterized by Jimmy and Che's *egoísmo*, or their egotistic and more self-centered mentalities. This provides a backdrop for their approaches to fatherhood, as Jimmy is ashamed of his incarceration and tells his brother *Paco* to tell his son that he is dead, and Che is so preoccupied with his own masculinity and homophobic tendencies that he temporarily severs his relationship with his son because he cannot accept his sexual identity. Che even questions if Jes' sexual identity is God's way of punishing him for his previous wrongdoings, and he continuously feels threatened and disgusted by the idea of Jes having a boyfriend. This disgust and rage materializes itself physically at the hospital when Che sees Jes' boyfriend Jordan, which results in a verbal and physical altercation. Taken together, these two approaches to fatherhood result in delayed, conflicted, and unsatisfactory father-son relationships. Jimmy's relationship with his son is off to a problematic start, given that he spends the first few years of his son's life in jail. Jimmy's young son repeatedly tells him that he is not his father, and Jimmy struggles to establish a relationship with his son. In Che and Jes' father-son relationship, the two have what appears to be a strong relationship characterized by open communication and mutual respect until Che discovers that his son is gay. Che's inability to accept his son temporarily severs the relationship, and in both films the conclusions allude to foreshadowing of better relationships between both Jimmy and his son and Che and Jes. In *Mi Familia* and *La Mission*, viewers see the more negative, sinister, and oppressive side of *machismo*, meaning the aggressive, dominant, and problematic masculinity that manifests itself both within intimate interpersonal relationships (husband-wife and boyfriend-girlfriend relationships) and also within their relationships with their sons.

One important theme that arises from the five films is what Heidi Denzel de Tirado refers to as the "patriarch's coming-of-age tale."[51] Although she argues that this plot is rarely found within Latino television representations, it was a strong component in all five films. In each of the films, the fathers have to deal with a variety of trials and tribulations that force them to re-evaluate their approaches to parenthood and make changes to improve their relationships with their children. Although this theme is less pervasive, albeit still present in *Mi Familia* and *A Better Life*, the father characters in *La Mission, Tortilla Soup*, and *Quinceañera* evolve from their original patriarchal modes of action and parenting to become more patient, tolerable, and accepting fathers.

Overall, representations of *masculinidad* and *paternidad* in these films ebb and flow between positive and negative representations of fatherhood, masculinity, and communication. Although some of these representations are positive in that they provide positive archetypes of Mexican fatherhood and disrupt previously detailed representations of negative, false machismo, this is short lived, given that these representations are situated within larger dominant stereotypical representations of Mexican men as immigrants, day laborers, thugs, and criminals and Mexican families as patriarchal and rigidly structured. In these movies, a paradoxical representation of Latino fatherhood is constructed and represented. In their analysis of the paradoxical representation of *Ugly Betty*, communication scholars Stacey K. Sowards and Richard D. Piñeda describe the importance of *Latinidad* in popular culture representations and both the positive and negative aspects of these representations.[52] For example, Sowards and Piñeda, in building upon the work of scholars Calafell and Gaspar de Alba, note that *Latinidad* can be both a commodification strategy and a strategy to explore identity and identifications between and among multiple similarities and differences in various Latino groups. However, similar to what occurs in *Ugly Betty*, *Latinidad* in these films becomes a commodification strategy so that the filmic representations of Mexican American fathers and families can simultaneously speak to multiple audiences. In these films, Mexican American culture is homogenized and singularly represented via immigrant struggles to attain the American Dream, community struggles rooted within gang violence and racism, and family values that are stereotypically and undoubtedly traditionally Mexican. Arlene Dávila notes that the stereotypes of Latino/a families often represent Latina/o families as Catholic, traditional, conservative, immigrant, and Spanish-speaking, which characterize the representations of all of the families in the five films selected for analysis. Moreover, consistent with other media representations of Latino/a populations and groups, *Latinidad* (or Mexican *Latinidad* specifically) is rooted within dark skin as a signifier of ethnic identity, a blending of the Spanish and English language, traditional Mexican foods, and traditional Mexican music. Therein lies the paradox: although there are both positive and negative representations of Mexican fatherhood in these three films, these representations simultaneously provide new ways of envisioning and witnessing Mexican fatherhood *and* reify and perpetuate media and cultural stereotypes of Mexican/Latino men as bandits, thugs, criminals, and immigrants. Thus, the positive nature and potential of these films is short lived.

CONCLUSION

Media representations of minority groups are vastly important as they have the potential to create the themes and messages that we and others use to make sense of the world.[53] The representations of Mexican fatherhood in these five films portray both positive and negative fatherhood archetypes, those rooted within both caring and supportive fatherhood and aggressive, dominant fatherhood. Despite the positive fatherhood evidenced in *Mi Familia* and *A Better Life* and the problematic, yet redemptive fatherhood represented in *Mi Familia, Quinceañera,* and *La Mission,* the positive success and implications of these *paternidades* are limited because they are situated within dominant stereotypes of Latino men that frequently serve to marginalize or demonize Latino men within the larger American consciousness. Only with more diverse representations of Latino families will the democratic potential of communication and mass media be fulfilled.

NOTES

1. Pew Research Center, "Statistical Portrait of Hispanics in the United States, 1980–2013," Retrieved from http://www.pewhispanic.org/2015/05/12/statistical-portrait-of-hispanics-in-the-united-states-2013-key-charts/.

2. Arlene Dávila, *Latino Spin: Public Image and the Whitewashing of Race* (New York: New York University Press, 2008).

3. Michelle A. Holling, "El Simpático Boxer: Underpinning Chicano Masculinity with a Rhetoric of *Familia in Resurrection Blvd,*" *Western Journal of Communication* 70, no. 2 (2006): 91.

4. Ibid., p. 91.

5. Sarah Eschholz, Jana Bufkin, and Jenny Long, "Symbolic Reality Bites: Women and Racial/Ethnic Minorities in Modern Film," *Sociological Spectrum* 22 (2002): 299–334.

6. Marco Portales, *Crowding Out Latinos: Mexican Americans in the Public Consciousness* (Philadelphia, PA: Temple University Press, 2000).

7. Holling, "El Simpático Boxer," p. 92.

8. Ibid., p. 92; Heidi Denzel de Tirado, "Media Monitoring and Ethnicity: Representing Latino Families on American Television (2000–2013)," Retrieved from http://nuevomundo.revues.org/66165; Dana E. Mastro & Elizabeth Behm-Morawitz, "Latino Representation on Primetime Television," *Journalism & Mass Communication Quarterly* 82, no. 1 (2005): 110.

9. Patricia Zavella, *Women's Work & Chicano Families: Cannery Workers of the Santa Clara Valley* (Ithaca, NY: Cornell University Press, 1987); Norma Williams, *The Mexican American Family: Tradition and Change* (Walnut Creek, CA: AltaMira Press, 1990).

10. Zavella, *"Women's Work,"* pp. 1–15.

11. Williams, "*The Mexican American,*" p. 2.

12. Holling, "El Simpático Boxer," p. 94.

13. Ibid., p. 94.

14. Geri-Ann Galanti, "The Hispanic Family and Male-Female Relationships: An Overview," *Journal of Transcultural Nursing 14*, no. 3 (2003): 180–185; Ismael Navarro Nuno, "Que Dios Guíe Sus Manos [May God Guide Your Hands]," in *Healing Latinos: Realidad y Fantasia*, eds. David Hayes-Bautista and Roberto Chiprut (Los Angeles,: Cedars-Sinai Health System, 1998), 159–169.

15. Celia Jaes Falicov, "Mexican families," in *Ethnicity and Family Therapy*, eds. Monica McGoldrick, Joe Giordano, and Nydia Garcia-Preto (New York: The Guiliford Press, 2005), 229–241.

16. Ibid.

17. Galanti, "The Hispanic Family," p. 181.

18. Holling, "El Simpático Boxer," p. 96.

19. Galanti, "The Hispanic Family," p. 283.

20. Ana Castillo, *Massacre of the Dreamers: Essays on Xicanisma* (New York, NY: Penguin Books USA Inc., 1994).

21. Gloria Anzaldúa, *Borderlands/La Frontera: The New Mestiza* (San Francisco: Aunt Lute Books, 2012).

22. Olivia N. Saracho and Bernard Spodek, "Challenging the Stereotypes of Mexican American Fathers," *Early Childhood Education Journa*, 35 (2007): 223–223; Alfredo Mirandé, *Hombres y Machos: Masculinity and Latino Cultur* (Boulder, CO: Westview Press, 1997).

23. Rick A. Cruz, Kevin M. King, Keith F. Widaman, Janxin Leu, Ana Marie Cauce, and Rand D. Conger, "Cultural Influences on Positive Father Involvement in Two-Parent Mexican-Origin Families," *Journal of Family Psychology* 25, no. 5 (2011): 731–740.

24. Scott Coltrane, Ross D. Parke, and Michele Adams, "Complexity of Father Involvement in Low-Income Mexican American Families," *Family Relations 53*, (2004):179–189.

25. Cruz et al., "Cultural References," p. 8.

26. David T. Abalos, *The Latino Male: A Radical Redefinition* (Boulder, CO: Lynne Rienner Publishers, 2002), p. 155; Leandra H. Hernandez, "It Wouldn't Change a Thing: The Role of Identity Politics and Gender Politics in Mexican-American Women's Decision-Making Experiences about Prenatal Testing," (doctoral dissertation, Texas A&M University, 2014).

27. Matthew C. Gutmann, *The Meanings of Being Macho: Being a Man in Mexico City* (Berkeley: University of California Press, 1996), p. 57.

28. Dana Mastro, "Effects of Racial and Ethnic Stereotyping," in *Media Effects: Advances in Theory and Research*, eds. Jennings Bryant and Mary Beth Oliver. (New York: Routledge, 2009), 325–341.

29. Ibid., p. 325.

30. Eschholz et al., "Symbolic Reality Bites," p. 299.

31. Mastro, "Effects of Racial," . . . pp. 327–328; Mastro et al., "Latino Representation."

32. Stephanie Greco Larson, *Media and Minorities: The Politics of Race in News and Entertainment* (New York: Rowman & Littlefield Publishers, 2006), p. 57.

33. The translation for *mandilón* is "man wearing an apron."

34. Christine List, *Chicano Images: Refiguring Ethnicity in Mainstream Film.* (New York: Garland Publishing, Inc., 1996), p. 21.

35. Ibid., p. 21; Larson, *"Media and Minorities,"* p. 59.

36. Larson, *"Media and Minorities,"* p. 59.

37. Holling, "El Simpático Boxer," p. 95.

38. Rosa-Linda Fregoso, *MeXicana Encounters: The Making of Social Identities in the Borderland* (Berkeley: University of California Press, 2003); Holling, "El Simpático Boxer," p. 95.

39. Angharad N. Valdivia, *Latina/os in the Media* (Malden, MA: Polity Press, 2010).

40. Ibid., p. 71.

41. Gregory Nava, *Mi Familia*, Film, directed by Gregory Nava (1995).

42. Chris Weitz, *A Better Life*, Film, directed by Chris Weitz (2011).

43. Peter Bratt, *La Mission*, Film, directed by Peter Bratt (2009).

44. Maria Ripoll, *Tortilla Soup*, Film, directed by Maria Ripoll (2001).

45. Richard Glatzer and Wash Westmoreland, *Quinceañera*, Film, directed by Richard Glatzer and Wash Westmoreland (2006).

46. The fact that less than 10 movies returned in the original web search is a telling factor of the under-representation of Mexican families in American cinema.

47. Laura Lindenfeld, "Visiting the Mexican American Family: *Tortilla Soup* as Culinary Tourism," *Communication and Critical/Cultural Studies* 4, no 3 (2007): 303–320.

48. Lindenfeld, "Visiting the Mexican," p. 314.

49. Alfredo Mirandé, Hombres y Machos: Masculinity and Latino Culture, (Boulder, CO: Westview Press, 2007), p. 134.

50. Ibid., p. 136.

51. Tirado, "Media Monitoring," p. 4.

52. Stacey K. Sowards and Richard D. Piñeda, *"Latinidad* in *Ugly Betty*: Authenticity and the Paradox of Representation," in *Latina/o Discourse in Vernacular Spaces: Somos de Una Voz?*, eds., Michelle A. Holling and Bernadette M. Calafell (Lanham, MD: Lexington Books, 2011), 123–144.

53. Valdivia, *Latina/os in the Media*, p. 73.

BIBLIOGRAPHY

Abalos, David T. *The Latino Male: A Radical Redefinition.* Boulder, CO: Lynne Rienner Publishers, 2002.

Anzaldúa, Gloria. *Borderlands/La Frontera: The New Mesiza.* San Francisco, CA: Aunt Lute Books, 2012.

Bratt, Benjamin. *La Mission.* Film. Directed by Peter Bratt. Written by Peter Bratt. Produced by 5 Stick Films Inc. and Tomkat Films. Sundance: Global Cinema 2009.

Castillo, Ana. *Massacre of the Dreamers: Essays on Xicanisma.* New York, NY: Penguin Books USA Inc, 1994.

Coltrane, Scott, Ross D. Parke, and Michele Adams. "Complexity of Father Involvement in Low-Income Mexican American Families." *Family Relations 53*, (2004): 179–189.

Cruz, Rick A., Kevin M. King, Keith F. Widaman, Janxin Leu, Ana Marie Cauce, and Rand D. Conger. "Cultural Influences on Positive Father Involvement in Two-Parent Mexican-Origin Families." *Journal of Family Psychology 25*, no. 5 (2011): 731–740.

Dávila, Arlene. *Latino Spin: Public Image and the Whitewashing of Race.* New York, NY: New York University Press, 2008.

Denzel de Tirado, Heidi. "Media Monitoring and Ethnicity: Representing Latino Families on American Television (2000–2013)." Retrieved from http://nuevomundo.revues.org/66165.

Eschholz, Sarah, Jana Bufkin, and Jenny Long. "Symbolic reality bites: Women and Racial/Ethnic Minorities in Modern Film." *Sociological Spectrum 22* (2002): 299–334.

Falicov, Celia Jaes. "Mexican families." In *Ethnicity and Family Therapy*, edited by Monica McGoldrick, Joe Giordano, and Nydia Garcia-Preto, 229–241. New York, NY: The Guiliford Press, 2005.

Fregoso, Rosa-Linda. *MeXicana Encounters: The Making of Social Identities in the Borderlands.* Berkeley, CA: University of California Press, 2003.

Galanti, Geri-Ann. "The Hispanic Family and Male-Female Relationships: An Overview." *Journal of Transcultural Nursing 14*, no. 3 (2003): 180–185.

Glatzer, Richard and Wash Westmoreland. *Quinceañera.* Film. Directed by Richard Glatzer and Wash Westmoreland. Written by by Richard Glatzer and Wash Westmoreland. Produced by Cinetic Media and Kitchen Sink Entertainment. Sundance: Sony Pictures Classics (2006).

Gutmann, Matthew C. *The Meanings of Macho: Being a Man in Mexico City.* Berkeley, CA: University of California Press, 1996.

Hernandez, Leandra H. "It Wouldn't Change a Thing: The Role of Identity Politics and Gender Politics in Mexican-American Women's Decision-Making Experiences about Prenatal Testing." Doctoral dissertation, Texas A&M University, 2014.

Holling, Michelle A. "El Simpático Boxer: Underpinning Chicano Masculinity with a Rhetoric of Familia in *Resurrection Blvd.*" *Western Journal of Communication 70*, no. 2 (2006): 91–114.

Larson, Stephanie Greco. *Media and Minorities: The Politics of Race in News and Entertainment.* New York: NY: Rowman & Littlefield Publishers, Inc., 2006.

Lindenfeld, Laura. "Visiting the Mexican American Family: *Tortilla Soup* as Culinary Tourism." *Communication and Critical/Cultural Studies 4*, no. 3 (2007): 303–320.

List, Christine. *Chicano Images: Refiguring Ethnicity in Mainstream Film.* New York, NY: Garland Publishing, Inc., 1996.

Mastro, Dana E., and Elizabeth Behm-Morawitz. "Latino Representation on Primetime Television." *Journalism & Mass Communication Quarterly 82*, no. 1 (2005): 110–130.

Mastro, Dana E. "Effects of Racial and Ethnic Stereotyping." In *Media Effects: Advances in Theory and Research*, edited by Jennings Bryant and Mary Beth Oliver, 325–341. New York, NY: Routledge, 2009.

Nava, Gregory. *Mi Familia*. Film. Directed by Gregory Nava. Written by Gregory Nava and Anna Thomas. Produced by American Playhouse, American Zoetrope and Majestic Films. USA: New Line Cinema (1995).

Mirandé, Alfredo. *Hombres y Machos: Masculinity and Latino Culture*. Boulder, CO: Westview Press, 1997.

Nuno, Ismael Navarro. "Que Dios Guíe Sus Manos [May God Guide Your Hands]." In *Healing Latinos: Realidad y Fantasia,* edited by David Hayes-Bautista and Roberto Chiprut, 159–169. Los Angeles, CA: Cedars-Sinai Health System, 1998.

Pew Research Center. "Statistical Portrait of Hispanics in the United States, 29180–2013." Accessed from http://www.pewhispanic.org/2015/05/12/statistical-portrait-of-hispanics-in-the-united-states-2013-key-charts/.

Portales, Marco. *Crowding Out Latinos: Mexican Americans in the Public Consciousness*. Philadelphia, PA: Temple University Press, 2000.

Saracho, Olivia N., and Bernard Spodek. "Challenging the Stereotypes of Mexican American Fathers." *Early Childhood Education Journal* 3, (2007): 223–231.

Sowards, Stacey K., and Richard D. Pineda. "*Latinidad* in *Ugly Betty*: Authenticity and the Paradox of Representation." In *Latina/o Discourse in Vernacular Spaces: Somos de Una Voz?*, edited by Michelle A. Holling and Bernadette M. Calafell, 123–144. Lanham, MD: Lexington Books, 2011.

Ripoll, Maria. *Tortilla Soup*. Film. Directed by Maria Ripoll. Written by Tom Musca, Ramón Menéndez, and Vera Blasi. USA: Samuel Goldwyn Films (2001).

Valdivia, Angharad N. *Latina/os in the Media*. Malden, MA: Polity Press, 2010.

Weitz, Chris. *A Better Life*. Film. Directed by Chris Weitz. Written by Eric Eason. Produced by Lime Orchard Productions. USA: Summit Entertainment (2011).

Williams, Norma. *The Mexican American Family: Tradition and Change*. Walnut Creek, CA: AltaMira Press, 1990.

Zavella, Patricia. *Women's Work & Chicano Families: Cannery Workers of the Santa Clara Valley*. Ithaca, NY: Cornell University Press, 1987.

Index

About the Contributors

Fernando Gabriel Pagnoni Berns currently works at Universidad de Buenos Aires (UBA)—Facultad de Filosofía y Letras (Argentina), as Graduate Teaching Assistant of "Literatura de las Artes Combinadas II." He teaches seminars on American Horror Cinema and Euro Horror. He is director of the research group on horror cinema "Grite" and has published articles on Argentinian and international cinema and drama in the following publications: *Imagofagia, Stichomythia, Anagnórisis, Lindes* and *UpStage Journal* among others. He has published articles in the books *Horrors of War: The Undead in the Battlefield*, edited by Cynthia Miller, *To See the Saw Movies: Essays on Torture Porn and Post 9/11 Horror*, edited by John Wallis, *The Cinema of the Swimming Pool*, edited by Pam Hirsch, *Dreamscapes in Italian Cinema,* edited by Francesco Pascuzzi, *Reading Richard Matheson: A Critical Survey*, edited by Cheyenne Mathews, among others.

Canela Ailen Rodriguez Fontao holds a degree in Arts at the Facultad de Filosofía y Letras, Universidad de Buenos Aires (UBA), Argentina. She is a member of the research group on cinema CIyNE and has published articles on Argentinian and international cinema and television in publications as *lafuga* and in books such as *Cine y Revolución en America Latina*, edited by Ana Laura Lusnich and *Bullying in Popular Culture: Essays on Film, Television and Novels*, edited by Abigail Scheg. She is a lecturer specialized in horror TV and cinema.

Lynda Goldstein is an Associate Professor of English and Women Studies teaching at a campus of The Pennsylvania State University. She is the author of essays on popular culture, queer studies, and feminism in several edited collections: "Graphic/Narrative/Hisotry: Defining the Essential Experience(s) of 9/11" in *Comics as History, Comics as Literature*, ed. A. Babic; "Raging in Tongues: Confession and Performance Art" in *Confessional Politics*, ed. I. Gammel; "Getting into Lesbian Shorts: White Spectators and Perfomative Documentaries by Makers of Color" in *Between the Sheets, in the Streets: Queer, Lesbian, Gay Documentary*," ed. C. Holmlund and C. Fuchs; "Singing the Body Electric: Buying into Pop Cult Bodies" in *Building Bodies*, ed. P. Moore; "Revamping MTV: Passing for Queer Culture in the Video Closet" in *Queer Studies: A Lesbian, Gay, Bisexaul, and Transgender Anthology*, ed. B. Beemyn and M. Eliason, and "Not 'Knowing Her Place'" in *Women and Media: Content, Careers, Criticism*, ed. C. Lont. She is delighted to be included in this collection.

Justin J. Hendricks is a Pre-doctoral Fellow in Sociology at the University of Florida where he studies family, gender, and social theory and philosophy. His interests include the constraints and production of family within various contexts, images of family, and how societal influences (including media) produce family in specific ways. His previous research has focused on fathers working within the education system and he is currently working with video as a means of exploring conceptions of family among foster care alumni. Other interests include new empiricisms and materialisms, qualitative methodologies, social theory as a means of inquiry, and post-structural theory.

Leandra H. Hernandez is an Associate Faculty member of Communication in the Department of Arts & Humanities at National University, San Diego. Leandra is a media studies and health communication scholar whose health communication research centers on reproductive rights, prenatal testing, and shared decision making. Her health communication research has been published in *Communication Research* and is forthcoming in Gilchrist-Petty and Long's book *Contexts of the Dark Side of Communication*. Her media research interests include media representations of and constructions of gender, race, and ethnicity, particularly in reality television shows and films. Her research about media representations of gender in *Toddlers & Tiaras* and *Duck Dynasty* has been published in Slade, Narro, and Buchanan's book *Reality Television: Oddities of Culture* (2014). She also has a chapter about digital interactivity, social media, and *Toddlers & Tiaras* fans forthcoming in Slade, Carroll-Givens, and Narro's book *Television, Social Media, and Fan Culture*. Leandra enjoys teaching courses such as Latin@ Communication Studies, Popular Culture, Gender & the Media, and Intro to Women's Studies.

Shirley Hill is a Professor of Sociology at the University of Kansas, where she teaches classes on families, social inequality, medical sociology, and qualitative methods. Examining the consequences of economic, racial, and gender inequalities has been the overarching theme of her research. Professor Hill has published articles and books that examine various aspects of African American family life. She is the author of *Black Intimacies: A Gender Perspective on Families and Relationships* (2005), *African American Children: Socialization and Development in Families* (1999), and *Families: A Social Class Perspective* (2011). More recently, she published (with coauthor John Rury) *The African American Struggle for Secondary School 1940–1980* (2012). Her current research focuses on health attitudes and behaviors in the context of African American family life.

John W. Howard III is an Associate Professor in the School of Communication at East Carolina University and Program Director for the minor in Leadership Studies. His research has examined the intersections among gender, soldiering, and nationalism and is transitioning into studies of gender and leadership. His publications have appeared in Women's Studies in Communication, Human Communication Research, Women and Language, and International and Intercultural Communication Annual.

Janice Kelly is an Associate Professor in Communication Arts and Sciences Department at Molloy College, New York. She is a licensed Certified Family Life Educator. She sits on the board as a member of Fathers Incorporated. She served as coeditor of Fathers and the Media, Fathering: A Journal of Theory and Research about Men as Parents. In addition, she published a documentary on Perceptions of Fathers in the Media: In Search of the Ideal Father for the Fatherhood Initiative Program with the New York States Office of Temporary and Disability Assistance Department. Interviewed on several radio programs and newspapers on the following topics ranging from The Affect of Sitcom Dads on Our Children's Expectations, Media Literacy, Improving Office Communication, and Women in the Workplace. Her works were published in the Journal of Advancing Women in Leadership, Scope, an Online Journal of Film Studies, Fathering Journal and Explorations Media Ecology. Her research and scholarship are in the areas of family communication, fatherhood and popular culture, race, gender and leadership, and intergenerational communication in the workplace.

Sarah Kornfield is a feminist media critic whose research has been published in journals such as *Women's Studies in Communication, Critical Studies in Media Communication*, and *Communication, Culture & Critique*. Sarah is currently teaching courses in critical methods, television studies, and gender at Hope College. Her research focuses on the portrayal and construction of gender within entertainment media.

Deepika Kulkarni is currently a medical student at the Morsani College of Medicine at the University of South Florida. Her prior research includes investigation of the metabolic complications of HIV-positive pediatric patients and HIV-exposed infants currently taking antiretroviral therapy. Her current research in medical school focuses on cardiovascular disease in diabetic patients. She continues to be involved in volunteering and service activities such as student-run free clinics, volunteering in hospitals and helping children with chronic illnesses.

Ralph LaRossa is Professor Emeritus of Sociology at Georgia State University. He is the author of, among other works, *The Modernization of Fatherhood: A Social and Political History*; and *Of War and Men: World War II in the Lives of Fathers and Their Families*. He also is the editor of *Family Case Studies: A Sociological Perspective*, and a coeditor of the *Sourcebook of Family Theories and Methods: A Contextual Approach*. He has received grants from the National Science Foundation (principal investigator) and National Institutes of Health (coinvestigator) in support of research on the social realities of fatherhood during the Machine Age (1918–1941) and on the experience of becoming a father in contemporary society. His most recent publications have focused on the history of fatherhood during and after World War II; the transition to parenthood; the social construction of the life course, the symbolic connection between fatherhood and baseball; the changing culture of fatherhood in comic strip families; the political economy of Father's Day and Mother's Day; the social transformation of childhood in the early twentieth century; and the theorizing process in qualitative research.

William Marsiglio is a Professor of Sociology at the University of Florida. He focuses on the social psychology of men's fathering, reproduction, health and fitness, and paid/volunteer work with children outside the home. He studies how men socially construct their identities as persons capable of creating and caring for human life in various settings. His books include: Nurturing Dads: Social Initiatives for Contemporary Fatherhood (with Kevin Roy, 2012); Men on a Mission: Valuing Youth Work in Our Communities (2008); Situated Fathering: A Focus on Physical and Social Spaces (Ed. with Kevin Roy and Greer Litton Fox, 2005); Stepdads: Stories of Love, Hope, and Repair (2004); Sex, Men, and Babies: Stories of Awareness and Responsibility, (with Sally Hutchinson, 2002); Procreative Man (1998), and Fatherhood: Contemporary Theory, Research, and Social Policy (Ed. 1995).

Laura C. Prividera is an Associate Professor of Communication, East Carolina University. She is also the Associate Dean of Graduate Studies for the College of Fine Arts and Communication and the Associate Director of the

School of Communication. Her research examines the social constructions of gender, race, and/or power in military, health and pedagogical contexts. Her research has appeared in Women's Studies in Communication, Health Communication, Women & Language, International and Intercultural Communication Annual, The Howard Journal of Communications and Texas Speech Communication Journal.

Peter Schaefer is an Associate Professor of Communication and Media Arts at Marymount Manhattan College. He received his MA and PhD at The University of Iowa. His teaching and research examines the intersection of popular culture and media from critical-cultural and historical perspectives. His work has appeared in journals such as Critical Studies in Media Communication, International Journal of Communication, and New Media & Society, as well as in several anthologies.

Heidi Steinour received her doctoral degree in sociology from the University of Florida with a specialization in family and gender. She currently serves as an adjunct lecturer and subject matter expert for the University of Florida and teaches family courses at the University of South Florida. Her research focuses on how cultural and organizational narratives that construct parenthood and work-life balance for both men and women. Additionally her work is devoted to advancements in qualitative inquiry and social theory. Heidi enjoys teaching courses such as Family, Work, & Gender, The Sociology of Families, Social Theory, and Social Problems.

Laura Tropp is a scholar on pregnancy, motherhood, and fatherhood studies with a doctoral degree from New York University. The focus of her work is on connections between popular culture, media technology, and families and parenting. Her book, *A Womb with a View: America's Growing Public Interest in Pregnancy* was published by Praeger in 2013. Her other work has explored such subjects as teen fathers in media, motherhood in popular culture, and postpartum depression on television. The author is currently a professor at Marymount Manhattan College where she is the Chair of the Division of Communication and Media Arts and teaches courses on media studies, motherhood and fatherhood studies, and popular culture. She also writes a blog on work-life balance and motherhood for Inside Higher Ed.